W9-AUZ-971

Sailing a Dream

Karl Livengood

Sailing a Dream
Copyright © 2015 by Karl H. Livengood
All Rights Reserved

Printing by Falcon Books

San Ramon, California

ISBN: 978-0-692-41759-1

Except for brief quotes used in reviews, no part of this book
may be reproduced by any means without the written
permission of the author.

PRINTED IN THE UNITED STATES OF AMERICA

ACKNOWLEDGEMENTS

My extended family played an important role by encouraging the writing of letters and emails during my voyages as they were passed or forwarded to their friends who read my writings with interest. These emails and letters became the well from which *Sailing a Dream* was drawn.

The Rossmoor Writers Group led by Mary Webb created a space where forward movement was expected and rewarded. Mary Webb read most of the book line by line and helped me fine tune my writing. The group gave me a supportive audience who listened and reacted as I read chapters at our meetings.

Meeting Deborah Medvick in the Writers Group and listening to her insightful responses caused me to use her services as a developmental editor. Her suggestions and insights have helped me create a deeper and more interesting book.

Finally to my wife Betsy who was my "first" reader, I offer many thanks for your editing skills and encouragement along the way.

PROLOGUE

The idea of writing *Sailing a Dream* was born in response to the loss of *JoJo*, our current sailboat, in the fall of 2009. A major part of my identity sank with *JoJo*. I needed a place and a way to put my self-confidence and my feelings about myself as a sailor and person back together. By going back into the letters. emails, and articles I had written, I took another voyage of discovery where my memories were deepened and heightened. There, I found the successful sailor I had been and so much more.

Sailing, for me, is ultimately a relaxing and mind expanding pursuit. By harnessing and staying in tune with nature's forces on the water, you and your boat are in motion and become one. Motion propels you through external space and time, but also opens up internal space for thoughts, ideas, and feelings to surface and become conscious. My sense of what is important in life took on more clarity and became more focused. The things I remember most fondly are the experiences of love and laughter that money can't buy.

It became clear to me that having a Dream and actualizing it had created the essential strands of my life, giving them form and direction. By piecing together my adventures, the people I met, and places I visited in the process of writing the book, the sweep of my life took on a greater and deeper meaning for me.

By slowly defining and then following my dream, I found in day to day life that I was able to maintain a greater, more finely tuned focus.

My hope is that the reader will come to understand the importance of having a dream, setting a goal that can lead you through the thickets of life and more importantly add significance and purpose to the events along the way. Accompany me along my journey, meet interesting people, find both the joys and effort involved in sailing, discover new places and cultures that will enrich your life as they did mine. Join me on board *Aurora* as did so many of my friends and family.

Most importantly, join me and my wife on an adventure of a lifetime accomplished by a couple motivated by a dream that took us almost 20,000 miles on the many oceans and seas of the world.

Discover the power of your own dreams and allow them to invigorate your life.

Table of Contents

PART 1 PADDLING MY OWN CANOE   1

1   A Perilous Night 3
2   Shipwreck 9
3   Dawning of the Dream 17
4   Back to the Land 27
5   Toward My Dream 33
6   Aurora Arrives 43
7   Discovering the Right Partner 55
8   Voyage to Mexico 63
9   Cruising the Sea of Cortez 71
10   Puerto Vallarta and Beyond 87
11   Back to Joanne 105
12   Experiencing the Sea of Cortez 117
13   Escape to the Baja 125

PART II LET THE CRUISING BEGIN   137

14   Beginning Our Cruising Life 139
15   Exploring Mainland Mexico 149
16   Tackling the Mexican Coast 165
17   Passage Along the Central American Coast . . 177
18   Costa Rica at Last 187
19   Isla Del Coco Adventure 209
20   Return to Mainland Costa Rica 219
21   South to Panama 227
22   Panama Still Darned Hot 245
23   On to Columbia 257
24   Life with the Kunas 267
25   Caribbean Coast of Central America 279
26   Sailing Into Guatemala 295
27   How About Belize? 309
28   The Yucatan 321
29   Rough Passage to Florida 331

PART III FAMILY FRIENDS HOME · 341

30   Sailing Up the East Coast 343
31   On to Nova Scotia. 359
32   Heading South for Warmth 363
33   Trekking Along the ICW 375
34   Bahamas Here We Come. 381
35   Back From the USA 399

PART IV AN OCEAN OF NEW POSSIBILITIES · 407

36   Preparations for Crossing Atlantic 409
37   It's a Big Ocean Out There. 419
38   Thoughts on the Passage to the Azores 427
39   Exploring the Azores 439
40   On to Portugal. 451

PART V EXPANDING THE DREAM · 459

41   Europe Here We Are 461
42   Returning to Ailigandi 477
Epilogue. 487

BLUE BOAT HOME

Though below me, I feel no motion standing on these mountains
and plains.
Far away from the rolling ocean still my dry land heart can say:
I've been sailing all my life now, never harbor or post I have
known.
The wide universe is the ocean I travel—and the earth is my blue
boat home.
Sun my sail—and moon my rudder as I ply the starry sea,
Leaning over the edge in wonder,
Casting questions into the deep.
Drifting here with my ship's companions,
All we kindred pilgrim souls,
Making our way by the lights of the heavens—in our beautiful blue
boat home.
I give thanks to the waves upholding me,
Hail the great winds urging me on,
Greet the infinite sea before me,
Sing the sky my sailor's song: I was born upon the fathoms,
Never harbor or port have I known.
The wide universe is the ocean I travel,
And our earth is my blue boat home.

Written by Peter Mayer, 1963
Copyright © 2002 Peter Mayer

PART I

PADDLING MY OWN CANOE

"It is the passions which do and undo everything.
If reason ruled, nothing would get on.
The passions in men are the winds necessary to put
   everything in motion, though they often cause
   storms."

—Bernard de Fontenelle, 1688

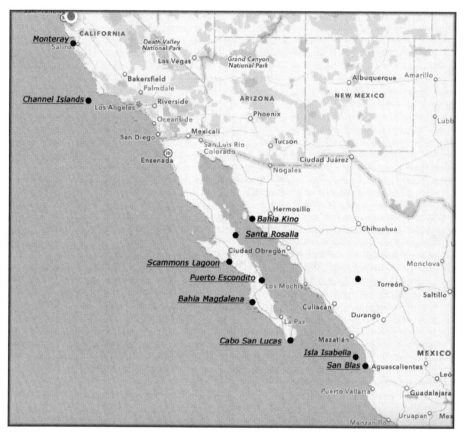

San Francisco to Manzillo

1

A PERILOUS NIGHT

"Calling Mayday, Mayday. This is sailing vessel *JoJo* stranded on a reef in Stillwater Cove near the Carmel Bay pier!" I shouted desperately. "Our position is 35.56 degrees north latitude and 121.94 degrees west longitude."

The Coast Guard responded, "Where are you located? How many people are aboard? Are you wearing life jackets? What is your position?"

I shouted back even louder, knowing that we were in big trouble and needed help pronto. "Coast Guard, Coast Guard, this is *JoJo* with two persons wearing life jackets."

Betsy loudly repeated our location information, but the Coast Guard replied as if they didn't hear us, and again asked our position. We looked at each other with frustration and fear. These repetitive transmissions were eating up precious time that we needed to save *JoJo* and ourselves.

*****

My wife, Betsy, and I had sailed our 1981 tan-hulled Catalina 36-foot sloop, *JoJo*, from Monterey Marina earlier that afternoon. There were problems with *JoJo*, but I thought we could find repair parts during our trip south to the Channel Islands. I was wrong. We couldn't have imagined that such a perilous night was ahead of us.

I had discovered these problems when we left *JoJo*'s San Francisco Bay berth. Our autopilot couldn't hold us on the assigned compass course, which meant that we had to steer by hand through the night to Monterey. Unfortunately, we were unable to

3

replace the autopilot while in Monterey, making our trip more difficult to accomplish. Luckily *JoJo* was in company with our "buddy" boat, *Lucky Lady*, owned by Rich, a real estate agent, and his wife, Sandy, a talented artist. They were our home dock mates in San Francisco.

As the sun began to set over the horizon in Carmel Bay, Betsy and I followed *Lucky Lady* into Stillwater Cove off the Pebble Beach Golf Course on the Monterey Peninsula to rest for the night. Large swells were rolling into the anchorage. We had hoped to tie up to a mooring, but the mooring field had been removed; only two moorings remained. The cove was not a good place to anchor because it was chock full of kelp that could entangle the anchor. *Lucky Lady* tied up to the round mooring buoy farthest from shore. Dismayed with the lack of good choices, I dropped our anchor to stabilize the boat. Betsy drove *JoJo* alongside *Lucky Lady*, trying to raft up to her. The violent wave action, however, caused our two boats to bang into each other, making it dangerous to remain rafted together.

As we motored away from *Lucky Lady*, I heard our windlass motor slipping while straining to pull the anchor up through the dense, tangled kelp. I worked feverishly to clear off the kelp from the anchor and the chain. I called Betsy for help, but our efforts failed when the anchor chain jammed in the motor. Problems were piling on top of us at a fast clip. I needed to disassemble the motor, but there was no time with so many crises facing us. I took several deep breaths to stay focused. I pulled up the chain and we reached down and cleared the kelp off the anchor. Then we were free to move on.

Dusk was closing in on us fast, and I didn't want to be drifting around in the turbulent waves in the dark. The outgoing tide was pulling fiercely on *JoJo*. We didn't have a second to waste. I spotted a mooring buoy closer to shore, meaning the water could be deep enough for *JoJo* there. That buoy called to me like the seductive sirens that lured Odysseus in the Straits of Messina. He put wax in his men's ears so they couldn't hear the sirens' seductive voices luring them to the rocks. I wasn't so lucky.

Yes, the buoy looked like the answer to our worsening dilemma. One fear, however, whispered to me as we motored toward our refuge. Was the buoy too close to shore? Recalling my experience with mooring buoys, I dismissed the fear, assuming there be would some deep water between the buoy and the shore. We tentatively approached our target, while intently watching the depth sounder.

"This is too dangerous," Betsy yelled. "I'm going to turn around."

"Let's go slow," I said calmly, trying to reassure her and myself. "Just take the boat up to the buoy, so I can grab it."

As I reached out with the boat hook to grab the buoy, I heard the sickening crunch of *JoJo*'s keel hitting the reef. My heart sank. We were hard aground. I ran back to the cockpit and took the helm, turning the boat into the direction of the waves. I revved the motor to full power, but *JoJo* failed to respond. She didn't move an inch. We were stuck on the reef!

I had to take swift action to save *JoJo*. I threw our inflated dinghy off the foredeck into the water and jumped down into it. Leaning over the lifelines, Betsy shoved a paddle into my hands. A second later a breaking wave crashed over my shoulder, knocking off my glasses and sweeping away the paddle. Betsy handed me the other paddle along with our long half-inch thick emergency towline. Still in the dinghy, I pulled myself hand over hand forward along the hull to the bow where the anchor was precariously swinging back and forth. Before I could get out of the way, the anchor grazed my head just missing my eye. I touched the small bloody cut and knew it wasn't a serious injury.

Next, I tied the nylon line around *JoJo*'s bow cleat and then, using one oar, I began clumsily paddling toward the mooring. It was impossible to keep the dinghy moving in a straight line. I grew more frustrated by the second with having to paddle with only one oar. I was getting nowhere fast! Then I realized that the towline dragging behind the dinghy was too short and had become wrapped in kelp. Escape from a tangled forest of kelp was like futilely struggling to get out of quicksand. The harder I tried, the more the maleficent kelp clogged up the line. While I struggled in the dinghy, Betsy revved the engine, trying to keep *JoJo* from being swept away by breaking waves toward shore and certain destruction.

Hearing *JoJo*'s Mayday, *Lucky Lady* motored off her mooring and anchored two hundred yards away from us. Rich and Sandy put together a four hundred-foot line with a float to pull *JoJo* off the reef as the tide rose. After slowly paddling the wildly rebellious dinghy out to them, I helped Sandy pull the line from under their boat and began clearing off kelp. I then piled the line into my dinghy. Rich attempted to start his dinghy engine to give me power, but it refused to start. Another effort to make things easier was thwarted, so I began the torturous trek paddling to *JoJo* using one oar. Reaching the end of the line, I dropped the buoy and the line in the water. By that time, I was tired, cold, and discouraged, but I doggedly paddled toward *JoJo*. I wanted to retrieve our half-inch line hoping to connect the two boats together.

After we spent an hour of relentless attempts to save *JoJo* on our own, the Coast Guard finally arrived. Their forty-five-foot patrol boat sat about one hundred-fifty yards away. I couldn't believe they just sat there watching the drama, not offering us any assistance. My frustration soon turned into anger.

Our friends Keith and Dodie appeared on the pier. We had planned to have dinner with them on *JoJo*. They stood watching with horror on their faces as helpless *JoJo* foundered near shore. Drawing on his U.S. Marine Corps training, Keith jumped into the water and waded in chest-deep water out to *JoJo*. When he reached the boat, he climbed up the transom. Springing into action, Keith secured the swinging anchor and then gave me another long line to lengthen my original emergency line.

I kept trying to connect *JoJo* and *Lucky Lady* but with no success. I saw *JoJo* being violently smashed from side to side as the waves broke and receded. Betsy wasn't faring any better on board in the cockpit. I wouldn't know about the danger Betsy was in until she told me several hours later.

JoJo's rocking and rolling forced Betsy to abandon efforts to hold our boat offshore by revving the motor. She climbed down the companionway ladder and gathered our wallets and other valuables into a waterproof ditch bag. Choppy waves rolled in one after another, slamming *JoJo*. Inside the cabin, Betsy was being thrown back and forth. Sliding on the wet floor, she fell, banging her knees and twisting her back. Betsy was sure she would break an arm or leg before being able to get off the boat. As if it was not already a treacherous situation, the carbon monoxide alarm went off, warning that the cabin was filling with the deadly gas. Betsy managed to scramble up into the cockpit and grab the radio transmitter.

"Get me the hell off this boat!" she screamed.

The Coast Guard heard Betsy's call and they ordered Rich on *Lucky Lady* to launch his dinghy and rescue her. Keith offered to take Betsy with him and wade back to shore, but she decided to have Rich take her to the Coast Guard cutter.

"Rich, don't come too close," Betsy shouted. "You might be hit when *JoJo* rolls on her side."

Hanging on outside the lifelines, Betsy timed her jump into Rich's dinghy as *JoJo* tilted to port side, just missing Rich. He paddled safely away from *JoJo* and moved toward the Coast Guard cutter.

I continued dragging the longer emergency line from *JoJo* to connect to the 400-foot line to *Lucky Lady*. I wasn't going to give up on *JoJo*. I doggedly kept paddling toward *JoJo*'s salvation, connecting the two lines so *Lucky Lady* could pull her off the reef. Rich was making much better progress with two oars, so I yelled to him to pull my line out with him. The final blow came when he refused.

"I'm under orders to take Betsy to the Coast Guard," Rich called back to me as he paddled on. I was devastated.

After I had been struggling desperately for at least two hours to save *JoJo*, neither the Coast Guard nor my friend would help me. I was physically exhausted and emotionally spent. I angrily refused the Coast Guard's loud hailer call for me to "Paddle over to the cutter."

"I'm too worn out and can't paddle anywhere!" I shouted to them.

The Coast Guard finally moved their cutter slowly toward me and in two minutes it was by my side. With aching, weak arms and legs, I climbed a ladder and boarded the patrol boat. The guardsmen pulled up the dinghy and placed it on deck.

As the cutter left Stillwater Cove, Betsy and I stood on the rear deck helplessly watching the incoming tide sweep our beloved *JoJo* toward shore. I winced; her fate was sealed. An incredible sadness welled up in me and threatened to consume me. All our hard work poured into *JoJo* would be lost. All the pleasure we had sailing her would be gone forever. The most fulfilling and transformative chapter of my life was ending.

2

SHIPWRECK

Wet, cold, and dazed, Betsy and I sat without saying a word in a very noisy compartment close to the cutter's engines. The guardsmen gave us blankets and ear plugs, which did little to comfort us after our terrifying ordeal with JoJo. I felt defeated and deflated in not being able to save our boat. Could I have done something more? Should we never have embarked on the journey with the faulty autopilot? Then anger bubbled through my remorse. Why did those who could have helped save JoJo fail to act?

After an hour aboard the cutter, we arrived at the Coast Guard dock in Monterey. Paramedics from the Monterey Fire Department met us and asked if we were injured. We were bruised and exhausted but okay. The cut over my eye had already scabbed over. Declining their offer to be taken to the hospital, we signed their release of responsibility form. Chelsea, owner of Pacific Coast Salvage, who had been talking with Betsy by radio and cell phone, came forward with salvage forms for us to sign.

"These are the standard salvage forms that have to be signed before we can go to work saving your boat," Chelsea said.

"Where do we sign?" I said with a knot in my stomach.

Neither Betsy nor I had the focus or energy to read the forms so we simply signed authorizations for the salvage company to save or salvage JoJo.

Keith and Dodie arrived and gave us long, caring hugs. They led us to their car and drove us to their townhouse not far from the harbor. Being sailors themselves they were tuned into how we were feeling. They didn't prod or probe; they simply stood by us, as we dealt with our loss. All Betsy and I had were the wet clothes on our backs and a few valuables. My wallet was still missing. When we arrived at the townhouse, we got out of our wet clothes and into hot showers. Keith and Dodie gave us some sweats so now we were safe and dry.

Betsy and I had met Keith, a tall, upstanding U.S. Marine Lt. Colonel, and Dodie, his obviously pregnant wife who had a delicious smile, at our daughter Leanne's wedding to Arnie, her husband, a Marine Major and a flyer of Harrier Jets in Keith's squadron. We became friends with Keith and Dodie over cocktails while sharing our interest in sailboat cruising. At the Monterey Marina two days ago, Betsy and I took them out to dinner, and we learned more about Keith's Master's Degree program at the Monterey Institute of International Studies.

Now sitting at their kitchen counter, eating leftovers and sipping hot chocolate gave us some energy to talk about what happened to *JoJo*.

"Keith, we want to thank you for wading out to *JoJo* and for securing the anchor and helping with the lines," I said gratefully. "Dodie, we're both so relieved to be here in the safety and warmth of your home with you two special friends."

"What a shame having your beautiful boat stranded on a reef," Keith said.

"Yes, we've put so much time and energy into renovating *JoJo* to safely make the voyage down the coast," I said, still wincing with sadness.

"Yeah, we both have worked on her," Betsy added. "I got some epoxy in my eye while we were fixing delamination in the deck. Karl has been working faithfully on her for years."

"When Dodie and I boarded *JoJo* in the marina, we could see the results of all your love and care," Keith said. "She had an almost new feel even though she was nineteen years old."

There was a pause in the conversation.

"Thanks for your support and care," Betsy said wearily. "We're both exhausted and need to go to bed."

We got up, hugged them, and shuffled off to the bedroom.

We had fallen into a fitful sleep and awoke about 3 a.m. trying to digest the tragedy that had forced its way into our lives. Going over in my mind the mistakes I had made was especially painful. I thought we could tie to a buoy so close to shore, but that put Betsy and *JoJo* into such a vulnerable, dangerous situation. I expected Rich to act as I would have acted. All this rehashing contributed to my feeling incompetent and deeply sad.

Still shaken by our ordeal, Betsy shared her feelings with me. As we commiserated with each other, a new thought suddenly popped up from the gloom and out of my mouth.

"Betsy, maybe now is the time to shift my focus from material things like *JoJo* where I invested four years of hard work and money to people and possibly to writing? Perhaps now is the time to reconnect with my social worker roots by volunteering to work with teenagers. Could this be the time to pull together all the logs, emails, letters, and stories of my travels on boats?"

"Yeah, it's time for a change," Betsy agreed. "You've certainly done your boating thing and after this experience my desire to sail lies shipwrecked with *JoJo*. There are safer ways to see the world."

I sensed relief in her sighs and slight smile.

"You're right about that," I said. "I'm hoping that recalling my earlier sailing successes and adventures will take some of the sting out of this failure and put it in perspective."

I fell back asleep feeling I could salvage the sailor part of my identity while creating a new direction for my life.

In the morning, Keith took time off from his studies to drive us on the famous Seventeen Mile Drive to Stillwater Cove just behind the Pebble Beach Club House. There we saw *JoJo* lying on her side like a beached whale on the sand, her keel missing, and side split open. My heart sank as I faced the stark reality that *JoJo* did not survive.

Chelsea from the salvage company came up from the beach and gave us an update. "The salvors have tied *JoJo* to the dock and to the buoy. We are now waiting for inflation bags to arrive so we can refloat *JoJo* and pull her off the beach in preparation for towing her back to Monterey later today. We piled what we have taken out of the boat on the blacktop in the parking lot. You can take what you wish."

Betsy and I sorted through the remains of our sailing life. Piles of sandy stuff were scattered around us. In a daze, we looked at the things, trying to decide what to take with us.

"Okay, how do we do this?" Betsy sighed. "Lots of it looks ruined to me."

"Well, we should save the most valuable things like the inflatable life jackets and the GPS," I responded. "Anything that's important to us should be saved." With heavy hearts we got to work.

A guy walked over to us saying, "Hi, I'm Tom, the harbormaster. Are you the owners of that wrecked boat on my beach?"

"Yes we are," I sheepishly replied.

"Do you know you are in a marine sanctuary?"

"I do now!" I said. "Well, it looks like the diesel and waste tanks are safely on the beach out of the boat, so there shouldn't be too much environmental damage."

Tom agreed, telling us, "The mooring buoy field was just removed two weeks ago and the buoy closest to shore belongs to the University of California at Santa Cruz. I asked them again last week to remove it, but as you know it is still there. They use it to tie up their small boats when students study the reef environment."

"Great, they left their mooring buoy in the bay with no warning signs about the water depth or danger from the reef," I said angrily.

The buoy indeed had been like a siren luring me not toward safety but to *JoJo's* destruction. I was furious about the university's negligence, but knew I couldn't fight such a large institution.

***** *****

Keith helped us put our few salvaged items into his SUV. He then took us to Target where we bought underwear and socks to augment our meager wardrobe. Later we returned to his home where we settled in talking with Dodie about the upcoming birth of their son. We definitely didn't want to even think about our disaster.

"Considering that this is my first pregnancy and I am over forty, my doctor and I feel that I'm doing really well," Dodie said.

Keith added, "I'm really excited about becoming a father, but it's a little daunting when I realize all the responsibilities and major changes in our lives involved in having a child."

"I remember those changes well," I said. "The lack of sleep and always having to be on the alert sticks in my mind. Keith, I'd like you to be a hands on father. I learned that being there with my kids was so important to me and to them. Don't be afraid to hold and care for your tiny boy when he comes."

"He won't break!" Dodie asserted. We all laughed.

Later we took our friends out for dinner at the Old Fisherman's Seafood Grotto on the wharf as one way to express our gratitude for their generous and warm hospitality and sincere understanding. Sometime during that evening, *JoJo* would arrive at the Monterey Boat Works and be deposited in the work yard.

After breakfast the next morning, Keith drove us to the work yard to see our wrecked boat and to search for my wallet and Betsy's jewelry.

There *JoJo* sat on the dry ground missing her keel. The huge hole in her port side allowed us to step inside the remains of our trusted companion.

"My God, our wonderful sailboat is now a total wreck," I said, gritting my teeth. "Let's see if there are any valuables still aboard."

What was left of the interior smelled strongly of diesel and was covered with gooey sand. I was overwhelmed by seeing my treasured boat destroyed and reduced to such a mess. I had to steel myself to focus on the task at hand. After pulling the heavy, limp soggy cushions out of the boat, I crawled into the forward cabin and yelled, "Betsy, I found the plastic bag with your jewelry. It's wet, but intact. My wallet, however, is nowhere to be seen."

"I'm so grateful you found the jewelry!" Betsy exclaimed. "Lots of it belonged to Mom."

Outside, Keith, Betsy, and I began the process of salvaging our brand new tan dodger still at its station protecting the companionway and cockpit. It had not been included on the insured list of equipment. As it was unharmed by its harrowing experience, we would be able to sell it later to another Catalina owner for a fair price. Sandy and Rich arrived and helped us to remove more equipment and lines. I felt like those people who lived on the North Carolina barrier islands in the 1800s who scavenged ship-wrecks for anything of value to supplement their meager exis-tence.

Captain Joseph Rodgers, a Marine Surveyor representing our insurance company, walked up. After taking one long look he de-clared, "Your boat is a total loss, but I'll be sure that you get the full insured hull value." Seeing my sad face, he added sympatheti-cally, "You know this is why you have insurance. Bad things can happen."

Joe's warm response and genuine concern buoyed my spirits knowing that I was hearing those words from a fellow sailor. His acceptance of me helped repair some of my wounded self-esteem.

Later, when we picked up our dinghy at the Coast Guard dock I found my glasses that had been knocked off by the breaking wave. They were stuck along the bottom of the inflation tube. We loaded the dinghy into the SUV, and Keith took it to his house. I added it to the other salvaged items undergoing water blasts with the hose to remove the sand and salt. Betsy and I rented a big van so we could haul us and all our salvaged gear back to Walnut Creek where our home was waiting for us.

*****

Deciding to act on my desire to work with teenagers, I volun-teered with the weekly Senior Tutors program at the Boy's Ranch residential program for delinquent youth. I felt I was making an important reconnection to strands of my life. Betsy got back into her art by joining a figure drawing class. For many years, she had spent her time working in civil engineering design but was now free to let her artist loose.

*****

A small miracle occurred two weeks after we returned home. I opened the mail one day and there was my wallet and all its con-tents. It had been found by the harbormaster washed ashore on Pebble Beach.

14

"Wow, some of our Livengood Luck must still be working," I gushed.

"Yeah, but it wasn't with us on that terrible night," Betsy replied.

*****

Just before Thanksgiving, Dodie gave birth to Cooper, a fine red-haired boy. Keith and Dodie gave us the honor of being his Godparents. Seeing and holding him a month later deepened our feelings for and connection with this wonderful family. A year later Keith, Dodie, and Cooper moved to Alexandria, Virginia. Keith began his State Department training for his new role as military attaché and pilot at the United States Embassy in Accra, Ghana. Betsy and I hoped to visit them in Africa after they'd settled in.

*****

After a month's time, I had enough emotional distance to reflect on the events around the shipwreck. In my opinion, the Coast Guard violated the practice of "good seamanship" by not helping me to secure *JoJo* and prevent her destruction.

We were in a marine sanctuary, and only by luck had I replaced the old fuel tank that began leaking before the trip. Because the new aluminum tank was much stronger, a fuel spill was averted, saving the environment from 30 gallons of toxic diesel. Again the Coast Guard did nothing to prevent this potential spill.

I remembered one Coast Guard Officer's statement. "We only save people, not boats." This hollow intention seemed to ignore the environment and put boat owners at more risk. Some of us want to do what is right for both the environment *and* ourselves. Actually the Coast Guard arrived on their cutter unprepared to help even us because they had no inflatable boat or dinghy capable of going into shallow water.

If Betsy had broken her leg or was too disabled to leave the boat, what would they have done to help rescue her? Her jump into the dinghy from the flopping boat also put her in peril.

Accidents are a series of events. In my case, tragic events compounded with poor judgment created a final catastrophe. We lost a grand sailboat that had given us many hours of sailing pleasure. She represented to us four years of hard work upgrading and replacing older and failing equipment. Such an investment was not totally insured. More to the point, *JoJo* was ground up and dumped in a landfill. What an undignified final end to a lovely boat named for my late wife and sailing partner JoAnne! What a punch in the gut for this passionate, experienced sailor whose life long dream to sail the seas was snuffed out in one terrible night!

3

DAWNING OF THE DREAM

How did sailing and traveling by sailboat become so firmly implanted in my mind and in my dreams? After all, I grew up in Aurora, Ohio, miles away from the closest big body of water, Lake Erie. Why did I have a burning desire to buy a sailboat? Why did I have to sail the seas? Here, "have to" are the operative words. Perhaps the print of Winslow Homer's *Boys Sailing* hung in my bedroom as a boy had a subliminal influence on me. My eyes were drawn to the scene of a sailboat cutting through the sea as white clouds hovered above. Homer captured the sloop's motion through the water while the boys' sprawling bodies spoke of relaxation and fun. At times I could feel myself on that boat with a smile on my face.

Then, I remember my early teenage years at Northwoods YMCA Camp in northern Ontario, Canada. Canoeing and canoe portaging were the main activities during the seven-week summer camp. I also had great fun sailing and racing small sailboats around the many camp islands. Our eight-boy cabin groups with one counselor (not much older than us) took trips on Lake Temagami, a large glacier-formed lake. It looked like an stretched open hand with its 2,000 miles of shoreline and about 1,500 islands of all sizes. Lake Temagami and nearby lakes were our playground. We explored the shoreline and camped on islands. We fished, and even drank water directly from the lake.

I can still feel the thrill of paddling hard, gliding so close to the blue water racing other cabin groups north to Bear Island where the losers had to buy Cokes for the winners at the Hudson's Bay Post. Of course, we were always the winners! Canoes were like magic carpets freeing us from the ordinary, allowing us to explore, and create new adventures. The lakes were our highways leading us always forward. It was here in the lake waters that the idea of using canoes and boats to explore and travel to new places was born in me. The excitement of discovering what lay across the lake or at the end of the portage or down the river though its rapids stayed with me. My emotional connection to those waters and possibilities sparked my dream to visit new places by boat and experience different cultures where I could learn about their rich history in person.

Later as an adult, I fueled my passion by devouring every book on sailing and cruising I could find. Irving and Electra Johnson's books and articles in *National Geographic* about adventures aboard their schooner, *Yankee*, captivated my interest. *Starbound*, a book written by Gordon and Nina Stuermer, told a compelling story of their family who restored an old fifty-foot-long wooden sailboat and sailed it around the world. These stories captured my imagination. The strong feeling of "Yes, I can do that too!" rose up in me and crystallized as an underlying goal of my life to sail long distances. Gordon Stuermer migrated from the pages of his book and settled into my consciousness, becoming my mentor and role model.

* * * * *

After completing graduate school in social work at Case Western Reserve in Cleveland, Ohio, in 1962, my new wife and I moved to the San Francisco Bay Area in California to work and later to start a family, eventually having four children. I was the assistant director of a youth center working with street gangs in San Francisco. The press of work and family life took lots of time, but the dream of sailing flowed like an undercurrent through my life, fed by my reading.

In 1970, I went to the San Francisco Cow Palace Boat Show where I joined swarms of enthusiasts examining all sorts of boats. The MacGregor Clipper Mk 21 sloop stood out in the crowd of boats. The Clipper's flared bow and sleek white hull pulled me to her. I imagined her cutting through the water heeling with the pressure of the wind. The special "boat show price" put her within my budget so I excitedly ordered a new boat from a factory representative. The Clipper had a white hull, one mast, a white mainsail on a horizontal boom and a loosely flown jib forward at the bow. A cast iron swing keel hung down from the bottom of the hull. When cranked up into the boat, it created a flat bottomed beach-able boat perfect for lake sailing. When under sail, the lowered keel would balance the changing forces of the wind.

A month later, my second wife and I trailered the boat back to the San Francisco Bay Area from the factory in Costa Mesa, Southern California. On our way back, I felt the urge to get her in the water. Morro Bay on the Central California Coast was nearby. Even though we didn't have a chart of the area, I was compelled to launch the boat into its element and feel it propelled by the wind. After I raised the mast and rigged the sails, the Clipper came alive and scooted across the bay. We were soon aground on a mud bar in the middle of the bay. Fortunately after cranking up the keel, I was able to happily sail the boat back to the launching ramp, proving the merits of its design. I was lucky but obviously needed to do more planning.

Whenever I had time, I sailed the Clipper in San Francisco Bay, learning how to handle its strong tides, often high winds, and many waves. The conditions on the bay were a challenge for me and the twenty-one-foot small boat. To sail my dream, I must master sailing in these conditions present on the world's seas.

On one excursion my Tunisian brother-in-law cried out with a French accent, "Le balance! Le balance!" in response to a gust of wind that heeled over the boat. My sister, Margie, let out a scream as a seal surfaced within arm's reach of the boat, peering at her with its dark brown eyes. I felt great involving my family in my passion for sailing.

Sailing became a fun family activity where I involved my children on the boat teaching them how to steer the boat and set the sails. I trailered the Clipper to Lake Folsom near Sacramento for camping weekends on an island with my kids as a special treat. My son David, with his usual abandon, jumped into the lake, and I threw him a line as we were sailing along. He loved being towed behind the boat in the warm water. Lake Shasta in Northern California was also a favorite for our family outings. Although we were having fun, the kids were learning more and more about sailing as they each took turns on the tiller pointing the boat toward an objective while keeping the sails filled with wind. Accomplishing this task was a necessary first step for anyone learning how to sail well.

The highlight of owning the Clipper came in February 1973 when I trailered her to Mexico with a crew of my coworkers from Catholic Social Service of Marin where I worked as a family therapist. I chose the Sea of Cortez between mainland Mexico and the Baja California Peninsula as a destination because its waters were protected and the weather would be warm. Being in the Mexican culture was another attraction. Here, the dreams floating in my imagination surfaced into reality.

The crew included my boss, Jim, a tall, slender and bearded fifty-year-old experienced sailor and boat owner whose playground was sailing San Francisco Bay; fellow therapist and friend Laurie, an attractive blond young woman with an adventurous spirit; her husband, Dick, an engineer with a slight surplus of seriousness, and my married UC Berkeley social work graduate student Bruce, who was full of fun. I was glad Jim was on board with all his experience. After all, this was my first cruising adventure, and he probably was more skilled than I was at the time.

As we were driving south through San Bernardino in the evening, suddenly my Jeep Wagoneer lost forward momentum after a sharp clank and some ominous rumbling sounds. I turned onto the emergency stopping lane as we rolled to a stop at the side of the freeway.

Looking under the Jeep I exclaimed, "Oh my God, the rear drive shaft is hanging down and scraping the pavement. No wonder we lost power."

We stood there dumfounded as traffic zoomed by. Applying my "Livengood Luck," I tied up the downed drive shaft and engaged the front wheel drive unit, allowing us to motor into town where we found an open garage. Fortunately, the mechanic could replace the broken universal joint from a part he had in stock. So off we went again until the drive line to the front wheels failed. This second failure shook my faith in the Jeep, but like a prepared boy scout I had bailing wire with me. I crawled under the Jeep and secured the broken drive shaft to the frame. Then we were off again to Mexico. Giving up on sailing in the Sea of Cortez? Never!

We crossed the Mexican border sometime after midnight and by late morning reached Baja Kino (Bay). It was glorious to see the sea shimmering in the bright sunlight. Excitement in me was bubbling over. I slowly backed the Jeep down the barren beach into the water and launched the Clipper off the trailer into the Sea of Cortez on its eastern side. We prepared for our voyage by loading our sleeping bags, food, and gear aboard the boat before we left.

As we looked out into the sea, a wave of feelings and thoughts washed over me. Wow, I'm really living my dream. What's it going to be like? Will reality live up to all the images I've been carrying in my head? Am I up to the challenges that lie ahead?

Bruce was put in command of the Jeep and trailer and I gave him instructions.

"Bruce, I want you to bring the Jeep and trailer on the ferry from Guymas across the Sea of Cortez to Santa Rosalia and pick us and the boat up in one week. Here's money for the ferry tickets."

"I'll be there. I'm looking forward to soaking up the sun and drinking lots of Mexican beer between now and then," Bruce said heartily laughing. He left and drove the Jeep and trailer south to Guymas for a week of camping on the beach.

Using a chart and compass as our navigation tools, we began our sail across the sea toward the islands of Tiburon, San Esteban, and San Lorenzo. The Clipper handled beautifully as she caught the wind and picked up speed. "This is great. Now we're really doing it," I exclaimed.

The interior of the Clipper had a V-shaped berth forward that was occupied by Laurie and Dick and two single berths aft, one on each side of the boat under the cockpit seats where Jim and I had to wriggle into the coffin-like spaces. Four people sleeping on a twenty-one-foot boat ended up pushing the envelope so we stopped at each island and camped on the beach. We cooked on a two burner Coleman stove or over an open fire. A small port-a-potty occupied most of the floor space in the boat. We used a small tarp to create the illusion of privacy for its occupant.

On day five, we reached the western Baja California shore and turned south toward Santa Rosalia. We soon discovered that the shoreline looked all the same and we didn't know where we were at that point.

After beaching the boat for the night, Jim said nervously, "Ya know, I'd feel much better if we actually knew where we are."

"I remember solving a problem like this in Explorer Scouts," I said. "By creating a north-south line using two sticks sighted on the North Star, I can find true north. I'll go and set one up on the beach." Dusk faded into darkness. The Big Dipper soon was visible and by aligning the two outer stars of the Dipper and moving higher into the sky five spaces, I found the brightest star which is the North Star. Everyone seemed relieved after I set up the line with two sticks in the sand.

In the morning, I oriented our chart to that north-south line. We were then able to see points on the coast and matched them with those on the chart. Voila! I felt competent having established our position, finally knowing our exact location.

Dolphins at Play

After an oatmeal breakfast, we pushed off from the beach. A large pod of dolphins soon surrounded us, surfacing and roiling in the water. What a magical experience to be so close to these wonderful creatures. Laurie and I lay on the foredeck pounding on the sides of the boat, calling, and whistling trying to entice the dolphins closer. Suddenly three of them leaped together forming a flower shape unfolding over the Sea of Cortez. The amazing sight delighted us!

As we enjoyed our dolphin encounter, Jim yelled out, "We're running low on gas for the outboard motor! We could be stranded out here!" He paused. "Wait, I hear an airplane. Let's all wave our orange life jackets as a distress signal."

It seemed to me that Jim's anxiety was being piqued by our having fun with the dolphins because he hadn't mentioned his concerns before that moment.

Dick and Jim began waving their life jackets over their heads attempting to signal the passing aircraft. I remained immersed in the remarkable moment of communicating with the dolphins.

"I'm not worried in the least, Jim," I said with confidence. "The onshore wind always rises in the afternoon and will eventually carry us to our pickup point at Santa Rosalia."

A half hour later, a 30-foot-long panga, a large fiberglass, open fishing boat appeared on the horizon filled with smiling fishermen who responded to our beckoning calls and waving arms. They were able to sell us enough gas to reach our destination, Santa Rosalia.

"Problem solved!" I said with a smile. "Looks like 'Livengood Luck' is still with us."

Located on the western shore of the Sea of Cortez, Santa Rosalia is about midway down the Baja Peninsula with a harbor serving as a terminus for the car ferry connecting Baja California with mainland Mexico, at Guymas. As the old copper mining community came into view, we could see the cast iron church and steeple designed and cast in France by Eiffel, the creator of the Eiffel Tower. The church and its tower had been shown in the 1889 Paris Exposition. Originally destined for Africa, the church was found by the French directors of the copper mining company disassembled in Belgium. In 1894, the structure was shipped in pieces to Santa Rosalia by boat and reassembled. The church became the town's principal place of worship.

After finding the harbor and tying up to a dock, we walked to a small restaurant and had a delicious dinner of tacos and fajitas washed down with potent Margaritas. Afterwards we walked further into town. I realized that I had left my camera at the restaurant. By the time we returned, however, the restaurant was closed.

Coming back in the morning, I asked the restaurant owner about the camera. "Senor, I took it to the Port Captain's office," he said. Sure enough, there it was behind the office counter, a testament to the honesty of Mexican people. By now many people knew that we, the *Norte Americanos*, had arrived.

In the morning Jim seemed agitated. "I'm worried that Bruce isn't reliable enough to bring the Jeep and trailer over to Santa Rosalia on time," he said nervously. "I'm going to ride the ferry across to Guymas and find Bruce to be sure he makes the connection."

"Jim, I really don't think your trip across is necessary," I said, thinking he was a bit crazy. "You know he's a responsible, married graduate student in social welfare."

"Well, I'm going now anyway," Jim insisted.

Because we had run out of our allotted time, we were unable to sail to our original destination of Mulege. Now we had to wait for Jim and Bruce. In the meantime, Laurie, Dick, and I took a 30-mile bus ride south to Mulege. An oasis-like town, Mulege is situated on the banks of one of the few rivers flowing out of the Baja California desert. Leaving the bus station, we walked along a dusty road next to the river in the shade of tall palm trees. At the end is a spot where the river joins the Sea of Cortez punctuated by a lighthouse resting on a volcanic cone. We wanted to see how people lived in Mulege and were not disappointed in our quest. We saw women baking bread in wood-fired brick ovens in their yards next to their small colorful houses along the river.

As we walked back toward the main square, Laurie said, "I know we all wanted to come to Mulege, but it may have been a mistake. We don't have a plan of how to return to Santa Rosalia in time for the ferry. The next bus north doesn't come until tomorrow."

"Good point! Why don't we try to find someone who can give us a ride back," I suggested. "I remember seeing a number of Gringos sitting on benches in the square."

After asking around, we found one couple who said nonchalantly, "Sure, come out to our hotel, and we'll take you. No problema."

As they rode off on a small motorbike, we caught a taxi and followed them. Our mouths dropped as we drove onto a dirt runway of a "fly-in-hotel," right up to their twin engine Beechcraft Bonanza airplane. We jumped out of the taxi, climbed up on the wing and squeezed through a small doorway into the back seat of this five-seater plane. We sat behind the pilot and his wife in the front seats as the plane zoomed down the runway and up into the air. What a fantastic treat seeing the turquoise blue Sea of Cortez shimmering below us, outlined by white sand beaches. Looking out of the left side of the plane, we saw a spine of rugged mountains jutting up 5,000 feet above the sea to frame our view. Taking in the expanse of the sea was a grand contrast to our close-up intimate view from the deck of the Clipper. What a multi-layered impression of our experience that sent shivers up my spine.

Beach Craft Bonanza over Sea of Cortez

Just imagine hitchhiking on an airplane!

Approaching the airport created by cutting off a mountain top above Santa Rosalia, the pilot warned us, "Expect some turbulence over the canyon at the end of the runway."

The sight of a wrecked plane littered on the left side of the runway emphasized his point! He came in fast with power to spare making a smooth landing. Thinking back, I can see that my "Livengood Luck" was riding with us again. Thanking these generous Americans, we strode past expectant taxi drivers, down the hill, through backyards to our waiting boat.

"Great to see you guys, wait till you hear what we've been up to," I greeted Jim and Bruce who just arrived with the Jeep and trailer. After sharing our Mulege adventures, I happily loaded the Clipper onto the trailer and drove the whole outfit into the ferry for a much faster trip across the Sea of Cortez to mainland Mexico. An uneventful drive north home to the San Francisco Bay Area was a welcome change from the breakdown-plagued trip when we began our journey south.

This maiden voyage in the Sea of Cortez convinced me that traveling by sailboat would be an adventurous way to see more of the world. I was hungry for more! After this ten-day trip where I had expected Jim's more extensive sailing experience to supplement my own inexperience, I realized that *I* should be and *had* to be the captain of my own boat!

4

BACK TO THE LAND

Following the sailing trip to Mexico in 1973, the desire of my second wife, Elaine, to move to the country initiated my growing interest in the "back to the land" movement. Elaine and I and our two children, Andy and Leanne, moved to Trinity County located in the mountains of Northern California. We hoped that living in the country would strengthen our marriage. We bought a 325-acre ranch in Hayfork that had an old Victorian style house, a huge one hundred-ton capacity hay barn, a drive-in shop, and other outbuildings. I quickly learned, however, that ranching did not produce enough income. Consequently, I applied for and was selected as the director of a day center for mentally challenged and mentally ill adults. I worked to keep the center open by securing grants and opening a six bed group home. I now had two jobs, running the center and the ranch.

The Clipper sat in the barnyard, but the demands of both jobs limited the time I could enjoy her. In the fall of 1976, I sold the Clipper to buy a backhoe. My marriage to Elaine was failing; being together was filled with conflict and pain.

My solution to gain some peace was to use 24 acres of undeveloped ranch property located across Hayfork Creek to build my own log cabin and a barn for the animals. For me, this "total involvement" therapy helped me cope with my feelings of disappointment and rejection.

First, I chose to build a barn for my half of the goats, rabbits, and chickens that populated the ranch across the creek. My friend Ken, who worked for me at the center, had built his own livable house for under five hundred dollars. We teamed up with my teenage sons, Doug and David, and cut ten standing dead pine trees that would form the central supports for the pole barn. I used the backhoe to lift the poles onto rebar pins embedded in concrete piers that I poured. The poles were interconnected with smaller timbers to form the basic structure. While attaching the roof rafters, I realized that everything seemed to be swaying in an alarming way.

Ken brought over a pickup truck load of 4x6 foot corrugated galvanized roof panels he had found at an abandoned lumber mill. Together we nailed them down and the structure stiffened, confirming son Doug's and my design. The whole 32x40 barn cost about $1500. The hard work, ingenuity, and achievement strengthened my sense of self-worth that had been steadily eroding in my miserable marriage.

*****

Building my 1,500-square-foot log house before winter was my next and more challenging task. My design called for a two-story structure having a cathedral ceiling in the front and two bedrooms and a bath upstairs to the back. Downstairs would be an open living/dining area with the kitchen to the left and the master bedroom and bath to the right. The logs were milled from 4x6 beams harvested by my neighbor, Claude. The finished logs had 3/4 inch grooves top and bottom, a half-round side facing out, and a tongue and groove side that composed the inside walls.

I enlisted Dick, the divorced father of one of my center clients, to help me build the house. He began living in his VW camper van near my ten-foot travel trailer next to the barn. After the foundation was poured, I needed more help to build my cabin. One night, I approached two long-haired, twenty-something guys who frequented the Hayfork Tavern where Dick and I hung out as the nights got colder.

"How would you guys like to help me build my log house?" I said.

"Sure, but how much can you pay?" the one named Mangey replied.

After thinking a moment, I said, "I can pay you a couple of bucks more than minimum wage per hour."

"Okay, it's a done deal!" said Mangey and his friend Ken, raising their beer bottles.

"See you tomorrow morning at eight," I said. "I am building the cabin across the creek from the Pony Ranch."

The next morning, we began building the cabin using the manufactured logs from Claude. The first logs were laid out and nailed down to the subfloor. Then each subsequent log was nailed down to its partner log below using ten-inch spikes about the thickness of my little finger. This repetitive process took lots of energy using a small sledge hammer to drive the spike into the groove in the log. We inserted 1x2 inch board into the grooves in the logs to seal the space between each log, and then repeated the whole very physical process again and again.

Setting 4 x 12 Rafters on Cabin

*****

Mangey and Ken became energetic stalwarts on the crew. They bought an old trailer "mobile home" and wanted to live in it on the few acres of land they owned down the road from me. Their problem was no one had a truck with enough power or traction to haul their heavy trailer up the mountain to their property. I volunteered to use my old D4 Caterpillar bulldozer which did the job.

"Thanks to you we have our home in place before winter sets in," Mangey said.

"Thanks to you guys and your hard work, I'll soon have a cabin to live in," I said.

We all worked hard to enclose the cabin before the onset of winter. We almost made it, but on a number of mornings, our first task was to shovel the early snow off the floor and out of the cabin.

Finally after we hammered down the last roof boards and covered them with thick tar paper, nailed the windows to their wood frames, and hooked up the wood stove to its metal flue, the cabin was now enclosed and had a source of heat. I could finally move in and leave the confines of the travel trailer. Feelings of joy and accomplishment flooded my body.

One night, I had a vivid dream of a young woman driving a sports car up my long dirt driveway to see me. Wow, what a great dream to have, probably in response to my loneliness. A few days later, a small, moss green Toyota pickup truck came up the long drive carrying Julie, the young, attractive, blonde woman who had bought baby goats from me in the past. Her bubbly personality brought a smile to my face.

She was stopping by to see how the cabin was coming along. "It's great, I love it," she said as I proudly showed her around. "I like the view from the kitchen windows looking out into the woods and over the pasture to the creek. I feel like I am surrounded by the forest, it's almost like living in a treehouse."

"Yeah, I was careful to place the house among the trees rather than cut them down since I like that same feeling," I agreed. "It's been a lot of work, but I'm really pleased with the way it turned out."

As she visited a few times more, I began to get the message that she might really be interested in me. Younger than me, Julie worked at the high school and she was also interested in raising animals. She was in an unhappy relationship with her husband, which seemed to be motivating her to look for a better alternative. Our attraction to each other grew daily.

As we talked about getting together, I pointed out our age difference, "Julie, I'm seventeen years older than you. That seems like a lot to me."

"Look, I don't think it's a big deal," said Julie. "You are only forty and you seem young at heart."

"I don't want to begin a relationship with you that has no real future," I asserted.

"I understand that," she said. "It's important to me, too."

Perhaps my "Livengood Luck" is working again, I thought.

Soon she moved in with her daughter, Jessie, who was friends with my daughter Leanne, still living across the creek with her mom. Julie's love and caring helped me repair the damages to my self-esteem. Our sexual relationship was easy and open. Julie and I lived together and cared for our animals for eight harmonious months. Unfortunately, just as Julie had driven up the driveway, about nine months later she drove away leaving a big painful hole in my gut. Julie's returning for occasional weekends would smooth over my wounded feelings temporarily, but she couldn't explain why she felt she had to leave. In the end, I felt the difference in our ages did matter, a lot!

My son David arrived to live with me in the log house after his mother and stepfather could no longer tolerate his defiant behavior that was encouraging his brother and sisters to act out the same way. David was fourteen years old, of medium build with a handsome face and a jokester smile. He did well on the farm. He loved to drive the tractor and cut wood, but his rebellious actions in the ninth grade at Hayfork High School caused a number of suspensions and eventually the assignment to a continuation school.

David was always pushing the limits with me, but more importantly with other authority figures. Our relationship was at times tense, but David seemed to value living with me. We continued to love each other through all his teenage difficulties even as I felt pushed to my limits. David remained with me through high school, then off and on during his young adulthood as he found work trimming trees. Later in life he would join me in my construction business. We would continue to have a good relationship and would survive the angst of his teenage years.

The dream of sailing again sustained me though the five long "back to the land" years of hard work and painful heartbreak. When I wasn't working on the ranch, on my house, or at the adult day center, I was reading books on sailing and cruising in a sailboat. I remembered my boyhood thrills of gliding over blue waters on Lake Temagami. In my mind and heart, I relived that first time I sailed out into the Sea of Cortez and saw my dream coming true. It was now time to put my life on a different course that would take me back to the water!

5

FULL SPEED FORWARD TOWARD MY DREAM

Bailing hay in the field on one suffocatingly hot afternoon, my old bailer kept jumping off its trailer hitch. Each time, I had to stop the tractor, get off, crank up the bailer's tongue with a jack, and re-attach it to the hitch. The constant toil in the searing heat burned in my mind, driving me crazy. This is NOT fun anymore, I thought over and over until I stopped the tractor and got off. "I'm burned out!" I shouted at no one. "I have to get back to my dream of cruising the world in my own sailboat." My marriage to Elaine was over, and my children were living with her. Seeing Julie, my lost love, around town was also painful. Hayfork's smallness was oppressive. "I have to get out," I sighed, sweat dripping down my neck.

A day later, I talked over my feelings of being worn out and discouraged with friends Bob and Linda, perceptive ex-hippies, who had worked for me at the center. "Buck up, Karl, it's time for a change," Bob said. "You've got to go for your dream, friend."

"You've reached a dead end up here and you have to follow your dream," Linda added.

Hearing my friends acknowledge my frustration and support my dream boosted my clarity and self-confidence.

"Yeah, you're right," I said. "It's time to change the direction of my life. I'll sell my log house, barn, and land, along with all the farm equipment. Then I'll have enough money to buy a cruising sailboat." I took a deep breath. "Yes, it's time for me to go for my dream!" I spoke with sure determination.

I immediately began to put my plan in motion. I placed my property in the hands of a real estate agent. I moved to Oakland with my son David, where we lived in a two bedroom apartment on the first floor of a duplex below my sister, Margie. It was a great location on Irwin Court just off Telegraph Avenue near the border of Berkeley.

Living on Irwin Court, a dead-end street with no through traffic, was like being in a small village surrounded by the bustle of the city where I could make friends in the neighborhood. Most important, I was only minutes from San Francisco Bay.

Joined on holidays and summer vacations by my oldest son, Doug, and my youngest son, Andy, we often had a crowded home. I was the chief cook when things were going well, but also the bottle washer when the boys neglected their duties. When my three daughters Darsie, Jeanne, and Leanne visited, they slept on the floor.

Soon, my neighbor David and I formed "Classic Renovations," a small carpentry business where I used the skills I developed while building my log house in the mountains. Our small business grew from referrals by David's brother-in-law, Larry, a professor at UC Berkeley. We became the favorite renovators for Larry's circle of UC Berkeley professors. The business financially supported me. It gave my kids opportunities to learn building skills while allowing me to take time off to pursue my sailing.

Being so close to the Bay was tantalizing. I could see fleets of boats being sailed as David and I drove to work. One morning I exclaimed, "Now it's time to get my own boat, David!"

I began my search for a cruising boat by reading about sailboats, their characteristics, construction, and sailing ability. Going to the water boat shows at Jack London Square on Oakland's waterfront helped me to compare the photos, diagrams, and descriptions of sailboats in magazines and books with actual boats. I could see and touch them, climb onto them, and ask questions about them. A number of "on paper" boats that attracted me did not fair so well in the bright light of reality. The skills I gained as a carpenter and builder sharpened my critical eye for detail in boats.

Poorly crafted wood joinery pointed to even worse problems lurking beneath the interior wood.

The design of one boat, the Nantucket Island 33, called out to me from an article in my favorite magazine, *Cruising World*. I wrote a letter expressing interest to the builder, Australian structural engineer and sailor Graham Shields, in Hong Kong. He sent more detailed drawings and pictures of the boat. My questions flew West to him; Graham's answers traveled back East to me. The next step was to see the boat in person. There was one small problem. None of these newly designed boats was in the United States, so I had to go to Hong Kong.

I called my mother. "Mom, how about taking a trip to Hong Kong with me?"

An inveterate shopper and traveler she said, "Yes, sounds like a great idea to me. I've always wanted to go shopping in Hong Kong." We would share the cost of the hotel room in Kowloon and explore Hong Kong together. Approaching Hong Kong's airport was a bit disconcerting because the plane had to thread its way between tall buildings just off the wing tips in order to land on a runway jutting out into the bay. As the plane touched down, Mom and I held our breath and clutched our armrests.

After settling in at the hotel, we walked along Nathan Road and gazed up at the amazing jumble of signs over the nearby myriad of small businesses lining the street. Mom immediately shifted into her major shopping mode.

"I have to buy Christmas presents for all eleven grandchildren. I better get busy," she said, eyeing the store in front of us.

"Mom, I've got to get back to the hotel to rest," I said. "Can you find your way back? Here's the hotel card. Come back when you're ready."

She nodded. "Sure, I'll take a taxi."

The next morning we took a taxi to Graham's office to arrange to see the boat. I was excited to meet him in person. As we talked about the boat, I sensed the depth of his expertise and commitment to building a great boat, a good sign to me. At the harbor, we found a water taxi to take us out to the Nantucket Island 33. It seemed like forever as we wound our way through hundreds of

Sampans, small wooden house boats moored in the Victoria Harbor Typhoon Basin. The floating community was connected by boards used as pathways to their neighbors and to shore.

We finally found the Nantucket Island 33. Instantly, I was taken by the look and feel of the sailboat with a small center cockpit and flush deck. She was beautiful! Her great sheer lines outlining the level of the deck spoke to me of speed. I imagined myself steering her as she sliced through the water. I tingled all over. Looking at the deck from side to side I saw that the boat took on the shape of a convex curve, higher in the center sloping to the sides of the hull, great for shedding breaking waves. This shape also created a very strong deck. A teak band below the cap rail, which covered the top of the hull to deck joint, accentuated the sheer line, helping the boat appear lower to the water. As I climbed down the companionway ladder into the cabin, I looked around and remarked to Graham, "Wow, what a great U-shaped galley. Besides being efficient, it has lots of handholds needed for cooking underway!"

"You're right," Graham added. "It's designed with a propane stove with oven, a double stainless steel sink, an icebox, and loads of counter space."

"I am amazed by the dining area," I said. "Looks like the settees can sit six to eight persons around the table."

"Here, next to the companionway ladder is the navigation area with real chart table and comfortable seat, a storage drawer under the table and space above to mount instruments," Graham pointed out. "Go forward and you'll see the nice two person V-berth with a hanging locker and dresser all closed off from the main cabin by a sliding door. It really creates a private space."

Then walking aft to the rear of the boat through the bathroom, I arrived in the aft cabin. "Graham, this is a comfortable cabin with double berth, a settee, and even a vanity with mirror. This space should really appeal to the ladies, hey?" He nodded.

I was amazed how my dreams expanded while being on this boat. It was so beautiful, so cozy. I felt at home. I knew that she would be *my* boat—soon!

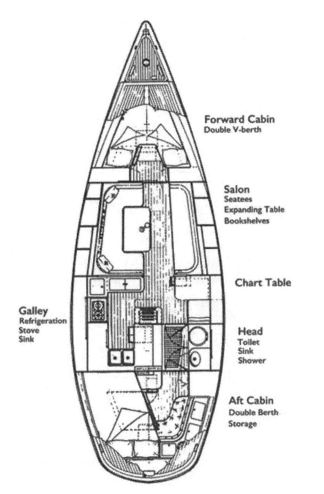

Forward Cabin
Double V-berth

Salon
Seatees
Expanding Table
Bookshelves

Chart Table

Galley
Refrigeration
Stove
Sink

Head
Toilet
Sink
Shower

Aft Cabin
Double Berth
Storage

Nantucket 33 Interior Layout

The interior bulkheads were finished in teak and the hull was covered with spruce tongue and groove boards mounted horizontally having a contrasting lighter tan color. What really attracted me was the homey, "mountain cabin" feel that was most inviting. I could have the water and land at the same time!

Seeing the Nantucket 33 was the first step of our meeting with Graham. He arranged for all of us to sail north on the South China Sea to the outpost of the Hong Kong Yacht Club that was surrounded by China. The next morning under bright sunny skies, we motored out of the Typhoon Basin into the sea where we picked up a strong breeze that filled the sails and began to heel the boat. Sailing in the flush decked center cockpit for the first time was a new and a bit unnerving experience. The seating position in an open cockpit was quite high off the water as the boat heeled in the breeze. Mom hung on and I wondered out loud, "Will this boat stay upright?"

"We don't have too much sail out," said Graham. "See how fast she's slicing through the water." He was trying to reassure me that all was well.

"Yes, you're right, she does have a good turn of speed," I agreed, feeling more at ease.

I saw that the Nantucket Island 33 was a very well made and compactly designed fiberglass boat. She is fun to sail and will be comfortable to live aboard, I thought. Both of these qualities are very important to me. Of course, more questions developed as I got deeper into trying to understand the construction of the boat. Using his structural engineering and sailing skills, Graham gave me detailed answers of how the boat was put together. The knowledge I gained being with Graham would help me for all the years of owning my own hull number 8.

Later in the afternoon, we anchored in the harbor of the Hong Kong yacht club located in the New Territories near China. We had a barbeque dinner overlooking the South China Sea and slept on the Nantucket overnight. In the morning, I had an exhilarating sail back to the Typhoon Basin.

Mom and I returned to Hong Kong and saw more sights. We even had "High Tea" accompanied by a string quartet at the magnificent Peninsula Hotel. Two days later, we took the long flight back to San Francisco. All the time, I couldn't stop talking about the Nantucket 33. Mom agreed that it was a great boat. I knew in my bones I had to have this boat.

When we arrived at U.S. customs at the San Francisco Airport, the agent looked at Mom's long list of purchases, turned to me, and said, "You mean, you actually let her loose in Hong Kong?" He smiled and waved us through!

Aurora at Anchor

Salon, Table, Library

Salon, to V berth

Salon, Table, Library

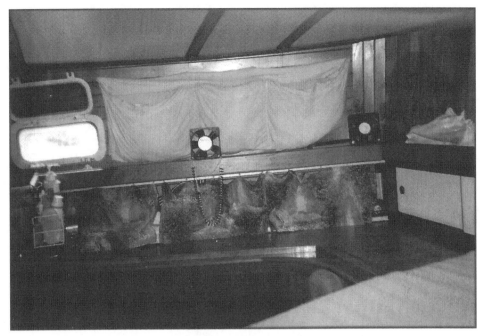

Aft Cabin, Seatee, Storage

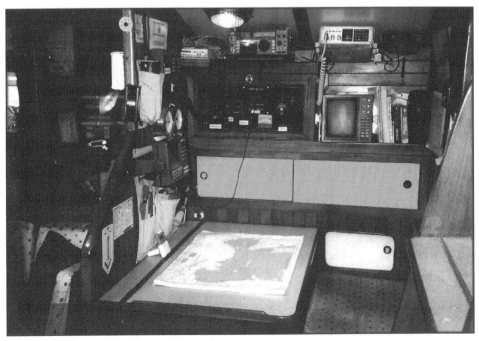

Chart Table, Radar, Radios

Paradise Island

Aurora in Turkey

When talking with Graham three months later, I quickly decided to buy the alluring Nantucket Island 33.

"I can offer you a boat at its current price of $50,000," said Graham. "This price includes the mainsail, the jib, two genoas, the large sails forward of the mast, and a cruising spinnaker. It can be delivered to Oakland as deck cargo on a container ship from Kaohsiung, Taiwan. If you wait any longer, I am going to have to raise the price about $10,000."

Fear that my dream could slip away if I didn't act pushed me to say yes right then. "Okay, Graham, I want the Nantucket for $50,000," I said. "We have a deal!" That was a lot of money for me at the time, but my dream was worth it. I could justify spending that much money only if my cruising dreams could become reality. Just having the boat tied to the dock and using it occasionally on weekends was not the cruising life I envisioned living.

In the nine months before my sailboat would arrive, I continued taking all the classes I could find related to sailing at the College of Alameda, a nearby community college. Peter, a professor of physics and an avid sailor, taught most of the classes. All these classes were offered at low community college prices in the evenings. The excellent instructors helped to prepare me to sail on the world's oceans and seas.

In Celestial Navigation class I made friends with Elmo Moorhead, a retired chemical engineer and avowed "health nut" who loved sailing, folk dancing, and hiking. Elmo became my accomplice on many future adventures. One afternoon, we sailed under the Golden Gate Bridge into the Pacific Ocean where we turned to the north along the Marin County coast. We wanted to test our celestial navigation skills using my plastic sextant.

"Okay, Elmo, take the first sun sight in the western sky," I said.

"Looks like it's 35 degrees between the lower limb (bottom) of the sun and the sea's horizon," he reported while I recorded the exact time of his observation.

We entered this data into the celestial navigation tables and then plotted the results on a nautical chart that put us on top of Mt. Tamalpais about five miles inland. I made another sextant reading but still could not find the error.

"Well, any time spent on a boat is a great time!" I said, grateful for another sail.

"Yeah, you got that right," Elmo agreed.

The Coastal Piloting class used ocean charts and taught us to select known places such as lighthouses and points of land along the shore. By determining their bearings in degrees from the boat using a handheld compass, we could triangulate the boat's position on the chart.

On Peter's boat, we learned Seamanship and Small Boat Handling by doing docking and anchoring exercises following the diagrams and theory presented in class. I learned to ease the anchor into the water as the boat moves slowly in reverse to make sure the chain doesn't become a tangled pile on the bottom that might foul (entangle) the anchor.

In Marine Weather, we studied meteorological theory to understand how to read fronts, lows, and highs shown on radio fax weather maps as well as how to read cloud formations to predict future weather. In Oceanography class we learned about the dynamics of wave formation and height prediction based on wind speed and fetch, the distance over which the wind acts on the water.

Elmo encouraged me to take a Spanish class. "You're wanting to go to Central America, Karl, so why don't you join my Spanish class taught by Lourdes Parra. She was born in Guanajuato, Mexico. She is a dynamic teacher and her classes are lots of fun. Lourdes teaches her community college classes in Berkeley and Richmond two evenings a week. You'll gain skills by speaking in conversation. Later she corrects your tenses and sentence structures."

"Sounds good," I said, deciding to take the class. After enrolling, I learned that an added bonus of Lourdes's teaching was a three-week summer class in the city of Guanajuato, lying in a valley of the Sierra Mountains in Central Mexico. I would definitely be on that trip.

Guanajuato is a Spanish colonial city built in the 1500s to support the rich silver mines in the surrounding mountains. Using the old mining tunnels and the skills of the miners, Guanajuato has placed the streets coming into the city and parking areas underground. The streets leaving town remained above ground thus minimizing traffic in the city center. The steep residential streets that rise straight up the hills from the valley floor are used only for walking or burro traffic.

Our classes became adventurous learning experiences in Mexican culture while living with Lourdes's aunt Rebecca and cousin Paco. They were under strict orders—"Never speak to students in English."

Rebecca was an elementary school teacher, and Paco was a computer expert. By carrying out Lourdes's instructions, they forced us to train our ears and voices in Spanish. In turn, Rebecca and Paco became masters at understanding and correcting our broken Spanish, creating a total immersion experience for all of us. Lourdes used a University of Guanajuato classroom for most of our instruction, but she was equally at home in cafés and parks and even on buses.

Once when taking a trip to Dolores Hidalgo on an intercity bus, we intended to sit with our classmates. Lourdes, however, had other plans. "I'll want each of you to sit with a Mexican passenger," she said, giving me a friendly shove.

Then saying to our seat mates, "Okay, *amigos, hablan con estos Norte Americanos*," she asked them to start conversations with us. Talk about living the language!

As we struggled to make ourselves understood, our friendly Mexican seat mates corrected our conversation of misplaced words and incorrect tenses with their smiles and chuckles. We all had a good time. Thinking about this exchange years later would still bring a smile to my face. The experience fueled my growing comfort with speaking Spanish and would help me to feel more at home in Spanish-speaking countries in the future.

*****

Back home in the San Francisco Bay Area, advertisements in *Latitude 38* for a Marine Electricity class caught my eye. I needed the class because it focused on the 12-volt systems that would be the electrical heart of *Aurora*. We learned about using tinned copper wire to limit corrosion in the salt water environment. Solar panels were another topic that caught my interest. I would need lots of power to run 12-volt refrigeration on my boat. Gino, my instructor, ran the electrical shop at Svendsen's Boat Works in Alameda.

After the last class, I talked with Gino. "Could I work for you at Svendsen's? I don't need a large salary, but I do need hands on experience."

"Sure, sounds like a good deal for both of us," Gino said.

Svendsen's is located on the estuary separating Alameda Island from Oakland to the East. For the next six months, I worked to put theory into practice. I installed and wired in sailing instruments, trouble shot electrical problems, and helped rewire and install a new engine in "a sinker," a sailboat that sank at dock when a worn out hose to the engine burst. Working at Svendsen's gave me the real life experience that prepared me for owning a boat and for cruising long distances without a mechanic on duty.

As I waited for nine months for my boat to be built and shipped, I thought about what to name her. I wanted a meaningful name. A name that spoke to me in terms of travel and adventure. A name with character that was not on everyone else's boat.

I decided to name my boat *AURORA*. Aurora is the name of my hometown in Ohio. It also signifies a new beginning of my life like the Roman Goddess of Dawn. *AURORA*, my boat, would enable my dream to come true. Another reason for choosing *Aurora* was to name her after the Aurora Borealis, the magical northern lights that reach out into the universe. The boat and dream would expand my own universe.

On September 2, 1981, *Aurora* left the factory in Kaohsiung, Taiwan, and began making her way to me over the vast Pacific Ocean. Her two-week voyage felt like forever to me.

6

AURORA ARRIVES

On September 16, 1981, the trajectory of my life changed forever. I finally met *Aurora*, my magic carpet for sailing the waters of the world. She would take me to the places, people, and experiences that I had only been able to read about in books. I was up at the crack of dawn on the day of her arrival.

I met a container ship carrying *Aurora* as it was pulled into the Oakland docks. I waited anxiously with a rented lowboy trailer truck and driver to receive my precious cargo. Looking up from the dock beside the ship, I felt like a kid getting a huge Christmas present. I watched wide-eyed as a large crane lowered *Aurora*—my boat. I held my breath, hoping the crane was up to its job. Thankfully, *Aurora* landed safely onto my trailer and the truck-driver securely strapped her down. She's here, she's really here, I kept repeating to myself.

Riding in the cab, I nervously watched as the driver navigated through the narrow streets along the Oakland Estuary. I kept looking back to check *Aurora* as he turned tight corners. I visually checked to be sure our oversized load fit on the lift bridge over the estuary. Finally, we arrived at Svendsen's on Alameda island where a travel lift crane picked up *Aurora* and deposited her on stands in the work-yard. She was ready for me to begin making her my perfect boat. I could hardly wait to put my hands to work on my boat and see my dreams turning into reality. Having *Aurora* here was just so sweet! All my plans had become an actual boat. *Aurora* would transport me into the world I wished to explore.

To get *Aurora* ready for launching into the water, I had to assemble all the parts that would make her seaworthy. Installing the bow and stern pulpits to the deck, threading the life lines through their stanchions, attaching the mast steps, painting anti-fouling paint on the bottom—each was a step forward. I was making *Aurora my* boat. The final step was having "Aurora" with a rising sun painted on the port and starboard hull and then "San Francisco" lettered on the stern as her home port. During the system check just before launching, I discovered only one problem—a light bulb had not been sufficiently tightened. I mentioned this to friends of mine and they said, "How many luxury cars could boast this level of quality?"

After weeks of anticipation, *Aurora's* launch took place on a sunny fall day. The sky was a brilliant blue. The air was crisp. It was a fitting day for *Aurora's* maiden sail with me at her helm. As the travel lift picked the boat up off her stands, she floated in the air before being deposited in her element. She looked smashing, like a model strutting down the runway showing off her best attributes—her sweeping sheer-line, her tawny teak deck, her white mast rising 40 feet above her deck.

After starting and running the Yanmar Engine, my business partner David and I motor sailed *Aurora* out of the Oakland estuary past the huge gantry cranes busy unloading other container ships, and then under the Bay Bridge with traffic roaring overhead. With the motor off, we sailed across the windy slot between the Golden Gate Bridge and Berkeley. *Aurora* came to life! I could feel her responding to the wind, surging forward toward the Richmond ship channel and her new home at Marina Bay. A boat slip on E Dock became *Aurora's* home and my base for outfitting her for the sea.

*****

I had been reading *Cruising in Seraffyn* by Lin and Larry Pardey. They describe their adventures on their 24-foot home built wooden sailboat. They were cruising just as I wanted to do. I was lucky to talk with Lin at the Oakland Boat Show.

"The most important thing is to cut loose from the dock and actually go cruising," Lin stressed. "Too many sailors only dream about cruising."

"Well, Lin, I am not going to be an armchair sailor," I vowed to her and to me.

While learning to sail *Aurora* later during the fall of 1981, I took out anyone interested for a sail on the bay. Community chorus colleagues, dock-mates, and my children, Doug, David, Darsie, Jeanne, Andy and Leanne, were among my guests. While sailing *Aurora* almost every weekend, I was also relaunching my children's love of sailing. They learned how to steer the boat, bring the jib from one side of the boat to the other (tacking the jib), and adjust the sails in response to the changing wind.

My oldest daughter, Darsie, loved to bury the rail, shouting, "Dad, we're really going fast," as the rest of us hung on.

"Loosen the main sheet, Darsie," I shouted back. "We are heeling so much that we could take on water. If *Aurora* leans over any further, the sails will be in the water and the boat could tip over."

Darsie reluctantly eased off the main sheet taking some of the pressure off the sail. While giving up some of *Aurora's* speed, her action reduced our angle of heel.

Leanne pointed to a large set of waves coming from a freighter and yelled, "Darsie, turn into the waves. Now everybody jump up!" As they did, the boat dropped off the wave, and my four kids were floating in the air experiencing a few seconds of weightlessness.

Sailing to Angel Island located off the Tiburon Peninsula was a special treat. Years later Leanne would reminisce about these trips. "Remember when we hiked up through the woods and then came out into a meadow where suddenly San Francisco filled our view? It was amazing that we seemed so close and the same time felt light years away."

David and Andy became experts at jumping onto the dock as we came into the slip then quickly wrapping *Aurora's* dock lines around the cleats to stop the boat. By docking *Aurora* under sail without the engine, I was practicing for a time when her engine might stall. Being able to handle a sailboat coming up to a mooring or into a dock under sail was a mark of the good sailor that I wanted to become.

One day as we were sailing just inside of the Golden Gate Bridge crossing the bay, a strong 40-knot blast of wind heeled *Aurora*. I fought the pressure on the wheel to keep the sails filled and our course straight toward Sausalito. I felt the limitation of the rudder's power in counterbalancing the powerful forces of the wind and swells. I also realized the limits of my own strength in being able to hold the wheel steady. *Aurora's* raw power, however, surged forward coming under my control. Strong exhilarating feelings of mastery and joy flooded my consciousness. In that one moment of time, I realized that *Aurora* and I were ready to sail into my dream!

Easing the sails and falling off the wind, I turned toward Raccoon Straits where the incoming tide was being squeezed between Angel Island and Tiburon, creating a strong rip tide current that bounced *Aurora* along as if running rapids in a river. Knowing that debris collects in rip tides, I scanned the water and caught sight of a log along for the ride. A quick turn of the wheel averted a dangerous crunch with the large, heavy, waterlogged object.

On another day, I took *Aurora* out through the Golden Gate at the end of a winter storm to test her and me. Elmo, Barbara, my then girlfriend, and her folk-dancing friend were the crew. As we sailed out into the Pacific in the shipping channel, the wind overpowered *Aurora*. I scrambled forward on deck to reef the mainsail and called back to Elmo, "Hold her steady!" *Aurora* wallowed in the incoming swells as I released the main halyard to lower the sail. I tied down the reef ties to secure the sail to the boom while taking my eyes off the horizon.

"Elmo, I'm not feeling very good, there's too much motion!" I shouted.

"Our dancer is hanging over the rail, puking his guts out," he answered.

"Okay, turn around and head in," I ordered. "This is supposed to be fun, isn't it?"

Aurora did well handling the rough seas and high winds, but some of the crew flunked the test.

Within six months, *Aurora* became my "live aboard home," allowing me to cut my living expenses and save more money for the cruising fund. During these years, my love affair with *Aurora* deepened as she became the one to grant my wishes to sail on the oceans and seas of the world. Another attractive attribute of my boat home was her cozy aft cabin that had a seductive effect on the women I was dating. *Aurora* and I were a "package deal." Love me, love my boat!

In the fall of 1985, after four years of practice and learning on *Aurora*, I felt that it was time for a serious sailing test for my boat and me, her captain. Elmo and I sailed *Aurora* out the Golden Gate and turned her south using the prevailing northwest winds to propel us to our first stop at Half Moon Bay about twenty miles down the coast. *Aurora* took to the ocean as the swells lifted her and gently set her down. After a good night's rest, we were off early for a longer sail riding the long swells and wind to Monterey Harbor. Arriving in the evening, we spotted the harbor entrance silhouetted against the lights of the Monterey Bay Aquarium. Motoring the boat in, we found our slip assigned by the harbormaster whom we had called earlier on the VHF short range radio.

On the next leg, reaching the anchorage behind Point San Simeon involved sailing overnight past Point Sur and the rock-bound coast of Central California.

That was a first for Elmo and me. My senses and awareness heightened as *Aurora* glided through the water in total darkness. The sound of the water bubbling along the hull and whispers of the wind rolling off her sails and rigging created a magical feeling of being suspended in a new reality. My mind opened, taking in the stars and the glow of the Milky Way, while my eyes kept a lookout for any fishing boats working in "our" part of the Pacific Ocean. A deep sense of relaxation and peace filled my body, relieving the temporary stresses of planning and executing the voyage.

At the end of the next day, pockets of daylight floated on the water as *Aurora* rounded Point San Simeon and glided into the anchorage sheltered by its bluffs and outlying boulders that broke up the incoming swells. The setting sun made the majestic Hearst

Castle glow as it stood on a high ridge overlooking the bay. The long pier used in its construction was our companion, jutting out from shore toward *Aurora*.

After a deep sleep making up for the broken sleep on our overnight sail, we continued on to Morro Bay. The short sail was easy because we used the giant Morro Rock as our aiming point.

"Morro Rock is the biggest and tallest object in view," I pointed out to Elmo. "It seems to have been randomly plunked down on that sandy beach by some giant force."

Elmo nodded. "Yeah it's so huge that I can't imagine how it got there."

Rounding the rock placed us in the entrance channel among playful sea otters swimming on their backs, cracking abalone shells with stones in preparation for lunch. Following the channel buoys into the harbor, we found the anchorage sheltered from the sea by dunes on the large sand spit. After dinghying ashore, we called my oldest son, Doug.

"Why don't you and Brenda drive over to Morro Bay for dinner with us. Be sure to bring my grandchildren Elise and Greg, so we can plan an outing on *Aurora* for them."

The children arrived the next morning for their sailing trip south past Montana de Oro State Park in the Coastal Mountain Range, which had shed huge boulders that cascaded into the ocean. As the swells rolled in bashing into the rocks, water flew up into the air creating iridescent rainbows that delighted the children.

"Grandpa, did you see that rainbow?" Elise marveled, pointing at the wave. "Look at all those colors."

Safe in his life jacket, Greg was glued at the bow looking intent on guiding *Aurora* on her course while watching the water slide beneath us. Elise and Greg took turns steering *Aurora* as the prevailing northwest winds off our stern carried us along.

Watching the kids made me feel that they were enjoying being immersed in my world of sailing. Was sailing in their genes, too? I wondered. Soon we entered San Luis Obispo Bay dropping anchor off the fishing pier at Port San Luis where we rowed two reluctant children ashore to be reclaimed by their parents.

After a good night's rest, Elmo and I continued south rounding Point Conception, one of the most feared capes along the West Coast. Lucky for us that day it was calm without the usual blasts of wind and conflicting waves that often make small boat sailing here a trying proposition. *Aurora* found shelter in small protected anchorage tucked in behind the cape located next to the main coastal railroad tracks. Unfortunately penetrating train whistles thwarted our attempts at sleep.

Before heading offshore to the Channel Islands National Marine Sanctuary the next morning, we sailed south into Ventura Marina where Leanne and Elmo's girlfriend, Lucy, were waiting. Leanne's smiles and hugs lit me up as I helped her aboard with her backpack.

"Dad, it's great to be here! What an adventure to sail out to some islands."

"It's wonderful having you aboard, sweetheart," I said. "*Aurora* is ready for a week of exploring Santa Cruz and Santa Rosa Islands. Let's get going."

Sailing off the eastern shore of Santa Cruz Island, I saw a large sea cave that looked big enough for *Aurora* to fit in.

"Hey guys, why don't we take *Aurora* into that big cave," I urged. "It'll certainly be a something new for all of us."

After assessing the waves and swells, I slowly guided *Aurora* into the cave's deep water. I kept an eye on the mast to be sure it cleared the ceiling. Safely inside, I relaxed a bit as my smile was followed by a sense of satisfaction. I had taken a risk and met the challenge of guiding *Aurora* into a sea cave. How great is that?

After we launched the dinghy, Elmo rowed Lucy and Leanne into an ever narrowing 800-foot-long tunnel burrowing under the surface of the island. I kept *Aurora* safe by using the engine to hold her position in the center of the cave while watching the mast move in lazy circles against the dimly lit ceiling as the sea surged in. The whooshing sounds of the incoming waves were in synch with my heartbeats that raced with excitement as *Aurora* danced in the cave's enclosing arms!

Later when climbing back onto *Aurora*, Leanne exclaimed, "Wow, Dad, the cave was really cool! We saw crabs climbing the walls, jellyfish in the water, and there was a bright shaft of light coming down from a crack above that gave the whole place a glowing blue color."

"Leanne, what a great experience!" I said. "I wish I could have gone, too."

I slowly drove *Aurora* out of the cave then along the shore to the Albert Anchorage where I dropped the anchor. After putting the boat in reverse to dig the anchor into the bottom, we dinghied ashore to hike on the island that is now the home of many beef cattle as well as deer and other mammals. The coastal Indians had used Santa Cruz and the other Channel Islands as offshore bases for fishing and collecting clams, abalone, and other shellfish, leaving a few shell mounds as the only remaining signs of their past presence.

In 1991, human remains found on Santa Rosa Island were radiocarbon dated to 13,000 years ago, some of the oldest human bones found in North America. These finds supported the theory that human migration had occurred by sea along the West Coast as well as inland crossing the land bridge from Siberia. Permanent villages may have existed closer to the ancient coastline which has now been swallowed up by the rising of the seas caused by the melting of the glaciers. Sound familiar?

Climbing a hill, we saw *Aurora* swaying in the bay as small blue waves came in.

I could picture her in other coves looking substantial and fit, knowing that I had guided her there. Together, we were going places off the beaten track. We would be a good team.

The cold, clear waters invited at least one hardy person to jump in. Adapting to the cold temperatures more readily than her dad, Leanne shouted. "Come on in, Dad, the water is great! Look at all those fish swimming under the boat. Swimming in the kelp is like slithering through a waving forest. Ooh, it feels like the kelp has a grip on my legs. That's scary."

I hung back enjoying the warmth of the sun streaming into the cockpit and called back, "Are you okay? Sorry, it looks like your Dad is chicken."

After five days in the islands, we returned Lucy and Leanne to Ventura and I sent them off to explore Pinnacles National Monument near Soledad on their way back to the Bay Area. Our thoughts then focused on sailing back north and home to keep Elmo's doctor appointment in a few days.

The sail down the Pacific Coast with its prevailing northwest winds and swells had been easy. As we headed up the coast, however, strong winds were on our nose. Everything went well until we left Monterey Marina and headed into steep six-foot waves that caused *Aurora* to surge up and down like a hobbyhorse. The pressure of trying to keep Elmo's appointment clouded my judgment when I made the decision to leave the marina. I was down below when I noticed water showering into the boat through the bow dorade air vent onto the forward bunk.

Running up on deck, I realized that we had forgotten to turn the vent opening around to face aft away from the waves. That's why the water was flooding into the boat. I worked my way forward to turn it. The motion of the bow was quite violent. I tried to time my approach by looking at the waves, but when I got there, the bow dropped off a large wave. I floated into the air with my right hand gripping the lifeline and the other arm extended to break my fall as the bow rose sharply on the next wave. My left arm took the brunt of the hit, causing me intense pain. I looked at my limp arm and knew that it was not in its usual location. I was in trouble.

I shouted to Elmo, "I've been hurt. I need help to get back to the cockpit."

"Stay where you are, I'm coming to get you," he yelled.

Elmo carefully assisted me to the cockpit and then down below where we applied ice to my elbow to dull pain and keep down the swelling. He ran back to the cockpit, turned the boat around, and headed back to the Monterey Marina in smoother seas because the waves now pushed the boat forward.

Calling the harbormaster on the VHF radio, Elmo said, "This is sailing vessel *Aurora* off Monterey. We have an injured crew member and need your assistance."

"*Aurora, Aurora,*" the reply came. "This is the harbormaster at Monterey. Come into slip 149. I am dispatching two staff members to assist *Aurora* into her assigned slip."

With *Aurora* secured in her slip, one of the staff drove me in his old VW bug to the community hospital where the emergency room nurses took over. One beautiful nurse was particularly gentle making me feel comforted as she helped me to the X-ray room and positioned my arm under the machine. One look at her and I was in love! The X-ray showed that the bones of my upper and lower arms were separated by a large space and no longer in correct alignment. My elbow was dislocated. Luckily, an orthopedic surgeon was at the hospital. After I was given a shot of a heavy duty Valium muscle relaxer, he reset my elbow and then put it in a cast.

*****

Going over the accident in my mind later, I realized I had ignored my mentor Gordon Stuermer's practice of "never leaving port when weather conditions will cause excessive stress on the boat or crew." I was now bearing the painful consequences of ignoring that rule!

A call to Oakland brought my son David to the rescue. We left *Aurora* in her slip at the marina, and David drove us home. With my arm in a sling, what could I do? My tendons and muscles had contracted following the injury. My arm would not straighten. I was concerned. How could I work or sail with one good arm?

Being a small building contractor who had no insurance, I was however fortunate to have my rehabilitation very kindly donated by my sailing friend Helene, a physical therapist who understood my situation. Many appointments followed.

"Hi, Helene, what is it going to be today?" I said, walking into the therapy room.

"Today is your lucky day, Karl," she replied. "Here's a heating pad to warm your muscles, then I'll put these electrode patches on each side of your elbow and give you some gentle zaps. Then I'll use an arm lock to straighten the joint."

"Whew, sounds like lots of fun," I said facetiously. "Let's get started."

"Okay, your arm should be relaxed. It's now time for the arm lock," Helene said. "Tell me when you reach your limit of pain, but please no screaming," she teased as she straightened my arm with increasing force.

I grimaced. "Okay, enough, enough!"

Thanks to Helene, my left arm would function well and be almost as strong as my right arm for many years to come.

The accident neither diminished my love of sailing nor altered my plans for cruising. Instead, it heightened my feelings of vulnerability and raised a sense of caution that more than balanced my left-over teenage "I am invincible" feelings. I learned valuable lessons. One, to be a successful sailor, you must think things through. In this case, I should have turned the boat around away from the wind and waves to decrease the motion before attempting to turn the dorade. Wearing a life jacket would have been a prudent idea! Weather, including wind force and wave height, are some of the most critical factors for a sailor to consider when making a decision to leave port. Such insights became my sailing mantras. They would serve me well on future ventures.

7

DISCOVERING THE RIGHT PARTNER

Another goal that I was pursuing before and after *Aurora* arrived was to find the right woman to accompany me cruising. Meeting female sailors was not too difficult, but getting the relationship elements right was a much more complex process. Communication and chemistry between mates were critical to the success of any cruising, and for that matter, any life venture. I wanted to be with a woman who really wanted to share the voyage with me. I imagined watching the sunset snuggled together on *Aurora* savoring the adventure of a lifetime. Not just anyone would do. As I looked ahead nine months at my self-declared cast-off date of Fall 1988, I began to worry I wouldn't have that special partner. None of the women I had been dating seemed to match my ideal mate. Early in 1988, however, my search looked like it would lead me to *the* woman.

For six years, I had belonged to the Berkeley Community Chorus and enjoyed the company of many colleagues there. I also dated a few nice women from the chorus. One night, we all gathered for an after-concert listening party at my friends' home. Groups of singers were drinking and talking throughout the house. Soon, I noticed a tall, statuesque, strikingly beautiful silver-haired woman standing close to me. JoAnne was a fellow singer. I wondered, Why haven't I noticed you before? The den we were in was getting more crowded and noisy, and JoAnne and I were being pushed closer to each other.

As we began talking about our performance of Faure's Requiem, JoAnne moved even closer. Looking into my eyes, she quietly said, "Have you had your older woman experience yet?"

I was taken aback but tried not to show it. Did she really say that? But I managed to mumble, "Well, no, but I might be interested." The door of possibility opened!

The next week, JoAnne and I met for dinner before chorus practice to get to know more about each other. As we walked into the restaurant together, I felt her upbeat energy and thought, Wow, what a woman! We were shown to a quiet table in the corner that had an intimate feeling. We sat across from each other, but as we talked, the space between us seemed to evaporate.

"I'm a foreign scholar advisor at UC Berkeley," JoAnne explained. "My office is located in the International House near the stadium at the top of the campus. I have been working there almost fifteen years. I love meeting and helping students and scholars with their adjustment to the United States and to the university. My daughter Betsy lives in San Francisco and we're very close."

"Why don't I tell you more about myself," I offered. JoAnne nodded, smiling. "I have a small contracting business and renovate older houses in Berkeley and Oakland. I am also a single parent raising two teenage boys, David and Andy, who frankly tend to drive me a little crazy with their rebellious behavior and smart talk. You know, it would be nice to have someone who can be a sounding board so I can develop some better solutions for getting through their teenage years."

"I can hear and feel your frustration," JoAnne said. "I've raised three kids and remember the challenge of their teen years. Maybe I could be a helpful listener."

"Boy, I'd really appreciate that," I said. We smiled at each other and I saw genuine interest in JoAnne's eyes. "One more important thing," I continued, changing the topic. "I'm a sailor and have been working hard to realize my dream of cruising in my sailboat, *Aurora*, to Mexico and beyond."

"Well, I like to travel and meet new people," JoAnne said immediately. "Perhaps cruising would be a fun way of traveling."

Relief moved through my body, and a smile spread across my face. Had I really found the right partner I hoped for?

As we continued talking, I was drawn in by JoAnne's smiling face and her luminous blue eyes. I could tell that she was being drawn to me. The force of our attraction was magnetic, pulling us closer. When it was time to leave for chorus, JoAnne decided to go home. I headed to chorus practice feeling a little woozy, and it wasn't from drinking the wine. My "older woman experience" had begun and I was ready!

As my relationship with JoAnne progressed, I realized that she wasn't an experienced sailor, although she had taken some sailing lessons and enjoyed our sails on *Aurora*. One day when we were sailing *Aurora* just out of the shipping channel next to Angel Island, JoAnne and I were in deep conversation. I happened to look over my shoulder but could only see the bow wave and the black sides of an outgoing tanker rushing by. It totally obscured the view of San Francisco and filled my whole field of vision.

I quickly stood up and yelled, "JoAnne, hold on!"

"Are we going to be okay?" she shouted, concern rising in her eyes.

"We'll be okay. I'm turning the boat into the waves," I shouted back.

The pilot on the tanker must have assumed that we knew it was there, because he had not sounded the ship's horn. My heart raced as *Aurora* climbed up the wave and then surfed down the tanker's wake. I grabbed the camera to record our near miss, catching its bow and six-foot tall wave. Settling down after all the excitement, JoAnne and I sighed and smiled at each other.

"That was a little too close for comfort!" said JoAnne.

"We'll get away from the shipping channel and go around Angel Island, then head for the marina," I said.

Safely back in the slip at Marina Bay about an hour later, I baked my special "Oregano Chicken" dinner for us with onions and lots of Oregano simmered in white wine. The chicken with green salad and white wine completed the menu. Holding up her wine glass, JoAnne smiled and said, "I've finally found a man who can cook."

I could be more expressive with JoAnne than with any other woman I'd known. Our deepening trust in each other allowed my whole body to respond freely in our sexual encounters as well as in my feelings. I opened some emotional doors I had slammed shut during my conflicted relationship.

My connection deepened with JoAnne during several months, and she invited me to live with her. I gladly accepted the invitation and began sharing a home with JoAnne in Oakland. Life was good. One day I showed JoAnne the large world map I had hung on the wall of the office. "This helps me to better visualize my sailing adventure," I said. She stared at the map and then looked at me.

"When I see the vastness of the Pacific Ocean I feel rather insignificant," JoAnne said. I felt the anxiety beneath her words.

"Yeah, I understand what you're saying," I said. "But, many sailors have crossed the Pacific west in the trade winds to the Marquesas and Tahiti." I was hoping this fact would help JoAnne see another perspective, but her stance told me otherwise.

Before JoAnne left for a summer vacation in New Hampshire with her mom, I asked her, "Would you join me when I sail down to Mexico in the fall?"

"I'll have to think about it while I'm at Mom's cottage," she said, as if she didn't want to talk about it.

"Okay," I said, not wanting to pressure her, but wanting desperately for her to go.

My stomach tightened as I remembered her tense reaction to the world map. Please, JoAnne, come with me, I hoped. I was on pins and needles as I waited to call JoAnne at her mother's cottage.

After a week, I called her. Before I could even ask about cruising to Mexico, JoAnne answered my question. "I'm sorry, Karl, but I can't leave my life on campus and my good friends. Leaving would also mean quitting my advisor job at Berkeley early. Leaving would drastically decrease my retirement income and future security." My heart sank.

After a long silence, I said, "JoAnne, I'm really disappointed, but I understand your reasons. Let's talk more about your decision when you come home." I hoped that by talking things out, I still might be able to change her mind.

*****

The tension between us was so intense it felt like a wall separated JoAnne and me as we sat on the couch talking about my sailing trip to Mexico. It was clear that she would not be coming with me.

"I'm sorry, Karl. but it's just not wise for me to join you on such a long trip at this time in my life and career," JoAnne explained firmly. "I have to be sure of my income for the future. I can't quit my job now."

I knew she was right, but I had to express the feelings building up inside me or I would burst. "If I don't sail this Fall, I may never realize my dream of cruising on *Aurora*. I paused, my heart pounding in my chest. "I may never have a chance to put all my study, practice, and hard work into action. I'm so afraid that if I stop now, I'll get stuck, and I'll be just another armchair sailor. That's not the life I want!"

JoAnne looked at me intently, first with anger and then sadness in her eyes. "I hear you, Karl, but that doesn't make it any easier for me," she said. "If you leave me for a sailing trip, what are you saying about the importance of our relationship?" Her words stung my heart.

"I feel really torn," I said with deep sadness. "Our relationship has grown beautifully and is important to me." I began to panic inside. I didn't want to lose JoAnne, but I couldn't lose my dream. I'd put it on hold for too long. "I'm sorry, JoAnne, I just *have* to do it," I blurted out before I could change my mind.

*****

I hated to leave JoAnne but within the next few days, I moved back to my boat in Marina Bay. A friend and fellow sailor, also named Karl, lived aboard his boat at the docks where I kept *Aurora*. He was also planning a trip to Mexico so we discussed our plans with each other. He had bought the 38-foot-long version of my Nantucket Island 33 sloop which he named *Eleuthera* for the island in the Bahamas. Karl was a nurse. His wife did not want to sail with him so he was taking a friend, another nurse, Anne, as his sailing partner. Although we did not intend to sail as "buddy" boats, we hoped to see each other along the way south. It was great to have a fellow dreamer on the dock who had to master the same set of tasks: equipping the boat, provisioning it with food, planning the navigation, and setting it up for long distance radio communication.

I had a lot to accomplish and keeping busy took my mind away from JoAnne and my inner conflict about leaving her. I needed to keep forward momentum or I might change my mind.

Having a limited budget meant that I could purchase only absolutely necessary equipment at first. A long range high frequency radio to connect me with volunteer ham radio operators and to the National Oceanic Atmospheric Administration (NOAA) long range weather forecasts was in that essential class of equipment. Useful things like a radar set and a roller furling for the jib would have to come later.

*****

Then again, there was the question of whether I would be sailing alone. Two years earlier, I had advertised for crew in *Cruising World* magazine. I had received a letter of response from a woman, Jean, whom I met during a short visit. She was a solid looking woman with a pretty face who stood about 5'6" tall with dark brown short cut hair. She had a distinct business woman's look that reflected a teaching job. Jean had left her husband and had been sailing with other men. I was sure I needed a sailing partner on the voyage to Mexico. Sailing alone as a single hander felt inherently too dangerous. If any serious accident happened, my life might be over. Jean was still available when I informed her that JoAnne was unable to go. She had just completed a teaching assignment in Thailand and had sent some of her luggage ahead to the San Francisco Airport (SFO). It was being held at U.S. Customs so she asked me to pick it up. Rushing to finish my last remodeling job, I didn't have enough time to get her luggage.

When Jean arrived at SFO, we went to Customs. An agent led us into a small room where he asked her, "Are these bags yours?"

"Yes, they're mine," Jean confirmed.

The agent opened a large suitcase and took out a number of plastic wrapped containers of Thai marijuana. "Are these yours?" he asked sternly.

"No, they aren't mine," Jean insisted. "My servant was angry when I left, so she must have put them there."

For some reason, the agent bought Jean's explanation and let us take the luggage minus the marijuana.

I stood there stunned, realizing that Jean had put me in a perilous situation. I felt betrayed. Did I make the right decision in taking her on as crew?

I didn't say a word to Jean until we were in the car. "I won't allow any drugs on my boat," I stated forcefully. "If the Coast Guard discovers them, they could seize *Aurora*."

"Look, it won't happen again!" Jean snapped. "Do you think that I'd expose myself and you to that kind of risk?

"I don't know what to think," I replied.

Thank God, I hadn't gone alone to pick up those bags. I would have probably been sent to jail. Every time I thought about the episode, I shuddered at realizing how close I came to being in deep trouble. But again, my desire to begin my voyage overcame the more rational thoughts concerning Jean's risky actions and behavior. The situation continued to provoke disappointment in myself for deciding to make the trip without JoAnne for whom I had a real feeling and trust. But my mind was set on leaving on the voyage. I would just have to live with the consequences.

8

VOYAGE TO MEXICO

After working to provision and prepare *Aurora* for the voyage south, my feelings of mistrust and trepidation lingered about having Jean as crew. However, I pushed forward and sailed under the Golden Gate Bridge out into the Pacific Ocean leaving San Francisco Bay with Jean. On November 9, 1988, it was a bright sunny day and the winds and swells were moderate. A great day to begin a new phase in my life and to put my dream into action. This was the beginning of a cruising adventure that would continue on for the next fifteen years with many changes of crew. *Aurora* was leaving her home and might never return to San Francisco Bay. This was a huge step for both of us!

Day hopping southeast along the Pacific Coast of California safely inside the shipping lanes was quite comfortable as the wind and swells were coming behind us from the Northwest. Jean proved to be a competent sailor. I taught her how to work the auto-pilot by aiming the boat on the proper course and then setting it to follow that compass heading. After spending the first night anchored in Half Moon Bay, we sailed out in the morning and into evening to reach Monterey Harbor where city lights on shore provided a bright outline, backlighting the marina and helping us to locate its entrance. In the harbor, we found other boats also heading for Mexico. We met a couple all the way from Alaska who were seeking to thaw out in the warmth found further south.

From Monterey, the next leg of the voyage was an overnight passage to Morro Bay enlivened by visiting dolphins who vied with each other to be closest to the bow of the boat. Riding on the bow wave, the larger ones nibbled on the tail fins of the smaller dolphins, chasing them away. I lay on the deck gazing down on them while they turned on their sides looking up at me. It was as if they were saying, "Hello, I see you." Later, we had more company on the sea. After following us for an hour that evening, the crew on the Coast Guard cutter launched its dinghy and paid us a visit as we sailed off Point Sur south of Monterey. Three young guardsmen climbed aboard to check our boat documentation, life jackets, flares, and other safety equipment. Jean had heeded my warning on drugs and *Aurora* had complied with all the rules, so the guardsmen departed shouting, "Good luck on your trip south."

Coming through the morning fog, we saw Morro Rock at the entrance to Morro Bay. We rendezvoused with my friend Karl and his mate, Anne, on *Eleuthera*. We found them having coffee and bagels at the Morro Bay Yacht Club. Karl and Anne said that their trip so far had been a good one.

Jean and I met my son Doug and his wife, Brenda, now in their mid-twenties, for dinner in Morro Bay. Their home is nearby in Atascadero. "Wouldn't it be great if you two could come to Mexico and cruise on *Aurora* in the Sea of Cortez," I said.

"Wow, Dad, we'd love to go," Doug said. "Brenda's mom could take care of the kids for a week or so."

"Great, let's do it when *Aurora* is in the Sea of Cortez," I said, overcome by the feeling that I was now really on my way. My visions of cruising were finally real, and I wanted to share them with my family.

*****

Continuing south to the Channel Islands National Park off Ventura, I anchored at Cueva Valdez on Santa Cruz Island. Keeping *Aurora* lined up in the center of the narrow cove required using the dinghy to deploy a second, stern anchor.

In the morning, I asked Jean if she thought we should leave. The barometer had dropped overnight indicating that we were in a low pressure area that could generate higher winds and waves.

"Well, the seas look okay from this vantage point in the cove," Jean replied. "Let's give it a try."

Sailing beyond the lee of the island, we found steep seas and strong winds blowing 30 knots steady with gusts to 40 knots. Beating back to a doghole, a tiny cove, we found the needed shelter at Hungryman's Gulch near Smuggler's Cove. The next morning, our departure was delayed by the propeller failing to turn when I put the transmission into gear. Opening a side hatch of the engine compartment, I used a flashlight to look at the transmission at the rear of the engine and found that the connecting bolts had loosened, allowing the propeller shaft to uncouple so the motor could not turn the propeller. This critical repair reminded me that my mentor, Gordon Stuermer, while sailing on *Starbound,* used a checklist to be sure that all essential equipment was in working order. It was time for me to follow his example.

Later that day, the wind and waves moderated, so off we sailed downwind, wing on wing. The wing on wing sail pattern looks like a wide V at the front of the boat that catches the wind coming from behind the boat. We sailed smoothly toward Santa Catalina Island off Los Angeles.

When we arrived at the island that evening, two serious looking harbor patrol officers boarded *Aurora.* "We have to put purple dye in your toilet," they said. "It'll signal us if any sewage is being discharged overboard. Storing it in your holding tank will prevent a heavy fine."

"Of course, we've been using our holding tank," I said.

A warm shower followed by breakfast at Sally's Restaurant in Catalina Town put Jean and me in the mood to explore the Wrigley Memorial Gardens set out of town against the hills. The spaces between large boulders were filled with succulent plants in tune with the arid character of the island. Some of the succulents were in bloom, creating colorful, bright blotches of yellow, orange, and red against the monochrome tan desert landscape.

My attitude about Jean was improving as I began putting the upsetting marijuana incident out of my mind. Jean, however, still distant toward me, kept our conversations centered only on the details of sailing *Aurora* and our next port of call. I was making my voyage, but the important close relationship parts of my dream were missing. My thoughts returned to JoAnne.

*****

Our passage past Los Angeles was marked with gobs of floating plastic trash on an oily surface of the sea as the low winds forced us to motor sail on our course past San Clemente Island toward San Diego Bay and the Southwestern Yacht Club. Arriving after ten in the evening, I found a berth and secured *Aurora* to it.

The club was very accommodating, offering us good food at reasonable prices, strong docks, clean showers, and access to chandleries where needed boat parts could be purchased.

I used this opportunity to work on *Aurora* by removing the small holding tank under the navigator's seat since it would not be needed in Mexico. The now empty space was dedicated to the storage of drinks, most importantly beer. I had the diesel tanks cleaned because black algae and water had been appearing in the primary diesel filter. The filter was doing a vitally important job of removing dirt from the diesel that could clog fuel lines and thereby stop the engine cold. I also climbed the mast and tightened a connection on the navigation lights that were essential for our night sailing. All this work was necessary because it would be difficult finding the parts and pieces needed to maintain *Aurora* in Mexico. Best of all, I knew how to do all these projects, which validated years of preparation and reinforced my confidence.

After leaving the marina, we sailed through the pitch black night along the Mexican Coast below Tijuana. I scanned the horizon thinking that I was following the bright stern light of another boat. As I continued on my course, however, I realized suddenly that I was watching a star. It now led my eyes to the mass of stars covering the black sky from horizon to horizon without any interference from artificial lights. Absent the moon's light, the coast appeared to be just a series of shadowed humps outlined against the starlit sky. I found myself wishing that JoAnne was by my side sharing this incredible moment.

Knowing the boat's position was very important. A dead reckoning log had to be kept by recording time, boat speed, and compass course because the Sat Nav was our only electronic navigational device, and it was limited to making position fixes (latitude and longitude) when the satellites pass overhead. As a rule, there are many hours between these position fixes. The dead reckoning log is used to compute the advances of boat position on the chart between the satellite fixes. Islands, points of land, and reefs are obstacles to be avoided. Entrances to bays and anchorages need to be identified.

One morning, I wanted to navigate into Scammons Lagoon that was used as a nursery by calving gray whales after a 3,000 mile migration south from the Alaskan Arctic. Here they give birth to their calves.

I called to Jean, "Do you see all those breaking waves on the shallows off the entrance to the lagoon? They're a sure sign that we shouldn't go in."

"You're right, Karl," Jean said. "A breaking wave could possibly turn us over or pound the boat onto the bottom."

"Yeah, I'm really sorry to miss seeing the whales after sailing all these miles. I yearned to get up close and personal with them."

We continued to sail into the evening past Isla Navidad as it was outlined against the glowing red sunset. We were making headway toward Magdalena Bay that is much larger and has an easier entrance according to the *Pacific Ocean Pilot Book*. The *Pilot Book* is a compilation of observations made by sailors over the past four hundred years giving the location of reefs, islands, and other obstacles as well as the expected weather patterns and wind directions. The *Pilot Book* became my sailor's "bible."

In the fluky winds, I hoisted a long sock that I had sewn to contain a multicolored, nylon spinnaker sail. I used a line attached to the bottom of the sock to pull it up using a pulley taking it to top of the mast. Being free, the sail caught the light wind allowing it to balloon out forward of the mainsail. Soon it harnessed the breeze, and the boat speed picked up, compensating for the loss of wind strength, which customarily happens in the evening. A deep feeling of calm surfaced in my body as *Aurora* ghosted along in the dark in tune with nature. Daily concerns evaporated from my mind and my thoughts expanded into the universe above and within. Memories of JoAnne, her caring and the feelings expressed in our conversations were in stark contrast to the limited empty relationship I had with Jean.

Entering Bahia Magdalena, we encountered a large body of water. Indeed, we could barely make out Puerto San Carlos across the bay set against the low shoreline to the East. Following the zig-zagging courses of fishing boats through the shallow water, we were led to the town and its anchorage. As soon as Jean and I went ashore, we learned that a squall had just passed, causing a 29-foot sailboat, *Yate Gavotte*, to drag anchor and be deposited by the waves on its side up on the beach. Approaching the scene, we saw that George and Ginny, its owners in their late fifties, were staring in shock as their floating home lay beached on its side vulnerable to total destruction by the pulsating surf.

"My, God!" George said. "We've got to save our boat. All our money, our dreams are tied up in her." The Mexican Navy and a large fishing boat were responding to radioed calls for help as many yachties on shore stood ready to assist.

"Can we save *Gavotte* by digging a channel in the sand from the boat out toward the sea?" George asked desperately.

A loud and overwhelming response from those assembled was, "Yes, we can!"

We all scurried to gather buckets, shovels, anything that could scoop sand and started digging. Soon a channel was made wide and deep enough to allow sea water in under *Gavotte*. Long lines were dinghied out to the Navy tug, which then pulled, dragging her on her side out into deeper water where she righted herself. This episode cost the owners $2,000, but with their only home being rescued, this was a bargain! A vital element in our survival as individuals and as a group were "Yachties," cruising sailors, working together because we all were traveling to new places and being exposed to many dangers lurking along the way. In other words, we were all in "similar boats."

Getting fuel in San Carlos proved to be quite difficult because the diesel hose from the dock would not reach out to our boat. Salvador, a young muscular Mexican man sporting an infectious smile, offered his services. "I'll do it for free," he said. He hauled eleven Jerry cans full of fuel and water in his row boat out to *Aurora*. After about three hours of hard work, we offered Salvador cans of soda, a pair of jeans, and added fifteen U.S. dollars which seemed to please him. After fueling, our other task was to make our official entry into Mexico—filling out forms and showing port officials our U.S. Coast Guard documentation for *Aurora* and our passports to immigration officers. Some of the officials were fishing for gratuities; one wanted a knife, and another five dollars for overtime, but in the end they settled for less. Others, however, just did their job, taking our smiles and *"Gracias, senor"* as their reward.

The next leg of the voyage was another overnight sail through the dark night. After I oriented the boat to its correct compass course, I chose a star above the horizon that lined up with the bow to steer by as *Aurora* sailed along the rocky coast toward Cabo San Lucas located at the tip of the Baja California Peninsula separating the Pacific Ocean from the Sea of Cortez. Reaching this cape is the goal of many cruisers. Rounding Cabo San Lucas was a thrilling experience for me, validating my trust in both *Aurora* and in the skills I had earned studying marine sciences and sailing *Aurora* in San Francisco Bay and in the Pacific Ocean.

We anchored among other cruising boats on the Sea of Cortez side of the cape off a beautiful curving white sandy beach. It seemed like a warm paradise, but here a few years earlier it was reported in *Cruising World* magazine that many boats had been wrecked on this beach by a sudden, southerly late season hurricane. One of those boats was owned by Bernard Moitessier, a famous French single hander, who had sailed non-stop around the world. He was named "the Vagabond of the South Seas." Many boats were saved but the crashing waves pounded others into submission, including Bernard's boat. The knowledge of these losses put me on high alert listening to my ham radio. I kept an ear open for any predictions of a wind shift from the south.

Aurora traveled 1,445 nautical miles from her home port on San Francisco Bay to reach Cabo San Lucas. We had completed the first long leg of our journey south. I was proud of our accomplishment and I was relieved that now *Aurora* was in the more protected Sea of Cortez.

9

CRUISING THE SEA OF CORTEZ

Sailing into the brilliant blue waters of the Sea of Cortez, I yearned to dive in and soak up the rewards of being in Mexico. It was drawing me in like a powerful magnet. I jumped in and snorkeled toward the famous rock arches, the iconic image of Cabo San Lucas. I saw a female seal with her pup lazing along about twenty feet in front of me. I leisurely followed them. Suddenly out of the dark, deep water came a large set of teeth streaking upward at me. Utterly vulnerable, I stopped. As those teeth rushed closer, I saw they belonged to a massive, black bull seal that must have felt his lady and offspring were in danger! Quickly flipping on my back, I vigorously kicked away hoping that if he did bite, only my flippers would be injured. Luckily for me, he saw that he'd proved his point and turned away. I was able to breathe some relaxing deep breaths as I swam back toward *Aurora*. My bull seal encounter made me realize that I needed to acquire a deeper understanding of the creatures I would be meeting in these waters.

Cruising boats filled the harbor at Cabo San Lucas making it the social scene for southbound cruisers enjoying the warm water, mild temperatures, and Mexican culture. Gringo headquarters ashore was Señor Suchi's Restaurant offering good food and dancing to a very loud band. In the mornings, the net controller of the local VHF Radio Cruisers' Net offered sailors a chance to check their boats and crews in, ask questions, and exchange tips on shopping, restaurants, and laundries nearby. After the Cruisers' Net, I used my time to tackle the maintenance list. Using my Hooka Air Compressor with air hose and mouth piece, I stayed underwater to change a protective zinc on the propeller shaft and to give the bottom a light scrub.

News from boats arriving from the north was not good. An Englishman who didn't believe the position computed from his sextant readings lost his boat on Cabo Lazaro as incoming waves pounded the boat onto sharp rocks. Thankfully, he was able to walk away alive in two feet of water. His boat, however, was a total loss!

Well rested after four days, Jean and I sailed overnight around the end of the Baja Peninsula to Los Frailes, a bay that offered shelter from the rising north wind. Attracted by a fire on the beach, we dinghied over asking to join in a beach party. We shared our bottle of wine with some lively Canadians from the Vancouver, British Columbia, area who also had headed south to escape their cold, wet northern winter.

While drinking wine and toasting marshmallows, we talked into the night with George, a gregarious sixty-year-old, and his wife, Ann, an attractive, fit woman.

"Our trip down the West Coast started off well, but off the Oregon Coast we got clobbered by storm after storm," said George. "The weather was so bad that the Coast Guard advised us to stay well off shore because there were huge breaking waves across the entrances to Newport, Coos Bay, and Brookings. Ann and I had no choice but to ride out the storms using a sea anchor to hold us steady as we ran *Gallant Gal* down the huge waves."

"So you and your boat were up to the battering of the storm," I said.

"Yeah, sometimes we had our doubts, but we were able to close off the companionway with hatch boards and stay below," George said, with the fear he had felt. "*Gallant Gal* shed the breaking waves and thank God we stayed safe and dry below."

I saw that Ann and George were still recovering from the trauma of their experience. Our own passage down the California Coast had been a cakewalk compared to their turbulent trip.

In the morning, we sailed north all day while using my preferred fishing method, trolling a heavy line and feather jigs to attract the fish off the stern of *Aurora* during the daylight hours. A

30-inch-long silver fish with longitudinal stripes struck the lure, then jumped out of the water and broke the line, raising the price of our fresh caught fish dinners. To solve this problem, I tied a bungee cord into the line to take up some of the initial shock caused when the lure was struck by the fish. This move improved our luck and ability to land fish. The Sea of Cortez has been known for exceptional fishing, and our stomachs longed for fresh fish. Years later, a friend of mine would catch his limit of wahoo, yellowfin tuna, and sierra in the same area bringing home 70 pounds of frozen fish!

We reached our next anchorage, Los Meurtos, "Bay of the Dead," in the moonlight using the glowing anchor lights of fishing boats as our guide. The lights were visible from ten miles away on this clear night, and we watched them growing larger and larger, pulling us into the shelter and security of the bay. Setting the anchor put *Aurora* into a resting mode, giving us time to go off duty and really relax. What a welcome relief after a day of sailing when heightened senses had been alert to the movements and noises of the boat under sail.

After we arrived in La Paz, Jean left to spend the next month including Christmas with her family in the United States. My youngest daughter, Leanne, flew in from California on vacation from Santa Catalina High School just in time for some cool, rainy days in Mexico. Gobs of rain flooded the streets, making wading a necessity for getting around. Ignoring the excess water, Leanne and I had a wonderful time exploring La Paz's many craft shops.

Lupe, a welcoming shop owner, took great pride in explaining the areas of origin for the outstanding ceramics and other crafts displayed in her shop.

"These plates are individually made," she explained. "As you can see, the faces are carved into the plates before they are fired. Then they are glazed and fired again. The villages in the mountains around Oaxaca specialize in this kind of pottery."

"Each one looks like it belongs in a museum," I said, admiring their fine craftsmanship. "But, I'm afraid that the prices put them beyond my reach."

"*Mira a todos los colores,*" (Look at all the colors) said Leanne, relishing a chance to speak some of the Spanish she was learning in high school and in summer classes given by her teacher Lourdes in Guanajuato.

La Paz was decked out with thousands of Christmas lights. Some were wrapped in ascending patterns around the palm trees, others were strung to outline buildings, while others were suspended between streetlight poles, creating long curving shapes along the Malecon promenade bordering the harbor. The water held our gaze as it reflected back dancing patterns of sparkling lights. Many Mexican families walked along the Malecon chatting, while children played "Catch me if you can," running at full speed in every direction.

Numerous former cruisers had "swallowed the anchor" and were now living ashore in La Paz. Leanne and I attended a *Los Cruisereros* Club Christmas dinner, complete with large roasted turkeys and all the fixings. This was a fund raiser to help Mexican children in an orphanage. After dinner, we joined a group of members walking to the orphanage with big bags of wrapped toys flung over our shoulders. As we arrived at the gate, the children played noisily inside a walled courtyard. Walking through the gate, we were greeted by about a dozen small children looking up expectantly at us. They flashed broad smiles and held open their outstretched hands. We gave a present to each one who immediately tore through the wrappings, squealing with delight.

"Dad, I feel like Santa Claus!" said Leanne. "It's great spreading joy to these orphan kids."

"Yeah, seeing their smiles and feeling their happiness is a priceless experience that melts my heart and makes me feel happy," I exclaimed. "I'm glowing all over!"

I've seen that wherever Americans are, they reach out to the local communities helping to fill unmet needs. We felt welcomed by our Mexican hosts, especially as we attempted to talk with them in their language. Our Spanish opened many doors by showing respect to the people we met during our daily trips into town.

*****

After Leanne left to return to her boarding school in California, I began planning my trip further south and to the east across the Sea of Cortez. The 256-nautical mile passage to the mainland of Mexico would require two overnights. With Jean still visiting family in the United States and not returning until I reached Puerto Vallarta, I needed to find temporary crew to help sail *Aurora* across the sea. I posted a small note requesting crew on the message board in Marina de LaPaz that raised a response from Jan, a German wind surfing instructor who had just completed his teaching job at a Sea of Cortez hotel. He was a twenty-two-year-old, tall, athletic, energetic, blond haired young man with a winning smile. Jan needed transportation across to the mainland where he could take a bus to an airport for his return flight home to Germany to continue his engineering studies. I thought Jan would be an excellent crew member because he understood the dynamics of sailing as well as the engineering involved in handling a boat.

I chose to leave La Paz after the northern storm had blown through. Continuing large swells, however, enlivened our ride south.

"Let's see who can make *Aurora* go the fastest surfing down the face of the waves," I challenged him.

"You're on," said Jan.

"Jan, I just hit 8.83 knots. Can you top that?" I bragged.

"Wow, it looks like my best speed so far is 8.51 knots," said Jan.

These speeds were well beyond *Aurora's* hull speed of 7 knots. It was exhilarating to be on a six-ton, thirty-three-foot boat that was acting more like a surfboard. *Aurora* lifted as the waves churned under her and surged forward and downward as she rode the foaming face of the wave. I felt like a kid learning how to get the most out of his new toy. As the waves subsided, we caught a twenty-four-inch Bonita that served as a good meal after being cooked in red wine. Anchoring *Aurora* at Los Frailes, we rested, waiting for the weather to stabilize before heading east across the Sea of Cortez to Isla Isabela on our way to the mainland.

With winds down to 15-20 knots coming from aft of (behind) the beam of the boat, Jan and I rode the rounded swells again in

Jan's Fish

surfing mode creating a fabulous ride. From the ham radio fore-casts, it was comforting to hear that a good weather pattern would hold. During the night, we would be more than one hun-dred-thirty miles away from land—much further than I had ever been. I ran the engine to recharge the low batteries drawn down by the autopilot and the refrigeration system. Monitoring and bal-ancing the ship's systems is an important aspect of long distance sailing. As relaxing as sailing can be, part of my mind was always paying attention to the needs of the boat signaled by strange noises, flopping sails, or heeling over too far.

Appearing about 3 a.m. on the second night, the flashing light of Isla Isabela's lighthouse was a welcome sight. By 4:20 a.m., we were a mile from the south end of the island where we backed our jib into the "hove to" position, stopping our forward motion and allowing us to drift in the current while we slept a few hours. Waking at 7:30 a.m., we motored into the anchorage located in a collapsed volcanic caldera, setting the anchor off a small beach near low cliffs marking the throat of the caldera. After breakfast, Jan and I swam along the cliffs seeing our first colorful tropical fish in the warm water. We scrambled ashore where a fishing camp was filled with welcoming men. Their catch of red snapper and small hammerhead sharks was lying on the beach waiting to be picked up by a larger boat from the mainland.

Isla Isabella Fish Camp

Climbing a low hill, Jan and I discovered Lago Crater, appearing to have been cut out of the earth by a giant round cookie cutter. Boobies and gulls preened themselves in the clear, fresh water. Isla Isabela had been featured in a Jacques Cousteau documentary. It now has a visitors' center and National Wildlife Preserve status but has no staff. Isabella Island is populated by thousands of red-throated frigate birds nesting in the low trees. The male frigate bird inflates his red throat to attract mates and has a distinctive black shape looking like the outline of a bat in the sky set off by their angular, swept back wings and forked tails. Hundreds of blue-footed boobies having a clownish appearance were nesting on the ground. All the birds were unafraid of us unless we approached them closer than an arm's reach.

Feeling like we were stepping into the Garden of Eden, we were careful not to disturb the inhabitants. Frigates are fish-eating birds that cannot dive into the water; they specialize in stealing food in flight from boobies or other diving sea birds. We witnessed many blue-green Marine Iguanas diving off the rocks into the sea. Such behavior occurs only here and in the Galapagos Islands off Ecuador more than one thousand miles south. Isla Isabella is isolated from the mainland and is indeed a special place. A unique environment for many creatures has developed there, causing their specialized adaptations over the centuries. They are living examples that validate Darwin's Theory of Evolution!

Sailing south toward our destination, San Blas on the mainland coast, took us through a fleet of shrimpers lined up in long rows dragging their nets along the bottom. They looked like grain harvesters moving down a field.

"Can anything escape from all those overlapping nets?" I wondered aloud to Jan. "Shrimp harvesting like this must have a major negative impact on the sea. These huge nets scoop up everything not allowing many creatures to survive the experience."

"What a waste of beautiful sea life," added Jan.

The river mouth entrance into San Blas was marked by a breakwater of huge, black volcanic boulders creating a narrow opening that magnified the swell. We carefully surfed through the gap, keeping *Aurora* straight with the swells to avoid the possibility of being broached, turned sideways, and possibly rolled over. We followed the river to a wide spot where shrimp boats were tied to long grey docks stretching out along the shore. We anchored in eleven feet of water in the middle. Jan and I took the dinghy ashore so he could depart for the rest of his trip home. We reminisced about our journey together as we walked to the bus station.

"We completed *Aurora's* first long offshore passage," I said. "What a treat to have you along as crew, Jan! I'm feeling very satisfied with our efforts and *Aurora's* performance. And, we had great fun turning her into a racing boat!"

"Yeah, feeling her surf was a thrill for me," said Jan. "Thanks for giving me the opportunity to sail her and to visit Isla Isabela. It's been a pleasure getting to know you, Karl." We shook hands.

"Goodbye and good luck, Jan."

I continued wandering through San Blas, the oldest Spanish port on the West Coast of Central America. The Spaniards used this harbor as a base to explore northward and across the Sea of Cortez to the Baja Peninsula. In San Blas, Father Junipero Serra began his journey to the Baja where he started building a chain of missions located a day's donkey ride apart. They would eventually stretch more than 1,500 miles north, all the way to San Francisco, California.

Ruins of a colonial custom house near the river and a fort on a high hill overlooking the harbor clearly marked the Spanish presence. The fort has volcanic rock walls complete with cannons, barrack foundations, other buildings, and a ruin of a cathedral with walls and some arches still standing despite missing a connecting roof. The jungle had crept into the cathedral creating an overlay of green softness against the blackness of its rock walls. Nature was creating its own triumphant cathedral by covering man's creation.

San Blas attracted surfers and other lovers of small Mexican towns. I met Americans, Canadians, and a few Europeans hanging out and soaking up the sun and warmth as well as cold Mexican beers. Many of these expatriates were habitués of a palm covered, pole structure *palapa* "Gringo" bar, with low walls open to the main square. Inside, I met two scruffy looking guys from Ireland, Sean and Paddy, in their late twenties.

"What brings you guys all the way from Ireland to San Blas?" I said.

"Well, one of our friends has been coming here to surf," said Sean. "He told us about the warm weather and friendly people.

We made the easy decision to escape the cold, damp winter weather of Ireland and to give San Blas a try for a while."

"Yeah, the long white beaches and warm blue water are hard to take," added Paddy, laughing.

"What about the beautiful Mexican women?" I said.

"Yeah, their radiant dark skin and black hair are very beautiful, but they seem rather shy," said Sean. "They really don't speak much English, and our Spanish is barely adequate to order dinner."

"Well, I'm here from San Francisco on my sailboat," I said, walking toward the door. "Maybe I'll see you two again around town."

While shopping for granola, my latest addiction, I found a small shop built on the outside wall of the central market owned by a young man named Chena who spoke some English. One of my more pressing needs was to improve my conversational Spanish. To do this, I offered to help in Chena's shop along with his two almost twenty-year-old assistants, Norma and Rebecca. Norma was a little spitfire who hoped to marry an American and move to the United States, while Rebecca was more serious and shy with an attractive smile. I helped them practice English, while they added many words to my Spanish vocabulary. We helped each other train our ears to the sounds of our new languages. My job was to serve customers by weighing and bagging their purchases. One day I noticed an older man who picked out some rice and beans then left without paying. I looked over at Chena with a puzzled look.

"Oh, I've been helping the disabled and poor as much as I can around here," he said. "For Sergio, I am also helping by paying his rent."

"Wow, Chena, that makes me feel good about being in a community with a person like you." I said with a smile. "I admire your helping and caring for those in need."

Outside of town one day, I waited for other tourists to join me in a thirty-foot-long *panga* (fishing boat) for a tour up the river through a jungle of mangrove trees that overhung the water. Motoring upstream, we saw many turtles sunning themselves on

Chena and His Shop

logs; a startled few dove into the water. Alligators on both banks and in the water swiveled their eyes to keep us in view. Black anhingas warmed and dried their outstretched sliver striped wings in the hot sun. All of us on the boat talked in whispers as we absorbed the creatures' behavior.

Following the river that moved like a snake through mangroves, we arrived at its source, the Tavora Spring. The gigantic spring flows out of a tall rock face, creating a large crystal pool of cool fresh water that is a great place to swim. I jumped in after months of bathing in salt water. Swimming in this fresh cool water left me with a squeaky clean sensation. Three-foot-long alligators lining the shore eyed me, heightening my sense of excitement. My boat companions kept watch to warn me of any sudden movements of these sharp-toothed creatures.

Tavora Spring is also the pure source of drinking water for San Blas. By the time the water is finally distributed in town through cracked and leaking pipes, however, it is polluted by contact with the soil. Sadly this type of contamination has made most of Mexico's drinking water impure.

After ten rewarding days in San Blas, It was time for me to continue sailing south.

"*Adios mi amigo Chena, buena suerte,*" I said. "Would you like to have a sail on *Aurora* before I leave?"

"*Lo siento pero.* I have to keep the shop open, but I'm sure Rebecca and Norma would like to go," said Chena.

Norma and Rebecca readily agreed take their first ride on a sailboat. We would make a short hop to Bahia Matachen. After boarding the boat, Norma draped herself on the aft storage box posing like a movie star. Rebecca, more interested in learning how to sail the boat, said, "Karlos, will you show me how to steer toward the opening of the bay?"

"Sure," I said. "When you turn the wheel to the right, the boat moves to the right. Begin by turning the wheel just a little so you can see how much the direction of the boat changes."

"Oh, I see what you mean," said Rebecca. "As I turn the wheel I can see the direction of the boat changing."

After an hour of sailing, I anchored the boat in Bahia Matachen.

"Thanks for the fun ride on your boat," said Rebecca. "I really enjoyed seeing San Blas from the sea and what sailboats look like on the inside. I had fun steering the boat, too."

"It's been a pleasure having you and Norma on *Aurora*," I said. "Thanks so much for helping me learn more Spanish. Making a connection with Chena and the two of you in San Blas has been very special to me."

"*Adios,* I hope to see you again someday," said Rebecca.

"*Lo mismo para me,*" I replied in Spanish.

Bahia Matanchen is a large shallow bay surrounded by beaches and palms. On the weekend, I dinghied into the beach and was amazed by the arrival of a large dump truck filled with many families. As soon as it stopped, everyone jumped out and ran happily to the water.

Three young boys about ten or twelve years old introduced themselves as Ernesto, Guillermo, and Jorge. "*Buenos dias, senor, esta possible que nostros usamos su dinghy cerca?*" (Can we use your dinghy if we stay close by?) Ernesto said.

Dump Truck Kids

"*Possible Vds, nadar?*" (can you swim?) I asked.

"*Si, senor,*" he said.

"*Esta bien,* it's okay," I replied.

Hours of fun began for the three boys, paddling, splashing, and swimming using the dinghy as their swim platform. I watched them from the beach, joining them in the water whenever I needed to cool down. Later after people had left the beach, I met a Mexican man picking up trash just as I was doing. I felt gratified that a local shared my sense of responsibility for the environment. He thanked me for cleaning up after the families and showed me where some empty trash cans were located.

After leaving the shelter of Bahia Matachen, I sailed alone leisurely south along the beautiful coast. White sand beaches were interspersed by dark volcanic cliffs, their reefs, like dark fingers, reaching out into the sea. The bright green jungle framed the coast as white clouds floated overhead, creating an alluring image of paradise. Anchoring in a bay not too far from the beach, I watched from the boat as people swam and body surfed on small waves. Soon, I caught sight of a woman who seemed to be swimming quite far from shore, coming closer and closer to *Aurora.*

Arriving at my boarding ladder, she said, "May I come aboard?"

"Sure, let me get you a towel," I said as she climbed up onto the deck. We introduced ourselves. Gwen was a nice looking, well-proportioned, brown-haired young woman from Winnipeg, Canada. She had traveled to Mexico by herself to soak up the sun and swim in the crystal-like blue waters.

"I was attracted by the sleek look of your boat and decided to swim out," she said. "What brings you all the way to Mexico from San Francisco?"

Wow, I thought. *Aurora* has a seductive effect on others, too.

"Well, I've had this dream of sailing my own boat to far away places," I said, beginning to tell her about my voyage so far. She and I shared a charmed space sitting in the cockpit surrounded by blue water and the vivid greens covering the shore.

After a beer or two I said, "Would you like to see the inside of the boat?"

Down below, Gwen exclaimed, "I'm amazed by the compact use of space and the homey feel of your boat. Wow, looks like I could cook great meals down here in this galley. It's small but has all the essentials of a full kitchen. Those couches on three sides of the dining table look quite comfy."

Looking into the forward cabin, I pointed out, "In here is a V-berth following the shape of the hull. On the port side is a hanging locker and across from it is a dresser with three drawers. Plenty of space for guests."

Walking through into the cozy aft cabin, the double bed, settee, and mirrored vanity seemed to seduce Gwen even more. Without a word, she pulled down her swim suit, dried her damp body on a nearby towel and lay invitingly on the bed. My eyes widened with surprise and my pulse raced with anticipation. My uncontrollable urges overcame my surprise as I lay beside Gwen. We gently explored each other's bodies, enjoying this impromptu intimate moment. Our bodies merged as our passions took hold. Lying beside each other, I wondered with a smile, "Who says that mermaids don't exist?"

"I only have one more day left in Mexico," Gwen whispered, meaning our first encounter would be our last. "Lying on the beach, I was fantasizing about how it would feel to be on a beautiful boat bobbing in the sea. I'm so glad I swam out. Being here was much better than my fantasy." She gave me a long, warm hug.

"Thanks," I said, smiling. "Becoming a part of your reality has been great! I've just realized every sailor's fantasy of being visited by a mermaid."

Was this Livengood Luck or what?

10

PUERTO VALLARTA AND BEYOND

Sailing alone the next day, I continued south still feeling charmed by my "mermaid encounter." I was seeing that I could handle *Aurora* by myself. Even the fish were attracted to my lure. I caught a 30-inch sierra mackerel and an even bigger yellowtail tuna. I hoped to find boats anchored in the bays indented along the coast to share my wealth of fresh fish with them. My refrigeration space aboard was now maxed out. I rounded Punta Mita that marked the southern entrance of Bahia Banderas, a large bay with Puerto Vallarta at its head. Sailing east to La Cruz de Huanacaxtla, I anchored with other cruisers outside the breakwater protecting a small harbor filled with fishing boats. I dinghied over to *Meander*, a nearby sailboat, where I met Len, the owner and captain.

"Len, how would you like a nice tuna fillet?"

"I'd love it," said Len. "The first rule of successful cruising is to never turn down fresh fish," he added, laughing. "Hey, live music is happening at Bananas Bar in town this afternoon. I'm going in. How about joining me? You can see the place just over there on the hill leading up from the water."

"Oh yeah, sounds good to me. I'll meet you there," I said, looking forward to an afternoon of fun with a new friend. Len took the tuna below deck, and I rowed by to *Aurora*.

Sitting in my cockpit watching the water, I saw a small pod of dolphins swimming by. I whistled and shouted trying to attract them. Ignoring me, they swam over to another sailboat where a large black Labrador Retriever was running and barking on the deck. Suddenly, the dog jumped into the water and began swimming with the dolphins gathered near the boat. They all swam together for about five minutes until the dolphins took off. The owner who had been watching the show decided to "retrieve" his retriever by leading him ashore with the dinghy.

That afternoon, following a parade of dinghies into the harbor, I joined a musical gathering at "Bananas." It was a fun bar, where cruisers and locals played their instruments while the audience sipped Margaritas and *Pacifico cervezas*. Len was sitting at a round wooden table so I joined him.

"Thanks for the tuna," he said. "I've been wondering, Karl, what brings you to Mexico?"

"Well, I'm living out a lifelong dream I've had of sailing my own boat to foreign places," I said. "I want to meet new people so I can learn about them and understand their cultures."

"That's an ambitious agenda!" Len said. "I'm here for the warm weather and water and looking for a chance to meet a woman who would like to join me. I find sailing alone a rather lonely affair."

"Sounds like you've got a plan," I added. "My current crew, Jean, is off visiting her family, but I'm discovering a sense of relief at being alone. It seems that I left the right woman back home in Oakland."

"Oh, really?" Len said quizzically. He turned to the music. "I really like the Mexican guitar player. He's so expressive. It seems like his fingers are flying over the strings."

"Yeah, this guy's jazz riffs really soar," I said. "My body is swaying and my fingers tapping as I take in the music. What a great way to spend a tropical Sunday afternoon!" I got up from the table to leave. "I'll be sailing to Puerto Vallarta tomorrow so look for me in the marina."

"You bet I will," Len said. The next day, while sailing deeper into Bahia Banderas toward Puerto Vallarta, I was amazed by three forty to fifty-foot-long humpback whales spouting water into the air. Their tails flipping nearby made loud cracks and huge splashes. I was thrilled to be so close! Then one whale surged up and leapt out of the water. The forty-ton weight and power of these grand mammals was awe inspiring. I had never been this close to a whale. I instinctively knew not to get any closer. I sensed the abandonment of their playfulness and joy. They might not be aware of my boat's presence. I didn't want to disturb them in any way. As I sailed on, I waved good-bye.

By following the glide paths of airliners coming in to land at Puerto Vallarta's airport, I located the narrow entrance channel into the marina just in front of the airport on my chart. The scene around the marina was dominated by new high rise apartment and condominium buildings under construction. Workers were everywhere mixing concrete, hauling it in buckets up the rickety scaffoldings, and pouring it into forms to create the structure of the building.

I went to the marina office and asked about laundry facilities.

"The new washer and dryer have arrived, but no one can be found to hook them up," the secretary informed me. "Everyone is busy working on the new buildings."

" I'll install the machines," I volunteered, "if I can be the first one to use them."

The manager happily gave me the tools and wire, and plugs, so I got down to work. I dreaded having to drill through a solid concrete wall with a light duty drill. I was amazed, however, that the carbide-tipped bit zipped quickly through the wall without much effort. I wondered how this could happen? While I was watching the workers mix cement on the ground, the answer came jumping out at me. They were using beach sand loaded with salt to mix into the cement. No wonder the concrete was so weak. Looking around at all the new buildings, I just shook my head, wondering how strong are they really? Would they continue standing when rocked by the earthquakes common in the area? For my efforts installing the laundry, I received free dockage for the remainder of my stay, clean clothes and sheets courtesy of the laundry machines, and my first job in Mexico. I was proud of myself for living off the local economy and conserving my meager funds. What a deal!

* * * * *

The Puerto Vallarta marina had collected a number of cruisers on their way south to Costa Rica so I was able to copy their charts to update my current cruising information. We also pitched in helping each other with small projects, sharing expertise, and solving problems by creating good solutions. Having fresh water on the dock motivated my boat-cleaning genes into action. I scrubbed and rinsed the deck and hull to remove all the salty grime that had been accumulating during my many months at sea. The clean dinghy received three coats of protectant to shield it from the intense southern sun. Water from the hose on the dock was fresh but contaminated like most water in Mexico. When filling my drinking water tanks, I used an inline filter on the hose and then added drops of microdyne, a sliver iodide solution, to the tanks to kill any unwanted critters that were sure to cause Montezuma's Revenge in my tender gringo intestines.

During Jean's absence, I realized that cruising by myself was not as lonely as I had feared before starting my adventure. I was enjoying setting my own schedule and focusing on the needs of *Aurora* while preparing for her voyage south. Being alone, I had a greater impetus to make new friends among the cruisers on the dock. I met Julie and Ed, a vibrant couple in their late sixties from northern British Columbia who were standing next to their red homemade steel ketch, *Wanderer*. They said they were old Mexico hands who spent their winters on their boat absorbing the life-giving warmth of Mexico.

*****

I decided that now was a good time to have a "Margarita Party" on *Aurora*. I invited Ed and Julie along with Len and his new friend, Loreta.

Passing around the first round of Margaritas, I said, "Let's introduce ourselves."

Ed, a stocky sixty-something, pleasant looking man, volunteered to go first. "Julie and I live on the Straits of Georgia north of Vancouver, British Columbia. We live and sail on *Wanderer*, our two-masted steel ketch that we built and launched from our front yard. I'm a retired airline pilot, but now I'm flying float planes that take folks to isolated lakes and rivers in Alaska during the summers."

"That sounds like an exciting job that allows you to escape to Mexico over the winters," I said.

"Yeah, we both love Mexico," said Julie. "I'm a retired nurse. I loved caring for people and raising a family, but I'm enjoying retirement even more."

"I'll go next," offered Len. "I'm from Sausalito, California. I'm a mechanical engineer taking a few years off to cruise *Meander*, my wooden sloop. I want to cruise while I'm still young enough to handle the demands of sailing and anchoring. This is my first time in Mexico and I just met Loreta in Puerto Vallarta." Loreta flashed a smile.

"Well, yes, I'm Loreta. I came down here to practice my Spanish and meet new people. I guess Len fits into that category. Back home in Santa Fe, I'm an interior designer working with a partner who's now covering for me. I just took a bus up to a furniture-making village in the mountains above Puerto Vallarta to find a source for the hand carved chairs, tables, and headboards that some of my clients would really like to have in their homes. I've also done some sailing and would like to try more in this tropical environment."

"That sounds good to me," said Len. Then everyone turned to me.

"Okay, I'm Karl from California. Besides making killer Margaritas, I plan to sail south through Mexico and Central America over the next few years. My crew, Jean, will be returning in a few days. We'll see how that goes." I took a sip of my drink.

"Well, I've had enough Margaritas to tell this story," Ed said. "One day, the float plane engine failed, forcing me to land near the shore of Hudson Bay in Canada, north of the Arctic Circle. I was able to paddle the plane to shore and anchor it while I waited to be rescued by a buddy in another float plane."

"You must be a great pilot!" I remarked.

"Yeah, I guess so," said Ed. "I was rescued, then later a mechanic and I were flown back in to fix the engine. We were able to fly the plane back to its base."

"Nothing like success to make your day," I said. A moment of silence passed.

"I'm beginning to feel a little woozy," said Loreta. "How many Margaritas have we had?"

"Yeah, what's your secret ingredient?" asked Len. "They're the best ever."

"I guess it's the whipped egg whites I blended into the mix that give it extra body and smoothness," I shared. "Of course, large amounts of tequila help too." We all laughed.

I saw the potency of the Margaritas demonstrated as I watched the cruisers wobble down the docks when they left one by one.

That evening, I received a call on the ham radio from a ham operator in the United States informing me that my father's prostate cancer was worse. I called my parents' home in Naples, Florida, and talked with my sister, Margie.

"Dad's cancer has metastasized into his bones, and he is receiving radiation therapy," she said with sadness in her voice. "We're not sure that the doctor caught it in time."

"Wow, I'm so sorry," I said, surprised. "I wasn't prepared for that news. Bone cancer is a nasty disease that causes lots of pain. Keep me informed though the ham radio operator, Margie." The jovial effects of the Margaritas had worn off with hearing about Dad.

* * * * *

Jean was soon to arrive, and the boat was a mess. It was time to clean up *Aurora*, but the beautiful sunny weather, the white clouds passing overhead, and the warm fresh breeze wafting through the boat tempted me to put off the job. A thought whispered to me. Did I really want Jean to return? Probably not. But, I tried to focus on setting *Aurora* back to ship-shape condition. These thoughts continued drifting from the tasks at hand to the voyage ahead and to my doubts about Jean. Was she a suitable partner in my most meaningful life venture? And then I thought about JoAnne whom I left in Oakland.

When Jean arrived by taxi from the nearby airport, I walked up the dock to meet her. She was relaxed and chatty about her family, but I was disinterested. Being away from each other had reinforced my feelings of independence. Jean didn't seem that interested in what I had been doing. I brought up the cruise south and outlined where we would be going.

In the morning, our first destination was Yelapa on the other side of Bahia Banderas. Yelapa is a community built by hippies in the hills above a small bay. Houses cling to the steep slopes, set among the live oak trees. Anchoring off the beach, we discovered that the slope of the hills continued down into the water, forcing me to drop a stern anchor in the shallow water near the beach and a bow anchor in deeper water out in front of *Aurora*. I set two anchors this way in case the winds shifted to an offshore direction during the night. The stern anchor would hold the boat in place keeping it from drifting out into deeper water.

Later, while climbing up the hill, we saw that the hand-built houses reflected the vision and varied skills of their owners. It seemed that building inspectors were confined to the larger towns and cities. Roads were not a part of Yelapa's community. The only access for residents was by boat and then by trails winding up into the hills. The houses were handmade with local natural materials: poles, sticks, rocks, and palm fronds. Not a glass paned window was in sight. The warm tropical climate made for "easy livin'" and a totally laid back atmosphere. Walking along the trails, Jean and I said hello to Sandy and Joe who invited us into their funky house for tea. They sported the venerable hippie look—long hair, tie-dyed clothes, and lots of handmade jewelry.

Sandy told us their story. "After we retired, we wanted to live in a warmer climate and to stretch our Social Security dollars. We migrated from the Los Angeles area to Mexico where the basic necessities of life are much cheaper. We're living off the grid with our neighbors and we've created a great community. We help each other and have lots of fun socializing. Our mantra is, 'I'd rather have a *palapa* in Yelapa than a condo in Redondo.'"

"Wow, sounds like you've hit on a great way to live!" Jean exclaimed.

"Yeah, we've eliminated cars, noise, and pollution from our lives, so what could be better," Joe added. "We love reading and hiking to the Mexican village higher up the mountain. Their weavings and other crafts are so colorful and creative."

"Yelapa feels like real community to me," I said. "Places like this are hard to find in California. People up there just don't seem to have the time and perhaps the interest to get to know their neighbors." I finished my tea. "Well, we need to get going. Our next stop is about fifteen miles away and getting there before dark is important. Thanks for the tea and interesting conversation."

"Great meeting you both," added Jean.

* * * * *

In preparing for my sea adventure months earlier, I had learned that helping children and adults along the Mexican coast was a part of the lore of the community of cruisers to which I would belong. Articles and letters in *Latitude 38* magazine published in Mill Valley, California, stressed that bringing useful things for these isolated communities is much appreciated. As we stopped in Corrales at the southern entrance of Banderas Bay, a crowd of children met us. We gave the smiling children school supplies of paper, pens, pencils, and crayons, that were part of our stash I brought to treat children along the way.

José, the father of one of the kids, came forward.

"*Hola señor*, I have two Cabrillos that I caught this morning. I would like to trade them for some laundry soap and coffee."

"I think we have enough to trade," I said. "I love fresh fish."

"Okay, sounds good to me," Jean said. "I'll get you the laundry soap and coffee."

Other valuable trade goods included hats, jeans, and sun-glasses because they cost so much money in stores. We could exchange those items for fresh fruit and vegetables, and if we were really lucky, rock lobsters.

We made the next hop south to Tenacatita, a large bay deeply carved into the coastline. It has several anchorages where many cruising boats had anchored behind the islands to enjoy the warm water and sunny days, protected from the rolling Pacific swells. Here, we began visiting boats and meeting more of our compatriots. It was nearly sundown when we joined a potluck cocktail party on the deck of *Meander*, my new friend Len's boat.

"Hi, Loreta and Len," I said coming aboard. "It's great to see you again. I'd like you to meet Jean. We're sailing together."

"Nice to meet you, Jean, I'm Loreta. I decided to join Len on his cruise south."

"Hi, I'm taking some time off from teaching to sail in Mexico," said Jean.

"You might say I'm an interior designer on an extended field trip in Mexico," Loreta continued. "I'm so excited about the new condos I saw in Puerto Vallarta designed by Eduardo Giddings. They are hanging off the mountainside overlooking Banderas Bay south of Puerto Vallarta. He's created curving fluid forms using concrete and stucco with native materials like bamboo incorporated in the walls to allow breezes to circulate in the house. The couches are concrete shelves attached to the walls covered with cushions. Mexicans are so creative. Their ideas will keep my interior design studio going for years."

"You're right," I agreed. "Those condos seemed so organic the way they followed the folds of the mountain. What a spectacular setting. Each one has a clear view of the water and the sunsets."

Loreta and Jean continued talking so I took Len aside. "How are things going with Loreta?"

"It's kind of amazing," Len whispered. "We seem to have all the right chemistry."

"Great!" I said softly. "You're a lucky guy."

Looking down at the water I noticed the surface was roiling nearby. It was a "bait boil" that occurs when large fish drive smaller bait fish to the surface. Soon, pelicans were diving into the churning water, scooping up their dinner, all sure signs that yellowfin tuna were joining them in the feast.

"Len, can I borrow your fishing rod and catch us some dinner?" I said.

"Sure. I'll get it. Good luck."

I jumped into my dinghy with Len's rod and rowed quickly toward the voracious sea birds. A feathered lure dragging behind the dinghy attracted a yellowfin tuna. It struck my bait. Setting the hook securely into its mouth, the 30-inch tuna dragged the din-ghy and me through the water for several minutes until it finally tired out. I pulled the fish close to the dinghy's side, grasped the fish by its gills, and threw it into the dinghy. I quickly covered the flopping fish with an old shirt that I kept aboard. Moments later, the fish stopped struggling.

Rowing back to *Meander*, I yelled, "Hey, Len, I've caught a nice yellowfin tuna. Would you and Loretta like some?"

"No thanks, not this time," he called.

"Okay," I shouted. "Jean, let's head back to *Aurora*. I've got a fish to clean."

Jean and I had yummy sashimi and steaks for broiling to spare!

Continuing to sail south the next day, *Aurora* reached the now famous resort of Las Hadas, off the port city of Manzanillo, where the 1979 movie *Ten* starring Bo Derek and Dudley Moore was filmed. White adobe cottages with red tile roofs dotted the hill. For five dollars a night, we anchored off the resort and were able to use its pools, showers, and other facilities.

The next morning while eating a light breakfast on onboard, I decided to tell Jean how I was feeling about the trip with her.

"Jean, we need to talk about the trip and our future together." Jean put down her coffee cup and gave me her full attention. I took a deep breath and resumed talking. "A couple of things are on my mind. One is that my dad has bone cancer, and I may need to go back to the United States."

"Oh, that's really too bad. I'm sorry to hear this," said Jean. She took a sip of coffee. "What's the other thing?"

"Well, after a lot of thought, I feel that you are not the right per-son for me to continue my cruise with," I said gently. "The emo-tional aspects of our relationship have been too limited for me."

"I felt that too," Jean said. "You seemed distant, and I wasn't prepared to open more of myself to you. I've been in the habit of having more casual fun relationships with men."

As Jean and I talked I was relieved to be finally expressing my-self. I went on and told her everything.

"I feel cheated, in a sense," I said. "I've put so much energy, time, money and planning into the cruise of a lifetime. I realized, however, that I wanted and needed more on the emotional level." I paused. "You're a good sailor, Jean, and we worked well together, but that's not enough for me." My disappointment clarified what was really important to me.

"Okay," Jean said cooly. She stood up and walked up on deck. I followed. Turning toward me, Jean said, "I'm going to see if I can find a berth on another boat."

Without another word, she jumped into the dinghy and roared off toward the other boats. Later I learned that Jean called a friend who happened to be in Mexico to pick her up.

*****

I realized I wanted it *all* now but was paying the penalty for having impulsively settled for less when I left JoAnne behind. I was happy and relieved to be on my own again. My thoughts and heart returned to JoAnne. I so missed our emotional closeness. I missed the feelings that emerged in our moments of physical tenderness. I missed the passion our bodies expressed to each other. It was time to go home! This was the time and place for me to turn *Aurora* around and head north again to find a safe place to leave her before returning to the States.

The next day, I began sailing north. I felt sheepish, hesitant, and afraid but decided to use a ham radio phone patch through a radio operator in California to contact JoAnne. Our difficult conversation would be even more awkward with having to say "Over" when changing from one person speaking to the other, while the ham radio operator listened. I could barely control the butterflies in my stomach. What if she wouldn't talk to me? What if she never wanted to see me again? What if?

"Hello?" JoAnne said. It was wonderful to hear her voice. I was so nervous that that I blurted out everything in one breath.

"JoAnne, this is Karl calling from Mexico. How are you? I've asked Jean to leave *Aurora*. It didn't work out. My father has taken a turn for the worse as his prostate cancer has metastasized into his bones. It's time for me to come back to the United States so I can help Mom with his care. Over." There were a few seconds of silence. Please talk to me, JoAnne, I pleaded to myself. She spoke.

"I'm sorry to hear about your dad, but I'm happy that you're coming back, Over," JoAnne replied. Every inch of my body sighed with relief and gratitude.

"JoAnne, I feel like such a fool for leaving you when I did. It was a big mistake. Over."

"Yes, it was!" JoAnne said. "But Karl, why don't you stay with me when you come back to Oakland? Over."

"I'd love to. JoAnne, are you sure that is what you really want to do after everything that I have put you through? Over."

"Let's give it a try," JoAnne said softly. "I can pick you up at the airport. Over."

"Great!" I almost shouted. "Now I'm really looking forward to coming home. Thank you so much. Over and Out."

I had left JoAnne to do my "cruising thing," so her decision to take me back into her life was a humbling experience, giving me further insight into the depth of her caring for me. How could I have left JoAnne behind when *she* was the key to making my dream complete? It took this painful mistake for me to understand that whatever we're doing in life is most meaningful when shared with a lover, a partner, a friend, a compatriot. Facing life with another makes so much more possible.

*****

My son David, responding to his dad's call for assistance, flew in to meet me after I reached Puerto Vallarta. Together we provisioned *Aurora*, this time taking on cases of Pacifico beer direct from the beer trucks that were supplying the sport fishing boats at their nearby docks. For ten dollars and a case of empties, we received a fresh case of 24 bottles that cost less than fifty cents a bottle. The price of beer had proved to be an accurate measure of the relative value of different currencies.

"These bottles of Pacifico are less than half the price of those back home," David exclaimed. "We are going to be happy campers!"

David's great sense of humor and easygoing temperament were an effective antidote for any remaining tensions that had built up in my relationship with Jean. David's positive relationship with me validated the hard work I had invested in helping him through the anger and angst of his teenage years. It seemed like a testament to both our perseverance through the process and our love for each other.

Sailing north toward San Blas, I chose to anchor *Aurora* in Matanchen Bay. Ocean swells breaking across the entrance made it too risky to enter the tricky river channel into town. Matanchen Bay was quite shallow, forcing us to anchor almost a half mile from shore. Going to town involved rowing in and finding a safe place to leave the dinghy—at a *palapa* restaurant on the shore. After I took a bus into town, Chena was surprised and happy to see me again, and his cute assistant, Norma, seemed quite attracted to handsome gringo David. It was a kick watching them try to communicate using hand signals and passing the dictionary back and forth. David's Spanish vocabulary consisted of adding the letter "o" to English words!

That night we took Chena out for dinner and later had a few drinks and sang Mexican folk songs with his friends. Afterward, David and I caught the last taxi on the square. Driving out of town, we arrived at the Matanchen beach in total darkness. There was no moon at all that night.

"David, there's the dinghy right where we left it at the *palapa*. let's drag it down to the water," I said.

"Okay, Dad, I'll row out into the bay, but I can't see *Aurora* anywhere."

"We should head in the general direction of where we left her," I said. "The problem is the only lights I can see are those on the far shore shining from cars driving along the highway by the beach."

"Are those shark fins sticking up near the dinghy?" David said with alarm.

"I don't think so," I said. "I'll bet those fins are the wing tips of large manta rays sticking up out of the water. Don't worry. I saw

8-foot-wide manta rays whose wing tips broke the water in Banderas Bay in the daylight that look just like these fins."

"Dad, do ya see those dim lights over there? It looks to me like a sailboat outlined against the faint lights on shore.""Yeah, I can make it out now. Let's row over there," I said. "I'll knock on the hull."

"Hi, sorry to bother you," I said. "We own the sailboat that should be anchored near here. Have you seen it?"

"Yeah, your boat is anchored right over there," the owner said, pointing the beam of his flashlight to reveal *Aurora* anchored only about one hundred feet away.

"Thanks so much," I said. "I feel kind of stupid, but the boat was totally lost to us in the blackness of the night."

We were relieved that *Aurora* was safe and sound. We had imagined that she had dragged her anchor and drifted away. Black nights play tricks in the darkness of our minds.

"David, I'm going to buy an automatic solar powered anchor light that will lead us to the boat on future dark nights," I promised.

* * * * *

After David left to fly back to California, my sailing buddy, Elmo, from El Cerrito, California, arrived in San Blas. He would accompany me on the voyage north along the Pacific Coast and then back west across to the Sea of Cortez.

"Elmo, so great to see you!" I said, giving him a hug. "Thanks for coming down here to exercise your sailing muscles. Do you remember the seamanship, weather, and navigation classes we took together? Did you ever think that we would be together on *Aurora* in Mexico?"

"Well, you did seem pretty serious about sailing the world, judging by all the questions you asked in our marine science classes," said Elmo. "Remember after *Aurora* arrived and we sailed her out the Golden Gate in that storm. It was then I knew you weren't just fooling around."

"You're right, I wasn't! I've provisioned the boat so we'll start sailing tomorrow."

After sailing two days and nights, we arrived at Isla Partida north of La Paz on the Baja Peninsula and entered its large lagoon cautiously as darkness enveloped *Aurora*. Elmo and I closely watched the depth sounder and the anchor lights of other boats before choosing a spot that seemed far enough from the dark outline of the shore and the other boats.

In the morning with a cup of coffee in my hand, I climbed up into the cockpit, looked astern, and spotted a reef about ten feet away.

I called to Elmo with alarm, "Come up and see this. We're lucky that we didn't hit this reef last night!"

"Karl, if you look more closely, the reef seems to be moving and flashing in the morning sun," Elmo said, smiling.

I looked again. "Oh my goodness, that's a large school of tiny silver fish undulating in the moving water."

We had a good laugh and thanked our lucky stars that this was the reef that wasn't.

We sailed up the winding channel to La Paz into the cruisers' anchorage where *Aurora* joined the fleet. Anchoring near *Oceanis II*, we rowed the dinghy over and met Jacques and Mariam Ebert, an attractive couple in their late forties, from Montreal, Canada. Mariam's dark hair and skin tones gave her a gypsy-like appearance while Jacques was slender with a handsome muscular look. They had been in Mexico a number of years with their teenage son and were anchored in LaPaz for a while.

Together, we visited the Elberts' favorite restaurant and talked about our adventures. Also I wanted to know about their boat.

"Your boat looks like it's made from ferro-cement. Was it hard to build it? How did you sail it to Mexico?"

"Well, I'm a structural engineer, and we built the boat when we were on assignment in Vancouver, BC," Jacques explained. "It's built like most concrete structures with steel rebar for strength covered by cement shot onto the steel core. So we sailed it down the west coast much like you did. We sort of fell into staying in La Paz because Mariam has developed her massage practice while I'm helping cruisers fix problems on their boats. Our budget is very tight so we need this income to survive, but we can also leave La Paz and cruise the sea when we have the time."

"It sounds to me that you've found a way to make it in Mexico," I said. "Lots of cruisers have that goal. I have to return to the United States, and I'm wondering, Jacques, would you check on *Aurora* while I'm gone?"

"Sure, I'd be happy to," he replied. "We're anchored close together so no problema."

"Great, I'll feel much better knowing you're here while I'm there," I said with a wink.

The next day Elmo and I were off the water and on airplanes. He was flying back to California and I was headed to Guadalajara and then on to my folks' home in Naples, Florida.

A stopover in Guadalajara proved to be both interesting and perplexing. I wanted to see the ceramic and glass making *puebla* of Telaquepecque that I'd heard about located outside the city. Blown glass vases, goblets and ceramics of all shapes and sizes spilled out of the shops and factories onto the streets creating a complex collage of brilliant colors. I bought a colorful yellow and blue pottery vase for JoAnne, who loved arranging flowers. I found the right bus back, but as I was riding along the realization hit me that I'd forgotten both the name of my hotel and its address!

I began asking passengers, "Which stops are in the central district?"

"This one," offered a passenger, so I got off near a park that I recognized and I saw the hotel. Finding it unleashed a flood of relief.

I flew into Naples, and my sister, Margie, met me at the airport with news about Dad. "He is failing, is in more pain, and is on morphine. His driving privileges have been withdrawn after two recent minor accidents."

"Wow, I'm sorry to hear that," I said with sadness. "I hope that I can help you and Mom with Dad's care. I know that he'll be angry about losing the independence that the car gave him."

Fortunately, Dad was still able to focus on his twin loves of reading and classical music. He spent many hours listening to the

Faure Requiem, a favorite of mine, too, since singing it with the Berkeley Chorus. We often sat together just listening to this and other works. I could feel the melodic "Pia Jesu" soprano solo soothing his soul in preparation for its journey.

My listening centered my feelings and concerns about Dad and JoAnne. I believed that I had been able to be there for Dad and Mom for the time being. Next it would be time for me to open myself to JoAnne. I knew that she belonged in the heart of my emotional life. Would JoAnne be open and able to respond to my longing?

11

BACK TO JOANNE

As the airplane flew over San Francisco Bay, I felt my heart pounding in my chest. I was approaching a critical juncture in my life. How would JoAnne react when she saw me?

I walked down the ramp and immediately saw JoAnne in the crowd of greeters. She was smiling when she saw me. I smiled back and walked up to her saying, "JoAnne, it's great to see you. It's been a long time." We gave each other a quick hug and were swept into the throng of passengers heading to reclaim their baggage. So far so good, I thought, letting out a relaxing breath.

"I'm glad you've come back, Karl, but it's been a tough six months," JoAnne said as we slowly walked to the car. "I felt really abandoned by you. Thank God for the support Mom and Betsy and all my friends gave me."

Once inside the quiet of the car, I responded.

"I *did* abandon you, JoAnne, and I made a big mistake. I feel like a schmuck. My desire to sail, to live out my dream overrode my feelings for you. I rationalized my thoughts about what was really important for me."

"Well, Karl, my feelings of anger and hurt as well as my love were cut off when you left," said JoAnne, her voice cracking. "I couldn't express them directly to you. Crying and talking with my friends just wasn't enough to relieve the pain." I could feel JoAnne's pain in my own heart.

"I'm really sorry, JoAnne. I understand what you were feeling. Jean turned out to be an emotional cripple, and I couldn't trust her, so my deeper feelings for you have lain dormant, too."

JoAnne struggled to hold back her tears. I took her hand in mine.

"Seeing you, Karl, brings up feelings I've held in check. You do realize we had something special back then."

"Oh yes. Right now, I feel unworthy of receiving those feelings, but I missed our special connection—our conversations—the support we offered each other."

We embraced each other and a long kiss sealed the moment and renewed our connection. It was time to go home.

*****

We walked slowly up the path to the front door of JoAnne's house. Once inside we sat on the couch and talked more.

JoAnne seemed distant. She was flexing her hands. "You seem tense right now, JoAnne, can you say what's on your mind?"

"You're right, I am tense," she said firmly. "You left me high and dry, Karl. You left with *that* woman. The whole thing didn't make sense to me. You left our real relationship for a fantasy."

Wow, she got that right, I thought as my stomach churned.

"I do feel bad and guilty about the leaving you, about ignoring your feelings and putting you in a vulnerable position," I said softly. JoAnne's shoulders relaxed.

"I can see that on your face and in your body," she said.

"Yeah, I'm feeling very ashamed," I continued. "Saying I'm sorry probably isn't enough, but I am truly sorry."

JoAnne sighed. "This has been very intense. I need a moment to take some deep breaths." We sat on the couch holding hands in silence for a few minutes.

When we stood up, JoAnne moved toward me and put her arms around me. We managed a real hug and then a loving kiss. She can forgive, I realized.

"Ahh, it feels good to be able to let go and breathe again," I whispered with relief. "It's so good having your soft body next to mine."

"Yes, my body is happy too," said JoAnne. "I love to nuzzle against your neck and take in the power of your embrace." She took a deep breath. "It feels like it's time to go upstairs."

Some of the disappointment and tension between JoAnne and me dissolved as our passions took hold of us. My whole being responded to hers. The intensity of our sexual feelings, an intimacy based on our attraction and love, helped bridge the gap that I had created by sailing away from our relationship.

Lying in bed together, I knew that JoAnne's depth of caring for me and her ultimate ability to accept and love me would be my salvation. Her love helped to assuage some of my guilt, allowing us to continue to enrich our relationship.

Over the next months, being able to express how much we cared would open doors to an even fuller relationship. Our common interests in music, politics, and friends as well our liberal humanitarian approach to life deepened our love. Honest communication enhanced our relationship that was also pulsating with attraction.

Later, I discovered the role that JoAnne's 87-year-old mother, Madeline, played in influencing her decision to give our relationship a second chance. Madeline and JoAnne were very close, like sisters, confidantes, that support each other's lives.

One day, JoAnne said, "Karl, can you help me repair Mom's couch?"

"Sure, I'd be happy to. What's the problem?" I asked.

"Well, it seems that the webbing supporting the seat cushions has broken loose," she replied. "I asked Mom about it and she said that she and her ninety-year-old friend George spend a lot of time on the couch. So I asked her, 'What are you two doing on the couch?' Mom said, 'That's none of your business! I don't talk about that with anyone, not even you.'"

"Wow, she sure put you in your place, and she looks like she's really alive," I remarked with a wide grin. "I've always thought that Madeline really liked me and approved of our relationship."

*****

Soon after arriving at JoAnne's, I began working again as a contractor to pay my share of expenses and to start refilling the now empty cruising kitty. As winter warmed into spring, future sailing plans evolved while talking with my children.

Darsie, my oldest daughter, told me, "Dad, Greg and I have set the date for our wedding. It'll be on the Saturday immediately after our graduation from UC Berkeley in June."

"Wow, what great news! You two make a great couple. I've enjoyed spending time with both of you, having dinners and barbecues together, seeing your love and affection for each other. Your mastery of those tough anatomy courses at UC Berkeley certainly allowed me to exercise my parental pride genes."

"Thanks, Dad, for all the compliments," Darsie said, blushing.

"I'd like to do something special to honor your marriage, Darsie," I continued. "How would you and Greg like to have a honeymoon cruise on *Aurora* on the Sea of Cortez?"

"Wow, Dad, we'd love going cruising on *Aurora* in Mexico! I've heard that fishing is killer in the Sea of Cortez."

"Great, I'll begin planning our trip," I said, giving my daughter a warm hug.

*****

I walked Darsie down a grassy aisle past family and friends seated on the lawn. Each step took us closer to Greg standing in front of a collection of tall roses in Oakland's Rose Garden near Lake Merritt. The woman minister performing the ceremony acknowledged the depth and length of Darsie and Greg's commitment to each other. I was a proud and happy dad and now father-in-law watching as these "kids" took a step into adulthood. I would be there to support them whenever needed.

The reception followed at the Lake Merritt Boat House overlooking the lake in downtown Oakland where Greg's six handsome brothers raised cheers and toasts. Being the oldest, Greg had set a good example and even changed the diapers of his youngest brothers. He was the leader of this pack of boys.

I offered my toast. "Congratulations to Darsie and Greg. You two hold a special place in my heart. I feel fortunate to be gaining a wonderful son. Let's all drink to your happiness and health!" The room filled with cheers.

The next day we left on a flight to La Paz, Mexico.

I sent Darsie and Greg by cab for two nights at La Concha, the old governor's mansion converted into a hotel, nestled along the beach opposite the entrance channel to La Paz. I stayed on *Aurora* getting her ready for their honeymoon sail. Giving them the captain's aft cabin affording them more privacy was only the beginning of a wonderful trip north toward Loreto.

The June weather was perfect. The warm water enticed this athletic couple into snorkeling explorations whenever the boat was anchored. The dinghy allowed them to explore the shoreline

"Mexican Gothic"

and reefs while casting a lure where they hoped fish were hiding. While they were trolling one day, a large tuna struck the lure. As the bungee stretched, Greg began to haul in the fighting fish as it jumped and twisted in the air eventually tiring itself out. I released the sheets holding the sails to slow down *Aurora*. Hand over hand, Greg pulled the fish next to the boat. I reached down from the deck and gaffed it through its gills, and then carefully hoisted it aboard.

"Boy, I don't want to lose this fish," I yelled. "It's a beauty!"

"Wow, what a fish!" Greg exclaimed.

"Greg, it's the largest tuna ever caught on *Aurora*," I said. "Congratulations, maybe it's a wedding gift from the sea!

"It's the biggest fish I've ever landed," bragged Greg. "I can't wait to show pictures to my brothers and friends. Are they going to be jealous!"

"I'd better conk it on its head so it won't jump off the deck," I said, picking up the heavy winch handle.

The deed done, I took a great picture of Darsie and Greg standing on the foredeck holding the 36-inch-long yellowfin tuna and the gaff, mimicking the classic *American Gothic* painting by Grant Wood from 1930. Wood's iconic painting showed a stern faced farm couple standing in front of their barn, the man holding a pitchfork, as the Depression was deepening in America. In contrast, Darsie and Greg's faces beamed with pride and joy.

*****

Together, we explored a tiny fishing village along the arid shore, a place of stark beauty, featuring tumbled boulders stacked into fanciful shapes. The Baja desert, while not exactly green, does have stunted trees and cactuses that relieve the monochromatic tan and brown colors of the rocks and sand. The towering Sierra Gigante Mountains rise some 5,000 feet just a few miles from the shore of the Sea of Cortez, providing an impressive backdrop to our view from *Aurora* when anchored or sailing.

After anchoring the boat in Puerto Escondido, I waited for my youngest daughter, Leanne, to arrive. I had arranged for her to come by bus from the airport at La Paz. I was just preparing to leave *Aurora* and walk up to the highway to meet the bus when I saw her arriving in a VW van filled with young men. So I jumped in the dinghy and used the motor to speed over to the sea wall.

"Hi, Dad," Leanne cheerfully greeted me. "I met this friendly Mexican guy, Guillermo, a college student, on the plane. He offered to take me along with his friends to Puerto Escondido."

Noticing my puzzled and concerned look Guillermo said, "Everything is okay. We had a fast trip to Puerto Escondido in my van. We are headed for Loreto so it was no problema to bring Leanne here."

"Thanks for bringing her, but she's only a junior in high school even though she may look older," I said, seeing that he seemed quite taken by her.

"Yeah, I was wondering, but she does seem older," said Guillermo. "She has a good Spanish accent and we had an interesting conversation."

"It's great to know that she's using her Spanish, but having her arrive with a van full of guys is still scary for a dad," I said.

"I understand, señor. I'll be going. *Adios,* Leanne, *buena suerte.*"

It seemed that this young man's attraction to Leanne's pretty face, slim body, and long amber hair might become a regular event when she meets other young men while traveling to see her dad in Central America in future years.

* * * * *

The next day was hot and the pool at Tripui, a trailer park located in Puerto Escondido, was most inviting so we all walked over to swim. I met Bob and Peetie, a couple in their seventies, as we luxuriated in the water. They mentioned their trailer was located in the park. I told them about *Aurora* and introduced them to Greg, Darsie, and Leanne.

Somehow their having a large van came up in our conversation so I asked them, "Would you be able to take us to Loreto? Darsie and Greg have to catch their flight back to California. I'll pay for gas, and I've heard that the fish tacos there are really tasty."

"Sounds like a winning combination to me. Let's do it," Bob replied.

Having more people than seats in the van made for a cozy ride to Loreto. With the rumors about the fish tacos deliciously validated, I had fun delivering our "cargo" to the airport. I also had a chance to learn more about Peetie and Bob, two really hip older folks who came to Mexico to stretch out their Social Security dollars and to enjoy themselves in a new culture. Both were outdoorsy types who used their small sailboat, *Vela*, to explore this area of the Sea of Cortez.

Being alone on *Aurora* with Leanne gave time to talk. "So how are you enjoying boarding at Santa Catalina in Monterey?" I said. "You've been there three years now. How are your friends Eileen and Sunny?"

"I still like school and really have fun rooming with Eileen," Leanne reported. "She's a good student so we study together a lot. She encouraged me to run on the cross country team with her. I'm enjoying the challenge of getting into shape for the five-mile races."

"Wow, I'm impressed that you are running," I said. "It's great exercise, but you never seemed interested in sports before. I'll have to thank Eileen when I see her,"

"I also love studying photography," Leanne continued. "I still would like to be a photographer for *National Geographic*. Remember my trip last year to Washington, D.C., to visit Anna? You said that shopping wasn't enough of a reason to make the trip, and that I had to spend time in museums and to expand my understanding of the government. Well, visiting the exhibits at the *National Geographic* offices really sparked my interest in photography."

"I remember your excitement when you returned," I said. "Photography is a great profession and an interesting hobby which I enjoy myself. It focuses my attention on the surroundings. I'm always looking for interesting shapes and colors. The pictures help my memory and keep me in touch with the images and feelings from places I've been."

"Yeah, it does that for me too," Leanne agreed. "I like working in the darkroom with the pictures and making them special by emphasizing their most interesting parts."

"I'm glad that you are friends with Eileen. I'm still in touch with some of my school friends even though it's been thirty years since I graduated."

"Sunny and I are planning to go to Grandma's in Florida to do a special senior project after Christmas," Leanne added. "Grandma said that we could volunteer as classroom aides with the young migrant children at the Immokalee Child Care Center."

"Helping others and working with children feels like a good plan to me," I said. "By the way, your good grades and active participation in your classes makes me proud." I hugged her, feeling glad to see my daughter evolving into a strong, sensitive, and creative woman.

*****

We left to sail north together for a week of exploring the small coves along the shore of the Sea of Cortez. We found a "Cruiser's Shrine" on the beach at the head of one cove.

"Leanne, look how they used bits of flotsam and more than a few beer bottles to build it," I pointed out. "Sailors seem to have plenty of beer bottles in this hot, dry climate."

"Dad, this shrine seems a little weird to me. Why would people want to make it?"

"Well, seems that we humans tend to leave marks like cairns or temples in isolated places," I said. "It's almost like the animals who need to mark their territory."

"You could be right, Dad. I've seen axe blazes on trees in the forest where I used to live in Trinity County. The Hoopa Indians and the early homesteaders both lived near our cabin."

Leanne wasn't interested in steering the boat until the wind came up causing *Aurora* to heel and pick up speed. She jumped up from her seat in the cockpit stating, "I'd like to drive now. I love feeling how the boat picks up in the wind and surges ahead. It feels alive. This is great fun!"

"Too bad there are no other boats out here to race," I said. "I bet you could beat them."

*****

My twenty-year-old daughter, Jeanne, a more serious young woman, flew in after Leanne left for her own solo journey with Dad. After a hug, I said, "Great to see you, Jeanne! How have you been?"

"Okay. It's wonderful to be here in Mexico and escape the heat of the Central Valley. I've been working for Mom in her fabric shop in Davis so I haven't had any vacation since college ended."

"I've been looking forward to spending some alone time with you," I said. "When all of your brothers and sisters are together, we have lots of fun, but the fooling around seems to be our main focus. We don't see each other often enough, and I'm hoping to catch up with you and to get a better sense of where you are going. How are your classes at Pomona?"

"I'm really enjoying my French classes," Jeanne said. "My Advanced Placement French classes at Davis High School were great so now I'm taking upper division classes. This fall I'll be spending a year abroad in Strasbourg, France. My goal is to enter the university there with regular French students rather than just taking the easier classes taught by professors from Pomona."

"Wow, Jeanne, that's an ambitious goal. I'm proud of you."

"Thanks, Dad, I want to learn as much as I can because I want to teach French in high school. I also am enjoying singing in the concert choir. We have a great director and many good singers."

"You have a beautiful voice, Jeanne. I remember your madrigal concert in Davis where you sang a solo. I'm so glad that you're continuing to sing. It's something you can do throughout your life. Remember when I sang with the Berkeley Chorus? It was most enjoyable, and I met JoAnne there." I smiled remembering how lucky I was to have JoAnne in my life again.

I turned our conversation back to our sailing trip.

"Jeanne, we're going to sail south toward La Paz. Then I want to head for the offshore islands where there will be stronger breezes at night. The summer heat is building and sleeping will be more comfortable there."

"At least we can jump in the sea during the day to cool off," Jeanne said.

"I've made air scoops from light weight nylon spinnaker cloth for both the forward and aft cabin deck hatches," I continued. "The wind will funnel through them down below like a natural air conditioner. They should help cool us some at night."

We had some good sailing under ideal conditions of moderate wind and small waves perfect for a sailor of Jeanne's limited experience. The dazzling blue beauty of the Sea of Cortez enveloped us, releasing sighs of pleasure and smiles of happiness. Gliding along in the rippling water mesmerized us as soft sounds filled our ears.

I reflected on how wonderful sailing has been for bringing me closer to my children. Being able to share this relaxing environment with them where they can experience my love for sailing is opening doors into my life. I feel like I'm inspiring a love of sailing in them.

*****

We anchored *Aurora* near friends, Jacques and Mariam, on *Oceanis II* in La Paz. They had watched *Aurora* when I returned to the United States and JoAnne last year. The next day, I took Jeanne to the airport where I would meet JoAnne coming to join me for a two-week holiday. How would she like living on a sailboat in Mexico?

12

EXPERIENCING THE SEA OF CORTEZ

Wanting JoAnne to have a great time, I made reservations at the Hotel California on a side street in La Paz. It looked okay from the outside. Perhaps, I was swayed by the Eagles song of the same name. It would turn out to be more of an adventure than I had anticipated. We found ourselves in a rather barren room. A thin, lumpy mattress sitting on a concrete shelf posed as a bed. A much needed fan hung from the ceiling, but it had no switch. I noticed two wires sticking out of the wall. As I touched them to each other, a bright spark welded the wires together, starting the blades to rotate at an ever increasing speed. We were cooling down, but the whirring blades sounded and felt like an airplane propeller was over our heads! During the night, I had to tiptoe through an army of large cockroaches on patrol in the bathroom. Fortunately for us, they remained at their post in the bathroom while we were safely in bed. In the morning, we woke to Mexican families in the courtyard using open air stoves to prepare meals next to a washing machine connected by hoses to the building.

"JoAnne, I'm not sure this Hotel California experience has given you the impression I was hoping for," I said not wanting to disappoint her.

"Well, the important thing is we survived it," she laughed. "This has been a very unusual introduction to Mexico, Karl. Let's hope we can find better hotels in the future!"

"It can only go up from here," I responded.

Walking along the Malecon along the edge of the harbor, we called out to Jacques and Mariam anchored out on their boat, *Oceanis II* . I asked them for a lift in their dinghy out to   *Aurora*

117

anchored nearby. Inviting us aboard and talking with JoAnne, Mariam found a compatriot interested in meditation and natural healing.

"Here's a book I wrote," said Mariam, handing a copy of *Self-Healing for Sailors and Sailorettes* to JoAnne. "It offers my recommendations for using herbs and mineral supplements.

"Mariam, thanks so much," said JoAnne. "I'm very interested in natural healing. I'll read it so we can talk about it."

Several dinners together on our boats followed over the next few days. We learned more about our friends' past lives in Quebec, Canada. Jacques was an engineer and Mariam owned a small health food store. After building their ferro-cement boat, they sailed it down the west coast to Mexico. Being fluent in Spanish, they had lived aboard their boat in La Paz for a number of years and had many Mexican friends.

"One of our friends has invited all of us to their home for their one-year-old daughter's birthday party," Mariam announced one evening. "Would you like to come?"

"Sure," JoAnne smiled in agreement. "We'd love to go. What a great way to get to know a young Mexican family."

After dinghying into the dock, the four of us walked to a dirt residential street where high walls surrounded the houses. I was wondering what we would find on the other side of the walls. José and Consuelo, the birthday girl's parents, met us as we entered the gate. They proudly showed the kitchen, dining room, and living room in their middle class house. José had a small business in La Paz while Consuelo taught in an elementary school.

The birthday party for one-year-old Alicia was a major event complete with two guitarists entertaining the assembly of about twenty friends, relatives, and their children. The enticing aroma of barbecuing pork filled the air as Mariam introduced us to most of the guests. When the meal of pork tacos washed down with Pacifico beer was over, Alicia was set down on the table next to her birthday cake. People gasped as she stuck her hand into the cake and began smearing frosting into her hair.

"Karl, they're quite permissive parents, don't you think!" JoAnne whispered.

"Yeah, and I've noticed the children seem to be the primary focus for most Mexican families," I said. "Even poor parents dress their children very well."

Older children were blindfolded and given a broomstick for a chance to break the colorful star-shaped piñata hanging from a tree branch. An adult pulled the rope to raise and lower the swinging target.

Everyone shouted encouragement. *"Mas fuerte, bueno, bueno!"*

After so many blows, the piñata swung in a weakened condition. Alicia was given her chance. The piñata was lowered to her height and she wasn't blindfolded. With a wild swing of the stick, she broke open the pinata releasing a torrent of candy cascading onto the patio. An avalanche of squealing children rushed in to scoop up the spoils. Smiles danced on their faces as they shouted, *"Dulces, dulces!"* (Sweets, sweets!)

The party ended after we all sang *Cerrito Lindo* and other folk songs accompanied by the guitarists. Saying, *"Adios, amigos,"* to everyone we shook hands and thanked our hosts for their hospitality.

"What a great party, Mariam," I said. "Everyone had so much fun. Thanks for inviting us to see what happens behind the walls that we see from the streets. I'm sad that tomorrow we'll be heading back to Puerto Escondido, but JoAnne's vacation is only for two weeks. Sharing La Paz with you two has been very special."

"The party gave me a feeling of what Mexicans are really like," said JoAnne. "I'd love to experience more. And I'll miss spending time with you, Mariam. We have so much in common."

The next morning, we left La Paz and sailed north in a wide channel between two islands. The water ahead seemed to be standing up about two feet higher than its usual level. Grabbing the binoculars, I saw hundreds of dolphins jumping and swimming along the water's surface, each creating its own splash and causing the rising water.

"JoAnne, look at this. I have never seen so many dolphins together. It's such an amazing sight!"

"Wow, the Sea of Cortez is indeed a magical place," said JoAnne looking through the binoculars.

"Dolphins are so social," I mused. "They seem to enjoy being in a pod. It's like they're trying to outdo each other and saying, 'Look, I can jump higher than you! My splash is bigger than yours. Look at me.'"

"I feel more and more a part of the sea, in touch with its inhabitants, swept into its wonder, surrounded by its beauty," said JoAnne. "I'm more relaxed and happy as each day goes by. I'm amazed by the major changes in my life. Sometimes, I feel a bit schizophrenic with one foot in the past holding on for dear life to the familiar, while the other foot is being swept forward as I am screaming and kicking into an unfamiliar future. At those times, I feel uptight and a bit anxious about the unknown. But for the most part, I'm feeling very open to learning new things."

"Wow, I have seen you struggling at times, JoAnne, but it feels great that you are up to the challenges," I replied. "I hope that I'm a good and supportive teacher!"

"You are, Karl. I appreciate your patience, and I love this cruising lifestyle." I was so relieved and happy to hear these words coming from Joanne. I was even more optimistic that we could have a grand life together.

JoAnne, *Aurora*, Sea of Cortez

The sights and wildlife recorded in the book *The Log from the Sea of Cortez*, written by John Steinbeck and biologist Ed Ricketts after their six week's trip on the sea, still exist. Their expedition on the Monterey fishing boat, *Western Flyer*, nearly 60 years ago, spoke of the same impressions of this stunning meeting of land and sea. Sparkling blue waters surrounded by striking boulders marking the shoreline were the perfect venue for showing Jo-Anne the joys and rewards of cruising. I was hoping that such beauty would also convince her that cruising was worth the risks and angst of leaving her close friends and family, the predictability of life ashore, and the comforts of her shoreside home.

When we arrived in Puerto Escondido, I introduced JoAnne to Peetie and Bob who were now living on their own land near Tripui in a small trailer. A large *palapa* structure (vertical poles holding up a framework supporting a roof of palm fronds) covered the trailer and sheltered a large stone-paved patio that they used for their living room in warm weather. These friendly folks were living on the Mexican economy, raising some of their own food, and catching fish as their main source of protein.

With Peetie and Bob aboard their 24-foot sailboat, *Vela*, and Jo-Anne and I sailing *Aurora*, we set off together to explore hidden places known to them along the shore and on nearby islands. At our first stop, we dinghied together to a hot spring bubbling into the sea along the shore.

"Be careful of the hotspot next to shore. It's okay further away," Bob warned us.

Climbing in, we luxuriated in the warm pool surrounded by rocks placed by other cruisers.

"What could be more relaxing?" JoAnne said serenely.

Later, we saw ancient rock paintings of fish and deer adorning a cliff face. A small herd of wild burros joined us on our hike. The creatures had adapted to this harsh environment.

They issued plaintive calls whenever any member of the herd became separated from the group. Maintaining the herd was the basis of their survival because their collective knowledge was used to find fresh water!

Vela

Our five-day trip ended in Honeymoon Cove. JoAnne gushed, "This is one of the most spectacular anchorages in the Sea of Cortez. I'm looking through the clear aquamarine water right to the white sand on the bottom. I just saw three sea turtles and all kinds of fish. Look at that manta ray flying out of the water. Did you hear the loud splash?"

Bob and I took advantage of the clear water to spear enough fish for our two dinners and a round of fish tacos. We had a fabulous time.

Back at Peetie and Bob's home base near Tripui, we took advantage of the swimming pool and restaurant, even having a chance to dance to live music.

"I really like free dancing to the fast ones," I said to JoAnne. "I feel so loose and creative."

"Yeah, it's fun," she said, "but sometimes it's hard to figure out where you're going to move next. The slow dances are more relaxing. Besides I enjoy the closeness of our bodies."

"I'll second that and raise you one," I said with a smile as I pulled her close to me.

Walking back to the dinghy after the dance, we found a drunken man crawling on the dinghy dock begging for a ride out to his boat in the anchorage. We decided to help him by rowing him out to his boat. We knocked on the boat's hull, and his wife appeared. The look on her face said she was not at all happy to see him.

"Why didn't you leave the jerk on shore?" she said, grudgingly hauling him aboard.

When we were back on *Aurora*, I thought more about the drunken man's situation and talked about it with JoAnne.

"It seems that some cruising sailors can slide into alcoholism as their plans of cruising long distances fade into oblivion. I can see that their lives become clouded in an alcoholic haze. I feel troubled when I encounter those lost people because a wasted life is not a pretty sight anywhere! Seeing them brings out my social worker training when I tried to help people with these problems."

Putting the trip in perspective, I was thrilled as JoAnne became enthralled with the Baja and Sea of Cortez. She enjoyed the freedom *Aurora* supplied in moving our "house" from place to place. Sailing under perfect wind and wave conditions provided a perfect introduction to cruising for her. My only concern was how would she handle being on the boat when nature flexed her muscles?

* * * * *

It was time for us to reluctantly to fly back to Oakland and our work-a-day lives.

It was hard to leave an idyllic place and time to plunge back into the demands of schedules, projects to complete with time deadlines starring at you. Where do the parts of ourselves that reveled in the world of the Baja find continued nourishment?

13

ESCAPE TO THE BAJA

In 1990, JoAnne and I needed a break after a year of hard work since being in the Baja last year. I was anxious to be on *Aurora* again. We borrowed our friend Gina's small Toyota pickup truck with an old camper mounted on the back to drive to Mexico. We hoped it would be a relaxing trip. The truck had been sitting in Gina's yard for years but still ran pretty well. Stepping back from the vehicle, we saw that the camper almost overwhelmed its host. Gina said yes to our request, and we were on the road to Mexico the next week.

Becoming comfortable driving the top heavy vehicle was a challenge as we made our way south. After crossing the U.S.-Mexican border, we wandered through the back streets of Tijuana until we finally found Highway 1 heading south. We felt free and easy in the rural countryside as we passed through vineyards in narrow valleys that cut into the coastal hills. What a sharp contrast to the urban jumble of Tijuana! About fifty miles from the border, our carefree adventure was interrupted suddenly when a dozen Mexican Army soldiers leaning on their rifles stopped us at a drug check point located on a barren stretch of the highway.

Two soldiers came forward with one asking, *"Donde esta su licencia de manajar y el papele de registracion por su coche?"*

After checking our driver's licenses and registration papers, one soldier ordered, "Please open the door. We must search your camper."

My heart raced as I whispered to JoAnne, "Remember, I hid that sawed-off shotgun in a rear storage compartment under the seat. Try to be cool and follow my lead." She agreed with her eyes and a slight nod.

My sons Andy and Dave gave me the gun to protect *Aurora* and their dad from the rumored threat of pirates along the Pacific Coast of Mexico. Foolishly, I hadn't declared the gun at the border, knowing of the Mexican authorities' sensitivities to weapons coming into their country. JoAnne stepped outside to get a breath of fresh air while I watched the soldier as his search of the cramped camper continued. He was getting warmer, coming closer to my hiding place, and I was growing more nervous.

I was beginning to panic, so I asked JoAnne, "Don't you need something to drink?"

She looked a bit confused but said, "Yes."

With my heart pounding hard in my chest, I took out three cold sodas from the refrigerator and offered one to the soldier. *"Quieres un 7 Up?"*

"Si, señor, gracias." He accepted it and thankfully was distracted from his search! He climbed out of the camper and said, "You are now free to leave."

"Gracias, senor," I said, a smile spreading over my face.

With a quick look at JoAnne and a nod of my head, I said, "Let's hit the road."

Driving away from the soldiers, JoAnne sighed, "Phew, that was too close for comfort. I hope that's the last we see of soldiers."

"Me too! Perhaps, my Livengood Luck is still working."

The irony of our encounter with the soldiers was that a young hippie couple, long hair, scruffy clothes and all, in the car in front of us were not searched and were waved through the check point. And I had thought that having gray hair was a "get of out of jail free" card. Later we told Stan and Sue this story as we camped together at a nearby campground and had a good laugh.

"We've decided not to carry any drugs in Mexico," said Stan seriously. "Mexican prisons are not for the fainthearted. You have to have a family nearby to support you or the money to buy your food."

"Yeah, I've heard that the prisoners have few rights and that conditions are primitive at best," I said. "We'll be leaving in the morning on our way to our boat at Puerto Escondido on the Sea of Cortez."

Highway 1 is a wild and lonely stretch of highway known for its steep drop-offs without guard rails, *vadas* (fords) that cross stream beds in lieu of bridges, gas stations spaced about two hundred miles apart, and cows and burros wandering on the highway that transverses the open range. Breaking one of the survival rules of the Baja, we were driving in the dark to reach our next stopping point. As I was driving the camper down into a *vada* and then up the stream bank, our headlights outlined a large black steer who stood transfixed facing the right shoulder, blocking our side of the road. Unable to stop, I whipped the steering wheel to the left to miss it then whipped it back to the right to stay on the road. Our hearts shifted into overdrive! In addition to luckily missing the steer, we were rewarded for venturing across the desert as darkness fell by seeing the flaming red-orange sun setting over the edge of the plateau while outlining solitary saguaro cactuses.

One day later, we stopped at the oasis village of San Ignacio where JoAnne and I stayed in a small hotel on the main square and ate dinner at a small restaurant that appeared to be in a family's living room. While we were sitting in the square after our dinner, some children came over to ask questions about where we were from and how we liked Mexico.

"*Esta la favorita de nosotros,*" (It is a favorite of ours) I said.

"*Venga con nosotros a mir la Iglesia,*" (Come with us to see the church) one child said.

The church stood tall at the end of the square bathed in the orange light of the setting sun. Its luminance contrasted with the stark, darkening desert landscape.

"Okay," I said, walking hand in hand with the children to the end of the square where we found a plaque on the front of the church. "JoAnne, I'll translate the plaque. Mission San Ignacio Loyola was built in 1728 as part of the chain of missions initiated by Fr. Junipero Serra. Let's go inside."

We walked up the steps and went into the church. Touching the wall I said, "Look at this wall. It must be four feet thick. Feel how cool and quiet it is. The ceiling must be thirty feet high. What a cool place to find respite from the burning heat of the desert."

"It's so peaceful," said JoAnne. "Let's sit down for a while. Look at the stunning gold retable behind the altar. It frames paintings of Mary and early saints. Imagine the effort it took to build this stout sanctuary in this small town."

"Yeah, I can feel the importance of this place to the people who live in this inhospitable desert," I said.

Through the owner of our small hotel, we learned about pre-Columbian cave painting located in the mountains at a place called San Francisco de la Sierra. His friend Enrique had a van and could take us up there on dirt roads off Highway 1. We were anxious to go in the morning.

Leaving early, we drove into an unusual layer of fog that obscured the view of the surrounding mountains. After bouncing more than twenty miles over rough roads through stark, rocky desert, we followed a snaking switchback dirt track climbing up the mountain. We arrived at a small ranchero, happy to find their outhouse. After paying an entrance fee, Enrique was given gate keys that allowed us access to the steep trail up to the site. Climbing through large boulders, we turned a corner, and right in front of us was a large overhanging cliff covered with ancient drawings called Cueva Del Raton.

"Wow, this is amazing!" JoAnne and I exclaimed, pointing at the cliff.

"Look at the large crouching mountain lions painted in black," I said. "Those red deer with huge antlers, they're larger than life size. Can you see the black human figures looking up at them?"

"Karl, what about the shaman-like figure divided in half? His left side is red and the right side is black. His fingers are pointing skyward as if he's receiving a message from the gods."

"Yeah, I see him, but what about that strange figure with a human body that has a large snake's head coming up from its shoulders then arching downward in a U-shape. Very strange. I'm wondering what it represents?"

The fact that the cliff was so far from the nearest source of water showed the importance of expressive art to the aboriginal inhabitants of this arid, isolated place high in the mountains. We felt privileged to see the paintings and to get an idea of the importance of animals and of myths in their lives.

*****

Continuing our trip through the Baja, we finally reached the shore of the bright blue Sea of Cortez at Santa Rosalia. I felt great returning after being here on my sailing trip seventeen years ago. We found a nice small hotel overlooking the water. From our balcony, we gazed at the magic of the sea's sparkling color. What a relief from the monochromatic desert landscape.

Taking a walk through town, I reacquainted myself with the shop lined streets after taking JoAnne to see Eiffel's iron church and the small harbor where I had landed on my first sail in Mexico. Stepping back into this scene reconnected me with many warm memories of that important first sailing adventure that had strongly influenced the course of my life. From here, we drove onto Mulege, taking in the splendor of that oasis. I told JoAnne about the thrill of hitchhiking out of town on an airplane. After lunch, we drove on to Puerto Escondido where *Aurora* lay at anchor ready to be awoken from her winter's rest.

JoAnne, Bob, Peetie, Karl

After finding Bob and Peetie again, we spent the afternoon in the shade of their *palapa* catching up on each other's lives. Peetie was one of the original flower children who grew up listening to Khrishnamurti in Ojai, the "Shangri-La of Southern California," a community of America's first "New Age" people.

"After achieving a 'Mystical Union' during a health crisis in Ojai," Peetie said, "Krishnamurti rejected organized religion in any form since he felt it controlled and limited the mind's search for meaning. Instead, his thought was that through deep meditation our minds would discover the meaning of life and true happiness."

I could see that Peetie had placed these principles in practice by living an intensely involved life based on input from all her senses. Peetie's life force radiated from her whole body, especially her face and deep eyes, drawing us in to experience her calmness and grace.

Bob, a more matter of fact, athletic kind of guy, took us in his dinghy out to the *Aurora* where we discovered that she was in amazingly good shape after being at anchor for almost a year. She looked clean and sleek against the background of the harbor's defining cliffs and piles of boulders.

"Thanks, Bob, for looking after *Aurora*, but her safety also has something to do with the honesty of the Mexican people," I said.

"You're right about their honesty," Bob said. "It's been a pleasure keeping an eye on her. I enjoyed rowing out in my dinghy. It's great exercise."

In a short time, our clothes and provisions were stowed aboard. In the morning, we were ready to sail. *Aurora* had other ideas, however, as I pulled up the anchor with JoAnne at the wheel.

I called back to her, "Okay, turn the boat."

"It's not turning!" she shouted.

I noticed the wheel just spinning in her hands without creating any response from the rudder. I immediately dropped the anchor back in the water and rushed back to the cockpit where my hunch that the steering cable had broken was confirmed.

"Wow, it broke while we were in shallow water rather than further from shore where anchoring would not have been possible!" I said. "Are we lucky or what!"

After applying cable clamps to mend the break in the cable, we motored out of the harbor and into the sea. A rising breeze filled the sails, pulling us toward Isla Carmen located two miles away. The sensation of *Aurora* responding and moving with the wind raised the hairs on the back of my neck.

The gypsum quarry on Isla Carmen is one of the largest in the world, supplying raw materials to wall board (sheet rock) manufacturers in the United States and Mexico. We saw large bulk carriers being loaded at a long pier. These large ships are among a few commercial carriers on the Sea of Cortez. South of Isla Carmen lay Isla Danzante, a long narrow island with a sheltered cove in its middle named "Honeymoon Cove" where we had anchored with Bob and Peetie last year. Here, I was amazed to see my friends Ed and Julie from British Columbia at anchor in their red hulled schooner, *Wanderer*. I had not seen them since our "Margarita Party" in Puerto Vallarta more than a year earlier. After anchoring, JoAnne and I dinghied over to their boat.

Wanderer

"Hello, Julie and Ed," I called up from the dinghy. "I can't believe you're here, too. What a nice coincidence being in the same anchorage with you." I turned to JoAnne. "This is my sweetheart, JoAnne."

"Nice to meet you, JoAnne, and it's great seeing you again, Karl. Welcome aboard," Ed said with a warm smile and beckoning wave.

"When did you return to Mexico from your place north of Vancouver?" I said.

"We've been here a couple of months ever since the weather began to get colder up in Canada. Seems like we want to come down to Mexico earlier and earlier each year," Julie said. "How about you?"

"We just got here. This is JoAnne's second trip to the Baja," I added.

"What a treat it's been! I love Mexico and the Sea of Cortez," said JoAnne. "Its remarkable quality seems to rise from the shimmering water and leads my eyes to the mountains beyond. The air is so clear that I feel that I can see forever."

After Margaritas and more conversation, JoAnne and I returned to *Aurora* for dinner.

I had been thinking about asking JoAnne to marry me and decided "Honeymoon Cove" had the beauty and attractiveness needed to be the right place to make my formal declaration. We loved the coziness of the anchorage being almost surrounded by the island and the still clear water where sea life abounded. Stillness magnified the impact of the scene. The charms of the Sea of Cortez created an enchanted moment. JoAnne said with a big smile, "Yes, I will marry you."

I responded with a "Whew," and held JoAnne in an embrace, giving her a long kiss.

"Wow, now my life is complete!" I said, smiling broadly.

My relationship with JoAnne had become a great source of happiness and joy. I was thrilled that we would be able to formalize our commitment to each other. Behind JoAnne's acceptance was knowing that her mother Madeline loved me.

I later learned that she had told JoAnne, "Go out and live a new life with Karl. You and I have done so many wonderful things together that I will always carry them in my memories." Madeline's encouragement was selfless because JoAnne's living a sailing life with me would mean long periods of separation from her.

The next evening, we accepted Ed and Julie's invitation to dinner. We made it our announcement party, floating in "Honeymoon Cove" on the warm Sea of Cortez. Having cruisers Ed and Julie present at this special moment made it feel like JoAnne and I were cementing their friendship and being accepted into the wider group of cruising sailors.

*****

After putting *Aurora* back to bed in the harbor of Puerto Escondido and saying our goodbyes to Bob and Peetie, we took to the road again driving north. I noticed that the camper was lurching strangely over the bumps in the road. We stopped and I looked under the truck. I saw that a steel bracket holding a rear spring had broken loose. I found a backyard garage. The owner confirmed that he could fix it. I was thankful that Mexican mechanics have so much experience keeping old machines on the road.

Moving again, we drove high into the mountains to cross over the Sierras to the Pacific side of the Peninsula. Rounding one curve, we were forced to stop by a large motor home resting on its side against the bank cut into the mountain. Talking with the motor home's owners, we found out that no one aboard was injured.

The driver told us, "An oncoming pickup truck was passing another vehicle and was on my side of the road. I was forced into the embankment to avoid a head on collision, but I'm afraid that the pickup truck lost control, skidding over the edge and down the mountain." Looking down on a gruesome sight, we saw the pickup and an earlier wreck of a bus splattered down the steep slope. Wrecks remain wherever they come to rest, creating a bizarre rusting graveyard.

"I realize that driving Highway 1 is a lot like playing Russian Roulette," I said. "We've taken a number of chances on this highway, so let's travel here only when absolutely necessary."

"Oh yeah, I agree," JoAnne said as she let out a sigh of relief.

We faced a more immediate problem when at a planned stop for gas there was no electricity to run the station's pumps.

"JoAnne, I've done some quick calculations. I think that we can make it to the next station."

"I'll keep an eye glued to the gas gauge so you can keep yours on the road," JoAnne replied.

The camper rolled into the station with only fumes to spare. A group of eight to ten-year-old children mobbed us and soon were cleaning our windows for coveted small change. Many of these kids were earning money to help their families survive. We learned that they lived in a small village located behind the huge boulders off to the north and went to a small one room school.

Later on, at home, I reflected on my growing feelings of being a more complete person, of joining our two halves together to form

Gas Station Kids

a more interesting and complex whole. Our marriage would formalize the commitment that already existed between us and announce it to those in our world.

*****

On October 11, 1990, surrounded by our families crowded into friends Vangie and Bill's living room in the Berkeley Hills overlooking San Francisco Bay, JoAnne and I were married, repeating vows we had written. Our friend Judge Mac McKinnon added his own thoughts garnered over the years, increasing the meaning of the ceremony. With senses heightened, JoAnne and I experienced the depth and rightness of our public commitment to each other that shone in our smiles and feelings of joy.

More friends came later to the reception spilling into the lower back garden owing to the limiting size of the living room. Looking down from above, I witnessed a moving stream of people, talking, smiling, hugging, and drinking. Pam, a soprano soloist with the Berkeley Chorus, sang lovely cabaret songs during the reception while her audience gathered around the piano. The intimacy of the setting enhanced the impact of the beautiful songs, creating a charmed space. What can be better than listening to a lovely singer's mesmerizing music? The kitchen staff at International House where JoAnne worked catered the reception, providing Middle Eastern hors d'oeuvres that were washed down with champagne.

JoAnne and I continued our celebration in a small hotel in Marin County across the bay. Here, I realized the impact that Livengood Luck had on the course of my life.

*****

Six months later in April 1991, UC Berkeley was facing a budget crunch and began retiring higher salaried staff to cut their expenses. For us, things were beginning to fall in place.

"If I retire from International House now, UC is offering me a golden parachute that adds extra years of service credit toward the calculation of my retirement income and an additional cash bonus," JoAnne explained with a smile.

"Perfect!" I said. "I think you should go for it. Now you have the retirement income you've needed to feel secure. Your income will supplement my savings and other income to fill up our cruising kitty. Compared to many, we'll be on a tight budget so let's rent your house as a furnished long-term rental. It can join our income stream."

* * * * *

All the details of closing accounts and of centralizing our stateside affairs were put in the capable hands of our friend Barbara, who had retired earlier from International House. Our small monthly payment to her helped her out a bit and she was glad to be in regular contact with her best friend, JoAnne.

* * * * *

Preparations made, *it was time for making the journey of a lifetime.*

PART II

LET THE CRUISING BEGIN

SO THIS IS CRUISING

Casting off the umbilical cords tying us to shore

Leaving harbors to expand our experiences of the world

Sailing to new and distant places

Overcoming the challenges of weather, navigation, mechanical systems

Making new friends who enrich our lives

Creating lifetime connections filled with rich common experiences

Creating memories that fill the spaces in our minds

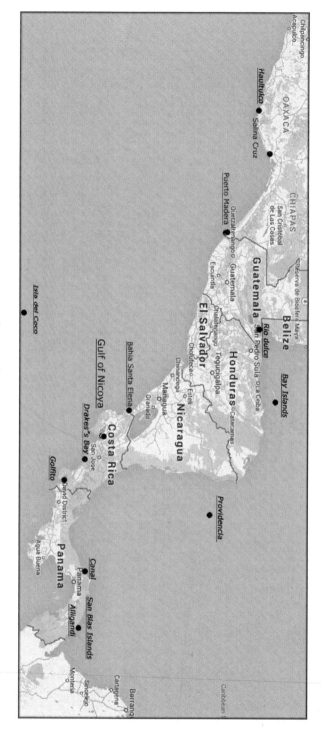

Coast of Central America

138

14

BEGINNING OUR CRUISING LIFE

In June of 1991, JoAnne and I were ready to begin our journey south to Baja, Mexico, ready to start a new life on the sea sailing on *Aurora*. Strong feelings of anticipation dominated my thoughts. JoAnne's feelings were mixed with some anxiety.

"I feel like I'm standing on the edge of a cliff looking out into a hazy future that attracts me, but I'm wondering how I'll cope with the sailing and lifestyle if things get rough," JoAnne said.

"I can hear how you feel," I said. "But, I have the confidence in myself and in you that together we can deal with whatever comes our way."

We loaded my old 1978 Toyota station wagon up to the roof with our clothes, boat gear, and some provisions. A mouse would have had a hard time getting inside.

"I feel like my whole life is being crammed into this little car," JoAnne exclaimed.

Having pared down my own belongings when I moved aboard *Aurora*, I sympathized, saying, "Yeah, but it feels great getting down to the bare essentials and being on our way."

The wet spring that year made our trip down Highway 1 a scenic adventure through the Baja desert in full bloom. The heavy saguaro cactuses boasted bright red and yellow flowers adorning their skyward reaching arms, silhouetted against the horizon. The more bush-like ocotillo reached some twenty feet in height with their branches creating intricate patterns that pricked our imaginations. Were they birds or dancing spirits? Occasionally, white bloom-covered spears of the soaptree yucca drew our eyes to their startling beauty against the golden desert landscape.

We drove through an area with giant natural formations of sand and rose colored boulders that seemed to defy any logic about how or why they were there. Some boulders over one hundred feet high were surrounded by jumbles of smaller stones. Our eyes and brains searched valiantly for recognizable and predictable shapes and patterns, but "Mother Nature" had been in a more random spontaneous mood, unlike mere terrestrial engineers.

After several days of driving, we arrived back in Puerto Escondido on the west coast of the Sea of Cortez where *Aurora* was anchored. We were greeted by friends Peetie and Bob, still living in their trailer overlooking the water near Tripui.

"It's great to see you two again," JoAnne said as she embraced Peetie then Bob. "I'm so happy to be here with you, our two sailing buddies!"

"Well, it's hugs all around. My dreams are coming true," I said beaming. "Having JoAnne here with me as my wife means so much. We're really ready to begin cruising. What could be better than to have good friends to start us off on our adventure."

It took several dinghy trips to transfer the contents of the station wagon onto *Aurora*. We hoped that all of our portable worldly possessions would fit. JoAnne was a master at finding safe places for all the stuff. With everything securely tucked away we could sail without fear of things raining down whenever the boat heeled. Having a sailboat as a home meant our immediate universe didn't have the rooted stability of a house. Although homey, comfortable, and compact, *Aurora* still could tilt forty-five degrees to the horizon.

Aurora was well designed in Australia for the Southern Ocean where 40-50 knot winds can generate huge waves. She was very *stable*. I recalled sailing over-canvassed (meaning with too much sail up) once in the San Francisco Bay where sudden gusts of wind of 50 knots or more came sweeping down the Sausalito Hills. In response, she'd heeled past forty-five degrees with the rail under the water and the sails almost horizontal. Hanging on while releasing the mainsheet from its cleat was my most difficult task I'd had to manage at that time. With the wind pressure let off the mainsail, *Aurora* righted herself immediately. I'd told JoAnne about that experience, but it would take time before she'd be able to overcome her fear that heeling might someday cause the boat (her home) to tip over.

Having the station wagon at the dock meant that we could easily buy provisions and tour some of the desert between the Sierra Gigante Mountains and the Sea of Cortez. Loreto was the nearest town of any size so we visited there often, feeding our newfound addiction to fresh fish tacos. A small craft shop featuring colorful prints of fish caught our attention. Real fish are dipped in fabric paint and used to create these wall hangings. In fact, they used some of the same types of fish that we had eaten or seen swimming among rock reefs extending from shore.

We met Joan, an expat American in one of the shops. She lived along the beach in an interesting house filled with wall hangings and other local art. Walking into Joan's home was like stepping into an art gallery. Her imagination, along with her love of things Mexican, created a warm, brightly colored atmosphere that nearly pulled our eyes out of their sockets!

*****

Less than a month into our preparations, a family reunion in Ohio sent us sailing down to La Paz to catch a flight to Cleveland located twenty-five miles northwest of my old hometown of Aurora, Ohio. We joined our extended family at Aunt Betts and Uncle Jack's house overlooking a small lake just outside of town. Betts called the gathering "The Bloomin' Reunion," and gave us all bright red tee shirts with yellow flowers. We even entered the town's 4th of July parade and won first prize in the family division. All of us had a wonderful time reminiscing about our growing up in this special place.

Talking with my brother, Lou, I asked, "Do you remember swimming in the river in the pool next to the railroad bridge?"

"Sure, I remember diving off the cement floor of the tunnel into a pool that we created by damming up the Chagrin River," he answered. "What I remember is carrying all those heavy rocks."

"Remember how we spent days fishing, hiking, fort building, and exploring? We could disappear into our 'wilderness' for hours on end with no adult supervision," I recalled.

"Yeah, what a great time we had!" Lou said with a sigh.

My nephew Steve quizzed me about sailing and expressed his interest in joining us on the Sea of Cortez.

"Why don't you fly to La Paz, Steve?" JoAnne encouraged him. "You can have the forward berth, and you can stay with us as long as you like."

"Great, I'll try to come down in a few weeks!"

As I left our reunion, a wave of nostalgia swept over me. Indeed, Aurora had been a magical place in which to grow up and to expand my self-confidence. It felt good inside to have named my sailboat *Aurora*.

*****

Upon our return to La Paz, our friend Elmo from the Bay Area picked us up at the airport. He had come down to join us and to view the total eclipse of the sun that would happen in a few days. We sailed north on *Aurora* to Isla Partida far away from any artificial lights where we anchored in its lagoon. We dinghied ashore to a sand beach, joining a small crowd of cruisers who had already gathered to witness the sun's journey behind the moon. We were armed with Mylar reflective sheets that protected our eyes and the camera from the intense light of the sun.

"Look, the sky is getting darker and darker," I pointed out. "See those shadow bands that are rolling across the beach. They're caused by the moon's mountains passing in front of the sun, creating thin slot-like crescents of light. Watch now, the shadow bands are gone just as the last sliver of the sun disappeared behind the moon. Against the blackness of the moon, the fiery corona of the sun is shooting visible solar flares out into the void of space."

"Awesome!" Elmo gasped. "We're seeing that the sun is indeed a huge ball of living fire."

In the darkness of the eclipse I observed, "The planets Earth, Venus, Mars, and Jupiter are lined up in a straight line in the heavens with the Sun and Moon. It feels to me as if we're standing on the edge of our solar system. It's an ecliptic."

JoAnne asked, "What's an ecliptic, Karl?"

"It's a great circle formed by the orbits of the heavenly bodies in space," I explained. "From our vantage point, it looks like a straight line."

We all stood watching in awe this inspiring display of our solar system in action.

"It's just amazing. We're witnessing a unique moment in time and space!" exclaimed Elmo. Just then someone yelled out, "I see Elvis." The crowd of eclipse watchers was jolted into laughter and the party began. The sun slowly emerged from behind the moon, transforming dark back into day and causing the birds to sing as if it were morning. This eclipse was a once in a lifetime experience that we witnessed in our own "backyard" under the most ideal conditions. I learned later that the other eclipse watchers who had paid thousands of dollars to fly to Hawaii and other places in the world had their view obstructed by clouds or fog. In Mexico, we were indeed fortunate that clear skies made a spectacular show possible on a small island in the Sea of Cortez.

Just maybe, Livengood Luck had some influence on making this extraordinary experience happen.

*****

After anchoring back in La Paz, Elmo took a taxi to the airport. Elmo was soon replaced by my twenty-four-year-old, tall, handsome nephew Steve who was brimming with high energy for an adventurous week with us. Sailing north again, we stopped at Isla Partida, taking advantage of the protected waters of its lagoon. At times Steve seemed to be more fish than human, spending hours snorkeling in the lagoon. Living in Colorado Springs, Steve had apprenticed himself to a master classical guitar maker for a number of years. After striking out on his own working in a small shop, he was developing a clientele willing to pay up to $5,000 for his handmade classical guitars. Being the social young man that he was, Steve had some difficulty handling the loneliness of his solitary work. This vacation would give him a much needed change of pace.

Sailing further north, we anchored off Los Isolates, an island inhabited by sea lions. About a hundred of the sleek creatures covered the rocks. Steve and I went ashore and walked among the female sea lions and their babies, keeping our distance from the much larger bulls that fortunately seemed more interested in sleeping at the time.

"Uncle Karl, you've got to get into the water with these guys," Steve called out from a pool where mothers and their babies were performing an underwater ballet.

Playing with Sea Lions

Under the influence of Steve's enthusiasm, I decided I had to overcome my fear of sea lions, caused by a scary experience at Cabo San Lucas. I joined Steve in the water. What a thrill, watching these graceful swimmers arc and turn, spiraling through the water. They brushed against us as they flashed by. We were lucky that the bulls remained ashore, not seeing us as a threat. JoAnne joined the fun. Having such a close and enjoyable interaction with aquatic mammals in the wild was a highpoint of my amazing Sea of Cortez experience. I would carry this wonder with me forever.

As we were leaving the anchorage, two black and white orca whales surfaced off the island, as if to say, "We can top that experience for you!"

I had never seen the Orcas' high black dorsal fins in the Sea of Cortez before. They swam around the boat surfacing, leaping out of the water, and blowing huge spouts to mark their presence. *Aurora* felt smaller than usual in the company of these two playful whales clearly having fun. We just sat in the cockpit enjoying the show!

Steve took over the helm as we continued north. He was gaining the feel of how the *Aurora* handled while I taught him how to tweak each sail to reach higher boat speeds. While not actually racing at the moment, we were like most sailors with the innate desire to maximize speed while pushing the performance ability of the boat through the water.

"I want to harness the power of the wind," I called out to Steve. 'I like feeling like *Aurora* is flying through the water." A huge smile filled my face. I felt my heart lifting and opening.

"It's like soaring, breaking free, moving beyond the confines of daily life," Steve called back.

In the afternoon, we anchored off the small fishing village of Agua Verde connected on the Baja side to civilization by a small gravel road that really was just a bulldozer track cut into the side of the mountain, overlooking a narrow valley carved out by a stream. The lack of rain had reduced the stream to a series of pools among the rocks. The houses were rough pole *palapa* structures covered with palm fronds as roofs and sides providing basic shelter in this temperate climate. As we walked up the beach to a small store, we felt like "Pied Pipers" as a giggling group of children accompanied us with two holding JoAnne's hands. We bought boxed milk and two papayas, throwing in some extra candy for the kids.

Steve's rudimentary Spanish brought smiles as he attempted to answer a shower of questions composed by their young minds. "Where are you from? What kind of work do you do?" The children's limited contact with the outside world seemed to make our visit all the more important to them.

Back aboard, we moved *Aurora* to a more sheltered anchorage next to a cliff face in a narrow bay cut into the land. Fifteen burros stood under the overhang of the cliff sheltered from the hot sun. Later the sun dropped behind the mountain, and the burros wandered off to forage for supper and to find the water that kept them alive in the Baja desert. We would miss the braying that had announced their presence in this snug, comfortable bay.

On our return to Puerto Escondido, Steve's week long adventure had come to an end. Steve would begin his return trip home to Colorado.

"We'll miss your boundless energy, Steve, your interesting conversation, and infectious smiles," JoAnne said, giving him a hug.

"Thanks for having me on *Aurora*, Uncle Karl. I really loved sailing and being here on the Sea of Cortez with you both. Keep me in mind if you ever need a crew member again."

"Our future plans are pretty fluid, but you'll always have a berth on *Aurora*," I said shaking his hand, patting his back, and hugging him.

* * * * *

Back in Puerto Escondido, we reconnected with Peetie and Bob and through the "Cruiser's Grapevine" learned that our friends Mariam and Jacques had been shipwrecked in late June. A sudden *chubasco*, a violent storm from the North, had broken their anchor loose allowing their boat, *Oceanis II*, to be thrown onto the rocks outlining the bay. A nearby fiberglass Beneteau sloop was declared a total loss, but our friend's homebuilt ferro-cement hull had survived with only one sizable hole. The cruising community at Puerto Escondido responded to Jacque's radioed call for help by organizing a flotilla of boats that brought pumps, plywood, epoxy, and other needed patching materials. Through their combined efforts, the hole in the side of *Oceanis II* was temporarily patched using a plywood sheet with epoxy to seal the leaks; the water was pumped out and the boat was pulled free of the rocks then towed to Puerto Escondido. All the contents of the boat were removed, rinsed in fresh water, then dried in the sun; finally a permanent patch was fabricated to make *Oceanis II* whole again. All of this was accomplished with an expenditure of a minimum amount of money while using a maximum amount of donated labor thus saving Jacques and Mariam's floating home, *Oceanis II*!

At a pool party at Tripui, JoAnne and I had the opportunity to thank some of the group as they proudly told their tales of helping save *Oceanis II*. Many of them expressed the same feeling that, "There but for the grace of God go I." All sailors know that they might be exposed to sudden weather changes that cause high winds and abnormal waves! JoAnne and I were not beginning our adventure without risks.

As if to punctuate that point a squall forced its way through the anchorage.

JoAnne wrote this impression to her daughter, Betsy, "A terrible squall hit this area with winds about 30 knots. It hit without much warning. We had to take down our large sun shade mounted over the deck and batten down the hatches. It was quite a struggle, but we did it, so there was no damage. Another boat wasn't so lucky. It lost its dinghy and its anchor dragged and the boat went aground on the rocks. Fortunately, they got it off before there was any serious damage. Pretty exciting stuff! My first squall...we were so busy securing everything that I didn't have time to get scared."

15

EXPLORING MAINLAND MEXICO

I wanted to expose JoAnne to more of the beauty and culture of Mexico, so I planned a trip using the old Toyota to drive on the Mainland across the Sea of Cortez. We drove south to La Paz. After staying one night at a comfortable, small downtown hotel, we boarded a ferry for an overnight crossing to Topolobompo. Rather than sleep in uncomfortable chairs, we had bought air mattresses and picked out a spot on deck near the pilot house for sleeping.

Before the ferry embarked, I told the first mate, "I'm a sailor and I'd like to see the pilot house."

He said "*Si, señor,*" and invited me in.

While I was looking over the instruments, the mate pointed to the radar mentioning, "*Esta se rumpio,*" saying the same about the depth sounder, meaning that both were broken. The captain would not know the depth of the water and might have trouble identifying ships in the vicinity of the ferry. What was even more alarming, one of the ship's two engines was inoperable so if the good engine failed, the ship would be dead in the water. Maneuvering the ship in close quarters could be very difficult since this ship didn't have any bow thrusters. What an interesting development! The Mexican crew seemed quite comfortable with the situation.

Our car was already aboard the ferry, somewhere in the middle of the car deck, so our only real choice was to stay aboard and to offer up some prayers. The crossing was quite smooth, and I noticed no real problems in the operation of the ship from our station near the bridge. But, arriving in Topolobompo, as the captain tried to turn the ship toward the pier, it quickly ran aground in soft, black mud. Several back and forth movements were necessary to break the ship loose so it could reach the dock. What a relief it was to finally make it to the dock in one piece!

By now it was dark as we drove into Los Mochis looking for a motel that had been recommended by friends. I stopped and asked a street vender for directions. We soon reached the motel and had a welcome night's rest. In the morning, we found the train station in El Fuerte where the train would take us to the Copper Canyon high in the Sierras, one of North America's most spectacular train rides. The train was nicknamed "*El Chepe.*" The *Chihuahua al Pacifico* Railroad took several decades to construct the three hundred-ninety miles of track rising more than 2,000 feet from sea level while bridging 39 rivers, ravines, and streams, and burrowing its way through 86 tunnels dug into cliffs and mountains to keep the tracks going forward in seemingly impossible terrain. JoAnne and I waited for the train to arrive with a mixed group of people. Locals were returning to their homes in the mountains loaded with big bags of goods bought in the city. Tourists from all over the world were hauling their backpacks and suitcases.

We talked with a young Dutch traveler who said, "Riding *El Chepe* up to the Copper Canyon will be the highlight of my trip."

"You're right, this will be a special trip," JoAnne said.

Riding the train was the chance for me to videotape this wonderful adventure. The sights were breathtaking as the tracks followed narrow canyons just above streams cascading down the steep incline. My desire to shoot the best scene pushed me out onto the swaying platforms between cars. From there, I was able to hang over as far as possible to capture images of the train as it rounded curves while the trees and rocks became a blur, sped over high bridges that caused me to hold my breath until the other side was reached, or disappeared into dark tunnels that filled with diesel smoke and noise. The track even made a loop de loop in one location passing over itself to gain needed altitude. What an amazing experience!

Inside the train, JoAnne had met a Mexican family who spoke English and were eager to talk. They were from Culiacan, a city further south toward Mazatlan on the Sea of Cortez. The handsome father, Alfredo, was a college sociology professor. He loved to talk. "This is my wife, Christina, who's a nurse," Alfredo said proudly. "Let me introduce our three children. My oldest boy is Guillermo who is ready to go to college, his brother is Jorge who attends high school, and their sister is Consuelo who is in middle school."

"Pleased to meet you," said JoAnne. "I'm a retired foreign student advisor from the University of California in Berkeley. It's been my pleasure to help many students from Mexico. We're going to stay in Creel. We've booked a room at Margarita's. Where are you staying?"

"We're also stopping in Creel at Margarita's," said Alfredo. "I'm not sure that you're aware, but from my perspective as a sociologist I can see that drugs and their transportation are going to be a big problem in Mexico. You may not know it, but the demand for cocaine in the United States is beginning to be filled by gangs down here."

"Wow, that's a very disturbing development," said JoAnne. "We in the U.S. don't seem to know an effective way of stemming the demand or treating the drug problem. I only hope that the Mexico I love will survive the experience."

The train made several stops along the way where the local Tarahumara Indians shyly offered baskets and carvings for sale. While turning their faces away from cameras or keeping their eyes down, they attempted to sell their handicrafts. Perhaps, they were worried like many indigenous people that cameras could steal their souls?

At one stop, we walked to the rim of El Barranca de Cobre (The Copper Canyon) to look almost a mile down into the canyon which is seven times larger than our Grand Canyon. In total the canyon is three hundred-seventy miles long by one hundred-fifty-five miles wide. Composed of six separate canyon systems, it covers a large part of Northern Mexico in the State of Chihuahua.

Our new Mexican friends accompanied us to Creel, a small town in the mountains close to the canyon. Here, we all disembarked from the train, were sort of swept into a van, and taken to Margarita's guest house. When we arrived, we saw Margarita standing on the stairs like a general sizing up her new passel of guests. Using her sharp eyes and considerable experience, she began assigning guests to their rooms. We felt like army recruits awaiting our commands. JoAnne and I were satisfied with our assignment in a separate log house with a bath located at the rear of the property while our Mexican friends were given a large room overlooking the front of the guest house. We joined the family before dinner for a walk out of town through fields where horses grazed. Alfredo, who had forgotten to bring his camera, gave us a roll of film. We were drafted into being the "official photographers" for his family.

Against the mountainside, I noticed black smoke stains going up the rocks above cave entrances.

"What causes those stains?" I said.

"Those caves are where Tarahumara Indian families live. The stains are from the smoke of their fires," said Alfredo.

Later at a large rock shaped like an elephant's head, I captured Alfredo and his boys on film climbing to the top and posing. They smiled and said, "Whiskey" at the critical moment which was their family's picture-taking ritual.

Our lodging included our dinner, breakfast, and a bag lunch. The warmth from the kitchen seeped into the dining room and was a welcome feature at this mile high altitude because our bodies were adapted to the heat of summer along the Sea of Cortez. Alfredo arranged for a van tour for our families after breakfast, and because JoAnne and I only had one day to see the area, we intended to make the most of it!

We were driven to a spot down where a river had cut a deep canyon into the Sierras that now towered over us. Following a footpath along the river, we used large stones placed by the Indians to cross the shallow water. On the other side, a dark pine forest covered the slopes and was interspersed with large boulders whose journey down to the canyon floor had been arrested by trees. Rounding one of these house sized boulders, we almost walked into a Tarahumara woman selling her painted carvings on pine bark. She held them out in front of her where we could see the fascinating designs in bright paint. Charmed by her shy smile and her crafts, we bought two carvings after halfheartedly negotiating a slightly lower price. Negotiation was expected, but we felt the prices were already low, and that the Indians really needed the money.

Hiking on further, we first heard a dull roar in the distance and then saw mist rising through the trees. Suddenly before us was a one hundred-foot-high waterfall. Peering over the edge of the cliff, we saw that the force of the stream propelled its water into space sending it crashing and splashing onto boulders lining a small pool below. Rainbows flashed in the mist. Back in our van, we visited a Mission Church in a tiny community in a high mountain valley. The walls of the Church were covered with murals portraying the Virgin Mary and the saints beside Indians hunting in the mountains. Here Alfredo, our professor friend, hopped onto the pulpit to give an impromptu lecture, exercising his arms and sense of humor for our amusement. Outside, about fifteen Indian children gathered with their soiled, sticky hands outstretched expecting small coins from us. Struck by their ragamuffin appearance, we all unloaded our pockets into cupped hands while hoping that their buying candy wouldn't be the only result of our generosity.

Further on, we hiked up to an occupied cave dug into the cliff face and with some misgivings went inside following our van driver. I felt that we were intruding into the Indians' very private space. A small fire was burning, providing flickering light on the walls and some warmth in the cave that had an oppressive, dark, close feeling to me. A grandmother was in the back taking care of her grandchildren who shyly came forward to welcome us.

After stepping through the cave entrance, I said, "JoAnne, it feels like we're entering the stone age; everything is so basic. They have only one small chair and their beds are made of stuff piled on the floor of the cave. I'll put some peso notes in the ceramic bowl near the door." The money was our "offering" to help the family and to temper our feelings of guilt arising from having invaded their home.

Outside our eyes adjusted to the bright sunlight. Once in the van Alfredo told us, "The Mexican government has attempted to resettle the Indians into houses, but many have refused to give up their caves or have returned to them after being moved out."

"What do we 'modern people' really know about lives lived so differently from our own? It seems to me tradition and culture are the strong influences that form and bind the Tarahumara together in this environment where they have lived for thousands of years," I speculated.

Rushing back to Creel, we just made the outgoing train. Jo-Anne charmed an accommodating conductor who held the train as I sprinted to Margarita's to retrieve our luggage. Our schedule had been a little too tight! But luckily we made it. After riding *El Chepe* back down the mountain, JoAnne and I found the car where we had safely parked it next to the station.

Guadalajara was our next destination. We drove south along the Sea of Cortez and then turned southeast on Mexico 15, a divided 4 lane, *cuota* (toll road). As we climbed up to the central plateau, the road surfaces became rougher and rougher, sometimes forcing us to drive onto the farmer's tractor tracks paralleling the *cuota*.

At a gas station, the attendant reported, "We've had torrential rains that flooded the ditches and washed away the road bed."

What was usually a three-hour trip stretched out to become an eight-hour marathon, forcing the old Toyota to struggle over the bumps, skirting "Volkswagen swallowing" holes while dodging oncoming trucks and buses and fishtailing through sticky mud. In gathering darkness, we arrived at the outskirts of Guadalajara unsure of our hotel's location.

At a stoplight on a wide boulevard, I rolled down my window to ask a taxi beside us, "*Donde esta el* Hotel Frances?" After a momentary consultation with his passengers, the driver motioned for us to follow him. We weren't really very far away, but following him through a maze of one way streets to the hotel filled us with gratitude. We waved and shouted, "*Gracias*," as the cab sped away.

The bellman met us at the door, unloaded our bags and took us into the 500-year-old Spanish colonial hotel. Our stylish and clean room was on the second floor overlooking the grand Plaza Central. The furniture was antique while the walls had painted flower borders near the high ceilings. This room more than made up for the cockroaches and cement furnishings at Hotel California back in La Paz. The pleased expression spreading on JoAnne's face and her words, "Wow, this is a great room," were sufficient reward to me as I felt her estimate of my ability to choose hotels rise before my eyes. One important thing about JoAnne was that she didn't hold grudges, and as we have seen, she had the capacity to forgive my mistakes.

We had one piece of business to do in Guadalajara. We needed to find a galvanizing factory that could clean and re-coat *Aurora's* 400 pounds of very rusty anchor chain as well as the anchor now resting in the back of the station wagon. We had an address and a map, but that was only the beginning of our quest since only half of Guadalajara's many dirt streets were officially named in this rapidly expanding city. Once I had pointed us in the general direction, I began asking at gas stations and even asked a policeman, *"Donde esta la Fabrica Galvanizador?"* Using my "many points of information" location method, we finally found it. Sr. Valentin, the manager, promised the chain would be ready in two days.

Now it was time to play and soak up the culture in Guadalajara. Strolling in the huge central plaza was great fun as small bands played, the fountain's waters danced and sprayed, and statues looked down on all the action.

"Look at that mob of children blowing and racing after their soap bubbles. Now they're chasing the pigeons," exclaimed JoAnne.

"What a riot of colors is created by the children's helium filled balloons bobbing in the breeze," I observed.

The explosion of life seemed to overwhelm our senses forcing JoAnne and me to sit down and to allow all of these sensations to be absorbed into our happy minds. We were seeing a much more expansive expression of feelings as the children's joy lit up their parents' faces. Laughter filled the square, breaking through the normal boundaries that people set. Everyone seemed to be related to everyone. Humanity was at its best!

Later, we walked over to the multilevel Mercado Central where drinking a beer at an outside table became a Mariachi Serenade. A group of older men with guitars, mandolins, trumpets and even a stand-up bass, gathered around our table to play and to sing Mexican folksongs. Smiles filled their broad faces outlined by huge mustaches. Their instruments were supported by ample bellies. They surrounded us, and we were immersed in the music.

"I feel so welcome and at home here," JoAnne gushed.

Our smiles matched theirs as we felt the remarkable warmth of the moment.

A group of about twenty life-sized, bronze stampeding horses stood against the backdrop of a grove of trees behind the Mercado with nostrils flaring, their hooves poised in motion, as their tails streamed in the wind. It was the most dynamic and forceful large work of art that I had ever seen!

After a wonderful dinner in the quiet, tree shaded central courtyard of the Hotel Frances, we walked across the plaza to the ornate Municipal Theater to watch a performance of the *"Ballet Folklorico de Mexico."* From our level, seats were set in tiers rising to the vaulted ceiling. The Baroque decorations danced across the tier fronts competing with the colorfully costumed dancers performing their regional dances. Each group's regional costume set them apart, and their dances preserved important aspects of their culture. The presentation of the dances exposes the multifaceted nature of this complex, rich country so steeped in artistic expression.

Walking back to the hotel in the cool of the evening, I asked JoAnne, "What other country has so many artisans and artists, dancers, and musicians overflowing into the streets and parks, all expressing the joy found in life? Add in that sweep of history from the Pre-Colombian to the Colonial to the Revolutionary and Modern Periods, I think creating one of the most fascinating places on the planet in my estimation!"

"I love all the complexly colored crafts and watching the expressions on people's faces. So much joy and love is communicated with their broad smiles and twinkling eyes. I was mesmerized watching the dancers' beautiful smiling faces," Jo-Anne added.

*****

After collecting our now heavily galvanized chain, JoAnne and I drove three hours east to Guanajuato in the Sierra Mountains near Leon where I had taken Spanish summer classes in the early 1980s. I had called Rebecca with whom I had stayed, arranging for us to spend two nights with her. As we walked up the steep street to Rebecca's house, I told JoAnne about the street, Calle Tecolote.

"JoAnne, this is the same street on which in 1810, a ragtag group of Indian revolutionaries led by Father Hidalgo and Sr. Allende marched into town. The Spanish overlords retreated to the Granary surrounded by high, thick walls and fired down on the invaders. A miner named Pipula placed a slab of stone on his back and inched toward the thick door where he placed and ignited a dynamite charge. You can see his statue on the hill just over there. With the door blown away, the Spanish were defeated in the first battle of the Mexican War of Independence."

When Rebecca opened the door, she recognized me with a big smile and embrace, welcoming us into her house.

"Rebecca, *este es mi esposa, JoAnna*. JoAnna, this is Rebecca, Lourdes's aunt," I said.

"*Mucho gusto, JoAnna y Karlos bien venida,*" replied Rebecca.

Rebecca took us on a tour of her house. My memory confirmed that not much had changed over the years in this typical Mexican house as we walked up the stairs to the main floor where the kitchen, dinning room, and living room were located. The construction was of cement blocks covered with stucco, typical of most Mexican homes, with wood used only for interior doors and furniture.

"Rebecca, do you still take in students?" I said.

"*Si, hay muchos.*"

Bedrooms and baths on the lower floors were rented to students from the University of Guanajuato to supplement her retired teacher's pension. Rebecca and Paco lived on the top floor.

Potted plants in bloom filled the patios, bringing color and fragrance into the house. The views from the rooftop looked over the city toward El Jardin, the central garden square and the nearby churches. Her son Paco, a thirty-year-old computer programming expert for the State of Guanajuato, lived at home and contributed to the running of the house.

Rebecca and JoAnne spoke Spanish together in the large kitchen with a work table in the center, while I helped with the translation of JoAnne's questions. Soon, both were deep into making delicious Chili Verdes.

We were joined by Lourdes, our Spanish teacher from Oakland, who is Rebecca's niece but more like her sister due to their similar ages. What fun it was for me to reconnect with wonderful friends from years ago in their homes in Guanajuato, one of my favorite places in Mexico. Paco came home from work, and the kidding and jokes began. Paco's role with Lourdes's language students had been to keep the conversation light and fun so we learned more of the young person's hip vernacular that helped us on the streets when meeting people or trying to understand conversations. All of this language training certainly helped me find my way in Mexico by helping create a level of comfort in meeting people and asking them questions such as needed directions.

The next day, Lourdes took JoAnne and me on a guided tour of Guanajuato.

The liveliness of the street culture included mimes and the *Cervantinos* (students dressed in Medieval tights and velvet jackets) whose playing guitars and singing swept us along. In the El Jardin (the central plaza) we stopped for some coffee. Leaving El Jardin, we walked past the University of Guanajuato, the second oldest in Mexico, and continued to muralist Diego Rivera's birthplace and museum down the street.

We found its rooms furnished in the late Victorian style that coincided with his birth in the 1880s. In pictures of his family, we could easily pick out Diego with his enormous head and frog-like face. From these beginnings, he became Mexico's most famous and productive muralist. His fame spread to the United States and led to a not so happy encounter with David Rockefeller.

Rockefeller commissioned Diego to paint a mural in New York City but had it painted over because Diego had included Leon Trotsky, a Bolshevik, among its subjects. Trotsky was involved in the revolution against the Russian aristocracy, but later Trotsky opposed Stalin's dictatorship. He was eventually killed by Stalin's henchman in Mexico. Sometime later, Diego and his fiery wife, Frida Kahlo, abandoned the United States to become the "toasts" of Paris.

Lourdes took us to El Callejon del Beso.

"On the Callejon, forbidden lovers kissed across the narrow street. For that act of parental defiance, the young woman was killed by her enraged father!" said Lourdes.

"I would call that a real tragedy of the heart!" JoAnne said.

"Let's go to El Mercado," said Lourdes. "It was designed by Eiffel as a railroad station, but the tracks were never laid, so the building has become the central market for Guanajuato." Walking up stairs, we were able to look out over the colorful food market below. Lourdes led us to her favorite clothing shop. "Here you can buy beautiful shirts," she said. They hang today in my closet ready for special events as a reminder of that day.

*****

JoAnne and I drove the old Toyota out of Guanajuato higher into the mountains to the small city of Dolores Hidalgo, passing a team of oxen cultivating a cornfield and a group of burros loaded with madrone branches being led by a woman down from the tree-line above the road. For many, cooking over wood fires is a way of life. At Father Hidalgo's house, a National Museum, the central displays were documents showing his involvement with the Indians and his proclamation against slavery in 1811, fifty years before Lincoln's Emancipation Proclamation.

Potzcuaro, our next destination, is surrounded by volcanic mountains and lies next to a large lake. Tarascan Indians live around the lake and on its islands. Each of their villages specializes in crafts taught by Fr. Quiroga, dispatched there in the mid 1500s to clean up the mess created when the Conquistador Nuno Guzman killed many members of the tribe for resisting being impressed into slavery. Guzman's treatment of the Indians earned him a trip home in chains to face a Spanish court. The surviving Indians are flourishing making pottery, weaving cloth, creating wood and paper mache sculpture, and making and painting highly polished lacquer bowls and plates. Their work was displayed in an old convent, now a regional handicraft museum where young university students serve as the docents. Climbing the hill adjoining the main square, we found "*once*" (eleven) patio workshops where apprentices are learning their crafts. The central square across from our hotel forms the lively center of Potzcuaro inhabited by strolling musicians playing their guitars and entertaining the families snuggling together on park benches in the coolness of the evening.

As we were driving through the volcanic mountains the following day, an intense thunder and lightning storm illuminated the peaks while dumping rain that flooded the highway as we passed through villages. Finally arriving in the dark at Lago Chapala, a favorite locale for American ex-pats, we found Hotel Nido that had immense bathrooms with ten-foot ceilings complimenting the large rooms, where I had stayed in 1971. With the light of sunrise, I was shocked to see that the shoreline of the lake had receded about one hundred feet leaving docks suspended over ground rather than water. Guadalajara uses the lake's water as its water supply and had grown so much that its thirst now overwhelms the sources of water feeding Lago Chapala.

Going on to San Blas nestled along the Pacific Coast, we drove down the mountains on a twisting highway until we reached the coastal plain. The highway dove into a jungle of palms, hibiscus trees, and vines that enveloped us in a tangle of green with accents of oranges, yellows, and reds. Arriving at the resort of Las Brisas, we found a lovely hotel right on the beach. Our room and balcony overlooked the breakers rolling into the white sand beach above a patio filled with purple bougainvilleas and red hibiscus.

We found my friend Chena at his family home on a dirt street close to the center of town. I introduced him to JoAnne and he introduced us to his mother who no longer works at the family's vegetable/fruit stand. She runs the household filled with her children, grandchildren, and other relatives. Since she is short like most Mexicans, one could have easily underestimated her power, but when Mama speaks the family listens, including her eldest son Chena.

I arranged to meet him for a spicy dinner at Chef Tony's on the square.

"Chena, have you continued to help the less fortunate of San Blas?" I said.

"*Si*, helping them is an important part of my life," said Chena. Everyone seems to know and respect Chena who thrives in this supportive environment.

After dinner, JoAnne and I danced with our bodies moving to the rhythmic music of three guitarists at a new *palapa* night spot under a starry sky in the warmth of a tropical summer evening. Talk about Romantic!

Morning found us checking in with Chena at the fruit stand to say, "*Adios, amigo,*" and confirm the directions that he gave us for a trip to Mexicaltitan, the island birthplace of the Aztec Nation. Driving on small highways through a maze of shallow lagoons along the coast, we reached the end of the road where a group of *pangas* waited for customers. In our case, they charged ten dollars for ferrying the two of us out to the island located in the midst of very rich shrimp breeding grounds. Originally named Aztlan, Mexicaltitan is about fifteen blocks square. On the main street, we found a restaurant featuring, you guessed it, "Shrimp!" The shrimp salad looked great until we realized that peeling about one hundred small shrimp was part of the price of eating it. During the peeling and eating process, JoAnne and I each consumed many small Pacifico beers, to help keep up our motivation and slake our thirsts.

Retracing our route to the Baja, we arrived back to Puerto Escondido and *Aurora*. JoAnne had been creating menus and lists of staple food items like powdered and boxed milk, coffee, and tea. It was time to prepare for our sail south to Costa Rica. After buying all the needed supplies in Loreto and hauling them back to *Aurora* anchored at Puerto Escondido, I sold the "one hundred dollar" Toyota station wagon for five hundred-eighty dollars.

(approx. 1,740,000 pesos) to a gregarious school teacher, Enrique, who had flagged us down when we were driving around town.

After deciding to come down for a last minute visit, my son David and his friend Tony, in his mid-twenties, drove an old 1967 Karmann Ghia convertible down Highway 1. South of the border, they passed through a checkpoint with their beer bottles raised high, now in their full, hang loose, "this is Mexico mode." Further along, the nut securing their generator pulley came off causing the pulley to fly off just as they reached the crest of a long hill. Coasting down the other side of the hill, they found a junk yard at the bottom where the owner searched his boxes to find the missing parts. These parts supplemented by their stash of bailing wire and duck tape was used to keep the Karmann Ghia running, encouraged by their inherent optimism.

Near Loreto, David saw my old Toyota Corolla driving along so they flagged down the new owner, Enrique, asking him, "Where can I find my dad, Karlos?"

Enrique said, "Follow me," and led them down the highway. Arriving at the shore, David blew his car horn, waving his arms to announce his arrival. I dinghied over to pick them up. David's first act on the boat was to climb the mast to the spreaders and jump off into the inviting water. David embodies the fun of thinking and being young. Their stay on the boat featured many opportunities to swim and fish, and I might add that much time was spent laughing as JoAnne and I enjoyed their antics and jokes.

David told me later, "When we crossed the border back into the United States, the Customs Agents looked under the car with mirrors. Guess what they saw? Tony and I looking down at them through the large hole in the floor!" It appears that duct tape had failed to do its job.

Next my oldest son, Doug, and his wife, Brenda, flew into Loreto for six days of sailing south to La Paz. Both were very excited to be on *Aurora* so they took over steering and helping trim the sails as we rode the north winds moving us easily along in the calm seas. Having a strong son, to raise the anchor with the hand operated windlass, was a treat for me. At San Evaristo anchorage, Manuel came over in his outboard boat and sold us five

Aurora—Sea of Cortez

just-caught lobsters for fifteen dollars that had our eyes popping and mouths salivating. What a tasty treat emerged from the boiling water of our largest pot, as each one of us had our own lobster to submerge in a buttery dipping sauce.

We were motoring into the La Paz entrance channel just past the La Concha Hotel when the engine again stopped due to air that somehow was being introduced into the diesel fuel lines cutting off the fuel flow.

I shouted to Doug, "Drop the anchor when we reach the side of the channel. There it'll be safe to bleed the air out of the system."

This problem continued to annoy me as all known sources of an air leak had been eliminated, but the problem continued. Taking a berth at Marina de La Paz, Doug and Brenda could easily connect with a cab to the airport and I could work on the boat. JoAnne and I took them out for a final, fresh flame-grilled whole fish dinner with mango salsa. Many years later, Brenda's eyes would light up whenever her trip on *Aurora* was mentioned. JoAnne and I would savor our memories collected in Mexico.

16

TACKLING THE MEXICAN COAST

JoAnne and I would be sailing more than 1360 nautical miles along the Pacific Coast of Mexico. The coastline was open to the crashing waves and swells generated thousands of miles to the west in the vastness of the Pacific. Harbors and calm bays were scattered along the coast. We would stay within sight of the coast most of the time; however, she and I would be traveling alone most of the time. I felt prepared and JoAnne trusted me. She didn't question the decision to make our own plans, while many other boaters only traveled in groups of buddy boats like wagon trains for their whole voyage.

As part of my final preparation for the long trip south to Costa Rica, all systems had to be checked to insure their maximum reliability since we would be sailing offshore away from marinas, our main source of supplies and help. Here, all the studies I made in preparation for sailing my dream would be put to the test by the reality encompassed in sailing thousands of miles. Before beginning the voyage, I recorded *Aurora's* engine hours (1469) to track the use of the engine so I could determine when to change oil or buy fuel. I read the current log reading of 7351 nautical miles sailed, and I would use the log as it advanced to track *Aurora's* progress on the nautical charts. Our planned trip down the Coast of Mexico would be to Puerto Madera, the last Mexican port before the northern border of Guatemala.

Our new friends whom we met at Tripui, Duane and Peggy sailing on *Amourette*, were also making their first cruise to Mexico. They stopped by our berth at Marina de La Paz and asked us to sail with them across the Sea of Cortez to San Blas on the Mexican mainland. By sailing with a buddy boat on this offshore passage, JoAnne felt a greater sense of security knowing that there would be someone nearby to offer help in a crisis. Both crews had all been listening to weather forecasts on our High Seas Radios and decided to leave on November 4, 1991, in an improving weather pattern. Motoring to the end of the La Paz peninsula then raising the jib, we were greeted by rising 25 knot winds causing a rough ride through the high waves. The weather pattern had not improved enough. After a tough day of *Aurora* being slammed by the waves and having her home jumping and sliding about, JoAnne had to confront some of her fears about the ultimate safety of being on the boat. We had departed from the more sheltered waters of the Sea of Cortez and were now sailing into the open Pacific Ocean where the rough day we had just experienced could reoccur. What a way for her to begin our long journey south!

Luckily, the wind moderated by swinging behind us, causing the boat's motion to mellow and providing for a more comfortable ride. As darkness fell, we followed *Amourette* into the anchorage at Los Meurtos (the bay of the dead) using the guidance provided by their radar. JoAnne had come through when I needed her help at the wheel with both of us earning our peaceful sleep in this calm bay.

Looking out at the seas the next morning, we all agreed the waves seemed too high. Our visual information was confirmed on the High Seas Radio by reports from other boats and satellite weather forecasts to the north, all of which dictated that we remain at Los Meurtos, so I used this time to work on the Autohelm self-steering.

Our day of rest improved everybody's attitude. JoAnne caught up on some reading. At one point we talked about the challenges of the day before.

"It's really great to catch my breath," JoAnne said. "I'm feeling a little more centered. The rough weather yesterday really scared me. I'm finding it difficult to overcome the fears that were stirred up."

"Yes," I agreed, "overcoming fears is part of becoming a good sailor, and it takes experience and time. I hope that once you're able to see how *Aurora* and I react in larger waves and higher winds, JoAnne, your confidence will grow in my abilities and your own strengths."

"That sounds reasonable enough," said JoAnne, " but fear often isn't reasonable."

"I hear you, JoAnne, but expressing your fears will help me understand them so I can support and reassure you."

Wind and sea conditions improved the next morning, and we began our 254-nautical mile voyage east to Isla Isabella, located twenty miles off the coast of mainland Mexico. After motoring our boats out of the wind shadow caused by land, we were able to sail all day until 9 p.m. when I had to start the engine to compensate for a drop in wind which usually happens with the setting sun. Tracking our progress using Sat Nav, I plotted *Aurora's* position on the chart through the night. We were in constant radio contact with Duane and Peggy. We verified our position based on the boat's compass course and speed over the bottom.

In the blackness of the night away from lights on land, the stars were our companions. Sitting in the cockpit, we saw the Big Dipper with the two bright stars that form the right side of the Dipper's cup pointing to the North Star higher in the sky. By using my fingers at arm's length, I measured the distance from the bottom of the Dipper to its rim and then used that distance to mark the five spaces in the sky arriving at the North Star. Dropping an imaginary line straight down to the earth creates the direction of True North. Looking to the south, I also saw the three stars that form Orion's Belt and then the millions of stars of the Milky Way, scattered clouds of stars spread across the heavens. It was a spectacular night!

With very light winds the next morning, we decided it was a good time for a brief swim in the clear blue waters.

"It feels eerie being suspended here with over a thousand feet of water below me," I said. "I can't see whether any sharks are lurking below," I called out to JoAnne as she watched me swimming from the boat. "Keep your eyes open!"

"At least, I can see sharks if they're close by, but my fears about sailing aren't so easily allayed," she said.

The weather continued to be fair as the second night of motor sailing progressed into the flaming red of dawn silhouetting Isla Isabella against the eastern horizon. We arrived at 8:20 a.m. two days after leaving Los Meurtos. The knot meter showed a log reading of 255.7 miles, one mile more than the predicted distance I measured on the chart. Soon we were visited by a boatload of smiling fishers from the fish camp on the beach who wanted some hats in trade for 5 lobsters and 3 fish. All of us were very happy to make the trade!

A late season hurricane, Nora, generated large swells as she traveled north up the southern Pacific Coast of Mexico. *Aurora* began to rock and roll as the waves bounced off the rim of the volcanic caldera that encompassed the anchorage. These swells limited our island visit to only one day, forcing us to set off for San Blas early. Arriving at high tide, we surfed the rounded swells through the entrance and then anchored off the shrimp boat docks in the center of the small quiet harbor.

During the night, higher winds and tides moved through the harbor causing the anchor to drag. *Aurora* drifted onto a sandbar, lifting her enough out of the water that she heeled over as the tide went out. JoAnne and I almost fell out of bed, catapulting me out of my peaceful sleep and into my "save the boat" mode. First I launched the dinghy and threw a second anchor into it; second I rowed away from *Aurora* where the water was deeper and pushed the anchor off the dinghy into the water. Getting back to the boat, I clambered back aboard and used the windlass to pull at the anchor while JoAnne started the engine to try to move the boat off the sandbar.

After our exertion of muscle effort and motor power failed to break *Aurora* loose from the sandbar, JoAnne calmly said, "Why don't we just wait for the tide to rise and lift the boat off?"

I looked at her, puzzled, and took a deep breath. "You're right. Let's get back in bed."

JoAnne's observation of my efforts added a more objective perspective that I had seemed to lose in the heat of the moment. After first light, I retrieved the main anchor in the dinghy while Jo-Anne ran the engine in gear. Suddenly, *Aurora* broke loose from the grip of the sandbar and came charging along, submerging me and dragging the bow of the dingy under the water. JoAnne didn't have time to react to my shouts of "Put the engine in neutral." Talk about an adrenalin rush!

The remnants of Hurricane Nora passed over us with torrents of rain, but not much wind. The sea state (wave height) outside the shelter of the harbor was another issue making a five-day wait necessary for the seas to return to normal. Our first order of business that morning was to dinghy over to *Amourette* for a drink and a bit of self-congratulation for our successful crossing of the Sea of Cortez.

"I think we really got the weather right although Nora was maybe a little too close for comfort," Duane noted.

"We sure did have a mellow passage in the sea, but our encounter with the sandbar last night interrupted our sleep," I said. "I'm not too happy with Nora."

"It was sure comforting to me to have you guys nearby on my first overnight passage," said JoAnne. "I rather liked motoring on the smooth sea and being embraced by the stars. It certainly wasn't the scary experience I had expected. But sometimes I do feel apprehensive and scared when I think about the overall picture of our trip, but I've decided to take it one day at a time. I'm gaining faith in myself everyday as I learn more about sailing."

"I enjoyed crossing too. The expanse of the universe is so amazing when it's really dark out there," said Peggy. "Light really is a form of pollution when you're trying to take all the universe in."

The next day we went ashore. After I showed JoAnne around the town of San Blas, we began to hike up to the old Spanish Fort and Cathedral Ruins overlooking the harbor. A flock of children joined us, holding our hands while talking excitedly in Spanish. "*Mas Dispascio,*" (more slowly) was our phrase of choice as we tried to answer their barrage of questions. "*Si,* we are from the *Estados Unidos.* We have *una braca de vela* (a sailboat). *Se llamo es Aurora. Y si, nosotros gustamos* Mexico." (Yes, we like Mexico)

Cathedral Ruins—San Blas

After tracking down our friend Chena and wanting to take advantage of the good restaurants in town, we took him out to dinner.

"I would like to own a Natural Food Shop," Chena said. "I think it would do well with all the Gringos who come to San Blas to surf. Some Mexicans are beginning to be concerned about what they eat."

"Yeah, I can see the need for a Natural Foods Store," I said. "Sounds like a great idea to me."

Finally, after five days, shrimp boats began to leave the harbor, indicating it was safe to return to the sea. The weather fax data confirmed the sea state had moderated. So we pushed off alone to continue our trip down the coast with a pleasant wind off the stern.

When we reached the center of Banaderas Bay off Puerto Vallarta as darkness began covering the sea, suddenly without any warning, the wind and waves did a 180 degree shift from the north to a southerly direction causing *Aurora* to slam headlong into six-foot waves. She rocked violently like a "hobby horse." Having no safe place to seek shelter in the gathering darkness, my only choice was to continue sailing.

After being tossed every which way down below, JoAnne looked out from the companionway at me, screaming, "If you think this is fun, you're crazy!"

I held my head and grimaced showing my understanding that we certainly were not having fun. "Why don't you try to go to bed?" I said sympathetically. "I can handle the boat alone."

I continued slowly to motor the boat south through the night trying to minimize its motion to help JoAnne get some rest. The wind dropped in the morning as we reached Bahia Chamela, a large bay scattered with tree-covered islands where we could anchor in a calm spot. After a swim and a restful sleep, we had a smooth downwind sail "wing on wing" (with both the main and jib sails held out on opposite sides of the boat catching the wind and looking like a V on the front of *Aurora*) to Las Hadas Resort near La Punta in Manzanillo Bay. We arrived in the late afternoon. We dinghied into the marina the next morning. We ordered pizza and Margaritas from the waiter and had lunch by an amazing swimming pool populated by islands and waterfalls. Iguanas scampered over the rock islands providing visual entertainment while strumming guitarists filled our heads with lively sounds. What a contrast to being bounced around on *Aurora*!

JoAnne smiled. "It wouldn't take me too long to get used to *this*!"

I gave her a big hug in agreement.

Later, we walked up the hill and toured the main lobby of the hotel. Looking out from a terrace, we took in the gigantic scale of the place which featured hundreds of white stucco villas cascading down the hills. It was easy seeing that luxury has its advantages!

After receiving a clear fax satellite photo showing that the area south was free of clouds, we set off for an overnight sail to Isla Grande, near Zihuatenjo. As the wind decreased in velocity, most of our progress was made by motoring. Along the way, we saw flocks of red-necked phalaropes migrating south from the Arctic Ocean. These birds are the size of small ducks with a sharp bill and red patches on their necks. The flocks flew in an undulating formation swooping down to the water then rising up. At that point they had come about five thousand miles on their journey.

JoAnne remarked, "I'm glad we had our bird book handy. These birds seem to have a lot of energy. Can you imagine traveling that far?"

"Well, here they are. The distance they fly is really amazing to me too and look at how many birds there are in the flock—perhaps thousands," I said.

During the night, a large cruise ship, lit up like a floating city, passed inshore of us on its way to Zihuatenjo. We realized there could be big ships in this alongshore shipping lane. In the dawn, the large port of Lazaro Cardenas appeared on the port side of *Aurora*. With our eyes, we followed the track of a freighter into the harbor. An entry in our Pilot Book mentioned that Lazaro Cardenas had been an honest and revered president of Mexico. Unfortunately it is a rare occurrence in this country to have an honest president.

As we closed in on Isla Grande, it became apparent that the island was off its charted position. Sat Nav readings are much more accurate now when compared to the old surveys of the 1800s that depended on sextant sights and time readings that were far from exact. Anchoring in a south-facing bay off a curving beach, we found a calm anchorage that allowed us to catch up on the sleep we missed on our overnight passage. In the early morning, we were awakened by a loud drill instructor shouting a cadence, "Hut one, hut two, hut three." Peeping out our port holes, we saw about ten people vigorously doing jumping jacks on the beach. The Club Med decals on the side of their boat confirmed its identity that raised questions in my mind.

I asked JoAnne, "Would that really be the way that we'd want to spend a vacation?"

She rolled her eyes. "No way!"

Listening daily to the Central American Breakfast Club Net on High Seas Radio had been providing our main contact with the wider world by giving us interesting information from Costa Rica and Panama along with reports of the current weather patterns. Talking on the Net gave me a chance to ask questions of the Volunteer Net Controllers and other sailors who were tuned in at the same time. Their answers formed a web of "local" information we used to keep us safe and alerted us to places to see, and even gave us the names of good restaurants to be found along our path.

Soon, we set sail on *Aurora* past the new, high-rise resort of Ixtapa strung out along a long white sand beach. Ixtapa is an example of Mexico's mass tourist development that has created artificial cities dominating the beaches and landscape rather than fitting them into the natural surroundings. Tourists rarely go further than the beach and are missing out on the Mexican culture of towns, like Zihuatenjo, a lovely old fishing village that's nestled around its bay where we anchored. Instinctively, we avoided Ixtapa-like developments to seek out the older and more authentic Mexican towns where the culture has remained less disturbed and contrived.

JoAnne and I motored the dinghy into a beach near the downtown area of Zihuatenjo where four ten to twelve-year-old boys rushed down the beach to help us land the dinghy with big welcoming smiles on their faces.

Their leader said, "Can we help you find things in town? We're strong and can haul your large bag of laundry to the *lavanderia* and to guard your dinghy."

"What is your name? I asked.

"Me llamo es David."

"Great, you guys decide who will stay with the dinghy and who will accompany us into town," I directed them.

After some negotiating, they reached a decision on who would accompany us to the port captain's office and who would stay with the dinghy. The boys were all very excited to show us around town since they knew where everything was located. Their information proved to be very helpful to us. Their leader, David, pointed out a large mansion overlooking the bay as belonging to a police chief who had just been arrested and extradited to the United States for drug dealing and corruption saying, "I'm disgusted that he was not a good person. He was '*muy malo*' and used bribery to get the money for building such an big house."

The police chief's behavior justified his punishment in the boys' eyes. Their hauling our heavy Jerry jugs filled with water to the dinghy was welcome help. Finally for all their help, they only wanted cokes and some ice cream cones to which we added pesos producing their happy broad smiles. Two of the boys, David and Caesar, accompanied us in the dinghy out to *Aurora* where we served them *limonada* and cookies along with a tour of our boat.

"*Amigos*, this is the steering wheel and this lever next to it is the throttle. It controls the speed of the engine," I said.

"Is this the compass?" Caesar said. "I see it pointing toward N. Is that *Norte?*"

"*Si*, that is *Norte* and opposite it is South or *Sur*," I replied.

It was interesting that they seemed embarrassed by seeing themselves on my video. Perhaps that was a new experience for them. Each boy wanted to be a *launchero*, driving tourists around the bay when they grew up. These kids were both easier to communicate with in Spanish and more fun as they were less inhibited than adults.

In the anchorage, early one morning, our floating world was rocked by a large shore boat from the cruise ship that sped by within fifteen feet of *Aurora* jolting us awake.

During the day, we were visited by John, a single handed sailor anchored in the bay who had a fantastic tale to tell. "I fell off my boat in the Gulf of Panama and watched it sail away. I was unable to swim fast enough to catch it. After floating many hours in the warm water my calls for help were finally heard by the ship's doctor and his wife who were walking the deck on a passing cruise ship. I was finally found and taken aboard. Later my boat was found and towed as we both were taken to the entrance of the Panama Canal and dropped off."

John had a "Plax" bottle, which soon we realized was filled with vodka that allowed him to suckle as the day wore on. His mention of nightmares and problems after going into the water sounded like remnants of his scary experience.

Whether it was true or not, we took his story as a warning. Always have one hand for the ship by keeping one hand free to grab a lifeline or handhold, and in heavy wind and wave situations always wear a life jacket and a safety harness with a tether that attaches the wearer to the boat. The chance of surviving a fall into the ocean would be slim to none, especially if it occurred at night when your mate was sleeping.

17

PASSAGE ALONG THE CENTRAL AMERICAN COAST

After another overnight passage using the spinnaker in the daylight and the Genoa jib sail poled out after dark, we entered Acapulco Bay, anchoring off the yacht club. The club occupied a peninsula across from the city and had the essential facilities that cruisers need: a swimming pool, clubhouse with showers, and a bar/dining room. Our friends Gina and Tom from the San Francisco Bay Area met us to join *Aurora's* crew for our trip to Costa Rica. Gina brought a smoked turkey and cranberry sauce and other trimmings in her luggage for our Thanksgiving celebration.

"Gina, you are amazing!" said JoAnne. "Quite a feat. How did you do it?"

"Well, I found some really large plastic bags and some strong containers. They did the trick," she responded.

Sitting around the dining table on *Aurora* with good friends having a traditional Thanksgiving dinner in Mexico was a real treat thousands of miles from our homes in the United States. In the cozy space, JoAnne and I had heartfelt feelings of thanks for our friends' thoughtfulness in bringing the tradition of our lives at home into our new lives on the sea.

"So what are our sailing plans?" Tom said.

"As soon as I complete the check of all boat systems," I said, "the engine oil, the fuel tank levels, look over the rigging for any wear or damage, and when the weather forecasts predict moderate wind and waves, then we can begin our voyage south down the coast. We'll stay a few miles off shore just inside the shipping lanes in deep water. I should warn you that El Salvador and Nicaragua are each fighting civil wars, and that I've heard rumors on the radio that pirates may be operating off the coast of Nicaragua. Because we'll **be** close to the coast and will not stop in those countries, I think we'll be alright."

"Okay, with those risks in mind, I propose that we have a bon voyage dinner at the Yacht Club," said Tom. "I think we deserve a treat before we take on the hardships of the passage."

"What a great idea!" agreed JoAnne.

Aurora left at 2 p.m. on November 29, 1991, sailing in mellow 10-15-knot winds into the night. That first night, we were joined by the constellation of the Southern Cross rising above the horizon.

"JoAnne, do you see the five bright stars just above the curve of the horizon?" I said. "It looks like a cross with the lowest star closer to the sea. We're south of 20 degrees latitude so we can see all of it now."

"Yeah, I think I can see it," she said. "It's almost due south of us as I look at the compass. We can use it to guide us through the night."

Two days later we arrived in Bahia Hautalco, a developing resort area, and we decided to anchor out in the bay across from the village. That decision was immediately challenged by swarms of tiny no-see-ems determined to chomp on every bit of our exposed skin. These insects, tinier than a grain of sand, and a visit from the harbormaster helped us to decide that motoring over to the quay was the best option. But backing into the quay along the channel which was my first attempt to med moor (dropping the bow anchor first and then backing in) wasn't going well since *Aurora* was being pushed sideways by the outgoing tide.

Seeing our plight, four young Mexican men climbed on nearby moored boats and jumped aboard to help us fend *Aurora* off them. Using their arms and feet, these strong guys prevented us from crashing into them. In the pandemonium, I tossed a long line ashore to another of their friends so he could pull us in. While gathering valuable boat handling experience, we made friends with Victor who later wove great jungle hats out of green palm fronds for each of us and with Jésus. He became our main man by checking us in with the port captain, filling our propane tank, and taking care of *Aurora* when we went up to San Cristobal de Las Casas.

That night JoAnne complained, "I can't get to sleep. The surging waves are rocking the boat and reverberating under the pier sounding like a sea monster."

"You're right," I replied. "This is not the best place we've ever tied up, but we really had no choice."

With the aid of earplugs, we managed to get some sleep.

Gina was anxious to return to San Cristobal de Las Casas where she had volunteered in an orphanage as a young woman. Being very proficient in speaking Spanish, Gina bought our bus tickets in Hautalco. Taking the bus to San Cristobal high in the mountains near the Guatemalan border was difficult. It was standing room only at the start. Later, I was able to squish into a seat with Violetta, a cute six-year-old, and her younger sister after their mom gave me the okay.

After many passengers left the bus in Salina Cruz, we continued on with our own seats as we crossed the Isthmus of Tehuatepec, the low point between the northern and southern mountains that create a spine traversing the length of Mexico. Then the bus headed up into the mountains that defined the southern border of Mexico with Guatemala. By evening, the beautiful lights of San Cristobal spread out in the valley before us as we came over the last ridge. Upon leaving the bus, our tropically acclimatized bodies immediately registered that it was indeed cold at 6,000 feet. On top of that, our hotel had no heat but did have extra blankets as we took a crash course in climatic adaption which to the uninitiated could be called "shivering."

Up late in the morning, we had a good breakfast at the Café Bazaar in the arcaded central town square. Here Gina's mastery of Spanish helped us order our eggs cooked just right. We walked to the old Santo Domingo Church that was surrounded by Mayan Indians from the nearby mountain villages. They were selling colorful weavings, interesting pottery, and muscular wood carvings spread out on blankets. The Mayan women's bright costumes complemented their wares. JoAnne found a dark blue woven dresser scarf with red and yellow decorative patterns.

Gina and Tom visited the orphanage where Gina had volunteered as a college student.

"The staff has continued taking good care of the young children," said Gina. "I feel really good being here again. That summer with the children stands out in my memory—their sparkling dark eyes and smiling faces were all the reward I needed."

"Yeah, I love to watch and be with Mexican children," added JoAnne. "Their happiness and joy infects me, raising my spirits."

After a good dinner costing only four dollars for each of us including dessert and coffee, we returned to our hotel that was still cold, like living in a cave, but by snuggling under the heavy blankets our body heat was preserved.

Coming down the mountain in the morning, we had reserved front seats in the bus. We were shocked by the sight of large tractor trailer trucks that had been blown over on their sides by the force of the wind funneling between the mountains from the Gulf of Mexico through the low Isthmus of Tehuatepec. This "Venturi Effect" had increased the wind's velocity. These winds (called the dreaded "Tehuatepecer") would directly affect our sailing along the coast so we delayed leaving our mooring in Huatalco for Salina Cruz by two more days.

Finally leaving the harbor, we found the waves and wind were still too high so we sailed north around the point to discover a beautiful bay suggested by Jésus. After a quiet night's rest, we ventured into the sea and hugged close to shore to keep *Aurora* safe from the larger waves that would develop further offshore. Waves become higher and higher when the strong force of the wind has added time and a greater distance to act on the water's surface. This sailing tactic of staying close to shore is called "One foot on the beach," which we chose to follow all the way down the coast of Central America. Turning into Salina Cruz Harbor that evening gave us a brief blast of the funneling winds that reached 42 knots in velocity as we followed the big ship range (guiding) lights into the inner harbor where we anchored near the port captain's office. We were glad to feel the calm that engulfed our bodies after the boat stopped bouncing and rocking!

Aurora was underway to Puerto Madera by 6:45 am as the winds had moderated to 18 knots in the harbor and 20-30 knots outside. *Aurora* flew just along the beach. The depth sounder was our most critical instrument in the shallow water. Keeping an eye out for fishing nets and their floats was also important since we were transiting the near shore fishing zone. Aurora was speeding along, sometimes at 7 knots in the smooth water, while the wind continued blowing 20-30 knots directly off the land perpendicular to the course of the boat. Winds over the beam of the ship produce the highest boat speeds with minimal heel since the sails are let out to correctly catch the wind. Not tipping so much meant that JoAnne, Gina, and Tom were happy campers for the two days it took to reach Puerto Madera, Mexico's southernmost port.

*****

Arriving at Puerto Madera, we found it was a rather disorganized place as shacks and their rickety docks lined the entrance channel. A large banana loading pier at the end of a wide turning basin was surrounded by jungle. A Chicita Banana freighter left its pier coming out using a number of tugs to help it maneuver into the narrow channel past *Aurora*. The water was very inviting so we all jumped in for a swim and soaped up to get clean after two days of continuous sailing. The warm solar shower rinsed off the salt water and we all emerged sparkling clean.

Provisioning *Aurora* was our number one task due to the fact that we would be at sea for at least 5 days transiting more than five hundred miles along the Central American Coast. At the time, El Salvador and Nicaragua were fighting civil wars so stopping in those countries was not an option. With no fuel dock in the harbor, I enlisted the help of a young man, Juan, who brought 200 liters of diesel in drums in his pickup truck onto the dock. Using a hose, I siphoned the diesel from the drums down into *Aurora's* tanks. He also took Gina to a nearby town, Tapachula, that had a supermarket where she was able to restock our food supplies.

Gina also arranged for the delivery of 2 kilos of fresh shrimp for dinners underway.

We shared some of the shrimp with a friendly young man fishing off a dock opposite *Aurora* to use as fish bait. Gina and I had been talking with him when we took the dinghy back and forth to the boat. Jorge was a happy teenager still in school who came aboard to see the boat and told us he was interested in creating art. When we told him that Costa Rica (rich) was our destination, he remarked that we were leaving "Costa Pobre" (poor.) Ready to leave, we all wondered about his future.

With concern in her voice, JoAnne said, "What will happen to this great kid in this isolated little town so lacking in resources?"

Looking over at Jorge, I said, "He's ambitious, handsome, and seems to be bright. Those attributes should help him succeed." We all hoped that he would become the artist defined by his dreams.

By 4:30 p.m., the provisions were all stowed aboard and *Aurora* was ready to leave so we headed her down the channel into the sea. As the sun was dropping over the horizon, we were off the coast of Guatemala and saw a large barge that looked like it had been dropped into the sea. Its super structure had round windows scattered about randomly and strange masts poking up into the sky.

Tom wondered, "What in the world is that thing?"

"I'm guessing that it's the product of someone's imagination gone wild—or perhaps a deranged mind. Besides floating what could be its function?" I asked.

"Maybe it's a leftover from a *Star Wars* movie," Tom speculated.

During the next day, we caught an 18-pound Jack Crevasse about which our "Baja Catch" book warned, "Eating one would remind you of Charlie Chaplin eating his shoe in Alaska." We threw it back!

Toward evening, the Port of San Jose, Guatemala, came into view so we decided to enter and to anchor in a calm corner away from both the fishing fleet and the large freighters. Here, we could swim and have Tom's sautéed shrimp with garlic over rice for dinner. The port captain, however, had other ideas and was upset

JoAnne and Gina

because we had not asked for permission by radio to enter his port. It had been our custom in Mexico to just sail in and then find the port captain. He sent over a *panga* loaded with three armed soldiers to check us out and take our boat papers and passports into the office.

My rule number one was now being violated. Always keep your official documents with you! Gina's protests in Spanish were to no avail. The soldiers assured us that the passports would be returned, so we swam and had dinner, trusting their word. Soon, they did return with our papers and ordered us to leave the port immediately which we gladly did with clean bodies and full stomachs.

While sailing during the night, we were amazed to see a beautiful fountain of fire and lava, shooting up into the dark sky from Fuego (Fire) Peak in the mountains behind San Jose. The clouds were tinted orange and red by the eruptions of lava sparks and flames.

"What an amazing sight," exclaimed Gina. "It seems that 'Mother Nature' has more new tricks up her sleeve."

"Look at the subtle colors and how they change from moment to moment," JoAnne said. "Her palate is stunning. I wish I could paint like that." The show continued as we took turns on watch through the night.

The rising sun outlined Acajutla, El Salvador's major port. We headed out to sea to clear the reefs of Punta Remedios. A good weather report on the Breakfast Club Net also brightened our day. About noon as we were sailing off La Libertad, El Salvador, *Aurora* was boarded by Senior Grade Lt. Jimenez of the *Guardia Coastal de El Salvador* and two of his men. Their coxswain had expertly backed the patrol boat to the stern of *Aurora* while we held our breaths and sailed along slowly using only the mainsail to keep the boat stable in the swells. The tall, slender, handsome lieutenant who had been trained in the United States and spoke excellent English, checked our papers while his men looked into lockers and under the floorboards for drugs. Lt. Jimenez was very courteous and liked JoAnne who reminded him of his mother. He seemed anxious to speak more English and to show us his country.

"Please come into La Libertad—it is a safe harbor—I'd like to show you my town," the lieutenant said, issuing a warm invitation.

"We're sorry, but we can't come in," I said. "Gina and Tom have a tight schedule since they have already booked their return flight to California from San Jose, Costa Rica."

"It's too bad that you can't visit La Libertad, but I'll clear *Aurora* with other *Guardia Coastal* units operating off the Coast of El Salvador," said Lt. Jimenez.

*****

As we sailed off Nicaragua at night, JoAnne and I watched as the numbers on the depth sounder suddenly got smaller and smaller. I immediately spun the wheel turning *Aurora* 90 degrees to the right, out to sea, but the instrument kept indicating that the water was getting more shallow. Again, I reacted by turning 90 more degrees so now we were headed back on our original track until finally the depth became greater. After a while I turned back out to sea making a large loop around the entrance to a river that had deposited its silt in shoals far out to sea.

Later in the Gulf of Fonseca further south in Nicaragua, we noticed that the fishermen looked poorer by comparison to those of Mexico or Guatemala. During the day, we noticed a black speed boat seaward of us that appeared to be shadowing *Aurora*. Remembering the rumors of pirates operating off Nicaragua, we started watching through our binoculars, and I told everyone where our shotgun and ammunition were stored. We also changed our course and headed closer to the coast where we hoped to be safe. Finally after about two hours, the black boat sped away from us and entered a harbor that we had passed. We all looked at each other with sighs of relief.

"I'm very thankful they didn't come after us," I said. "Thinking of what might have happened is too dark to contemplate."

"Yeah, if they had wanted to take us, we wouldn't have had much of a chance," said Tom.

After dark, *Aurora* entered an area of many large mooring buoys for ships whose charted positions were in disagreement on our two charts. Tom became confused.

"Karl, wake up! I need your help," he shouted down the companionway. "It's really puzzling out here."

"Tom, where do you think we are?" I said.

"Beats me," he said.

"It seems that we should stay on our southerly course and keep track of the numbers on the buoys," I suggested. After a few minutes, I said, "That seems to be working. The number on the last buoy and the one in front of us follow in order and matches what is on the chart."

"You mean we really know where we are," said Tom with surprise. "Out of the confusion clarity emerges. We must be doing something right!"

Of course, this all happened at night when shoreside lights and those on the buoys could easily become mixed up, especially after one of us was awakened after insufficient sleep. We did have a two crew on and two crew off rotation because keeping awake was critical to our survival in our "one foot on the beach" navigation mode which put us very near to shore. We all felt good having survived these critical tests and now being close to our destination, Costa Rica.

18

COSTA RICA AT LAST

Sailing through two days of strong winds, we passed the last port in Nicaragua, San Juan del Sur. I began shouting challenges at the incessant winds as they reached 35 knots. Costa Rica was near and boy, we needed her shelter.

"Give us your worst, we can take it!"

I had to eat my words as we were forced to take down the jib and to pull the main down to its second reef position to reduce sail area just to keep *Aurora* upright. I'd had enough.

"Okay, wind, *Aurora* is tough," I shouted back, "but let's not go crazy."

Now sailing away from shore, we were more exposed to the winds and waves. It was a long ten miles across the Gulf to the entrance of Bahia Elena where we found at last a calm anchorage. We finally made it!

The bay is protected by low ridges of dry tropical forest backed up by higher mountains and is a part of Santa Rosa National Park in our destination country of Costa Rica. That land once belonged to Nicaragua's deposed dictator, Anastasio Somoza.

"Wow, it feels like we've entered paradise," JoAnne said. "Listen to the chattering monkeys. They seem to be greeting us. The piercing squawks of that flock of parrots sound like a whole village of people screaming all at once."

"It's been a struggle to get here, sailing five days and nights without a break, but you're right about being in paradise," Gina agreed.

We jumped into the 78 degree water that soothed our aching and dirty bodies as we allowed ourselves to relax and revel in our new environment. Before dinner, we sat on the deck sharing a bottle of wine. We continued to soak in the sight of waving palms and sounds of palm fronds speaking in the wind. The parrots and monkeys added their voices to this tropical symphony. The earthy smell of the forest wafted out to the boat, connecting us to land after our days at sea.

"At times it's been hard getting here, but you can't beat this place," said JoAnne. "It exudes a sense of calm. All the birds and animals feel at home here, and so should we."

"Yeah, it's great that our world isn't rocking and rolling anymore. My body is enjoying being at rest," added Gina.

"My mind is chilling out now that it's off duty," I said with relief.

A good night's sleep was another welcome reward. I was feeling some regret about having to leave so soon, however. Tom and Gina's homeward bound tickets made it necessary to arise early and to sail through the Bat Islands of the Golfo de Papaya to keep the appointment with a Port Captain of Playa del Coco set up by my radio friend, Maury, a net controller on the Central America Breakfast Club. We arrived with time to spare and broke out the bottle of champagne brought by Gina and Tom and celebrated the conclusion of our voyage together. They would leave us tomorrow when we dinghied them ashore.

"As captain, here's my toast, to a wonderful and skilled crew who went the distance," I said. For me, the toast was especially heartfelt since they helped us through the most dangerous part of the trip, so far.

Gina toasted, "Here's to our success, survival, and continued friendship."

At that point in my adventure, JoAnne and I had sailed 2,040 miles in twenty-seven travel days including fourteen overnights from Puerto Escondido in the Baja, Mexico, to Playa del Coco, Costa Rica. The trusty Yanmar Diesel engine ran a total of 361 hours while our average speed was 5.7 nautical miles per hour. Gina and Tom had been crew for a total of over 1,000 miles, covered in twelve travel days that included seven overnight passages, from Acapulco. Their presence added immeasurably to our safety and pleasure. The crew, though tired, was still in good shape while trusty *Aurora* had completed the voyage with no major problems, sailing her way through high winds and rough seas without complaint as did JoAnne's tomato, cilantro, and basil plants riding inside the dodger. My chest swelled with accomplishment and pride.

*****

After sailing past the unstable countries of El Salvador and Nicaragua, we were now in Costa Rica, a country having a stable constitutional democracy and being an island of peace in Central America. The roots of these different political outcomes between these countries were sown by the Spanish Conquistadors who had bred a strong class system based on their Spanish blood and the family ties among the new immigrants. Those ties and the prejudices that supported the immigrants kept the indigenous Indian populations stuck at the bottom of society thus insuring their later discontent. Costa Rica by not having as much gold, however, attracted fewer settlers and also had fewer natives to subjugate. A more egalitarian society developed here where even the governor tended his own garden. A democracy was created which was able to eliminate the army in 1948 and elect a President, Oscar Arias Sanchez, who helped negotiate the solutions to his neighbors's problems. The ending of the two civil wars in El Salvador and Nicaragua earned him the Nobel Peace Prize.

*****

After we all had dinghied ashore and said our "Goodbyes," Gina and Tom boarded the bus to the capital city of San Jose for their flight home. JoAnne and I walked along the beach to visit our radio friend, Maury Gladson, at his home located in the trees just behind the breakers, facing the bay where *Aurora* lay at anchor. At 87 years young, Maury had the mind and body of a much younger man. He was a fount of information on cruising the coasts of Costa Rica and Panama. His sharp mind had absorbed current information from the cruisers passing through and from his radio contacts with them. Maury's own cruising in the 1950s added a historical perspective that gave me a deeper understanding of how this coast had developed.

Maury was not the only expat American here as we discovered at a cruisers party at his house. We met an attractive couple in their forties who had decided to stay in Playa del Coco.

"Hi, we're Tom and Leslie," said Maury's friends. "We fell in love with this place and have created Pronto Pizza where we use a beehive, wood fired oven to cook the best pizza ever."

"Yeah, we had some the other night and can attest to that," said JoAnne.

"We also have a gift shop that sells local crafts," Leslie added.

"I'm interested in crafts," said JoAnne. "Are you going to be there tomorrow?"

"Yeah, I'll be there pricing the handicrafts."

"Great, I'll stop by and give you a hand," said JoAnne.

We also met Rick and Roy, two brothers who also decided to stay on after returning from a family cruise in the South Pacific. We were really attracted to these upbeat go-getters who had developed a boat building and repair facility, acquired a fish processing plant and a number of long line fishing boats that catch dorado (Mahi Mahi), tuna, and sharks. They even owned a restaurant/bar. Hearing of all the economic activity they had generated gave us a sense of pride in being Americans.

Roy gave us half a dorado for the barbecue in Maury's backyard. After dinner he presented a slide show of his travels on his 50-foot gaff rigged ketch, *Doubloon*. His words turned into images and deepened our connection with him. After Maury's wife died, cruisers had become his family. We joined that family and Maury invited us to Christmas dinner—another treat.

JoAnne and I took the bus to San Jose and picked up my daughter Leanne from the airport and brought her back to Playa del Coco for her Christmas vacation. I wanted her first time in Costa Rica to be special so we rented horses and galloped on the beach and later explored the town. One day by chance, a 35-foot motor trawler, *Sea View*, joined us in the anchorage. Jim, the owner, and his young crew, Dan, whom he identified as "my Nurse," had cruised down the Pacific Coast from Santa Catalina

Island off Los Angeles. Dan's designation as nurse raised questions in our minds that remained unanswered because Jim didn't have any visible disabilities. We became "buddy boats" heading south together and Leanne found a young man to share some of her time.

We filled our diesel tanks from pumps at the Flamingo Marina, our first opportunity to get fuel from an actual gas pump since Acapulco. We spent time on the beach at Playa Conchel. Interesting shells and warm white sand invited us to relax under our new beach umbrella. JoAnne and I watched Leanne and Dan having fun playing in the waves.

Later we rounded Cabo Vela and anchored off the beach at Playa Grande hoping to see the Volkswagen-sized leatherback turtles come ashore to lay their eggs in the sand after their migration from Indonesia across the Pacific. Leatherbacks are the largest living turtles and have skin and oily flesh covering the carapace rather than shell. Costa Rica is a major nesting site for the female leatherbacks.

Dinghying ashore through the surf, we met the challenge of keeping the dinghies perpendicular to the waves, thereby avoiding being flipped over. The turtles' tank like tracks heading up the beach indicated that we were indeed at the "right" beach. Body surfing and swimming filled our time as we waited for evening and the arrival of the turtles.

We waited almost until dark, but we saw no turtles. Disappointed, we headed back to our dinghies.

"Oh, my God, our dinghy motor is missing," yelled Jim. "Can any one see it?"

"It's not around here on the beach," I said. "Our motor is still locked to our dinghy. How lucky is that!"

That night, I heard a loud bump against *Aurora's* hull that reverberated through the boat. Was it made by a passing turtle thrown off course by the growing onshore waves? The waves grew stronger by 3 am. I was concerned by the more violent pitching motion and our unprotected location off the beach (a lee shore). I got up and decided to pull the anchor and head off shore. Feeling our way out in the dark to deeper water, I turned *Aurora* south and headed forty-nine miles for Bahia Samara where we found a sheltered anchorage. The next day *Sea View* joined us.

Jim told us about his experience. "We had a hard time pulling up anchor due to the size of the swells coming in."

His report confirmed that we had been smart to leave when we did. Now, all of us were looking forward to a good night's sleep!

Morning found our two-boat flotilla continuing south toward Cabo Blanco which forms the seaward flank of the Golfo de Nicoya, a deep body of water indented into the coast of central Costa Rica. Nearing the cape, I saw a dark structure in the distance. As we sailed closer, the outline of a wrecked freighter became clear. Soon, we could see that the hull had been driven high on the reef. We took the sight as a warning to keep an eye on both the depth sounder and the color of the water (dark being deep and light being shallow) as we threaded our way through the reefs. Navigating into the deeper waters of the Golfo, I turned *Aurora* toward Bahia Ballena (Whale Bay) and then drove toward the Bahia Ballena Yacht Club, a restaurant/bar. We rowed toward shore and tied our dinghy to a floating dock opposite the yacht club. Then, we pulled ourselves in using a continuous line that tied their aluminum rowboat to the jagged concrete steps and ladder hanging off the pier. Later the darkness and the 9-foot tide complicated the return to our boats, but after a delicious fresh fish dinner, we all agreed the struggle was worth the effort.

During the rough night, I rowed the dinghy out to deploy a stern anchor that kept the boat lined up perpendicular to the swells coming in thus minimizing the side to side rolling. In the morning, we moved *Aurora* across the bay to Heart's Beach. Its white sand, palm trees, and black lava rocks reignited thoughts of paradise in our minds.

Sailing further into the Golfo de Nicoya, we saw masts near Isla Gitana and decided to check out the anchorage and island. The island is owned by an ex-cruiser, Carl, and is under the care of his daughter, Linda, who manages a small restaurant that has a nearby pool open for visitors.

While we were drinking cold beers by the pool, family pets joined us looking for treats and affection. Linda told us their names so we could call them over. JoAnne called to Leanne and me, "Let's take a hike around the island."

So off we went into the forest accompanied by an unusual group of animals. Our "friends" included: a peccary pig called Miss Piggy; two long and skinny coatimundis, raccoon-like mammals, named *Flaco*, for thin and *Gordo*, for fat; and a dog. As we were walking along the trail with our friends, howler monkeys roared like lions overhead in the trees while white-faced monkeys scampered from branch to branch occasionally throwing sticks in our direction. We were surrounded by animals.

"Leanne, watch that stick. The white faces are sharpening their aim," I said.

"Thanks, I saw it coming," said Leanne. "Those guys seem to like making us jump out of the way. Their chattering sounds like laughter to me."

"White-faced monkeys move with such agility in the trees," I said. "Tree branches are their pathways as they zoom around."

While climbing a hill covered with scree, JoAnne slipped and slid down to the bottom. Miss Piggy became concerned and rushed over to lick her face before I could get there to help pull her up onto her feet.

JoAnne petted Miss Piggy, saying, "Thank you! You're so sweet."

The coatimundis were having fun doing a sort of dance as their bodies swished by each other and around our feet. We felt like Dr. Dolittle as we hiked through the jungle leading our animal menagerie who accepted us as compatriots. I feel high just thinking about the experience.

*****

While at anchor that night, Leanne and I watched torpedo-shaped forms streaking toward *Aurora* shedding streams of phosphorescence that created intricate patterns in the water. As these forms got closer to the boat, we realized that they were dolphins playing with each other and using our boat as a hiding place. We stared in amazement. After diving under the boat, the dolphins reappeared, rushing toward their friends. Our eyes followed their luminescent trails that crisscrossed forming momentary glowing shapes that dissolved into darkness. What an unforgettable moment to share with my daughter.

"Dad, that was really amazing! I've never seen anything like it."

"Yeah, what a show. Nature always surprises us. I'm so happy that we're here together to see it!" I said, giving her a hug.

In the morning, we sailed toward Puntarenas and timed our entrance into the estuary with the incoming tide that we rode up the river to the Costa Rica Yacht Club. The boat boys came out to help us tie *Aurora* to the bow and stern buoys that would keep us parallel to the current. Soon, the crew was cooling off in the pool with Jim and Dan who later joined us for dinner at the club's restaurant. This marked the end of Leanne's vacation on *Aurora* and her dalliance with Dan over the past two weeks.

After breakfast, while standing and waving our arms on the edge of the highway, we were able to bring the San Jose bound bus to a stop. Soon, the bus was climbing up into the coastal mountain range as the narrow road switched back and forth, following the folds of the mountain. Costa Rican drivers are known for their willingness to take chances. Their risky actions raised our level of anxiety as they passed on curves and committed other suicidal gestures. We changed the song lyric, "Do you know the way to San Jose," to "We hope to make it all the way to San Jose!" We cringed and winced at the crazy chances they took.

A taxi from the bus station took us to Hotel Don Carlos where friends Anne and Doug from Oakland, California, were waiting to greet us. Anne was a student at UC Berkeley and lived at International House where JoAnne worked. They became fast friends. Anne is a good looking dark-haired woman who is a college librarian. Doug is a brush cut, athletic young man who loves golf and riding bikes. He is an avid photographer who manages a photo store. They met on a geology field trip sharing that interest. JoAnne and I joined them in the lounge that sported cages of macaws and parrots. Over beers we planned our two-week adventure in Costa Rica. Ron, the desk manager, volunteered his help by sharing his considerable local knowledge. Soon, our itinerary included most of the spectacular sights in Costa Rica.

In the morning with hugs and goodbyes, we sent Leanne off by taxi to the airport while Doug and Anne joined us for a return bus trip to Puntarenas where *Aurora* was moored. We would begin our exploration the next afternoon on an old Blue Bird school bus. The jovial bus driver enjoyed using a loud air horn as he followed the Pan American Highway north before turning off on a dirt road that climbed 5,000 feet up to the Monteverdi Cloud Forest Reserve. This bus was the lifeline for the nearby community of Santa Elena, carrying packages, large and small, that were dropped off on doorsteps. The driver also picked up large metal cans of milk headed for the cheese factory higher up the mountain.

Monteverdi boasted an international staffed research station that studied the unique ecosystem there. A four-wheel-drive Toyota Land Cruiser took us further into the mountains to *Pension Flor Mar*, owned by an original Quaker settler's family from Alabama. They came here in the 1950s to establish dairy farms and a cheese factory to support a safer way of life far from the nuclear armed United States then involved in the dangerous cold war with the Soviet Union.

After an early breakfast, we rented knee high boots to foil the mud in the cloud forest, and we began the self-guided trail into the reserve before the one hundred person limit for that day was reached. The hiking trails were small streams filled by light rain. We were soon overtaken by a group guided by a wonderful Tico biologist who allowed us to join them. His narration deepened our understanding of the cloud forest. The tall trees were covered with layers of vines, mosses, and air plants called bromeliads, creating a profusion of colors and textures that almost demanded being captured by our cameras. Both Doug and I were drawn into action. Clouds swirled around us as we glided through the softness of the forest. Moisture dripped from every surface sustaining all these living things.

Adapting to the Cloud Forest

"Look over there," said the guide. "See those Avocado pits littering the ground? I'll bet that the famous Resplendent Quetzal, the National Bird of Costa Rica, is close by. Its ridiculously long tail resembles a work of art."

We were only able to catch a flash of red and green up in the canopy since the Quetzals are so successfully camouflaged in their environment. Walking on cut tree rounds kept us from sinking too deeply into the mud created by small streams channeling surplus water out of the forest. We felt suspended in this misty environment where everything was thriving and growing. Our senses were absorbed into the shapes, colors, and sounds that seemed to overwhelm us, filling us to capacity, bringing smiles crinkling on our faces. The memory of this day more than lingers on!

Over time, the Quaker farmers had allowed the forest to expand into their pastures creating a second growth area accommodating even more wildlife. Just outside the reserve, we came upon the Hummingbird Gallery displaying photographs taken of the birds and animals inhabiting the area. The hummingbird feeders were in full use by hundreds of the tiny iridescent birds feeding and inviting photographers to take amazing pictures of the many different species. The brilliant rainbow colored feathers were captured in stop action shots.

*****

Back on *Aurora*, Ann, Doug, and JoAnne took the bus into town to gather supplies for our next adventure. Continuing south in the morning, we made it to Bahia Herradura where I anchored *Aurora* to escape the strong south wind and waves that had slowed our progress.

Doug remarked, "That 'native' village ashore looks like a CIA training camp."

"Yeah, there's something unnatural about it," I responded.

Later we found out that it was the film set for *1492, The Conquest of Paradise*, a movie about Christopher Columbus starring Gerard Depardieu and Sigourney Weaver. In the evening as the winds diminished, I announced, "Let's pull up the anchor and continue sailing south through the night since the seas are calmer."

We arrived off Manuel Antonio National Park as the sun rose over the hills bathing the seas in a pinkish glow. Anchoring in the crook of Cathedral Head, we were opposite the "Second Beach" where sounds of monkeys and birds drifted out to greet us. Going ashore by dinghy, we hiked up the trail watching a mob of white-faced monkeys scamper and chatter above us. We climbed onto the higher headlands and were rewarded with spectacular views of small islands scattered across the bay set like emerald green jewels in the blue Pacific beyond. Sliding down the steep trail on the opposite side, we saw the "Third Beach" appear covered with white sand interspersed with black volcanic reefs slithering toward the sea and backed by trees whose branches spread out toward the water. It was later that we learned these trees could drop a caustic sap on unwary bathers.

"This is the most beautiful beach I've ever seen," I remarked.

Then we all exclaimed, "This must be paradise!"

"I never used the word 'paradise' as much as when we were here in Costa Rica," I said.

The warm water and gentle waves did seem to fit the bill for our next activity so we went in for a swim. Lying in the water, we lazily watched the white clouds pass.

"That one looks like a whale," exclaimed Ann. "See its head, broad back, and tail."

"How about that one over there? Can you see a huge bird with wings?" Doug said, pointing. "What a relaxing way to spend an afternoon!"

The next morning at breakfast, we were joined by Ted from the 30-foot sloop *Egret*, anchored nearby.

"May I come aboard? I've been in Costa Rica for four months now, and I'd like to share my impressions with you."

"Great, welcome to *Aurora*!" I said. "How about a cup of coffee?"

"Sure, that would hit the spot," said Ted holding out his hand. "I assume that you'll be heading south for Golfito. There's a good anchorage off the Hotel Las Gaviotas where the cruisers hang out. There is another place called the Jungle Club located on a hill just across the bay. When you sail into northern Panama just south of Costa Rica you'll find a cruising couple who are homesteading on an island and will welcome visitors."

"Thanks," I said, "for all the info! Having destinations like these will sure make our voyage more interesting."

Back on shore, while we were lying on the beach, an emerald green snake slithered across someone's beach mat as we blinked back at many docile iguanas checking out the sunbathers from the edge of the tree line. Leaving the beach, we hiked up the Mirador trail finding a two-toed sloth with her baby moving slowly up in a tree.

"These guys must be the original couch potatoes," Doug observed.

"Yeah, it looks like speed isn't in their vocabulary," said Ann.

A much larger, four-foot-long iguana that looked like a steel plated, spiked monster spiced up our hike as it sunned itself on a rock. We watched curiously as it flicked its forked tongue at us as if saying, "Beware!"

A ranger on the trail explained that Costa Rica has protected about one-fourth of its land area as national parks and nature reserves so seeing a profusion of animals and birds is almost inevitable. These facts combined with the friendly demeanor of the Ticos, short for Costa Ricans, mean the country has become a very popular tourist destination. A bonus for them is income for people who provide many needed services like food and lodging to tourists.

*****

Motor sailing on our way back up the Golfo de Nicoya in *Aurora*, I was brought to attention by the loud buzzing of the engine alarm. My first response was to shut down the Yanmar diesel and then to throw open the cover of the engine compartment. The problem almost jumped out at me. The alternator's belt was loose and the bracket holding the alternator was now limply hanging down on the front of the motor. I saw that the bracket's bolt had sheared off at the face of the engine meaning that the remainder of the bolt now was flush stuck in the engine's metal case. I knew that to fix this problem, I would first have to drill out the bolt end. Then, I could turn a tap into the hole to cut new threads for a larger and stronger bolt to hold the bracket and alternator in place. The whole operation took about an hour to complete as *Aurora* slowly sailed along.

"Let's see if it works," I said. "Doug, press the starter while I watch to be sure the alternator turns." Doug did as I instructed. "Okay, it's spinning! The bracket is holding. Hooray!"

I rewarded myself with a quick swim shouting, "*Tres* cool!"

Detouring over to Heart's Beach, we used the lights of Heart's house to guide us in so we could anchor for the night behind the reef. Everyone was very tired so we slept in and rested the next day. Later, taking advantage of a shift in wind direction, we sailed back to Puntarenas and our mooring at the yacht club.

Having completed the sailing portion of our itinerary with Anne and Doug, we all returned by bus to the capital of San Jose and a rented new Toyota sedan. Climbing northeast into the mountains, we found the charming town of Gracia where a red metal clad church was located on the main square. We were now in the coffee growing region where the climate is much cooler and drier than on either coast. It's an ideal place to tour and to live. Responding to the rumbling of our stomachs, we headed for a pizza restaurant nearby and were greeted by the owner, an Argentine ex-mining engineer. He had started a new family on a farm close by. He made a great pizza that fueled us and put us back in a traveling mood.

Sarchi, the next town, is famous for the production of the traditional brightly painted ox carts, the national symbol of rural life in Costa Rica. We were disappointed to find all the factories closed, but we stumbled on one whose gate was still open so we wandered in to look at the buildings and some old ox carts on the grounds. We were hoping to see this factory from another age.

A man came out of his house and said, "*Hola*, I am the owner, Jorge. Would you like to see my factory?"

Big smiles were our answer! "Oh, *si señor! Por Cierto*, for sure."

Jorge led us into a big shed filled with old machines connected by large, long belts to pulleys on skinny drive shafts suspended from the ceiling. Pulling a long lever, he engaged the large water wheel located in a small stream next to the building. In an instant, the whole place jumped to life with a roar. I couldn't contain the smile on my face. The spindle shafts and pulleys began moving at high rates of speed. By throwing other levers, Jorge made each machine in turn come to life, as saws, planers, sanders, and drills began whirring, ready to shape the pieces of wood needed to create an ox cart. These machines were manufactured in the mid 1800s in Massachusetts so seeing the whole factory was like arriving by time machine back into the early stages of the Industrial Revolution.

Doug said, "These machines are over one hundred years old and still function well in the 1990s. It's so amazing!"

"What a great place you have here! *Muchas Gracias*, Jorge, for your tour." I said. "*Adios*."

The active volcano Mt. Arenal was our next destination. It dominates the town of La Fortuna lying at its base. The whole town had turned out to celebrate its patron saint, St. Bosco, with a large colorful parade of flower covered floats. Amongst the crowd, we discovered Melvin who spoke a little English.

"We'd all like to see some toucans," I mentioned to him.

"I have a friend who has some in his back yard flying free during the day enjoying the mango and other fruit trees, but they sleep in cages during the night," he replied.

Melvin drove us there, and I was able to feed a toucan a piece of an orange. The toucan grabbed it with the end of his large bill, tossed it up in the air and caught it so it could then slide down his throat. Given their bright colors, large green circles around their black eyes, and oversized beaks, the whole effect was both comical and amazing.

"Close up, toucans appear to be clowns with wings," Doug remarked.

We had hoped to see an eruption of Arenal, but clouds impaired our view. Seeing posters advertising tours, I found a young man named Gambino who took people up the mountain on the side opposite La Fortuna where the sky should be clear. We signed up for a trip up the following night.

So off we went in an old van with about ten people. Soon we were driving up the back side of Arenal on a rough road carved into the lava and pumice, stopping about half the way up. As dusk descended, we hiked across the lava rock strewn ground, amazed to see tiny orange orchids peeking through the rocks. Hiking up the slope as close as we dared, our group was halted by the lava wall created by Arenal's last big eruption. We set up our cameras here and waited for something to happen.

Suddenly, the ground began to shake, and a low rumble grew into a roar that filled the now dark night sky with sparks and fire. Red hot boulders arced their way towards us. My mind was frantically attempting to calculate their trajectory to determine if we were safe. The boulders fell to the ground, tumbled down the steep sides of the volcanic cone and continued to bounce all the way down the mountain shooting red sparks in our direction as they tumbled.

Were we safe because of physics or was it Livengood Luck?

Ann, an avid amateur geologist, commented, "If I have to go, what better way than to be cast in molten rock like the inhabitants of Pompeii!"

Fortunately, our guide, Gambino, knew his stuff, and he was sure we would be safe. The rumbles, however, tipped Doug's tripod over, and my video camera automatically shut off limiting our ability to capture this remarkable event on film or tape.

On our drive back to La Fortuna, Gambino stopped the van in the darkness by the side of the road. He coaxed us to slip and slide down a muddy bank to the stream below where we immersed ourselves in the steaming hot, flowing water heated by the volcano.

"Does it get any better than this?" JoAnne exclaimed. "What a very remarkable evening. It's so relaxing lying here with the stars filling the sky above."

The experience was made all the more memorable when we discovered the little scratches on our behinds left by the fine pumice that was washed under our swimsuits by the swift current.

The next day while on the way to San Jose, we arrived at a fork in the road with no road signs to indicate which way to turn. Stopping the car to ponder the map, I got out hoping another driver would come along and be able to point us in the right direction.

We waved down the next vehicle, a Toyota Land Cruiser, "the National Vehicle of Costa Rica," and the driver told us to turn right. He then asked, "Have you seen Jerry Livengood from Illinois? He's my friend who's visiting Costa Rica."

I said, "No," but I remarked to JoAnne, Doug, and Anne, "What are the chances of finding a person in a small Central American country looking for someone with my same family name? Livengood is a little more unusual than Smith." We all laughed.

The drive took us across open, gentle hills of Bermuda grass that were scattered with tall Guanacaste trees, the national tree of Costa Rica that looked like giant umbrellas against the blue sky. At one point, a huge rapidly moving cloud of chartreuse came into focus as a breathtaking flock of several hundred cacophonous parrots flew overhead. Stopping for lunch in the middle of nowhere, we found a restaurant complete with perching toucans and good food. Carrying on, we motored though a teak forest planted and maintained as a renewable cash crop.

Arriving back at our now favorite Hotel Don Carlos, Anne and JoAnne opted to spend the next day exploring colonial homes and visiting the history museum, while Doug and I were up at 5:30 am ready to join a *"Rio Tropicales"* white water rafting trip on the Rio

Pacuare that flows down the eastern slope of the Continental Divide to the Caribbean Sea. Along the way, after stopping for a hearty breakfast of eggs with black beans and rice, we were trucked down a bumpy gravel road to the river's edge.

Blue inflatable rafts waited along with Geraldo who issued life jackets and paddles along with instructions saying, "Listen to your guides and paddle when they say to since your paddle power will help steer the raft."

Geraldo, an Olympic class kayaker, had the task of picking up any of us who might be thrown out of the raft in these class three to four rapids where large waves are produced when the water slams onto and shoots up and over huge boulders. Just as he had said, our paddle power helped keep the raft on course down the tongues of calmer water and kept us from being turned sideways in the rapids. Being sideways was to be avoided at all costs since the raft could overturn throwing us into the water and causing our bodies to be slammed into the rocks. Shimmering pools between rapids allowed us a chance to calm down and take in deep breaths while absorbing the beauty of the surroundings: the rocks in and along the river, tropical trees, and toucans, hawks, and other large birds flying overhead in this wild area. Moving through the rapids and pools, paddling our raft under waterfalls to cool off, and stopping for lunch at a site made and maintained by a local Indigenous tribe from the surrounding mountains were the highlights of our trip. Our guides left our extra food for their use creating the feeling that our trip had indeed left only a small "footprint" on the earth.

Soon JoAnne and I parted company at Hotel Don Carlos with Annie and Doug who set off to further explore Costa Rica. We, instead, took a plane back to Oakland to be with JoAnne's 89-year-old mom, Madeline, who was having trouble surviving her latest hospitalization.

As the family rallied around to encourage her recovery, Madeline's strong will and toughness brought her through. Spending two weeks at home with her reassured us and also gave us a chance to see friends and the opportunity for me to buy a radar set for the boat which we hauled back to Costa Rica.

When we returned to *Aurora*, I installed the radar on the mast at the yacht club in Puntarenas. Here we also met George, a retired policeman from Los Angeles and Akiko, his first mate from Japan, aboard their heavy weight cruising boat, *Camille*, a 38-foot Atkins. They had taken the offshore route past the Tehuantepec in Mexico. Over drinks and dinner, we learned about their passage. JoAnne and I both could feel the emotional impact on them of the voyage.

George began. "We were sailing *Camille* about one hundred miles offshore when the wind started to howl and waves intensified causing the boat to heel over, and then the mainsail ripped. I had to turn out to sea and run with the wind while using our motor to help steer the boat. Things were flying about in the cabin as *Camille* was catapulted off the huge waves. I had trouble keeping her on course when the engine's transmission gave out with a loud screech and then a resounding clunk. So we just kept being blown about and ended up about three hundred miles off Costa Rica. Both Akiko and I were terrified, but with some good luck, we had drifted toward Cocos Island where we spotted a group of fishing boats. One responded to our call for help and took us in tow. The five hundred dollars I gave them to tow us to Punta Arenas was the best money I ever spent!"

As he was telling his story, I kept thinking, I'm really glad I used the close to the beach tactic to transit the same area where our conditions were manageable.

"Wow, what a terrifying experience!" I said. "It's really every sailor's worst nightmare, not being able to control your boat when at the mercy of Mother Nature's most violent conditions. Thank God you made it back to Costa Rica since the next safe harbor south would have been the Galapagos Islands about five hundred miles away."

"Yeah, we decided we'd had it! Our bad luck brought us close to losing our lives. We've made the decision to sell *Camille*. We'd like to buy a farm near Quepos."

"Sounds like you made the right decision," I responded.

Their misfortune certainly validated my previous decision to use the "one foot-on-the-beach" method for navigating *Aurora* down the Central American Coast to Costa Rica.

While at anchor off Puntarenas, a small cut on my ring finger had become infected. I saw that a red line ran down the finger into my palm. Not a good sign. Remembering that a doctor and his wife owned a neighboring boat, I jumped into the dinghy and drove toward their boat. The doctor and his wife were just leaving so I held up my hand. He immediately saw the problem and told me to return later. Coming aboard, I shared introductions. They were Jim and Sue from Dana Point, California, while their young crew were Paul and Gloria from Seattle, Washington. After Jim gave me a course of Ampicillin, I stayed to talk.

"Our crew is looking to buy their own boat," said Jim. "This was really a test cruise for them, and they really like the cruising lifestyle."

"I might be able to help them find a good boat," I said. "My friends, George and Akiko, are selling their Atkins 38, *Camille*, a heavy duty cruising boat."

"Where are they located?" said Paul.

"They're moored at the yacht club," I said. "I know they'd be interested in talking with you. George monitors their VHF radio."

JoAnne and I were eating dinner at the club when George and Akiko came running over to our table.

"Have a seat, you look very excited," I said.

"Well, we just sold our boat to a nice young couple, Paul and Gloria," said George. "Thanks for telling them that *Camille* was for sale."

"Really, that's great!" I said. "Did you get enough money to buy the farm?"

"We sure did," said George. "We want you to come and visit us after we're settled in."

"You can bank on that," said JoAnne. "What a great reason to return to Costa Rica later next year."

"Great, let's keep in touch by radio," offered Akiko. "We'll have our High Seas Radio at the farm."

*****

JoAnne and I again sailed south off on our next adventure toward Quepos, stopping for rest at Bahia Herradura where the *Aurora* joined the replica vessel, *Pinta*, in the anchorage. We found that the young English crew from Bristol was very hospitable and invited us aboard. They introduced us to Janet and Libby, the "captain's floozies" (a nautical term meaning a promiscuous woman). The crew had been drafted as extras for the *1492* movie and had good things to say about the "stars."

After anchoring in Quepos Bay further down the coast, JoAnne and I dinghied into a dock where we were met by my younger sister, Margie, her friend Leslie, and my mom, Kathryn, who invited us to stay with them at Hotel Byblos in the jungle near Manuel Antonio Parque National. We tied the dinghy to the pier and accompanied our hosts to the luxury of soft beds, air conditioning, French cooking, a pool surrounded by jungle, and of course their great company. What a pronounced upgrade from our more Spartan life on *Aurora*!

In the evening at the pool located in a pocket carved out of the jungle, I called out, "These cicadas are so loud that they're drowning out our conversation."

Margie, ever the jokester, said, "What'd ya say?"

Living with the tropical birds was a new experience. They seemed to accept us to their environment as they swooped down to drink from the pool, flying past our heads dripping water on us as they flew off.

Unfortunately, our fun and comfort came at a price. Upon returning to the dock, we discovered our dinghy had been mortally wounded after being swept under the dock by winds, waves, and tides causing leaks in its flotation tubes from rubbing against the dock. Trying to stem these leaks became an ongoing task that taxed both my ingenuity and patience. Returning to *Aurora*, we found that she had been broken into and that some of JoAnne's jewelry had been stolen. Thank goodness, the thief did leave the radios and navigational gear essential to our continuing voyage. An interesting aside is that our homeowner's insurance in the USA covered the loss in Costa Rica.

Leaving Quepos Bay, we looked for a suitable anchorage nearby, but a rocky bottom foiled the anchor's first attempt to set. Heading to another spot off a beautiful beach, we hit an uncharted reef, stopping *Aurora* "dead in her tracks."

After I backed *Aurora* off the reef, she struck another rock with the back edge of the keel. We finally were able to move forward into deeper water. Initially, I was very concerned about whether the boat was sinking so I left JoAnne to check the bilge which was thankfully dry.

I called up, "The boat is okay. We're not sinking."

"But I'm not okay," JoAnne cried. JoAnne had been thrown into the steering wheel causing her teeth to make a nasty cut through her bottom lip. She was bleeding.

Seeing blood dripping down her chin, I grabbed a towel to mop it up and some ice to keep the swelling down. I drove *Aurora* into deeper water where we could stop and anchor safely. After giving JoAnne a big hug and making sure she didn't need stitches, I dove down under *Aurora* to inspect the damage. I saw that a six-inch chunk of fiberglass was missing on the front of the keel and there also was some damage to its thin trailing edge.

By radio, I alerted our Tico friend, Douglas, who worked at the Yacht Club in Puntarenas of our problem. He made an appointment for us at a local boatyard that constructed and repaired Fiberglas boats. There, I drove *Aurora* into the stands, mounted a cart that rode the rails laid under water. Secured to the stands, *Aurora* was winched up and pulled out of the estuary on the marine railway then deposited on land allowing her to dry out in the tropical heat. Checking out the damaged area, I found a small piece of shell imbedded in the mushy fiberglass.

The Fiberglas crew did a good job grinding out the damage to solid fiberglass and then applying many layers of resin-soaked fiberglass tape much like bandages to fill in and then cover the injuries. *Aurora*, now stronger than ever and with new bottom paint, was ready for another year or two in the sea.

JoAnne's wounds also healed after a while, but Mother Nature still wasn't so forgiving. Puntarenas was shaken by a 5.6 earthquake that caused its sand spit to wave and roll like the ocean that we could clearly see as well as feel. The plasticity of the sand spit gave the term "solid ground" a whole new meaning. My greatest fear was *Aurora* had fallen over, but she stayed steady on her stands.

The old saying, "Problems come in groups of three," seemed to be true for us this time! But, just maybe, Livengood Luck foiled the earthquake.

19

ISLA DEL COCO ADVENTURE

JoAnne was called back to California because her mother's rehabilitation in a nursing facility was not going well. At the same time, my Berkeley friend, Elmo, flew to Costa Rica as planned for our trip to Isla del Coco.

Located three hundred miles offshore to the west of central Costa Rica, the remote island totals fourteen square miles of volcanic terrain rising out of the Pacific Ocean forming a twin-peak mountain. I was attracted to the island's isolation and the reports of its beauty from other sailors. Early sailors were drawn to Isla del Coco by its fresh water, coconuts, and fresh fruit that they needed to replenish their meager stores and to prevent the scourge of scurvy. Later sailors, probably pirates or using the more gentlemanly term "privateers," had the same intent in mind, but with an added purpose. They needed a safe base away from the prying navies along the coast and a place to stash their surplus treasure.

Captain Edward Davis of the ship, *Bachelor's Delight*, along with his buccaneer surgeon-naturalist, Dr. Lionel Wafer, was on Isla del Coco between 1683 and 1702. Rumors spread that they had buried tons of loot somewhere on the island. Captain William Dampier, who succeeded Captain Davis, organized a much larger pirate enterprise involving as many as 1,000 men. These pirates terrorized the Pacific Coasts of South and Central America, adding more booty to the buried loot. The last depositor was Captain Bennett Graham who had been sent by the British Navy to survey the west coast of South America, but instead he diverted his ship *Devonshire* into the "pirates' trade." Finally three British "men of war" ships were sent from England to capture Captain Graham who in desperation gave a woman named Mary Welsh the map locating the shaft dug into a subterranean cave at the head of Wafer Bay. Mary Welsh and the map disappeared with the sweep of time, seemingly lost somewhere in the unwritten pages of history.

Preparing *Aurora* for the voyage, Elmo and I pulled the boat into the fuel dock at the Yacht Club where an English photographer asked me, "Could I use the boat as the back drop for photographing my model from Venezuela?"

Glancing over, I saw a beautiful, olive-skinned, dark-haired young woman.

I smiled at the photographer and said, "Our time is limited by needing to catch the outgoing tide, but if you hurry you can use the boat for your photo shoot."

"I'd like you to be in the pictures holding the steering wheel," he said.

"Ok, I'll raise the sails while *Aurora* remains tied to the dock so it appears that we're sailing." The "fee" for the use of the boat and my "bod" was to be copies of the pictures that the photographer promised to send.

I wildly thought, Wow, at last, I've found out what I want to do when I grow up. Months later reality set in when no photographs arrived so my incipient career as a model evaporated with the same lack of pretense with which it had begun.

Elmo and I followed the channel buoys as we motored down the estuary on the outgoing tide into the deeper water of the Golfo de Nicoya. A fair wind propelled us to Bahia Herradura where we again anchored among the Columbus ships.

"Elmo," I said, "it's like we've been transported back to the 1400s except that *Aurora* doesn't fit in, being made of fiberglass."

We were invited aboard the *Santa Maria* by Richard, the captain, and Peter, his first mate, for tea and a tour of their ship, a reconstruction of a sunken French fishing boat. It had been re-floated with a new superstructure added for its role in the movie *1492*. The original *Santa Maria* was one hundred-fifteen feet long, a Spanish Galleon of Noa design, a much heavier vessel with a very high stern. A bare breasted young lady carved on the bow sprit now rested quite appropriately next to the captain's bed in the aft cabin.

"This is really a small ship!" I told Elmo. "Can you imagine it sailing on the long trip back to England before the hurricane season in the Caribbean? The passage could be very uncomfortable since the *Santa Maria* has a rounded bottom with almost no keel to stabilize her motion. Life and work on the ship would be very difficult."

"Even a smaller boat like *Aurora* with its five thousand-pound keel would be much more stable on a voyage like that," observed Elmo.

After wishing the crew good luck, Elmo and I rowed back to *Aurora* to prepare for our own voyage and to barbecue a juicy steak for dinner.

*****

We sailed for most of our first day as a fair wind propelled us on our westerly course toward Isla del Coco, "Treasure Island." About five hundred previous expeditions had searched the island for pirate treasure without success.

I recalled Joe Nold, a sailing friend, telling me of his Isla del Coco experience. "In the 1950s a group of guys just out of college caught the 'treasure bug.' We secured a sailboat on the East Coast of the United States owned by the parents of one of the crew. We had a wonderful time sailing it south through the Caribbean and then west to the Panama Canal. After going through the canal, we sailed northwest out to the island. Equipped with shovels and picks, we spent a few weeks digging holes in likely places without finding even one doubloon. Finally our food supplies began to run low which forced us to sail back to Costa Rica. This grand adventure holds a mellow place in my mind."

A more notable visitor to the island was Franklin D. Roosevelt who came in 1935 on the Battleship USS *Huston*. On this, his third trip to the island, he caught a one hundred-ten-pound sailfish that he had mounted then hung in the White House. Another famous visitor, Jacques Cousteau, spent two months in 1987 researching the waters, being especially interested in the large schools of hammerhead sharks. It remains unclear why these huge fish are attracted to the island. Cousteau left behind carvings on a boulder indicating the name and dates of his expedition. These hammerhead shark schools continue to attract dive boats filled with brave divers who swim among the sharks. The sharks must have plenty to eat since divers do not appear to be on their menu.

Our trip to Isla del Coco was not predicated upon finding buried treasure, but on our way there we did land a large 25-pound yellowfin tuna which provided us with eight wonderful meals. In mid passage about one hundred miles offshore, *Aurora* became the floating home for five yellow-footed booby birds that roosted on the stainless steel bow pulpit. Moreover, by using the bow as their bathroom, the boobies not only mucked up their welcome but also ignored our invitations and pleadings for them to leave. Clearly stronger measures were needed, so "bird man" Elmo, clad only in his boxer shorts, charged forward with a boathook held like a lance imitating Don Quixote while slashing at the recalcitrant birds. Finally taking flight, they circled, attempting to land again, but "Sir" Elmo was there to beat them off. We could now attest that the learning curve of boobies was not very steep, but when faced with grit and determination, we humans could win out!

The next evening rewarded us with the sight of the smooth sea looking like undulating liquid glass reflecting deep blues, oranges, reds, and yellows as the sun set behind the clouds on the horizon. The changing patterns of colors drew our eyes into them, relieving the usual blank look of the sea extending to the horizon. Looking out from the cockpit was like viewing the sea through a fluid filled kaleidoscope. The following morning revealed the cloud capped, two-thousand-foot twin peaks of Isla del Coco rising out of the sea just where we expected them to. Feelings of "Wow, we made it!" played through our bodies while pride of accomplishment filled our minds.

Making our landfall in Wafer Bay, we joined eight other boats originating from many countries at anchor, the largest group of cruisers we had seen since Mexico. We were awakened from an early morning nap by a radio call for help from a Swiss woman whose son had scalded himself by knocking over a pot of hot water while playing with a soccer ball in the cabin. His mother's first response was to drop him overboard into the water to cool down his skin which was great first aid. We responded by launching our dinghy and taking over "Second Skin" bandages to cover his burns, all the while talking with the young mother who was stark naked.

Later, a doctor working on a shark dive boat returned her radio calls and took over the boy's treatment.

Peter, on the cruising boat, *Phoenician*, stopped by to give us a quick orientation to the island and told us that a B-17 bomber from WWII had crashed just below the saddle between the two peaks crowning the island.

"A good trail leads up the mountain to the wreckage," he said. "Look at this ammunition box containing live 50-caliber machine gun shells that I scavenged from the wreckage."

Elmo, a chemical engineer, expressed concern. "You know, these old shells could be unstable and would explode with disastrous results. You best treat them with care."

"Thanks for the warning!" said Peter, closing the box.

Elmo Cocos Island

We dinghied into the beach and followed a stream inland to an inviting pool where our salt incrusted skin welcomed soap and cool fresh water. We let our bodies "melt" into the delicious liquid. This bathing experience was a real luxury. *Aurora's* limited fresh water supplies inhibited our ability to stay really clean.

On our return to the boat, we found that anchoring over a narrow strip of sand in the middle of Wafer Bay had become more tenuous when the anchor chain wrapped itself around a rock and had gotten lost in the coral that lined the sides of the bay. Fortunately for us, Roger, on the English boat, *Freelance*, volunteered to untangle the mess while Elmo and I repositioned *Aurora* by pulling in the extra chain. Roger reset the anchor in the sand as we adjusted the scope of the chain so that the boat would remain safely over the sand.

"Thank you, Roger," I said. "I see that you're a real English gentlemen!"

With our home secure, Elmo and I decided the next day to hike up to the bomber site. The words "taxing" and "exhausting" best described the five-mile climb from sea level up to 2,000 feet on a steep, but well marked trail. Spectacular views of the sea, waterfalls, and nesting fairy terns flying through the trees on the ridge distracted me from feeling the pain of my aching muscles. Taking a newly cut trail into the jungle toward the crash site was tougher going, but water from a cool stream slaked our thirst.

B-17 Wing

Suddenly, large pieces of aluminum littered the floor of the jungle as wings, the fuselage, and four huge radial Pratt and Whitney engines emerged from the tangled green background of trees and vines. Climbing through the wreckage, I found the engine control levers with brown Bakelite handles in the remains of the cockpit, a 50-caliber machine gun and shells on the fuselage. Near the engines, I could see the propellers twisted and crumbled by their impact with the ground.

Sadness dampened our excitement when we realized that a number of young men had lost their lives here just as they had lost their bearings, wandering three hundred miles off their original course to fly down the coast of Central America. The crew had been assigned to take this B-17 to Brazil and then across the Atlantic to Africa to join the fight against Hitler's Nazi armies led by Rommel in North Africa.

The walk back down the mountain was a breeze for Elmo, the experienced hiker, while for me, the novice, the backs of my knees and legs were screaming and cramping with pain. Sliding down the trail on my butt helped to relieve the agony. What kept me going besides gravity was knowing that the pool of cool water awaited us in the river at the bottom. Water was indeed the universal solvent for dissolving pain.

When we were settled back on *Aurora*, rain came, first as a shower then a deluge, that washed off the salt and dirt on the deck and sunshade. I chanted, "A clean ship is a happy ship." The surplus water allowed us to fill the fresh water tanks to overflowing, a great luxury.

Later, new neighbors from the San Francisco Bay Area, George, Brenda, and friend Scott, came over to say hello. They were sailing the aluminum hulled *Avatar* and had completed their eleven-day voyage of 1,600 miles from Socorro Island off the tip of Cabo San Lucas, Mexico. After talking about their custom boat designed by San Franciscan Gary Mull, built in Sebastopol, California, they mentioned liking lobster and needing two strong steel fishing leaders that I could supply. Those two leaders would prevent their catch from biting through the line and were later exchanged for two lobsters which Elmo and I relished.

Later on I mentioned to Scott that, "I haven't been able to find or even catch a lobster."

"You know it isn't that hard," he said. "They hide in the rocks, usually in a hole with their head looking outwards. Come toward them from behind and just stab them with your fish spear."

"Sounds easy enough to me," I said with hope.

The next day following Scott's instructions, I dove near the boat and caught three lobsters, the largest one by using my gloved hand.

Holding it up, I yelled, "Elmo, look at what I have."

"Wow," he said, "my mouth is already watering!"

Swimming to the boarding ladder, I said, "Grab them so they won't get away."

Lobsters At Last

Finally, I completed a cruiser's rite of passage by capturing my own lobsters! This experience gave birth to more feelings of accomplishment and to the anticipation of eating luscious lobster salads and the chewing of succulent, buttery lobster bits so they might slide down my throat into my eager stomach.

Soon our social calendar was filled with cake and wine on *Avatar*. Later, we enjoyed Elmo's baked pineapple upside down cake, as we watched my recent sailing videos. The video footage displayed *Aurora* in motion while the boat herself was rocking and rolling in response to incoming waves. These two out of sequence motions made our guests a bit queasy.

"My stomach can't take any more of this. Stop the show!" Brenda pleaded. "I need to go to solid ground so my body can stabilize."

"Okay, we're out of here," I exclaimed. "All dinghies ashore!"

A hike ashore resolved the sea sickness issue. All five of us scampered up the stream, over and around a jumble of large boulders. Then we suddenly saw the stream leap off a sixty-foot cliff creating a waterfall that splashed down into the large pool at its base. Tiny droplets of water filled the air, forming rainbows where shafts of sunlight penetrated the jungle. Everyone dove or jumped into the pool and began splashing merrily. Swimming over to the edge of the waterfall, I allowed the water to crash onto my head and shoulders. It was indeed a delicious experience that beat out the residual tension in and cooled off my tropically heated body.

In coming years, we all would talk about this wonderful moment in time being so special and one that significantly enhanced our connection to Isla del Coco and to this planet.

20

RETURN TO MAINLAND COSTA RICA

All too soon, it was time to leave Isla del Coco and to return to mainland Costa Rica. First, Elmo and I circumnavigated the island with our eyes focused on the numerous waterfalls billowing down the cliffs into the sea while we were sailing just beyond the foam of the breaking waves that surrounded large volcanic boulders. The bright green trees covering the island created the illusion of a giant green emerald shimmering in a sea of brilliant blue water. Elmo and I felt fortunate seeing this unique microcosm where nature does her work with little if any interference from man. We anchored in Bahia Iglesias hoping to hike up through the jungle to the waterfall emerging from a tree-covered cliff high above, but one look at the incoming waves crashing on the beach persuaded us that a dinghy landing would be foolhardy and dangerous.

After a luscious lobster salad lunch, we raised anchor and began our voyage toward Bahia Drake on the Costa Rican Coast. Dark clouds on the horizon warned us to watch the developing squall being shown on *Aurora's* new radar as an encircling monster. Fortunately, it was neither too large nor carried too much wind to be a threat. The radar was proving to be a good local weather forecasting device by showing where the storm cells were located and their direction of travel. Using this information, I could choose to dodge the more violent cells that might have done damage to *Aurora* and her crew.

After sailing smoothly for two days, we arrived in Bahia Drake and anchored *Aurora* where Francis Drake had rested and re-provisioned *Golden Hind* on his voyage around the world in

1579. He started his voyage from England with five ships but was down to one, the *Golden Hind*, after losing the others to storms rounding South America or to wood rot. He had been busy sacking cities in Chile and Peru and capturing a Spanish treasure galleon that held eighty pounds of gold and twenty-six tons of sliver. His exploits earned him a knighthood in 1580 when he returned to Plymouth, England.

"You know, I feel honored to be sailing in such an adventurer's wake," I said to Elmo. "Just think about continuing to sail around the world in just one small ship. Imagine the confidence in his skills and those of his crew that he must have felt."

"I've always admired Drake's accomplishments," Elmo said. "His defeat of the Spanish Armada in 1588 really saved England, capping his long list of daring deeds."

Drake's Bay is a large open bay now ringed by a linear community of houses strung out along the beach that was backed by the jungle spilling down the hills. There, we found a small store with a telephone on the front porch facing out into the bay. I just had to call JoAnne.

"How's your mom?" I said when JoAnne answered. "Boy, it's great to hear your voice. You sound good. Can I assume that she's on the mend?"

"Wow, I wasn't expecting a call from you," JoAnne exclaimed. "You must be back on the mainland. Mom is doing much better and I'm feeling great, except I'm missing you."

"Yeah, I'll second that motion. Elmo and I are at Drake's Bay and will be sailing back to Puntarenas tomorrow. Were you able to buy the new refrigeration system for *Aurora*? The old one finally gave out," I asked.

"Yeah, I bought it. I'm returning on Wednesday," said JoAnne. "I'll see you at the airport!"

"Great! I've been storing up lots of kisses and more than a big squeeze for you."

Being apart was difficult because we enjoyed spending our time on *Aurora* together.

Exploring along the shore, Elmo and I found a small stream flowing out into the bay. It looked deep enough for the dinghy, so we headed upstream into the overhanging jungle. Twisting the dinghy among large boulders, we soon found our way blocked by a small waterfall.

"I can imagine the crew from the *Golden Hind* rowing up here and placing their water casks right there under the falls," I observed. "That flat rock would keep the casks upright while the falls would fill them with pure, fresh water."

"Wow, I can almost feel I'm back there with them," Elmo exclaimed.

After sailing back to Puntarenas again, Elmo and I then bused up the mountain to San Jose where we stayed at our "adopted home," the Hotel Don Carlos.

The next day, we rented a car and drove to the airport. We met JoAnne along with the precious refrigeration system that she had shepherded through customs. Our smiles reflected our joy seeing each other again after two weeks of being separated from our normal life of 24-hour "togetherness" on *Aurora*. Long hugs expressed our longing for each other. It was great to have JoAnne back in my arms.

Leaving the airport, we drove northeast into the mountains above San Jose to Santa Barbara to stay at Finca Rosa Blanca, a new Bed & Breakfast, designed and built by Ruben (the Cuban) an ex-cruiser and restaurateur from Berkeley, California. My sister and mom had given it rave reviews after their stay.

Looking it over, Elmo gushed, "To say it is spectacular would be an understatement. Its design does away with straight lines and rectangles and instead employs curves, circles, and ellipses for walls, windows, and even doors. The use of Costa Rican hardwood inside brings out their many deep colors that enhance the overall effect."

The honeymoon suite is located in a tower overlooking the coffee plantation. The tower is accessed by climbing steps cut into a tree trunk while a long curving tree branch serves as the hand rail. Added to all of the beauty, Ruben, a gourmet chef, a consummate host, and a tour arranger made our stay unique. Our lively conversations took him back to his earlier life in Berkeley and our mutual friends.

*****

Following Ruben's suggestions, we set off in two days to explore the coffee growing areas on the slopes of Volcan Irazu. Here the smaller coffee trees, the size of large bushes, are grown under taller deciduous trees that provide shade for slowing the ripening of the beans. The soil and climatic conditions of each plantation create unique flavors and aromas that excite coffee connoisseurs. Costa Rican coffee is ranked among the best in the world.

We made our way to the small town of Turrialba where we found a small hotel with clean rooms at a low price. A marimba band performed on the main floor as we ate dinner. After a large Tico breakfast of eggs, toast, black beans and rice, and of course good Costa Rican coffee, we were on the road to Guayabo National Monument, one of the country's most important archeological sites. A bubbling stream runs through the site and connects with a system of aqueducts that direct the water to cisterns. Cobblestone streets lead to the foundations of ancient round houses and mounds. Brilliant, neon blue morpho butterflies flitted about while proving to be elusive subjects for my camera.

While driving back through the forested mountains to San Jose, Elmo and I shared our impressions of our time together with JoAnne.

"What stands out in my mind," said Elmo, "was our experience at Isla del Coco. It was a thrill to explore an isolated island, the waterfalls, hiking to the B-17, finding and eating those luscious lobsters. I felt like we entered another world, remote from everywhere, where nature prevails. I couldn't ask for more than that!"

"Yeah, all of those sights and sounds flooded my perceptions," I said. "I felt awed being in the wake of Sir Francis Drake, imagining standing beside him taking in the same vistas. We had a unique experience. I hope that sharing the photographs with JoAnne will excite her imagination, too."

The time had come for Elmo to end his month's stay in Costa Rica.

The next day after taking Elmo to the airport, JoAnne and I drove to the Butterfly Farm in Alejuela not far from San Jose. A young man, who had stayed on in the country after completing his Peace Corps tour, developed the farm that raises and then ships butterflies in their pupae stage all over the world. Being with the butterflies in their environment of jungle foliage inside large screened enclosures was a unique experience since they sometimes landed on our arms or head. We became just another accepted part of their environment. Having these fragile, beautifully colored creatures so close at hand helped us feel that our spirits could also soar. A Tico, short for Costa Rican, biologist walked with us telling us all about them, deepening our understanding and enjoyment.

Arriving back on *Aurora*, we entered another reality taking care of our "house." It was time to install the new refrigeration system. Removing the broken compressor and all its components was the first task. Installing the new system was not difficult since the electrical wiring and holes for the Freon tubes already existed.

As I switched it on, I called out, "Hooray, it works," but its continued operation caused the Freon lines to frost over and the compressor to draw way too much electrical current. The next morning, Harold, a refrigeration expert who spoke English, came to the boat and provided the needed answer when he found that the factory set pressure of the Freon coolant was too high, thus causing the compressor to work too hard. Adjusting the pressure solved all the problems. *Aurora* was fully functional again.

Now it was on to the dinghy that had resisted all my efforts to patch the holes rubbed through its inflation tubes by the dock in Quepos. Because the dinghy was our essential commute vehicle from the boat to shore and back, JoAnne and I decided to order a new white Avon fiberglass bottomed dinghy from West Marine in California to be shipped to us in Puntarenas. The dinghy arrived in the custody of a customs agent. He was here to be sure that we took possession of it and intended to use the dinghy as part of *Aurora's* equipment. All of these official procedures were necessary to allow the dinghy to be imported into Costa Rica, free of import duties. One good thing about being designated a *"Yate en Transito"* is having custom duties on replacement equipment waived since that equipment is necessary for continuing our voyage. Over time this designation would save us many hundreds of dollars on customs duties in many different countries!

It was time to test all our new equipment. JoAnne and I sailed *Aurora* north in the Golfo de Nicoya where we anchored in a small bay surrounded by trees, nary a house in sight. Soon, another sailboat from England anchored near us. Ever the hostess, JoAnne dispatched me to invite its owner to dinner. Geoffrey dinghied over with a bottle of wine. Relaxing in the cockpit, we found out that before crossing the Atlantic Geoff had spent a summer transiting the canals and rivers of France. His mast was secured horizontally on the boat using crossed 2x4s to support it. He could now go under the many old bridges along his way.

"One day I pulled into a small town, tying up to bollards along main street," Geoff said. "Suddenly, a waiter from the café across the street walked over and asked me what I'd like to drink and eat."

"Amazing," I said. "Sitting here in the Golfo de Nicoya, it's hard to imagine. How were the canals?"

"Well, I loved the slow pace and being so in touch with the land and the people along the tow paths and in the towns," he said.

"You know, Karl," said JoAnne, "canalling sounds really attractive to me. Imagine traveling on the water without having to worry about heeling!"

"Yeah, it sounds great to me to," I said. "Let's do it someday."

*****

In the morning, we sailed on to Isla San Lucas, home of an abandoned prison. On the island, we joined a group of *bomberos* (firefighters) from Puntarenas who showed us through the prison dormitories decorated with prisoner paintings of Pele, the Brazilian soccer star, and some very beautiful, dark-haired, voluptuous women. One of the *bomberos* whispered that the paintings were made with the prisoner's blood. Another one of the *bomberos* removed a metal disk in the courtyard. A dark chamber was revealed below with a small metal ladder descending into it. Climbing down with some of the firefighters, I immediately felt the hot, stifling air adding to the oppression of the low concrete ceiling that made this "hole" a terrible place of punishment for prisoners who broke the rules. I was glad to escape from the claustrophobic space. After "spending time in prison," we all headed down to a beckoning beach for a swim. We also played an impromptu "football game" using a gourd for a ball. Just behind the beach were small houses where trusted prisoners had lived until the prison was moved to the mainland two years earlier.

"Some of these men cried when they were told that they would have to leave," a firefighter told us.

"Yeah, this is such a beautiful tropical island," JoAnne said. "I can understand the prisoners' reluctance to leave."

"Being held in a regular prison would be especially difficult for them," I said.

Back in Puntarenas, we accepted the firefighters' invitation to tour their firehouse. Greeted with shouts of *"Buenos dias Karlos y JoAnna,"* and warm smiles, we walked up the driveway. We learned that in Costa Rica, the firefighting establishment is paid for by the insurance companies to protect the property of their policy holders. The firefighters treated us to lunch and also gave us "Africanized" bee honey that the firemen had extracted from the walls of a house after they had killed the swarm. Down the hall in the firehouse, they showed us photos and badges of firefighters from all over the world who had stopped in for a visit.

"We firefighters are informal members of the fraternity of all firefighters and are welcomed by other firefighters wherever we travel," said Jorge proudly.

The warm welcome made us feel that we were at least honorary firefighters. Actually, I had been a volunteer fireman in my teens so perhaps I deserved that status.

*****

Our six months visas about to expire, JoAnne and I sat drinking wine in the cockpit of *Aurora* and looked back on our adventures in Costa Rica.

"What impresses me most," said JoAnne, "is the warmth shown by many of its people, the shop keepers, folks on the street responding to our questions about where we were and where was the next place we wanted to go."

"I feel privileged to have experienced the country's natural wonders protected by the good intentions of so many," I said. "Who could forget Mt. Arenal showing off her power? What about all the birds—there are more birds in Costa Rica than all of North America."

"Yeah, what about those monkeys scampering all over," said JoAnne. "I feel so lucky being in a country that values the natural environment and takes steps to preserve it. You don't see the mega-resorts here that we saw in Mexico."

"I feel special being able to live my dream with you and our wonderful *Aurora*," I said. "Life for me can't get better than this." Hugs came next.

21

SOUTH TO PANAMA

It was the middle of May, 1992, when *Aurora* was ready to head south. The tropical summer was upon us. We would sail along the remaining coast of Costa Rica and day hop into northern Panama before reaching the Panama Canal in southern Panama. Stopping in Bahia Drake, we met Canadians Heinz and Zan, aboard *Inzan Tiger*, a large custom-made sport fishing boat that took luxury to a new level with its huge interior spaces. Three ice makers supported their drinking habits as did the fifty cases of beer stowed in the bilge. Heinz came from Germany. His almost oversized personality and physique didn't quite fit with being an engineer setting up breweries around the world. Heinz came by his preference for beer honestly and was happy to share his wealth with us. Zan was a blonde, spiked-haired woman from Eastern Europe who projected a sense of being an Amazon while smiling in an engaging way. We agreed to see each other again farther south at Golfito.

Pacific white-sided dolphins surfing on our bow wave accompanied us sailing out to Isla del Cano. The joy flowing from their smiling faces and acrobatics was infectious and made us feel happy to be alive. These playful creatures treated *Aurora* like a big water toy. They dove under and hid behind the boat and then darted out to amaze us and to impress each other. The blue transparent water enhanced their performances. We clapped and whistled in appreciation.

Anchoring in a bay, JoAnne and I donned masks and snorkels. While skin diving in the clear water over coral reefs, we discovered a diverse population of angelfish, wrasse, sgt. majors, and small neon blue fish swimming among the hard and soft colorful coral branches. JoAnne excitedly pointed to the most vibrant fish in the scene below us that continually changed as a blur of shapes and colors undulated in the water. Coming up for a breath, we held hands and exclaimed, "Wowzer!" The wonderful scene we witnessed, reaffirmed our belief that Costa Rica's conservation efforts were being successful, an impressive realization in our rapidly polluting world.

After a long day's sail past Corcovado National Park, we reached the Golfo Dulce in southern Costa Rica. Entering the gulf through an intense band of rain squalls and lightning strikes, we approached the town of Golfito, one of the wettest places on earth. Following the recommendation made by a fellow cruiser, we anchored *Aurora* in front of Hotel Las Gaviotas. It would be a nice place to hang out with a clean pool, showers, a restaurant, and an ample bar. All of these amenities were offered to us by the smiling and helpful owners.

Inzan Tiger arrived the next day. JoAnne and I dinghied over to her. Heinz greeted us clad only in his briefest of briefs, sporting a bright orange tiger decal in a strategic spot. This gave us a greater understanding of the meaning of their boat's name.

"You've arrived at the right time," Heinz said with gusto. "We have a surplus of fish! Welcome aboard!"

"You guys are much better fishermen than we are," I said. "We'd be happy to take some off your hands." Meeting generous people like Heinz is among the many benefits of cruising.

"Why don't you come back later for a drink and some yellowtail tuna sushi?"

"We'd love to," JoAnne said, smiling.

Returning to *Aurora*, we transferred half of a 40-pound wahoo to our refrigerator. Its white meat would taste ever so good barbecued for our evening meal.

The next morning we joined Zan and Heinz in their fiberglass dinghy and toured Golfo Dulce in style. We stopped by to say hello to Captain Tom and his family who were living in an old gray PT boat from WWII. Walking up the beach, we met Tom who was clad in ripped jeans and sporting long white hair and beard.

"Welcome aboard," he said. "It's amazing when I beached this old boat ashore 38 years ago, I only paid twenty-five dollars for the property."

"What a deal!" we all exclaimed.

"My family feels it's great being members of the Golfito community," Tom continued. A deep tan made it hard to differentiate Tom from the locals.

The following day, Heinz drove us in his larger Boston Whaler skiff, powered by a 60 HP outboard motor, up the Rio Cato now filled with rushing brown water that had accumulated from last night's tropical downpour. Dodging logs, floating islands of plants, and other debris, we all focused our attention on the river. Toucans watched us from the jungle that lined the banks. Pink and white roseate spoonbills were fishing along the shore.

Coming to a cable ferry that was crossing the river, we stopped at a restaurant next to the landing where we washed down a fresh shrimp dinner with Tico beer.

We met Melvin, a local, who was cleaning a huge robalo that he had just caught in the river.

"Hey, you guys should continue further up stream where there are alligators and other wildlife," he said.

"Great, thanks for the advice," Heinz said.

So off we went. Rounding a corner, we came upon a stranded *panga* that had filled with water. Heinz used his bilge pump to empty the boat of water so that the family inside could head upstream to their corn patch. Further on we saw the swish of a large alligator's tail as it dove under our boat. Another alligator rushed into the water from his sunning spot on shore. A brave otter joined him, swimming into the mix and appearing to survive the experience.

Coming downstream, we approached the family of farmers who waved us over and gave us a bag of fresh corn.

"*Muchas gracias, amigos,*" I said.

"Looks like one kindness is being repaid by another," Zan added.

Pushed by the current, we moved faster through the water and we also knew the course of the river. Soon we were out into the Golfo and back on *Aurora*.

JoAnne and I left Heinz and Zan and dinghied over to Hotel Las Gaviotas. We met Tom and Ursula while having a drink at the bar. They were an attractive couple in their fifties from Marina Del Rey, California. They were staying at the hotel. Realizing that we were cruisers, Tom and Ursula excitedly began asking questions about the preparations we had made for our voyage. They were planning a similar trip after retiring in five years. This and other conversations like it gave us a chance to share some of our knowledge gained over the past few years.

The next morning, we met Tom and Ursula on the dock and began a hike up a mountain road to gain a more expansive view of the Golfo Dulce. Walking along, Tom revealed that he was an airline pilot who really wanted to slow down his life.

"The cruising life is a great choice for that, because you can definitely use your navigation skills on a boat," I said with encouragement.

"I'm from Sweden and work in the movie industry as a set designer," Ursula said. "There is a lot of pressure in my work, too!"

"You know, your blonde hair and blue eyes had me thinking you were Swedish," said JoAnne. "It's great to meet interesting people like you two as we travel!"

Up the hill, we found Miss Betty tending her garden in front of an open wooden house perched on the side of the steep hill. Her brown crinkled face lit up with a smile as she invited us in to her house. Within minutes of our sitting down in her living room her life story came spilling out.

"I arrived in Golfito twelve years ago from Alaska with my husband, Bert. We decided to stay on in the warmth of the tropics while soaking in the beautiful solitude of this isolated location. It's been lonely since Bert passed away a few years ago. I'm glad you stopped by. It's great to have company like you who speak English."

"Gazing out over the water and the surrounding lush jungle, a sense of peace enters my mind and heart, making me want to stay longer too," JoAnne said.

"Betty, you seem to have created your own paradise here," I said. "I also feel like staying."

Tom and Ursula sat silently, mesmerized by the view.

*****

The reality that our Costa Rica six-month visas were running out surfaced again. We needed to continue on to Panama. It was time to get serious about preparing for the 350-nautical mile voyage south to the Panama Canal. After hauling enough fuel and food on to *Aurora*, we checked out of Costa Rica with immigration and customs Officers.

Leaving Golfito in the early morning, we sailed in mellow seas and winds southwest along a peninsula that forms the border of Costa Rica and Panama. Memories of our stay in Costa Rica again flooded my head and heart. Who could ever forget our night on the slopes of Mt. Arenal when the volcano exploded sending red hot rocks shooting into the air? Also what about the ridiculously large bills of the toucans sticking out of the jungle cover as their beady black eyes tracked our every movement. And of course, the smiles and laughter of friendly Costa Ricans as they welcomed us to their country.

Rounding Punta Burica at the end of the peninsula into Panamanian waters, our lousy fishing luck began to change. A 30-inch yellowfin tuna struck the lure and arced into the air before biting through our "invisible" nylon leader, escaping. To remedy this defect, I substituted a new steel leader. As a result a ten-pound, 30-inch iridescent blue and gold spotted sierra mackerel was caught and could *not* escape. Our improving luck was due to some good advice on finding the right lure given to me by Rob, a fisherman-owner of a small resort back at Drake's Bay, Costa Rica.

We turned *Aurora* south toward Isla Paridita, inhabited by homesteaders Elan, Bella and Natalie Stern whom we'd heard about on the Cruiser's Radio Net. We saw a cloud of islands ahead of us that covered the horizon, making identifying the right island a more complex problem. Up to now, our passage along the Central American coast featured only a few islands, making navigation easier. We luckily found an important clue—a sailboat anchored off their Isla Paridita. We headed toward it.

Seeing us anchor across the bay, nine-year-old Natalie and her dad, Elan, dinghied over to welcome us.

"Hi, welcome to our small world," he said, extending his hand. "We bought the island you see across the bay in August 1991. Would you like to join us for dinner tomorrow afternoon?"

"Sure, we'll bring our fresh caught sierra and wine to add to the meal," JoAnne said.

Their homestead on Isla Paridita was located across from a beautiful, white sand beach on the larger Isla Parrida. While taking a walk on that beach watching out for alligators, JoAnne and I met Francisco and Theodoro tending their garden plots hacked out of the jungle.

"*Buenos Dias. Como Estas*? What are you growing?" we asked.

"*Hola*. We're growing bananas, yucca, vegetables, and rice," said Theodoro. "Come visit our homes."

Their *palapa* style houses were located on the next bay where the simplicity of their lifestyle became apparent. In this warm climate, only shelter from the rain is necessary while many essential foods such as mangos, bananas, and coconuts grow wild in the jungle, and the surrounding seas produce many types of fish. Later, we learned from Elan that Francisco and Theodoro had helped build their *palapa* structures. They offered to help Elan when needed and often shared monthly boat trips to the city of David to buy staples such as soap, coffee, sugar, wine, and cooking oil.

The next day we arrived by dinghy on the Sterns' white sand beach. Noisy barking and fervent tail wagging of Fifty, their mixed breed German Shepherd, greeted us. We began a week of making new friends who were living their lives in this unique tropical island environment off the coast of Northern Panama. Their life here was quite different from my own homesteading experience in the Trinity Mountains of Northern California in the 1970s.

Bella, Elan, Natalie

On Isla Paridita, the Stern homestead occupied a small clearing just behind the beach in a corner of their mile-long by a quarter to half mile-wide jungle-covered island. They built a native style coconut palm pole main house. The house had bamboo side walls, open windows, a dirt floor, corrugated iron roof, and a raised concrete cooking area using a wood fueled fire. A concrete floored bathroom with a flush toilet and shower completed the main house.

Another adjacent pole structure covered with palm fronds served as a dining/living/work room with a loft above and hammocks strung between the poles. Here, Elan used an iron spike in the ground to husk coconuts and then whack off their tops with a machete to expose the coconut meat. Two noisy green parrots occupying a spot near the entrance sometimes took hurtful nips out of unwary hands like mine that I offered in friendship. A large garden and chicken house were nearby along with a fire ring used to burn paper garbage. All waste food was being given to the chickens to be converted into wonderful, deep yellow-orange yolked eggs.

Our dinner with the Sterns was memorable. We enjoyed broiled sierra as we delved into talking about our past lives.

"Bella and I grew up in Israel," said Elan. "We both served as intelligence agents in the defense force before immigrating to California. We lived in Santa Barbara before buying our Mason 43 sailboat to sail in the Pacific. We enjoyed cruising to the Channel Islands off Santa Barbara. After a year or two, we decided to sail south so here we are in Northern Panama."

"Due to the promised sale of our boat, we rushed the building of our *palapa* house and the moving in process," Bella continued. "The potential buyer dropped out, leaving us short of cash here in 'paradise' which lacks drinking water in the dry season and features daily attacks of insects as the sun sets."

Listening to their story, we came to understand that young Natalie's education was being neglected by her parents. Other children were living too far away to become her playmates. Natalie had to invent her own fun with Fifty who was her constant companion.

The next day, a couple of local fishermen anchored in a neighboring bay came over asking to borrow a diving mask from Elan. These guys mentioned that they had lots of shrimp which they'd like to share. We dinghied over to their boat and offered to trade a bottle of brandy and a pound of coffee for some shrimp. They filled a plastic grocery bag full of shrimp and then another bag of red snapper was thrown in as a bonus giving us two more great meals. These generous men were in a happy mood, glad to talk with an American who spoke some Spanish.

I decided to help Elan with some work around his homestead the next day. I dinghied over and picked up Natalie, and took her back to *Aurora* for some "Grandma time" with JoAnne who had her art supplies, charcoal pencils, colored pencils, watercolors and brushes at the ready on the salon table. Soon, Natalie was laughing and having fun creating drawings of her companion, Fifty, and her tropical home.

When I returned to the island, Elan and I talked over coffee as he laid out plans for his clearing back more of the jungle near their house. Hearing the chickens' loud squawking in the jungle sent Elan for his gun yelling, "It must be a boa constrictor." Accompanied by Fifty, we ran toward the sound. Sure enough, his favorite rooster was being squeezed to death by a six-foot-long snake. The flock of chickens stood around in a circle watching and clucking, proving that chickens are not the smartest of creatures.

Elan shot, killing the snake. Then I uncoiled its grip on the rooster. "This chicken will be fine to eat. The snake hadn't begun swallowing it," I said.

Elan agreed. "Let's have it for dinner!" he said.

Returning to the house, Elan cut up the snake, dropping pieces in a big pot of boiling water to cook for Fifty's dinner. I plucked and cleaned the chicken for our dinner. These actions fit in with what I'd learned when homesteading—let nothing go to waste.

Dinghying back to *Aurora*, I retrieved smiling Natalie and Jo-Anne and brought them back to the island in time to prepare dinner. In the main house, Natalie proudly showed us her drawings and paintings that captured her impressions of the island. Bella and JoAnne began cooking dinner over an open fire. After having more than a few drinks to combat the effect of the sweltering heat, the cooks sang along with R&B music played on a cassette recorder. Gales of laughter followed.

As we enjoyed dinner a sudden rain shower passed over along with a loud explosion. We watched in awe as lightning hit a palm tree at the corner of the island about 30 feet from our table. The blinding flash caused all of us to duck down and hide under the table.

"I hope lightning only strikes once," I exclaimed with my heart pounding.

After dinner, it was time to say our goodbyes. I saw the tears in Natalie and JoAnne's eyes as they hugged each other. I, too, had a few tears as I parted with Elan, my compatriot, with whom I shared so much. Bella and JoAnne had a swaying embrace to the music in the background. As we reluctantly left the island in the rain, we promised we'd see the Sterns again someday. It was time for us to journey towards the Panama Canal.

Later that night when we were aboard *Aurora*, JoAnne reflected on what she had observed on the island.

"It was clear to me that Bella is drinking so much that she is either unable or perhaps unwilling to home school Natalie who seems to spend most of her time in the company of Fifty. At nine years old, she is obviously missing important building blocks of her basic education."

"Yeah, you're right," I agreed. "She is such an alive and intelligent girl. I hope she can overcome this neglect. Both Elan and Bella truly love her which does count of a lot in her young life. But you have to wonder if this island is the paradise they had hoped for? Or perhaps reality has intruded into their dreams overcoming their positive expectations."

*****

Voyaging further south, we stopped at a number of uninhabited island anchorages, occasionally accompanied by a native fishing boat. Our favorite anchorage, Bahia Honda, is in a larger bay indented into the mainland surrounded by mountains where the scars left by slash and burn agriculture stand out against the shimmering lush greens of the jungle. Bahia Honda is about seven hours by fast boat from the nearest town of any size. A village has grown up on a small central island in the bay whose tiny store sells essentials such as boxed milk, eggs, canned meats, and vegetables. A traveling priest visits the church once a month. A mobile health clinic on a boat was dispensing shots to the kids while we were there.

We anchored in a side bay near a small farm that was growing rice on the steep hillsides. Soon after anchoring *Aurora*, we were visited by a procession of dugout canoes bearing mangoes, papayas, bananas, eggs, and coconuts offered in trade for our sugar, laundry detergent, rice, tee shirts, and hats. The last two canoes to visit paddled up to *Aurora*. A powerfully built, nut-brown man flashed a wide smile. Domingo introduced himself and his three shy teenage daughters as we traded back and forth. A huge papaya, the size of a big watermelon, was too large for the galley so we stored it on deck. We conversed in Spanish about their isolated life in Bahia Honda.

"Domingo, *como esta su vida, aquí en Bahia Honda?*" I said. "How is your life here in Bahia Honda?"

"Well, *todas las días*, we have much work to do," he said. "Everything grows *muy rapidimente aqui*—even the weeds. I also fish in the Bahia. Fish provides us with good protein. My kids are growing up quickly, and I want them to be strong. You can see how well they paddle the *canoas*."

"*Si*, I can see that," I said. "How about school?"

"The government provides a teacher and a small school house on the island, so the girls paddle over there. They have learned to read and can do arithmetic. Our family is *esta muy forte*. We share lots of love," Domingo said fondly.

"I have enjoyed meeting you and your smiling family," I said. "I can see that you have a good life and a community here. *Buena suerte y adios amigo*."

I watched them paddle back to their home across from us, appreciating this special moment. This gracious, gentle family became lodged in our memories, symbolizing the spirit of the Panamanian people.

Later in the day, a young man came by canoe asking, "*Es possible* to borrow a diving mask so I can capture some lobsters?"

"*Si, es possible*," I answered.

"*Muy bien*, I promise to return the mask with a lobster as your reward," he said.

After we waited for days, he had not returned so we went to the village looking for him. No one seemed to know his whereabouts. This was our only negative experience with any natives in Panama. In the meantime, *Aurora* had acquired the look of a floating fruit market as many stalks of red sweet bananas hung from the boom and the bright orange watermelon-sized papaya rested on the deck. In the galley, every available space sported a mango or a coconut. It was time now to sail on to the Panama Canal!

We rounded Cabo Malo, "the bad cape," during the daytime to avoid the heavy northbound ship traffic from the Canal at night and to observe the effects of currents that might push *Aurora* off course. Cabo Malo was "a piece of cake," but as darkness fell the sky filled with lightning. I counted 20 strikes in a four-minute period, some radiating between the clouds and others ominously forking down into the water. Knowing that *Aurora's* mast was the highest target for miles contributed to our anxiety. JoAnne hesitantly took over the watch at midnight using the radar to help her play a "cat and mouse" game avoiding the intense storm cells generating the most lightning. The suspense was heightened by needing to avoid about twenty fishing boats strung out over the Gulf of Panama as we closed in on the Las Perlas Islands located thirty miles off the western entrance of the Panama Canal.

Coming up into the cockpit at first light, I said, "Wow, JoAnne, you did a great job of avoiding the lightning. I heard it cracking until I dropped off to sleep. If our mast had been hit by a strike, all our electronics would have been fried! I'm wide awake now. It's your turn to gather in some Zs."

"My eyelids are now at half mast, but I managed to stay awake with all the lightning. See you in a couple of hours," she said with a kiss.

While we were anchoring off a small village on Pedro Gonzalez in the Las Perlas Islands, a fisherman setting his nets near *Aurora* came by in his boat to be sure we saw them. Realizing that I could understand much of his Spanish, Enrique and I conversed as he stood in his boat and I sat on the deck with my legs dangling over the side. He told me about his hobby of searching for Pre-Columbian pottery on the island. He confided his story to me because telling his neighbors might lead *them* to discover the source of his treasures. I felt that he had to tell someone because it might just burst out.

"I've unearthed an untouched tomb containing many pieces of pottery," Enrique said proudly. "Some of my discoveries were bought by a museum in Panama City, and others were sold to a collector from the USA."

"I wish I had some extra dollars to buy some of the pottery," I said, hoping they were genuine. Without the extra dollars, however, it wasn't a real dilemma. JoAnne and I were happy that most of his pottery had remained in Panama on display in a museum.

We wished Enrique well as he paddled off saying, "I'll pull the nets up early tomorrow morning. Good luck on your voyage." With an early start the next morning, we followed a parade of pelicans moving across the sky like a ribbon undulating in the wind. They were heading eastward toward the mainland. "Where were they going?" we wondered aloud. Our answer soon appeared over the horizon. Numerous shrimp boats were pulling their nets through the sea, bringing thousands of fish to the surface. For the diving pelicans, it was breakfast time on the Gulf of Panama!

As we sailed closer to the Canal, we saw the horizon scattered with many large ships anchored and waiting for their turn to go through the locks at this major crossroads of world shipping. We grew more excited the closer we got to the ships. Soon, we could identify their names and countries of origin: China, Japan, Korea, Canada, Indonesia, and the United States. Bright orange lifeboats pointing down toward the sea rested on rails at the sterns of oil tankers. These capsules could be launched by the crew for their escape if their flammable cargo ever caught on fire.

Trying to find the outer sea buoy marking the entrance for the Canal was our more immediate task. "Trying" was the operative word because we could not see it in the charted location. We decided the buoy must be hidden behind an anchored ship. Talking by radio with Flamingo Signal, the official radio contact for the Panama Canal, we confirmed our current location and were told to continue to the Balboa Yacht Club located at Buoy 14 on the right side of the channel.

The yacht club has mooring buoys made necessary by the force of the tidal current sweeping in and out. These strong currents could easily pull yacht anchors out of the bottom. With JoAnne guiding *Aurora* up to the buoy, I was able to snag it with a boathook and pass our bow line through its ring pulling it back to the second bow cleat. We were securely moored at the entrance to the Panama Canal. The club sent out a launch to safely take us to the main dock using its abundant power to overcome the current.

Walking into the clubhouse, JoAnne and I were greeted by an Aussie. "You two look like sailors. Come join us."

"Great, we'd love to," we said.

Moving a forest of beer bottles and bringing up more chairs, we joined a large table filled with Aussie sailors heading west into the Pacific. We introduced ourselves to Bill McNeil, his son,

Andrew, and daughter, Julie. They had just been joined by a friend, Brownie, who had just flown in from Australia knowing only that the McNeils might be in the Canal area.

Bill told us his story. "After losing my wife, I began my second trip around the world. Brownie sailed with me on the first trip but can't seem to get enough of this life so here he is again. We're ready to start this leg of the voyage across the Pacific to Tahiti, a distance of 3,000 miles that will take us over a month."

"I'm very impressed," I said. "My own original plan was to cross the Pacific, but the long distances and uncertain weather patterns convinced me that cruising along the coast of Central America would be a better choice. So far we've had a great trip, and visiting Cocos Island three hundred miles off Costa Rica has been one of the highlights."

JoAnne and I gave them our beautiful ten-pound papaya as a farewell present and wished them bon voyage as they left.

After cool showers and a good night's rest, we found a taxi driver who knew the check-in procedures for the Canal. He took us on a pleasant day-long experience of securing a Canal Transit Reservation and the Panama Cruising Permit. Next, we needed to find four line handlers to control the four one hun-dred-twenty-foot-long lines that would secure *Aurora* to the sides of the locks.

That night in the club bar, we met Rogier, a young man from Doorne, Holland, and his friend, Frederico, from southern Brazil. After we bought them a few beers, they agreed to accompany us through the first two locks to the Pedro Miguel lock. In the morning we paid two Panamanian professionals recommended by the yacht club to work the two other lines. An advisor sent by the canal authority would complete our transit crew. All were brought out to *Aurora* by launch early the next morning. My job was to drive *Aurora* following the directions of our advisor, Jose "Peru" Mires, who kept in radio contact with the control tower personnel on the Miraflores Locks that coordinated the movement of all vessels.

Americans finished building the Panama Canal in 1913 after the French abandoned their attempt due to crushing losses of men to malaria and yellow fever, and the disappearance of money and material trying to conquer the seemingly invincible jungle. Each lock chamber is 1,100 feet long by 110 feet wide by 40 feet deep and is truly impressive when looking up from a small thirty-three-foot sailboat center tied in the lock chamber behind a massive freighter. It felt as if we were a tiny bath toy in a huge concrete tub. Our advisor carefully choreographed our movements. As we arrived in the lock, monkey fists on light lines were thrown down to our four line handlers who tied them on our long heavier lines that were then pulled back up and secured on bollards by canal personnel. As the lock filled, raising up *Aurora*, each of our line handlers kept taking slack out of his line, securing them to the boat's port and starboard fore and aft cleats. So far so good, I said to myself.

Panama Canal

With the lock full, a burst of black smoke announced that the massive propeller of the freighter in front of *Aurora* had begun to turn, sending out a strong wave of water straining our lines. *Aurora* surged in the turbulence like we were riding a rapids. Fortunately, the lines held and kept *Aurora* in the center of the lock. This was not the case for an unlucky sailboat crew whose line broke, sending their boat careening against the lock wall and causing serious damage to its bow. Viewed later in the boatyard at Pedro Miguel Boat Club, the injured boat looked as though a giant knife had sliced off about three feet of its bow. Not having that image in my mind made our passage through the locks less stressful!

After waiting until the freighter had exited, we were permitted to motor forward into Lake Miraflores. At the end of this two-mile long lake, we saw the Pedro Miguel Lock and Pedro Miguel Boat Club. Maneuvering through a spider web of lines that tied anchored boats to the docks proved to be the trickiest operation of the day, but we made it safely. With *Aurora* secured, we served sandwiches and drinks to all hands on deck as we talked about our lives and our transit. The boat club ordered a taxi and soon calls of *"Muchas Gracias y Adios!"* sent our temporary crew on their way back to Balboa, a classy end to a successful transit.

*****

The Panama Canal Commission built the Pedro Miguel Boat Club during the construction of the canal. The club had become a funky facility leased by its boat owning members. We chose this place as the summer home for *Aurora* because it provides slips, boat workshops, a clubhouse with showers, a communal kitchen, and a trading library. All of these assets are being used by cruising yachters as a base to store and work on their boats.

During a shared shower with JoAnne, I suddenly melted onto the floor with intense waves of pain radiating through my abdomen causing my knees to buckle. With a worried look on her face, JoAnne slowly helped pull me up off the floor. We were both alarmed by the fact that the only treatment we had was pain medication. Reading our onboard medical books, we deduced that kidney stones were the most likely cause of my debilitating pain, probably brought on by my constant sweating in the hot, humid environment. I had not realized that I needed to drink gallons of fluids to stay hydrated. Fortunately the pain subsided. In two days we would be leaving for a scheduled three-month "vacation" from *Aurora* to flee the suffocating heat of the tropical summer. Escaping Panama by plane to California and medical attention came none too soon!

*****

After arriving and occupying friend Barbara's extra room in her Berkeley apartment, visiting the doctor was my first priority. The doctor, who had suffered from the same problem, confirmed our kidney stone diagnosis. He prescribed drinking large amounts of fluids as a primary treatment. The intense pain phase had passed, and we took off on a road trip visiting friends and family all over the United States.

22

PANAMA STILL DARNED HOT

We were back in California after a three-month, eight thousand-mile cross country road trip where we regaled our hosts with many sailing stories. It was the fall of 1992, and we were ready to get back to *real* sailing. I was excited about shopping for needed parts and supplies that would improve *Aurora*. Two major items were purchased: a Harken Roller Furling System to roll in the jib much like a window shade from the safety of the cockpit and two new davits to be mounted on the stern used to hoist and stow the dinghy out of the water. These parts were shipped air freight to Panama City at a reasonable cost. Our time to leave soon arrived. We expressed our heartfelt thank yous and goodbyes to our friends Vangie and Bill, who had hosted us in their home for a month. When it was time to leave, our friend and home base coordinator, Barbara, drove us to San Francisco Airport for the return flight to Panama City.

The tropics had not lost any heat. A blast of hot air hit JoAnne and me as we walked off the plane. When we stepped aboard *Aurora*, we immediately saw that she had become an incubator over the summer. Mold was everywhere, inside and out, fed by the constant rains and oppressive humidity. JoAnne went into battle armed with a bleach sprayer and rubber gloves, while I began installing the new systems and doing other needed maintenance. Our bodies poured out sweat constantly, so we drank loads of fluids. Taking showers also cooled down our core temperatures. All of this activity could be filed under the general heading, "Aren't Boats Fun?"

We rented a small Toyota sedan to reward ourselves for all our diligent cleaning and repair work and drove toward Northern Panama along the Pan American Highway through small towns and lush farmland. The sparse development of Central Panama was clear with the lack of side roads off the highway. We did not go through a real city until we arrived in David ten miles south of the border with Costa Rica. In David, we reconnected with homesteaders Elan, Bella, and Natalie Stern whom we had met six months ago when they lived on Isla Paridita west of David. Remember the boa constrictor versus the chicken incident or the lightning strike during dinner?

These folks were now living in a spacious three bedroom house (rent three hundred dollars) in a nice neighborhood on a dirt street along with their German Shepherd, Fifty, who was Natalie's constant companion along with a few chickens scratching for bugs in the yard.

It was great to see them in much improved conditions as we shared hugs and smiles.

Natalie gave JoAnne a big hug, proudly saying, "I'm going to a great private school. I've made some nice friends. I walk to school with some of them and have fun at recess."

"My, your life has changed since you left the Island," said JoAnne with relief.

Looking content, Bella said, "Life is better for us since we finally sold the boat. I have a housekeeper who I pay fifty dollars a month for six half-day's work and she lives next door. Elan has been exploring business opportunities in David."

"Yeah, I'm looking into import-export opportunities," said Elan. "We'll show you a parcel of land that we're thinking about buying. We'd like to build our own house."

"I'd like to see it," I said. "I've had experience in designing and building my own mountain cabin during my homesteading days."

We had a wonderful reunion with the Sterns. Drinking lemonade in the shade of a tree, we talked about our adventures over the last six months. JoAnne and I were relieved and happy that their lives seemed more settled than when they had lived on Isla Paridita, now occupied by friends.

Seeking escape from the lowland heat, we crossed the Pan American Highway to the north driving up about twenty-five miles to Bouquete. Set in the mountains at 3,500 feet elevation, Bouquete sat at the foot of Vulcan Baru, the highest peak in Central America. In the premier coffee growing region of Panama, Bouquete was beginning to attract visitors and ex-pats due to its temperate climate and beautiful setting on the slopes of the forested mountains. The town has a few restaurants and a small hotel on a dusty main street. JoAnne and I relished the coolness of the air and the variegated patterns of trees and sunlight decorating the slopes of Vulcan Baru.

We drove back to David that evening for dinner with the Sterns. We were joined by a woman doctor, Gabriela, from Mexico and an Israeli friend, Jacob, who manages two stores in town. Sitting around the dining table, we broke into an interesting conversation as we were accepted as friends.

"How are you two foreigners finding life in David?" I said. "You seem to be successful."

"Because of a shortage of doctors here, and that I speak Spanish, I've been able to build a good practice," said Gabriela. "I feel accepted and have been making many friends."

"I'm glad to hear that," said JoAnne. "Karl and I have talked about moving to Costa Rica and perhaps Panama and have been wondering what it would be like."

"It's been a little tougher for me because I've had to learn Spanish," said Jacob. "But my employees seem to like me and I'm also making friends. Of course having Elan and Bella here has been great."

"I can see a real advantage in having old friends to help make the transition into a new culture," I said.

"We've found a beautiful lot for sale where we might build a house," said Elan.

"Let's go look at it tomorrow," I suggested.

In the morning after getting Natalie off to school, Bella, Elan, JoAnne, and I drove to the lot on a knoll overlooking a lake with a view into the distant mountains toward Bouquete.

"What a great spot," Jo Anne said. "I can imagine you being very happy here."

If the Sterns decided to stay in Panama, building a home on this lot would create another paradise rivaling that of their own island in beauty.

*****

A day later, we arrived back at the Pedro Miguel Boat Club and became immersed in the casual social life of the club featuring potluck dinners. We made new friends. Anne and Len were working in Panama while living on their boat. Anne graciously took us shopping and to the trail where mules carried Peruvian gold across the Isthmus of Panama to the Caribbean in the 1500s. Mac, cruising alone on *Joyride,* and Bill also alone on his boat *Phat Duck* shared conversation over dinner. It seemed to us that each of them was sort of stuck in the mellow social life of the club. JoAnne and I wondered when or if they would continue on their sailing adventures. In the midst of finishing all the projects on *Aurora,* JoAnne shifted into rescue mode saving a starving female dog, a poodle-terrier mix who bonded strongly to her new "mother." As we were faced with returning to the sea, Mac graciously agreed to adopt "JR," named for his boat, while JR was understandably confused and reluctant to leave her "mother."

Our friends Gina and Tom flew in from San Francisco and rejoined us as crew for the remainder of our Panama Canal transit and the sail to Cartagena, Columbia. Our first priority was exploring the historic center of Panama City. Here, many city squares were surrounded by two and three-story wooden houses with upper iron balconies covered with vibrant flowers and colorful laundry. A general refurbishing of the old city was underway with many streets being repaved with bricks.

Walking by the city hall where President George H.W. Bush was scheduled to speak after the US invasion of Panama and capture of President Noriega in December 1989, we saw that bullet holes still remained in the buildings. We learned that at the time, the police had tear gassed an angry mob of demonstrators, ending the ceremony. Bush was whisked away to safety. Despite these events, we felt welcomed by the Panamanians, most of whom were happy to be rid of Noriega, "a thug" in their eyes. The people we met were eager to talk with us about their frustrations with the current government's inability to get things done. Watching a procession of excited children walking to the cathedral topped our morning's visit causing smiles to break out that matched theirs.

As we prepared for our trip to Cartagena, I moved *Aurora* away from the dock. Gina and Tom helped me maneuver her through a web of dock lines out to a mooring buoy on the day before starting our canal transit. I wanted to avoid the last-minute anguish we had observed when other boats were forced out in a rush to keep their scheduled transit time. Our volunteer line handlers, Mac and Bill, from the San Pedro Miguel Yacht Club, were ferried out to *Aurora* along with the Canal advisor. JR, Mac's newly adopted pup, was left forlornly crying on the dock, not understanding what was happening. We all called out, "Mac will be back." With everyone aboard, *Aurora* rafted up to *Brittany*, a 44-foot ketch owned by Molly whose crew included her boyfriend, Jerry. We motored together into the lock, and each corner of our two-boat raft was secured to bollards at the top of the canal walls.

Everything progressed normally, and we exited the lock together. Casting off our short lines, we separated the two boats and began motoring forward into the Goddard Cut, a deep pass that had been made by blasting through the Continental Divide. We motored into the narrow cut, and without warning, *Aurora's* engine alarm started screaming indicating an overheating problem. I immediately shut down the engine causing *Aurora* to be adrift in this narrow part of the canal that had steeply carved rock sides. We helplessly watched large ships moving toward us. Our advisor called to his compatriot on *Brittany* requesting that they help by taking us in tow. I focused on the problem and found a stick had been sucked into the cooling water intake filter stopping all the water inflow. With an eighteen-inch-long screw driver and hammer, I drove the stick out of the filter. On further examination, I discovered that the impeller, the spinning paddlewheel, the heart of the cooling water pump, had suffered a terminal meltdown when it overheated after losing its normal cool flow of water. Working feverishly, I installed a new impeller. Bill started the engine. Much to my relief the temperature began to drop as the cooling water flow reached the engine. Again, my preparation had overcome adversity.

Since we were back under our own power, the tow lines to *Brittany* were cast off. Our advisor, a canal pilot in training, wanted to make up for the lost time, so he urged me to go faster.

"I want to complete the transit of the canal today," he insisted.

Bill increased the engine's speed and black smoke poured out of the exhaust pipe. I was alarmed because the smoke could indicate more serious damage to the engine.

"Bill, look at all the smoke. What's happening?" I said with alarm.

A retired merchant marine engineer, Bill reassured me, "It's okay as long as the oil pressure and engine temperature stay normal and they are."

We increased our engine speed, and soon the black smoke was replaced by the usual light grey exhaust mixed with the cooling water after blowing the black accumulated carbon out of the engine. Now out into Gatun Lake, the large fresh water storage reservoir at the canal's center, we took advantage of favorable winds to roll out our new jib which added another knot to *Aurora's* speed.

"Tom, *Aurora's* receiving a free water bath that I hope will remove some of the salt water barnacles and other marine critters that have taken up residence on her hull," I said.

"Yeah, it will sure save us a lot of scrubbing when we get to the San Blas Islands," Tom agreed.

* * * * *

After passing the Smithsonian Institution Tropical Research Station on an island along the way, we soon reached the Gatun

Locks. Another warm tropical downpour stopped, however, leaving enough daylight for us to transit these last three locks.

After the first lock emptied and its doors swung open, a large Canal tug powered into the lock followed by *Brittany* and *Aurora*. After the tug was secured to the lock wall, we maneuvered our boats close by the tug so their crew could tie us to its side. A large freighter pulled by four "mules," small heavy train engines, followed us into the lock and was held in place by these ten-ton mules.

"Wow, this downward trip seems so easy being tied to the tug," I said. "We don't even have to adjust our lines when the water goes out, and since we're in front of the freighter, we won't have to battle the turbulence created when they start their engine."

"Yeah, it's much safer than when the freighters go into the lock first," remarked JoAnne.

Soon, we exited the third and last lock and motored over across the bay to find space on the main dock of the Panama Canal Yacht Club.

After we were safely docked, our temporary crew said goodbye.

"Thanks, Bill, for your expert advice on the engine," I said, shaking his hand. "It surely made the trip less stressful for me." I turned to Mac. "And Mac, you are an expert line handler. Here's some money for the taxi trip back to Pedro Miguel. Goodbye and good luck with your own cruising in Central America."

"Same to you guys. We've had a great day on *Aurora*," said Mac.

JoAnne, Gina, Tom, and I hit the showers and had dinner in the club's dining room. A refreshing end to an exciting day transiting the most famous canal in the world!

The next morning we followed normal checkout procedures with the port captain and immigration officials. Their offices were a short walk from the club, but other yachties warned us to take a taxi because even groups of sailors were being held up by armed bandits in the center of urban Colon. We needed the official stamps that would permit us to continue our cruise south twenty miles along the coast to Portobelo, the second fortified port built by the Spanish in the 1500s to receive the mule trains carrying Peruvian gold across the Isthmus of Panama.

Located on a beautiful bay surrounded by hills on which forts were built, Portobelo was now being restored with funds from the Spanish and Panamanian governments. Guarding the entrance to the bay, the forts still had ancient cannons in place and watch towers ready to spread the alarm if English pirates such as Morgan and Drake happened to drop in for a "visit."

The Church of the Black Christ, a Catholic Church, was also being restored. It is the home of a Black Christ Icon that attracts many pilgrims. The Black Christ stands in the center of a room off the main sanctuary. Walking up to the statue, we saw scores of silver amulets signifying a limb or another part of the body to be cured adorning the base of the statue. These amulets represented the reason for each pilgrim's quest. We felt that coming here for them was a serious business. We could only hope that their prayers are answered.

After loading up with yeasty bread rolls and guava goodies made by ex-pats Jimmy and Gene, from Biloxi, Mississippi, at their bakery, we set off for Playa Blanca, home of ex-cruiser Mike Starbuck. I had talked on the radio many times with Mike on the Central American Breakfast Club while he was performing his duties as Net Control.

Mike helped keep order as cruisers called in with questions or offered suggestions about places to visit or avoid.

Mike had settled down at Playa Blanca with his wife, Sandra. They now had two young children. We joined five other sailboats at anchor and dinghied in to join a potluck party at the house he built just up from the beach. Being with other cruisers is always fun because we have so much in common. More important, though, we can share experiences with sailors who had thrown off the shackles of "normal life ashore" by cruising to far off places. Mike Starbuck was certainly one of those people. We met a weird guy who said he was ex-CIA and claimed to have shot at two Panamanians who approached his boat by canoe. I didn't know whether to believe him, but I felt sick to my stomach. I warned my crew to avoid him. We don't want people like that in our cruising community!

Talking with Mike, I learned that unfortunately, he had mistakenly built his current house on a beach property he thought he owned and now was being forced to build a new house in the correct spot. This one would be his masterpiece.

"Oh my God, Mike, I've built houses and know how much work it is," I said, understanding his situation. "I'm not sure I could start all over again."

"Yeah, it's not going to be easy," Mike said. "But this place is paradise for me and my new wife. My choice is to stay here and build." Mike's conviction was impressive. Later, we shared our respect for Mike's energy and dedication to creating a satisfying life for his family on a beautiful beach on the East Coast of Panama.

We left Mike's bay in the morning and sailed around a point entering the San Blas Islands, the home of the Kuna Indians who live on an archipelago of 365 islands scattered along one hundred-fifty miles of Panama's southeastern coast in the Caribbean. Our destination was Chichime Island located in a group of three islands surrounded by coral reefs. When we reached the island, we found an anchorage occupied by four other cruising boats. Threading our way through the reefs, we carefully followed a dark deep blue ribbon of water that would lead *Aurora* into the anchorage. We anchored near the larger island taking in the beauty of being surrounded by palm covered islands, their white sand beaches reaching into the sea.

We were sitting in the cockpit mesmerized by the scene when a canoe full of smiling Kuna women came out from their island to show us their *molas*, traditional blouse panels created by them. Looking up from the canoe, their brown almond-shaped faces were outlined with black hair and adorned with small tattoos and gold nose rings. Examining their *molas*, we saw they were layered with three or four pieces of fabric, usually black, orange, green, yellow and red, and were cut into intricate patterns through different layers of the fabric. Some patterns are abstract, others are of fish, animals, or birds that are snipped into the fabric so that the desired under color shows through. To finish the *mola*, its creator sews almost invisible, tiny stitches to bind the edges of the cuts. The sleeves and a bodice are attached to the panels completing the colorful blouse. Each one was an original work of art that made us want to see more.

Gina, our best communicator in Spanish, told the women, "We want to come to your island tomorrow to see all your *molas*."

"*Si, senora, esta bien,*" was their answer with smiles and gestures of friendship.

We took the dinghy ashore on the beach where the Kunas' dugout canoes were lying near their huts. We stepped into the Kuna culture, feeling its magical quality expressed by the simplicity of their lives and the inner joy seen in their eyes and faces. Here, the Kunas are a successful group of indigenous people tending the coconut trees on their island surrounded by the sparkling turquoise water of the sea. They live in thatched roof houses with bamboo walls, sleep in hammocks strung between poles, and cook over open wood fires.

I walked over to an elderly man and ordered a loaf of bread baked in half a fifty-five-gallon drum. He took Gina to visit his wife who had some stomach pains. She encouraged the ailing woman to visit a medical clinic on an island, ten miles away. The Kuna diet features fish, crabs, and lobsters found in the sea among the islands or just beyond the barrier reef that protects their island archipelago.

The psychologist, Carl Jung, seems to have been right when asserting, "We all carry archetypal memories from our earlier evolutionary existences in our collective unconscious." Walking through the coconut palms and smelling the sweet sea air, I felt myself being swept back in time to another, more primitive age as my mind and body resonated in these surroundings. I felt that I had walked here before as a wave of peace swept over me. I was home.

Seeing the *molas* strung on fishing lines gave us all time to really examine them and pick out the right design for each person on our Christmas lists. Being with these friendly gentle people enhanced a feeling of peace which enveloped my body. We all felt richer because of this visit to Chichime and our introduction to Kuna culture.

Leaving Chichime, we traveled further east to Coco Banderos Island located near the outer reef protecting all of the San Blas Islands from the full dramatic force of the Atlantic Ocean. *Aurora* approached the island from the west. We saw boats at anchor, but our sketch chart didn't clearly show where the pass through the reef was located. A call on my VHF radio raised Lee on a nearby sailboat, *LightHeart*. He came out by dinghy to guide us through the twisting channel between the islands leading to a deeper anchoring area in the center, now temporary home for eight other cruising boats.

We had fortuitously arrived on the day of a scheduled beach party potluck. Lee, his wife, Jane, and their children dragged driftwood logs to the party spot to serve as seats, a table for food, and the demarcation for a fireplace. Hadley, a cute blond nine-year-old, and her brother, Nichols, a tall suntanned eleven-year-old, had been following a daily home school schedule laid out by their mother. They told us their lessons focused on the history and geography of the places they visited. In addition, they were completing regular reading and math lessons. The children's sailing knowledge already included basic navigation, following a compass course, trimming sails, and a basic understanding of the mechanical systems of their boat. It was a real pleasure meeting and talking with these interesting and independent kids. Jane, their mother, had written several articles in sailing magazines describing her experiences of being the primary teacher on *LightHeart's* "floating school."

*****

At the beach party we met Nancy and Steve, an engaging couple aboard *Keeha* from Hawaii who encouraged us to spend more time in the San Blas.

"We've visited other areas with islands and palm trees," Nancy said. "But these islands are really unique especially because of the Kunas who have preserved such an intact culture."

"That strikes a chord with the amateur anthropologist in me," I said. "So far, the Kunas and their *molas* have fascinated me."

Their enthusiasm and information confirmed our decision to later return to Ailigandi Village located further east in a more isolated Kuna area closer to Columbia. We would then have enough time for a more in-depth experience.

Skin diving the reef off Coco Banderas took us into deeper water where the clouds of colorful fish moved as waves surged against the reef. Gina's first diving experience proved to be surprising and exciting when a large, harmless nurse shark appeared at the edge of the reef. Gina hurriedly swam back to the safety of shallow water. She joined JoAnne on an air mattress for a few moments until the mattress capsized throwing both of its riders into the sea amid gales of laughter.

Talking later, we agreed that the deep water contains all sorts of creatures that we may not wish to meet face-to-face. Also we needed to know more about them and be able to identify them for our safety's sake. But, at the same time, the deep holds a fascination that attracts us to its beauty.

23

ON TO COLUMBIA

Sailing overnight and into the next day was easy with our crew of four except when a small, severe squall barged into our path as we neared Cartagena's harbor entrance. As we were being blown off course, I began to doubt our position because the harbor had two entrances quite close to one another. On the VHF radio, I called a freighter anchored off the Boca Chica (small mouth) entrance who answered back confirming our position.

Our friend George on *Avatar* whom we had met at Cocos Island soon joined the radio conversation giving us detailed instructions.

"You can identify the entrance by locating the low fort on the right side," he said. "You'll notice that its cannons are trained on your water line still there ready to protect Cartagena from marauding English pirates of the early 1600s."

While we followed the buoyed channel into the inner bay, George came back to us on the radio with a warning, "Don't stop if you're approached by small boats. Yesterday, they swarmed an entering cruiser's boat and stripped off all their deck gear, fishing poles, boat hooks, winch handles, the works"

We had no trouble at all and arrived off Club Nautico where we anchored *Aurora* in an inner bay surrounded by the Old City of Cartagena to the east and the Modern City to the west. Club Nautico would be our "home" for the next month. Norman, a "laid back" Australian sailor, and his wife, Rosa, a fiery Colombian, owned the club. We were lured there by its slips, showers, laundry facilities, and restaurant/bar. Other cruisers biting on the same bait made Club Nautico a gathering place and a first rate hangout. Additional perks included Norman's orientation to the history and wonders of Cartagena and the use of his custom agent friend. For a reasonable fee, his friend took our papers and passports to customs and immigration agents for their approval and of course the requisite, all important official stamps.

Karl, JoAnne, Tom, Gina

*****

After arriving at the dock by dinghy, Gina, Tom, JoAnne, and I walked into the Old Town and headed for the Cathedral Basilica of St. Catherine. Its spire stood out, rising above the surrounding two- and three-story colonial buildings.

A young man named Jorge offered to be our guide and told us its history.

"Construction of the Cathedral began in 1577, replacing a humble structure of straw and reeds. Sir Francis Drake's attack in 1586 caused severe damage and delayed its completion until 1612. Look at the gilded altar shining with Columbian gold. The pulpit is made of Carrara marble brought here from Italy."

We absorbed the serenity of the space as we sat in the pews.

Next Jorge led us to the Palace of the Inquisition, now a museum documenting "man's inhumanity to man." The impact of seeing the instruments of torture up close such as the rack and a spiked metal cage-like device designed to squeeze against the human body was eerie and gut wrenching.

"See the drawings and paintings on the walls showing these horrible machines in action torturing their poor victims whose only crime against the Catholic Church was not 'weighing enough' on a balance scale," said JoAnne. "The effect shown on the victims in the paintings magnifies their impact. I'm feeling the terror of those victims spread through me."

"Wow, you've got that right!" agreed Gina.

Jorge continued, "Seven hundred people had lost their lives during the Inquisition in Cartagena as it had swept across the Atlantic from Spain after being initiated by Queen Isabella and King Ferdinand to purify the Catholic Church."

"What I've read about this period in Spain," I said, "tells how Spanish soldiers drove out the Jews and Moors who had peacefully lived together in Southern Spain for centuries, creating a literate and advanced society. The Jews and Moors had created water systems that irrigated the arid area and had brought Greek and Roman texts which they translated, thus spreading the knowledge of ancient philosophy, mathematics, and science that became the basis of learning in the late middle ages. This society was the beginning of the Renaissance in Europe. After the Jews and Moors were driven out of Spain from the 1400s to the 1500s, the majority could neither read nor write."

On the night of October 14, Gina and Tom treated us to a tasty fish dinner at El Anchor restaurant in the Old Town where we celebrated our second wedding anniversary. We were seated at a quiet table in the corner next to a marvelous painting of square rigged ships in the harbor.

Tom offered up a toast. "Let's drink to our second eventful voyage on *Aurora* and to the Kuna Indians who added so much color and interest to our experience."

"Let me add my congratulations to JoAnne—my wonderful wife and sailing partner," I said, looking deeply into JoAnne's blue eyes. "You are going a long distance to show me how much you care!"

Smiling, JoAnne turned and gave me a long kiss.

Our waiter, Sergio, responded to the celebration and brought "on the house" cups of hot flaming brandy to complete our meal. While challenging to drink, they added sparkle to the occasion. We then toasted Gina and Tom's flight home to Los Altos, California. They successfully ended their three-week tour of duty on *Aurora*.

✳✳✳✳✳

Being anchored out in the midst of Cartagena gave us a visual feast at night with flickering lights from the streets and houses onshore dancing on the water. Spotlights illuminating forts and walls made them command the blackness of the night. One of these nights in Cartagena particularly stands out in my memory when an intense thunder and lightning storm swept through the anchorage unleashing surges of driving rain followed by a loud bang. A sizzling bolt of lightning struck our neighbor's mast. He paid an unfortunately high price for having a larger boat with a higher mast as the mega volts of electricity fried his radios and other electronics. JoAnne and I felt sorry for their loss but were relieved that that no one had been injured and that *Aurora* had survived the near miss.

With the storm's passage, we accepted an invitation from Caroline, a plump, friendly retired Florida real estate broker, on her motor trawler, *Sana Vida* (Sane Life). We joined her on a day trip across the bay to Playa Blanca. Many Cartagenans went there for swimming and picnics. Swimming ashore we met some of Caroline's Rastafari friends who were members of a movement originating in Jamaica and Ethiopia. This movement has spread with the popularity of Bob Marley's reggae music and includes the spiritual use of cannabis. They invited us to join their party and to share their open fire barbecued fish dinner and bottles of rum. Guitars were out in force accompanying Columbian folk songs. The group swayed and sang, creating a mesmerizing mood while we sat on the sand absorbing the warmth of the sun and sparkle of the sea.

"Wow, these folks are having a great time!" I remarked.

"By the look of their raggedy clothes, they don't have much money," said Caroline.

"We Americans could learn a lot from them," said JoAnne. "Money isn't everything."

On the way back to our anchorage, we passed close to *La Gloria*, a beautifully restored, three-masted barque that is the school ship of the Columbian Naval Academy located in the harbor. The ship had just returned from the Columbus Five Hundred Year Anniversary celebration in Spain and the United States. Seeing *Sana Vida's* American flag, the midshipmen waved and yelled, "USA! USA!" from the rigging and deck.

We all cheered, "Columbia, Columbia!"

In a few days, it was our turn to fly to Bogotå, a city of seven million inhabitants, located at a 9,000 foot elevation in a valley in the Andes Mountains. Our friends Jaime and Julianna lived there. These friends were made through JoAnne's connection to International House on the UC Berkeley campus. They lived with their two teenage children, Tom and Annie, in a beautiful suburb on the north side of Bogota. Jaime, who took his degree in hydraulic engineering at Berkeley, is well known throughout Central and South America because he made studies of the desired location of ports and designed structures needed when the land meets water. Julianna is an American who coordinates the teaching of the English Language at the German school where their children are students. Their three-story townhouse is located in a guarded, walled development as are most other homes in this city where drug-generated violence is an incessant fact of life.

Our stay was fortunately uneventful and peaceful as Julianna shifted into the tour guide mode, taking us to the acclaimed Gold Museum. We saw the distinctive work of different tribes in creating human and animal figures. Many of these figures were used to carry powdered limestone which reacts with coco leaves when chewed by porters to produce a narcotic effect that enables them to carry heavy loads high in the Andes. The narcotics counteract the effect of the high altitude and produce more energy needed to haul their heavy cargo.

On another foray into downtown, we rode an aerial tram up the mountain then hiked to find the best spots to view Bogotå as it spread out below us. Julianna pointed out their walled neighborhood in the distance. Later, we drove out into a formation of large boulders that seemed to be arranged by nature for a teen's game of hide and seek. We found an open spot where we relaxed, sitting on blankets, sharing food, drinking wine, and talking with good friends who live in a much older culture that traces its influences back to the Spanish Conquistadors. I found their historical references fascinating and quite different from similar conversations at home in California where our young culture precludes those types of allusions.

We spent our last night in Bogotå at the seventieth birthday party of Jaime's mother who lived with his sister in a beautiful Art Deco three-bedroom apartment in an upscale area near the embassies of Great Britain and Germany. Jaime and his two brothers are responsible for their mother and sister's welfare, showing how a strong family in Colombia functions. At dinner around a large ornate table, we enjoyed the friendly banter and teasing among the family as well as delicious roast chicken covered with a papaya and guava sauce. After dinner, we were serenaded quite professionally by grandchildren playing guitars and maracas to accompany their singing of Colombian folk songs. Our stay in Bogota created many memories. Central to them all is the warmth and caring of this wonderful family who took us into their world.

Years later, we would learn that as medical students, Jaime and Julianna's daughter, Annie, and her boyfriend, Andreas, were car-jacked and kidnapped. They were taken to an ATM and forced to make a withdrawal. Andreas was locked in the trunk and they were taken into the mountains to a spot where many kidnap victims had been killed. Still sitting in the car, Annie kept talking to their abductors and convinced them to release both Andreas and her by saying, "We're studying to be doctors so we can help people. Please let us go." Thank God her plea would be successful!

After the San Francisco-like temperatures of Bogota, Cartagena seemed steamier than ever. My abdominal pain, first noticed in Panama, returned.

I asked Norman's advice and he suggested that I talk with Juan. "He's a good doctor who has his boat moored here," he said. "Why don't you ask him what he would suggest?"

I followed Norman's advice and found Juan. He was a pleasant looking man in his mid-thirties, sitting at a table opposite his boat.

"*Buenos Dias, mi llamo es Karlos,*" I said. "I have kidney stones that are causing me some pain. Norman suggested that you might be able to help me."

"*Hola,* my name is Juan," he greeted me. "I did my residency in internal medicine in Philadelphia. I have many friends in the States and many fond memories of my training at the University of Pennsylvania Hospital."

"Great, I would really appreciate your help because the pain is getting worse," I said trying to ignore it.

"I want to be sure of the diagnosis before we go further," Juan continued. " I'll write you some prescriptions for tests that you can get nearby." I smiled with thanks.

"So are you enjoying your time in Cartagena?" he said, changing the subject.

"JoAnne, my wife, and I really like the Old Town," I said. "It's so steeped in history. We sailed in past the fort with its cannons aimed at our waterline. I find it fascinating that the Boca Grande entrance to the harbor still has a chain across it just as in the days of the English and Dutch pirates. Adding in the forts on the hills, we can see that the Spanish were very serious about defending Cartagena. We've had some tasty meals in town."

"Let's order another beer," said Juan. "It'll help wash out your kidney stone."

We laughed. I got the feeling he was treating me to repay the many kindnesses he said he had received from Americans.

"You're my kind of doctor!" I agreed.

The next evening, I returned to Juan's table where by candle-light he studied the ultra sound test and X-rays of my abdomen.

"See, there are the kidney stones," Juan said, pointing at the X-ray.

"Okay," I said, "but what do I do now?"

"Drink gallons of fluids to flush out the stone and collect your urine so you can see when the stone passes," he replied.

"So beer is okay?" I said.

"Sure," Juan affirmed.

"I'll order another round," I said. And beer it was!

Unbelievably, the next morning, the kidney stone passed when I peed into a jar.

I called out to JoAnne, "Was this jar clean? It looks like it has a piece of granola in the bottom."

"You bet it was clean!" JoAnne called back.

I looked at the jagged, light yellow stone about the size of the end of my little finger that had passed through without any real pain. "Amazing!" we said together.

I saw Juan at his usual table that evening. "Juan, you are my kind of doctor," I said, joining him. "The stone passed this morning, and I feel great! I really enjoyed your beer prescription! *Muchas Gracias por su audar!* How about another beer?"

With *Aurora* now tied to Club Nautico's dock, we were drawn into the social scene there. Dan, a retired athletic looking tennis pro, and his wife, Marty, a lively retired teacher from Southern California, had arrived on their sailboat, *Vivid*, from Panama. After spending time with them at a potluck at the Pedro Miguel Boat Club back in Panama, we were able to nurture our budding friendships in Cartagena. We celebrated JoAnne's sixty-third birthday together at The Classic Restaurant in the Old City, complete with three musicians serenading us with folk tunes.

Walking after dinner atop the city walls, Dan remarked, "See how magical the Caribbean looks from up here. I love how the light glimmers on the waves creating patterns that fluctuate and expand as they move."

"Yeah, if we look down onto the old houses and winding cobblestone streets of the Old City, the lights expose more stable shapes," Marty added.

"What a unique treat to be embedded in this remarkable scene," JoAnne said. "The light seems to have a life of its own and is playing a game for us as we watch."

The next day, we joined a group of cruisers busing up to Castillo San Felipe de Barajas overlooking the city and the harbor. Built by the Spanish on the top of a steep rock hill to defend their treasure ships and Cartagena, the Castillo had huge cannons mounted in gun ports accessible by tunnels connecting to magazines that had been filled with black powder and cannon balls.

Our group fought through the gauntlet of vendors selling sombreros and other souvenirs. That was an easy task, compared to getting through a few men holding monkeys and one man holding a sloth. The slow sloth was not a challenge, but leaping monkeys suddenly were climbing all over us, grasping at our clothes and hair to the amusement of our friends. Their laughter stopped, however, when the monkeys climbed up their bodies, forcing them to experience being groped by an out-of-control animal. Fortunately for us, the monkeys' owners removed them for a few pesos.

Our tour continued on to dinner at a Brazilian restaurant. Before dinner entertainment featured two magnificent Spanish horses prancing around a courtyard in front of us.

"Who would like to ride?" said one of their riders.

I raised my hand, "*Si, mi por cierto!*"

Another sailor, Deborah, joined me.

We rode these smooth-gated Lipizzaner stallions descended from the Spanish Riding School in Cadiz, Southern Spain, around the courtyard performing for our friends.

"What a thrill to have ridden one of the world's best trained horses!" gushed Deborah.

"Yeah, that was an *amazing* ride," I exclaimed still high. "It would be great to be able to ride them in a bigger space so we could gallop with them."

Dinner featured all types of barbecued meat sliced off the skewers with swords. All the meat was tasty and tender except a cow's udder, which was like mushy rubber. Not very appealing at all!

We had one more unusual experience back in the harbor when we met Cliff from the *Logos II*, a floating evangelical missionary ship. He was a professional mariner from New Zealand. He gave us a tour of the ship where we met a group of young college-age missionaries from forty-seven countries. We also saw their extensive library of Christian books. Cliff invited us to dinner that night. We sat at long tables chatting with committed young men and women about their desires to improve the world by spreading the Christian message of love and compassion to their fellow human beings.

*****

Having thoroughly enjoyed Cartagena and the new cruiser friends we made during the last month, we were itching to get back to traveling. We moved on to Las Islas Rosario located about twenty miles to the southwest toward Panama. There I cleaned *Aurora's* hull which was covered with white marine worms and other growth fed by the pollution in the harbor at Cartagena. Using the new compressed air tank, buoyancy compensator, and regulator bought from Elan Stern in Panama, I could stay underwater for the longer periods of time necessary to scrape off the offending growth which would have slowed our progress through the sea.

Joseph, a harbor neighbor from Central France, joined us as we dinghied over to a nearby island where a fenced off area of the sea contained dolphins and sharks. Here, a trainer demonstrated the dolphins' intelligence and agility. Afterwards, these incredible animals interacted with a group of school girls from Cali, Columbia. Without any cues from their trainers, the dolphins answered the girls' squeals of delight with high leaps and well-aimed splashes. They delighted in playing with human beings, too.

24

LIFE WITH THE KUNAS

With her clean, smooth bottom, *Aurora* was ready for an overnight passage to Ailigandi Village located on a small island off the Darien Peninsula in eastern Panama. Ailigandi is off the edge of the "known world." The U.S. Defense Mapping Agency charts stopped further west toward the Panama Canal. To locate the island, I had to use hand drawn charts that Steve on *Keeha* gave us during our stay at Club Nautico. These charts gave the latitude and longitude coordinates of the pass through the reef close to Ailigandi.

Our last Sat Nav position was hours ago as the sun began to set. For a long time, I searched the reef ahead with my binoculars hoping to see a patch of smooth water confirming my dead reckoning course was correct. At last it appeared in the fading light. I steered *Aurora* gingerly through the narrow opening with JoAnne on high alert watching the color of the water. I scanned the depth sounder to be sure we wouldn't hit bottom. Soon, we were into the deeper water behind the reef. At the same time, we let out great sighs of relief.

"Wow, we made it!" we shouted with exuberant smiles.

"How about that for Livengood Luck!" I exclaimed.

After anchoring between two small islands in sheltered water, we had a quick dinner and poured our tired selves into bed. Each of us had stood watch five hours during the night before. As I fell asleep, my thoughts drifted back to the moment we saw the smooth water telling us that we could reach safety behind the reef. I also sent thankful thoughts out to Steve whose charts proved to be accurate. We had taken quite a risk in coming here, and I hoped that Ailigandi would live up to its advance billing. Again, skill and luck brought us through!

The early morning light revealed that we were in a new world populated by a fleet of about twenty Kuna Indian dugout canoes paddling out from Ailigandi to fish. A few canoes had colorful sails, but only one used an outboard motor. After breakfast, we motored *Aurora* over to Ailigandi Village that was covered with *palapa* houses near to the shore where canoes were tied to rough docks or to trees. We found a place to anchor just off the island. Soon, a canoe filled with Kunas paddled out to us bringing *molas* and other handmade craft items for sale.

"We want to come to your island to buy *molas*," I told them. Seeming to understand, they nodded, and returned to shore. A few minutes later a young man, Daniel, came out to us and invited us to buy bread and lime juice at his home.

"We'll come to the island soon," JoAnne said.

"Okay," Daniel said. "I'll be waiting for you."

After we dinghied in to the island, we tied up to the dock. A small, smiling, young brown-skinned child walked up to greet us. She took JoAnne's hand and led us into the village and to a small restaurant. Buying cold sodas was the order of the day. After Jo-Anne gave her a soda, the girl ran off to play with her friends., We saw a small health center next door. Walking across an open area, we found the school which we learned later the government of Panama had provided for the indigenous people of Kuna Yala, this semiautonomous region of Panama encompassing all the San Blas Islands. Here the Kunas live on densely populated islands with as many as 1,000 inhabitants, but families also own smaller islands that they use as coconut palm plantations like those we saw at Chichime. Coconuts are a currency for the Kunas.

While we walked through the irregularly shaped central area, we found there were no *molas* for sale. I asked a woman who was observing us, "Is it possible to buy *molas*?"

As soon as I finished my sentence, a crowd of women rushed out of the shade toward us holding up their *molas*. A sea of women and their *molas* ambushed JoAnne. They shouted "*Mira, Mira, Mira.*" (Look, look, look.) I moved in beside JoAnne to open up

Karl and Kids

some space, and she gave me a grateful glance. We began select-
ing the most interesting *molas* that caught our eyes from the
throng of women holding up their best work. To help make our
choices, I took some of the best and placed them on a bench so Jo-
Anne and I could really examine and compare them. The women
calmed down, and their hubbub subsided when they seemed to
realize that we were serious buyers. Our Kuna experience on
Ailigandi was different from the shy reactions of the Indians we
met on Chichime. We paid the asking price of twenty dollars each

for *molas* that looked like works of art and bargained for lower amounts for the simpler ones.

True to his word, Daniel arrived and seemed amused by all the hustle and bustle. When we reached our mola quotient, we went with him along a trail between families' fenced off living areas to his father and mother's compound where his sisters and their families lived. Their small store and bakery fronted on the path past their gate. In an open space inside children played and the women sat working on their *molas*. When we walked into the courtyard, I felt everyone's gracious smiles radiating a warm greeting to us. We shook hands with Daniel's father, Daniel Sr., who looked into our eyes. We instantly felt included in the warmth and joy of his home. His face was relaxed and his eyes radiated acceptance. With a few words, he organized a children's dance accompanied by flute and maracas in our honor. The kids moved and swayed to the music laughing and smiling. A circle of approving adults surrounded them.

Daniel Sr. brought out a carved wooden fish spear and a small model of a Kuna dugout sailing canoe to sell to me. They would occupy a prominent space on the desk where I would write about our sailing adventures. After we said our goodbyes, Daniel guided us to his wife's family compound where he lived. We received another warm welcome. Then, we walked on narrow paths to the library housed in a palm covered pole building with a concrete floor. Nearly 4,000 books were stored on rough sawn wood shelves.

The librarian had the recessive albino trait that I had previously read about. That trait is quite strong here due to the inter-marriage within clan groups probably brought on by Kuna's isolation. Albinos are called "Moon Children" by other Kunas. Daniel introduced us to Alberto, a short, white haired, fair-skinned man with an intelligent face. He gave us a short description of the Kuna Culture.

"Our culture is matrilineal as property is passed from mother to daughter, and when a man marries, he goes to live with his wife's family but in their own *palapa* inside the family compound fenced by bamboo sticks woven into a screen using strips of palm leaves. The women tend their small gardens on the island, take care of children, and make *molas*, both for the family and for sale as a way of raising the dollars needed to buy food and clothing. The men fish in the surrounding seas, harvest coconuts, and tend larger gardens allotted to each family located on the Darien Peninsula about a mile away."

"There aren't very many matrilineal cultures in the world," I said. "I would like to learn more about your tribe. Do you have any books about the Kunas?"

"I do," said Alberto, smiling. He handed me three books from a display table. "These were written by missionaries and anthropologists. I can lend them to you."

"Great!" I said. "We'll be here a week or so, and I'll be sure to return them."

After dinghying back to *Aurora* with our treasures, we decided to move further from the village to Islandia, a group of three palm-covered islands about two miles away from Ailigandi. In a lagoon near the outer reef, we found a deep spot large enough to anchor *Aurora* where the breezes from the Caribbean Sea cooled the boat and us. Our eyes feasted on the swaying palms close by

Islandia

and then onto the green mountains of the Darien nudging the clouds that the west winds from the Pacific pushed over them. We had found a paradise much like that of the South Pacific where warm water invited us to play and swim while the breezes and our sunshades kept the boat temperatures comfortable. First, however, we had to get to the task at hand of washing our new *molas* to remove the strong odor of wood smoke that spoke of their birth in the huts of Ailigandi. We hung them on the boat's life lines to dry. We had so many that Aurora looked like the inside of a mola shop. She had "gone native" which could also accurately be said about us.

The next day after breakfast, two Kunas, Eladio Anderson, about 50 years old, and his handsome teenage son, Irving, paddled their dugout canoe alongside *Aurora*. Eladio spoke excellent English, having been taught by his father who worked for the U.S. Army during WWII when the Panama Canal had been under threat of attack by German submarines. The army built runways for their spotter planes on the mainland and constructed observation posts for coast watchers on many of the San Blas Islands.

Eladio recalled his experiences for us. "The soldiers were very friendly, always smiling, drinking beer. They gave us kids gum and candy. We loved walking around with them, holding their hands and then running off, playing catch and other games like 'hide and seek.' My memories and those of my friends account for the special feelings Kunas have for Americans."

These warm feelings, historically, go back to the late 1800s when American whaling ships recruited Kunas as crew members. They often took the English family names of the crew as their own. Eladio's family name of Anderson would be quite unusual in the dominant Spanish-speaking culture of Panama. In the 1920s, the U.S. Navy did another good deed when the heavy cruiser *Cleveland* helped stop an invasion force of Panamanian soldiers from attacking a large group of Kunas who were in their canoes ready to defend their territory and culture. Panama wanted to suppress the Kuna culture and take control of the San Blas Islands. This action of the U.S. Navy prevented the takeover, permitting the Kuna people to flourish as the semi-independent indigenous group of people that control their own Kuna Yala territory.

From my reading, I learned that men form the Kuna governing council of elders. They meet in a large council house in the center of the village while administrative control is vested in the chief whom they elect. The chief has an office and, in the case of Ailigandi, a secretary who sold us a permit for two U.S. dollars to visit the village. Chiefs from all the islands come together to form a governing council for Kuna Yala. This Council of Chiefs interacts with the government of Panama.

I shared my readings with JoAnne. "The women control the money and the family while the men exercise control over the village and the whole string of San Blas Islands that compose Kuna Yala. An interesting distribution of power, I would say. Also I learned that the Kuna are the second shortest people on earth after the pygmies of the Kalahari Desert in southern Africa. They are also one of the most successful groups of Indigenous Peoples in the world." JoAnne smiled.

"Judging by their *molas*, I would add that they are one of the most creative groups, too," she said.

In pre-Columbian times, a more warlike tribe (probably the Embras) drove the Kunas from the Darien Peninsula onto the San Blas Islands which afforded them the protection of the surrounding sea. Here, their culture developed as they harvested the bounty of the sea, and continued to farm plots on the mainland.

Eladio and Irving stopped by *Aurora* during their daily fishing trips. We invited them aboard for something to drink.

I clearly remember sitting in the salon on *Aurora* with them as Eladio related this part of his oral history. "My grandfather and my ancestors were all born in the mountainous jungle of the Darien where they had fled at the time of the Spanish Conquest about 1540. Because our historical homes on the San Blas Islands made it too easy for the Spanish to attack and make us slaves, all the Kunas fled into the jungle." Eladio paused, taking a sip of lemonade.

"Almost 400 years later in the 1920s my father wanted to return to the islands that he had heard about in family stories. So he

Eladio and Irwin

asked his father to come with him. His father, my grandfather, refused to go because he was afraid that the Spanish would make him a slave."

As I listened intently to Eladio, I was overcome by seeing the powerful impact that oral history passed down through at least twenty generations had on my friend Eladio.

"You mean to say you have never been able to meet your grandfather?" I said.

"That's right," said Eladio softly. "He remained isolated in his village in the mountains with no real knowledge of the world outside."

Eladio's grandfather lived in the impenetrable jungles of the Darien Peninsula where even today rivers serve as the only roads. The Pan American Highway goes no further than Panama City meaning there is no overland link through to Columbia.

Daniel again greeted us on our second trip to Ailigandi. He guided us through a maze of pathways between the family compounds.

"These houses last about 60 years and the palm frond roofs must be replaced every fifteen years," he said.

Kids with Balloons

When we reached a clearing filled with children, I distributed the hundreds of balloons that I had brought to the village for them. They disappeared in a flash into the kids' outstretched hands. Each child took one for him or herself or perhaps for another sibling. They did not try to grab more.

As JoAnne and I watched them blow up the balloons, I said, "Oh my God, I hope they don't swallow them and choke."

"Oh, I don't think they will," JoAnne said confidently. Thank God they didn't!

Daniel had a bemused smile as he watched and helped children tie knots in their balloons to keep them inflated. He took us next to the new Kuna Cultural Center designed by an architect from Panama City. José, the director, showed us panels woven from palm fronds, wood carvings, and some beautiful clay sculptures made in classes held at the center.

After Daniel's tour, we dinghied back to *Aurora* and caught up with the Anderson family paddling out to see us in their canoe. The family included Eladio, his wife, Eloisa, son, Irving, and granddaughter, Evelyn, who brought gifts of seashells for us. We reciprocated with gifts of books for Eladio and Irving, used reading glasses for Eloisa who was having difficulty seeing her tiny stitches for making *molas*, and balloons for Evelyn.

Eloisa was amazed when she put on the eye glasses. "I can see!" she exclaimed in Kuna, beaming with joy.

Many Kuna women only speak their tribal language while most men also speak Spanish. Some (like Eladio) are fluent in English. Eloisa was fascinated by the inside of *Aurora*. She appreciated our buying two of her traditional *molas*. Sharing limonada on a hot day, we learned that most of their children had gone to college, and that their daughter, Evelyn, was a teacher on the island.

As they were leaving, Eladio said, "Please come to visit us at our blue stucco house on Ailigandi. Over there," he said, pointing. "You can see it from here."

"We'll come tomorrow," I said happily.

The next day on the morning Breakfast Club Radio Net, I had a long conversation about the Kunas with Maury Gladson speaking from his house in Playa del Cocos, Costa Rica. He told me of his experiences with them.

"In the mid-1950s, when my wife and I sailed to the San Blas Islands, I saw Kuna women bringing fresh water held in halves of coconut shells lining the bottoms of their canoes as they paddled from the mainland out to their home island. They had no other way of carrying water so we gave them some large plastic containers. They were thrilled!"

Hearing this story was just another indication of how primitive the Kuna culture was then. On our visits there, however, we saw fresh water being transported from a spring on the mountainside in white PVC pipes laid under the sea to a water tower where it is distributed in pipes to the family compounds. Quite an improvement!

The next day we landed our dinghy on Eladio's beach. Four generations of his family warmly greeted us in English, Spanish, and Kuna.

"I feel like Columbus arriving in the new world," I whispered to JoAnne.

Meeting everyone became a blur of names and smiling faces as we absorbed their warm handshakes and greetings. All were as welcoming and friendly as Eladio.

"It strikes me that Eladio and Eloisa have created an amazing family of bright, happy people," JoAnne whispered. "I could feel right at home here."

Afterward a son-in-law guided us to Daniel's bakery and two other small stores where we were able to replenish *Aurora's* galley with bread, boxed milk, and carrots. As we were walking back to the dinghy on a narrow pathway between family compounds, a woman opened her compound gate holding a mola in front of her that featured a pair of stylized fish on each side of a purple blouse that looked like it belonged in the Museum of Modern Art in New York City. Out came my last twenty dollar bill, and with smiles, the exchange was made. That mola blouse would hang for years in our entrance hall for all to see and marvel at.

Mola Blouse

On our last morning in the lagoon at Islandia, Eladio and Irving paddled up to say goodbye.

Looking up from his canoe Eladio said, "Someday my son or grandson may come and see you in the States."

"If we're home from our travels, we'd love to have them stay with us," I said. JoAnne and I felt conflicted about leaving in that moment. We wanted to stay and continue experiencing the warmth and hospitality of these unique people, but we needed to press on. The hurricane season would be coming all too soon to the Caribbean routes of our voyage.

Over the years, we would continue to send letters back and forth to the Anderson family. I would send garden seeds, and Eladio would mail *molas* for us to sell so he and Eloisa could help pay for their children's education in Panama City. In response to Eladio's questions about lobster traps, I would make a drawing of a lobster trap from Maine that adorned our back deck. In coming years, I would have a deeply felt yearning to return to the San Blas Islands and the village of Ailigandi to renew my friendship with Eladio and the Kuna people. Thankfully, I would return eighteen years later.

This special experience with the Kuna people took me from my dream of learning about other cultures into living with and being accepted by the Andersons and other Kuna families. The reality of the experience was beyond my expectations. It validated for me my basic values of being an open, kind, interested, and loving person in the world as I felt warmth and, yes, love reflected back from the Kunas we met. Of course, JoAnne shared these same values and feelings with me.

25

CARIBBEAN COAST OF CENTRAL AMERICA

In November, 1992, JoAnne and I were ready to sail back through the reef into the Caribbean Sea on a NNW heading to Isla Providencia, three hundred-seven nautical miles away from Ailigandi. Leaving Kuna Yala, we carefully lined up *Aurora* with Eladio's blue house and the end of Islandia to locate the opening in the reef. Fortunately, the seas were moderate as we motored through into deeper waters, and away from the sharp coral reef that could wreck havoc to *Aurora*. Once clear of the danger, we felt a great sense of relief. We sailed through the night. The next morning, we found that a swallow had landed on *Aurora's* life-lines. JoAnne approached the bird offering it some granola and water to sustain its energy. It looked so exhausted. Helping this tired bird was symbolically important to us. In most of our anchorages throughout Central America, swallows had flown out from shore to greet us with their bobbing heads and musical chirps while sitting on our life lines.

Providencia would be our next stop. Located in the Caribbean Sea, three hundred miles off the east coast of Nicaragua, this small island about ten miles wide by twenty miles long is controlled by Columbia. Providencia offered us a place to rest and resupply after our sojourn in the San Blas Islands. The ship's agent, Bernardo Bush, was our key to passing through the Providencia's reef into protected water. We had learned about Bernardo in Cartagena and alerted him by radio that we needed his assistance. He guided us through the reef by radio to a pier where the officials were assembled to board *Aurora*. After the formalities were completed, we took the boat out to anchor and dinghied in to meet Mr. Bush standing on the dock. Bernardo was a tall, charming, handsome black man. He handled the check-in formalities and joined us for lunch. We were fascinated by hearing about his African ex-slave and British explorer (possibly pirate) ancestors as we drank iced tea in a small cafe overlooking the harbor.

"My family has inhabited this area of the Caribbean ever since the first slaves were brought here by the British. My ancestors managed to free themselves and have been living on these islands for hundreds of years. You may not know it, but I'm a distant relative of your President George H.W. Bush."

"Wow," I said with a smile, "that's very interesting. Seems like the Bush clan really got around."

Later in our travels we would meet other Bush families scattered around the Western Caribbean making the same assertion.

"I just heard on the radio a sailboat named *Rondo* has struck a reef between Cartagena and Providencia Island which is essentially on the same course that you must have taken," Bernardo said, taking our talk to the present day and the realities of sailing. "Evidently, *Rondo* was pushed off course while its skipper was sleeping. The boat is stuck on the reef with a huge hole in its side."

"Wow, the *Rondo* crashing on the reef really validates my own decision to not sail long distances alone," I said, looking at JoAnne with gratitude.

Urged on by Bernardo to tour the island, JoAnne and I boarded the local bus, a brightly painted truck with seats on its flat bed covered by a brightly colored canopy overhead. The bus stopped whenever someone by the side of the road waved their arms, signaling to be picked up. Blaring Caribbean Calypso music from a tape deck added to the festive nature of our trip. We were immersed in a group of happy, singing islanders. Small farms surrounded with banana trees dotted the hillsides. On some farms we saw pens housing black pigs. Chickens were running loose everywhere. Driving by secluded beaches fringed with palm trees heightened the allure of this island for us.

Back on *Aurora* after our bus tour, we felt well-rested and entertained. Captain Blood, an older gentleman with a toothless smile, came aboard as self-proclaimed pilot to guide *Aurora* through the pass in the reef into the open sea. His friends named him Captain Blood because he was accident prone. He entertained us with his outrageous stories. Captain Blood had brought along a bag of oranges and a small stalk of bananas as farewell gifts. He took his leave by jumping into his aluminum dinghy being towed behind *Aurora*. Unloosening the tow line, he smiled, giving us a wave and shouting, "Goodbye and good luck!"

Under sail again, we set our course to the NW off the eastern end of Nicaragua which we rounded in good weather. We had decided not to stop on the Gorda Banks, a group of shallow reefs that broke through the sea's surface, because of deteriorating weather conditions and rumors of piracy in the area. In the morning light, we saw Guanaja in the Bay Islands Group of Honduras rising up from the sea and offering us shelter as we sailed along its barrier reef.

"I'm counting the small cays (islands) on the reef, JoAnne, so I can find the pass into Guanaja Town," I explained. "Do you see a good anchorage off Low Cay? The masts of other cruiser boats are right over there."

"Looks good to me. Let's go over and anchor there," said JoAnne. "We've just sailed three hundred-seventy miles in four days and three nights and it's time to relax. It feels good to set our anchor in a safe harbor."

Out of the jumble of stilt houses and their connecting boardwalks near shore, three young mulatto boys came paddling over to us in their dugout canoe.

"Hi, I'm Emmet and these guys are my friends, Sheldon and Omar. We'd like to be your guides in town. What do you think about that? We've lived our whole lives here and know where everything is."

"Sure, sounds good to me," I answered, responding to their smiles and Emmet's upbeat personality.

"Great," said JoAnne. "You look like nice guys."

Being able to understand the sing-song of their Creole-English dialect would be a big help to us.

So off we went with our guides to check in with the Honduras Immigration and Customs officials. It was a breeze clearing customs as "our boys" introduced us and knew the ropes. Then they led us on a search for my favorite breakfast food, granola. With hopeful smiles, they pointed out the cookie maker's house along the way.

"Her cookies are really good!" Emmet said, sounding like a seasoned salesperson.

"Should we buy some?" I said.

"Oh, yes!" Emmet said emphatically.

The chocolate chip-peanut cookies were excellent as testified by the boys smacking their lips and giving us wide smiles. Walking through the village, JoAnne and I learned more about the lives of these eleven and twelve-year-old boys. They had never been to mainland Honduras or even to the Island of Roatan which is only fifteen miles away. Their school teaches them in Spanish, the official language of Honduras while their "native" spoken language is an early version of English passed down by their pirate ancestors. The Bay Islands and Belize are unique to Central America due to their English influence in contrast with the dominant Spanish culture of most countries.

Emmet and Sheldon guided me as we took a dinghy ride across the bay to the shrimp processing plant where I bought a large bag of right-out-of-the-ocean fresh shrimp. With a dinner in hand, we ended our tour and headed back to *Aurora* with the boys.

"What are y'all going to do with all dem shrimp?" Emmet said with hope in his eyes.

"We're going to eat them," I said.

"We'd like some too," Emmet boldly said. "We'll help peel dem, okay?" JoAnne and I were pushovers for these smiling young boys who had been so helpful in town and so filled with upbeat energy.

"Okay, you all come over in two days and we'll all have some shrimp!" JoAnne said smiling.

*****

We moved *Aurora* about three miles down the coast to Sandy Bight (Bay) where other cruisers had anchored. The constant stream of small boats passing by told us that Guanaja didn't have roads. A small restaurant and bar standing on stilts in the bay was a magnet drawing in cruisers hungry for food and social contact. Here, we met Bev and Dave, a cruising couple in their sixties sailing on their 46 Cal center cockpit sloop, *Cloverleaf*.

"We've come to Guanaja from the Cayman Islands south of Cuba," said Dave. "I'm a mechanical engineer and worked for Bev's father at his cold storage business in Sioux City, Iowa."

"I'm Bev. I really love the freedom that comes with sailing off the beaten track. We're a long way from our usual haunts in the Bahamas."

"We'd like to learn more about the Bahamas because we plan to go there in a couple of years," said JoAnne.

Over cocktails and dinner, we explored common interests in cruising to new places.

The next day, Emmet and Sheldon showed up at *Aurora's* anchorage, making good on their promise to help us peel "dem shrimp." With their help, we had a great shrimp salad for lunch. Fascinated with our onboard library, Emmet found a book describing tropical fish to which he added the local names. He had a curiosity about life that was propelled by his bright, inquisitive mind. As his eyes darted around the boat, we could almost see the wheels of his mind turning. I was curious if he had access to many books in his school or home.

Using our dinghy with its five horsepower motor, the boys became our guides showing us around the bay.

"This small farm is raising pigs in wooden pens supported on stilts over the water," Sheldon pointed out. "Over there is a seventy-foot motor yacht. It was abandoned by its owner after a drug bust. Now, we are stripping off all of its copper and brass fittings for salvage. My cousins are helping so we can finish the job before it's towed out and sunk in deeper water."

They took us aboard. We saw that the interior hull coverings had been pulled away exposing the wiring and plumbing, most of which resided in piles on the deck. I wondered if these boys were driven by the genes of their pirate ancestors who took advantage of situations like this.

After arriving back on *Aurora*, Emmet and Sheldon said good-bye and paddled home for dinner.

* * * * *

Motoring further down the coast to Savannah Bight, we found a small town by the same name nestled against the steeply rising hills covered with grazing cows.

"Holy cow, those are the first ones we've seen in months!" exclaimed JoAnne.

As we went ashore on a beach, a young man came walking toward us.

"Hi, you look like Americans," he called out. "I'm David, an ex-Peace Corpsman. That's my new house over here, right on the beach. My assignment on Guanaja was to help people improve their homes in preparation for the arrival of electricity to replace the noisy generators used by most residents."

"Great to meet you, David," I said, shaking his hand. "We're impressed with your work and your new house. What a great location!" I marveled. "We're from the San Francisco Bay Area and have sailed all the way here."

"Guanaja is so isolated that most of our visitors are sailors," said David. "How has your trip been so far?"

"We spent a most fascinating week with the Kuna Indians in the San Blas Islands," said JoAnne. "I'd like to return there someday."

Stopping in a small coffee shop restaurant, we were surprised when looking out to see a large damaged sailboat, called *Sea Queen*, tied to two docks and bridging the gap between the two houses. JoAnne and I sat at a table. I asked a man at the next table if he knew what happened to *Sea Queen*.

"Well, I'm Sam, the owner of *Sea Queen*," he said. "The other night a storm created havoc in the anchorage when the increased wind and waves pounded the boats causing the anchors to drag.

A loose line in the water caught in the propeller as we tried to power into the wind and waves."

"Wow, just when you needed to overcome the dragging, you lost power," I said.

"Yeah, we were doomed," Sam said. "The wind and waves propelled *Sea Queen* onto shore damaging both a dock and her bow. On that night, we called for help on the VHF radio but it had sparked alive with calls for help. Everyone had the same problem and were using their engines to keep their boats from crashing into the docks and houses that lined the bay."

"I just realized that the storm JoAnne and I weathered on our way here was the same storm that damaged your boat," I said.

"Must have been," said Sam. "The worst of it is that the propeller shaft was bent after being abruptly stopped by the line. Unfortunately, repair shops were located miles away across the sea on mainland Honduras."

"Well, good luck with your repairs," I said as JoAnne and I got up to leave.

We learned later that Bob Bean, a retired fire captain from Long Beach sailing on *Windfall*, using his dinghy, had done his best to stabilize the boat by setting its anchor out toward to the windward. This effort stopped the constant bashing caused by the waves pushing *Sea Queen* into the dock. Bob became known as the "go-to-guy" whenever problems arose among his cruiser friends. His lovely wife, Janet, served as the VHF net control whenever a few of us were located in the same anchorage.

Reflecting on this incident, I realized that the weather was a major factor in determining how safe our cruise would be. Under duress too many things can go wrong. Perhaps, it was Livengood Luck that had us out to sea where we could handle the storm rather than in this exposed anchorage next to a lee shore.

Savannah Bight had become a gathering place for many of the cruisers JoAnne and I had met in Cartagena. Bob and Laurie on *Endless Weekend* suggested that we hike up to the ruins on Marble Hill that overlooked the bay.

Walking in that direction, we stopped and asked a twenty-year-old man named Daren with a short Afro hairdo if he'd like to be our guide. "Yeah, I'm happy to guide you up there," said Daren. "I know a lot about its history. Marble Hill was the home of the Payan Indians who were chased off the mainland before 900 A.D. by the more warlike Mayans. This defensive position is covered with large rocks and many caves that we can explore."

Scrambling among the rocks and trees, we found many pottery shards covering the hill.

"A National Geographic Expedition has already explored this hill," said Daren. "I think it's okay if you want to take a few shards back to your boat."'

"It feels great to have these pieces of history in our pockets," I said.

Walking back to Savannah Bight, we stopped in the coffee shop, joining Guy and Deborah, our friends on *La Coursaire*.

"How are things going for you two?" JoAnne said.

"Well, my ego got deflated in Guanaja Town when some boys asked us if they could be our guides," said Deborah. "We were ready to leave so we said no. Then as we were leaving one of the boys said, 'You sure look like Barbie.' So I smiled, but then he added, 'But you sure are old.'" Deborah rolled her eyes in disgust.

"Wow, that kid was tactless," said JoAnne. "You do look a lot like Barbie with your blond hair and trim body." I detected a slight hint of jealousy in JoAnne's voice. '

Heading out in our dinghy, we stopped at *Hotspur*. Karen and Fred greeted us and said they would soon conclude their cruising days so they could start a family. Fred, a boat mechanic, and Karen, a nurse, were planning to buy a home on the Chesapeake Bay where they could continue to sail *Hotspur*.

"How about coming over to *Aurora* for dinner?" I invited.

"Sure, we'll be over about five, okay?" said Karen, and I nodded.

When Fred and Karen arrived aboard *Aurora*, I wanted to test Fred's expertise.

"Fred, my Yanmar engine has a persistent problem of accumulating air in the diesel lines that eventually stalls the engine," I said, hoping he'd have a look and an answer.

"Let's see," said Fred. I opened the engine compartment for him. "The diesel return lines are missing," he said. "Those lines should run from the injectors back to the diesel tank. By installing the return lines, the extra fuel as well as any air will be returned to the tank."

During dinner Fred mentioned, "We have a dilemma. What to do with the dugout canoe that we found out at sea coming into Guanaja?"

After some weighing of options, our best decision was to give the canoe to the local net control of the VHF Radio Net who readily agreed to give it to a "deserving family," because canoes are the main source of their mobility and ability to fish.

*****

With Christmas approaching, we sailed *Aurora* over to Roatan Island where we found dock space at Romero's Dive and Yacht Club. From Roatan, JoAnne and I flew to Naples, Florida, for a family Christmas with my mom, my sister, Margie, and her friend Leslie. We were joined by my daughters Leanne and Darsie and Darsie's husband, Greg, who had all crewed on *Aurora* in the Sea of Cortez.

After the holidays, we flew back to Honduras, landing in San Pedro Sula. We found a travel agent who arranged a van trip to Copan, the site of Mayan ruins three hours away in the mountains near the border of Guatemala. I'd been wanting to see Copan after I saw it featured in a recent *National Geographic* article. It has the best preserved statues and stelae (stone trees) of any Mayan site. Copan's location next to a river on the floor of a valley makes it a pleasant place to visit from the nearby town of Copan de Las Ruinas.

After we had spent a night in a small hotel, our trip guide, Gorge, gathered us for the ride to the ruins. At the entrance gate to Copan, Victor, our handsome young local guide with a charming smile, strode toward and began giving us some background information.

"At its height, Copan was a city of 24,000 people that developed from 250 A.D. to 900 A.D. when the site was abandoned,"

Victor explained. "Like most Mayan cities, Copan was built in layers with the old structures filled in with rubble so the new structures could rise on top. This rebuilding occurred every fifty-two years when the sacred calendar, measured by two interlocking wheels, returned to its starting position."

Walking through the jungle into the site felt like taking giant steps back into the past.

As the trees thinned, suddenly a tan sandstone building came into view.

Victor continued, "This stele is covered with carvings and hieroglyphics recording the history of the kings who ruled this city-state. Over there is the hieroglyphic stairway built between one level and another that contains more inscriptions than any other structure in the world."

Eighteen Rabbit

We stood on the broad level plain in a valley surrounded with two to three-story structures on raised platforms that had been engulfed by the forces of nature prior to the structures being rescued from the grip of the smothering jungle. Stelae were standing in front of the buildings on the plain. These stone trees are slabs of stone about eight-feet high, three-feet wide, and four-inches thick covered with carvings.

"This is one of the most interesting stela and is dedicated to King Eighteen Rabbit who lived from January 2, 695 to May 3, 783," said Victor. "See how it's covered with glyphs telling of battles and other events during his reign. It's crowned with a statue of Eighteen Rabbit in his royal garb. That huge carved feather headdress proclaims his rank and his exalted status among Mayan rulers. Each ruler created a flurry of construction to mark and memorialize his reign."

The details of the carvings jumped out at us, due to the hardness of the limestone. It was an amazing sight considering the more than a thousand years in jungle weather. Victor then led us down a dark narrow stairway leading beneath the building where we discovered the tomb of another ruler long departed.

"Notice its stucco walls are painted a deep burgundy color that has survived along with paintings of Mayan warriors standing guard over a carved sarcophagus holding the royal bones," Victor said. "The downfall of Copan was probably brought on by incessant wars fought against other Mayan cities and the depletion of the surrounding soils."

Our tour with Victor was a delightful experience and an in-depth education about the meaning of the hieroglyphic writings. My journey to Copan would motivate me to read and study more books on the Mayans who comprised the dominant civilization in Eastern Central America from Honduras north to the Yucatan in Mexico. With my interest sparked, I wanted to learn about the Mayan history and culture so I could put what I was seeing into a more complete context. I also vowed to explore more Mayan sites whenever possible. It felt to me that I was earning another Master's Degree, although not from a university.

Arriving back on Roatan by small plane from San Pedro Sula, JoAnne and I set to work on *Aurora*. My tasks included reinstalling instruments that had been repaired in Florida over Christmas and the new GPS I purchased for finding our position anywhere in the world while also knowing our course and the speed over the bottom.

"JoAnne, the only thing this GPS can't do is cook breakfast!" I exclaimed. "What an advance it is beyond the older system. The GPS receives data all the time, so I can really know where we are. No more guessing!"

"That will be a real improvement," said JoAnne. "I'm already feeling more comfortable."

One day as JoAnne and I walked the path to the yacht club, we met Mona, a large spider monkey chained to a tree. We learned she had been banished from her perch overlooking the dining patio for being naughty by throwing sticks and other "stuff" at guests. Mona loved bananas and peanuts but was really more hungry for affection as JoAnne found out when she walked by a little too close to the needy monkey.

Without warning Mona suddenly jumped from her perch onto JoAnne's back. She clung to JoAnne much like a child except that the monkey's long arms wrapped completely around my wife's neck restricting her breathing. I tried unsuccessfully to peel her fingers off JoAnne's neck but was met with Mona's low growl and bared teeth.

As I ran back to the boat, I called out, "Stay still. I'm going to get some bananas."

Fortunately Mona's love of bananas was stronger than her desire for JoAnne's affection. The monkey untangled her stranglehold on JoAnne's neck, succumbing to the lure of bananas. Grabbing JoAnne's hand, I pulled her out of Mona's reach. I gently hugged her as her head sagged onto my shoulder. Both of us sighed deeply with relief.

After completing all our needed work on *Aurora*, we sailed her a few miles down the island to French Harbor. We anchored out with many of our friends in the lee of small cays on the reef that protected the island and our anchorage.

Improving weather gave me an opportunity to scuba dive with two friends along an incredibly deep coral wall with colors that were a feast for the eyes. These shapes and colors created a feeling of wonder at Mother Nature's ability to create and revel in such diversity. As I descended sixty feet down the coral wall, I suddenly became aware of an overwhelming fear. There was just too much water above me for comfort. As I stared down at my friends already on the bottom about sixty more feet below me, I thought, No way. I can't go down there! Taking some deep breaths from the air tank, I rose slowly upward, feeling calmer the closer I got toward the surface. I stopped on the surface and checked my equipment. Everything was okay, so I dove down to sixty feet again, my personal depth limit, enjoying the beauty of the coral.

While I was scuba diving, JoAnne was snorkeling with two friends.

"I had a wonderful time," she said later when we shared experiences. "The bright streams of the sunlight shimmering in the water made the pastel colors more vibrant."

Our ongoing guessing game was trying to figure out when there would be a break in the weather. Our trapped fleet of cruisers was itching to move on to explore the other Bay Islands of Honduras. A change in the steady flow of strong northers rolling down from the Gulf of Mexico was needed to release us. After a break in the storms finally came, half the fleet joined *Aurora* sailing off to Cayos Cochinos (Hog Cays) about twenty miles west toward the Honduran Coast. It was exhilarating to break free from harbor life and to be underway on a beautiful day toward a new destination waiting to be explored.

The Hog Cays did not disappoint us, as palm tree-covered hills rose above white sandy beaches surrounded by reefs forming a deep water lagoon between two large islands. We moored on buoys provided by the Plantation Beach Resort that were needed to protect the coral from anchors. In the morning before snorkeling, we explored the island, stopping at a medical clinic built of limestone at the land's end. We had learned that a nurse started the clinic. It serves this outlying island, but also draws patients from as far as one hundred miles away. Joanne and I delivered empty pill bottles to be used to dispense medicine to patients requiring long-term intervention for their chronic problems.

In the evening, we found all the sailors in the anchorage gathered on *Kennemer* for a floating potluck. We met the owners, Glen and his wife, June, in their late seventies, who were still sailing. Glen, an athletic avid windsurfer, often zoomed by *Aurora* on his tours around the anchorage. A retired nuclear scientist who worked at Oak Ridge National Laboratory in Tennessee, Glen would windsurf to work across an adjacent TVA Lake and then change into his "normal" clothes for work. We were impressed with his vitality expressed in a "go-for-it" approach to life.

Morning storm clouds billowing on the horizon forced us to scrap our plans to visit the Garifuna village across the lagoon. Instead, we cast off our mooring lines and sailed for the shelter provided by the island of Utila. As our sails filled, the twenty miles flew by as we were being driven by rising winds. The boat surfed on and down the growing waves. Deborah and Guy on *La Coursaire* helped us find our entrance through the reef by giving us detailed navigational instructions via the VHF radio. Utila seemed much cleaner than other Bay Islands towns and had only a single street fronting its harbor.

Later, we met Bradford Duncan, a tall distinguished looking man and the self-proclaimed "Resident Overlord of Utila," who told us proudly, "For twenty years, I've been working to develop and to keep Utila clean." He said, "Often I pay a crew to sweep the streets and collect the garbage." Duncan, an octogenarian, is hard to distinguish from the workers on his projects because he is a hands-on structural engineer.

"My lawyer in Dallas is the ex-Secretary of State, James Baker," he told me.

"Great to have friends in high places," I said.

Our visit to the Turtle Conservation Project gave us all the opportunity to meet Glen, a handsome, twenty-something Peace Corps volunteer with a great tan. He was working with a local conservation group that uses school children to help raise baby (fifty cent sized) Hawksbill and Green turtles into vigorous six-inch youngsters in only six months time. The turtles are kept in a net-enclosed wire structure in the sea that protects them from predators, while the children feed them flies and the bigger bugs collected from outside one particular restaurant. We all quickly decided not to eat there! The parents of these eight to ten-year-olds were pleased with their kids' new found interest. The kids were teaching the parents about how throwing plastic garbage into the sea posed danger to the turtles. Having grown large enough to dissuade most of their predators from trying to eat them, these wiggly turtles now were ready to be released from their pen into the sea. Glen's successful efforts and the hands on approach of the Peace Corps gave us all a good feeling about him and our own country. He was certainly one of the most respected and popular young men on the Island of Utila!

Just before leaving Utila, I walked up a trail overlooking the town and anchorage to take a few pictures. Two girls came whizzing down the hill on one bike, almost hitting me. One girl, about twelve years old with wild red hair, let out a stream of swear words as she passed. She cursed me for being in her way, sounding like ghosts of her crude pirate ancestors. I leaped into the brush to get off the trail and out of her way.

With improving weather and perhaps a haunting warning from those "pirates" on the bike, it was time to sail on to Guatemala.

26

SAILING INTO GUATEMALA

Sailing north along the Honduran Coast, we found two good anchorages before reaching the entrance to the Rio Dulce at Livingston, Guatemala. Timing our arrival at the period of lunar high tides was essential because the low tide depth of the sand bar across the Rio Dulce was said to be only six feet. We were concerned because *Aurora's* depth was 5'10", or perhaps more. At the Cabo Tres Puntas anchorage, bad news came over the radio, that *La Coursaire* was not able to cross the bar. Later, friends measured her depth at 7'2" so Deborah and Guy would have big trouble going in!

An action plan quickly evolved. We would all meet an hour before high tide in the morning, measure the actual depths, and mark the deepest channel into the river mouth. We would use anything that floated attached by light string with weights to hold it on the bottom. By following this path of floats over the bar, *Aurora* went through with not more than a bounce off the bottom, but *LightHeart*, drawing 6'6", got stuck part way in. A strong inboard engined power boat came out from Livingston to help. By using a halyard from the top of their mast, the boat crew was able to heel and then pull *LightHeart* over three sand ridges into deeper water. *La Coursaire* came next, running aground quickly and requiring all the tow boat's available power to bounce it over the shallows into the welcoming deeper water of the Rio Dulce.

Our group motored into the harbor off Livingston where officials were rowing out to check us in. Next, we went ashore for a celebratory lunch toasting our successful strategy of "one for all and all for one." We were ready to begin our of twenty-five-mile trip up the Rio Dulce to Lago Izabel.

Out on the street in Livingston, we heard a voice say, "Hello, JoAnne." Turning, we were amazed to see Mike Hughes, an Irish denizen of Berkeley's Starry Plow Pub, striding up the hill toward us.

Sitting together over a few beers, Mike recounted his story to us. "I've been in Nicaragua helping farmers rebuild after the recent earthquake. Some of these farmers were 'Contras' led by Daniel Ortega who are fighting right wing paramilitary groups supported by the United States. Things were getting rather dicey, so I got out of Nicaragua by slipping over the border into Guatemala." Mike took a few sips of beer.

"I'm not going to let a little war get in my way of delivering my help to those needy farmers," he continued, proud to support leftwing causes. "But, my money has run out, so it's back to Berkeley for me."

"Thank God you made it out," JoAnne said. "Be sure that you tell Barbara and my other friends at the Starry Plow that we have crossed paths in Livingston. Just think about the chances of that happening!" JoAnne and I were more than a little awed by Mike's bravado!

*****

Our business in town finished, we slowly motored up the Rio Dulce, penetrating into the interior through a canyon lined with towering cliffs and thick jungle. Snowy white egrets and gray pelicans flew overhead. After being out at sea for two years, it was thrilling to be on the river in such a lush and beautifully enclosed habitat. We moved along, passing canoes and larger outboard *pangas* carrying Mayan Indians and their provisions up and down stream. We saw many Mayan thatched roof houses complete with boathouses built to protect their dugout canoes. Scores of colorful green, yellow, and red parrots flew out of the jungle, adding bursts of color to the scene.

After stopping to anchor up a side stream named the Rio Tatin, we joined Deborah and Guy on *La Coursaire* to plan a dinghy trip up the tributary in the morning. We got up early the next day and set off in our dinghies. It wasn't long before we found that the Rio Tatin abruptly ended in a pile of rocks at the base of a steep hill. Here we met a group of Mayan Indians carrying supplies uphill on their backs using tumplines stretched across their foreheads to support the heavy loads.

A man who looked to be the oldest told us, "There is a large cave not too far away. You should see it."

"*Si, senior, esta un bien idea,*" I replied. What good luck I thought.

The man called over a fourteen-year-old boy named Wilbur and asked him to guide us to the cave. Agreeing, we all started out together, but JoAnne and Deborah were forced to turn back finding that climbing the steep trail wearing flip-flops was too dangerous.

"We'll wait for you guys at the bottom," said Deborah.

Guy and I continued up the trail through the jungle with Wilbur who was coughing due to the exertion. We passed more Mayans carrying rough cut lumber boards down to the water on their backs again using tumplines to keep their loads in place. We guessed these loads weighed about eighty pounds each. After arriving near the cave, we scrambled down a boulder-strewn riverbed under a large natural bridge cut through a cliff. As we walked into the cave, our eyes were drawn up to a ceiling that looked like dinosaur backbones protruding from the eroded limestone surface.

"Wow, Guy, this is really a spectacular cave," I said.

"I'm glad your Spanish is good," Guy said. "Otherwise we would have missed coming all the way up to this place."

The river continued through the cave until it suddenly disappeared, making a swishing gurgling sound under the back wall of the cave. We realized it must flow out at the bottom of the mountain where we left our dinghies.

While walking back down the mountain, Wilbur mentioned, "*Yo tengo una piedra de oro, quieres mirar.*" (I have a golden stone, do you wish to see it?)

"*Si,* Wilbur," I said eagerly.

Wilbur went to his house and returned with his rock of gold, really a crystallized fossil of a spiral sea shell. He wanted to sell it for the equivalent of one dollar. "Okay," I immediately said. Hearing my quick response, Wilbur tripled the price. I was being asked to pay the new price, because bargaining is the expected response in his culture. So bargain I did, we settled on a middle price, and the incredible fossil was mine.

"Wilbur, if you paddle out to *Aurora* tomorrow morning, I'll give you some cough medicine for your bad cough," I said with concern. "But if the cough doesn't stop, you'll need to see a doctor."

The next day on *Aurora*, JoAnne and I hoped that he understood our repeated warnings. We gave the cough medicine to Wilbur as promised. We also gave him a few small kitchen tools hoping they would prove useful for his family.

After motoring further up the Rio Dulce, we anchored opposite a hot spring that formed a warm pool at the edge of the river. We enjoyed our first hot bath in months and luxuriated in the pleasant water. As we sailed on, the Rio Dulce widened into a lake, which we crossed in a few more hours. *Aurora* arrived at Mario's Marina where most of the other cruisers had gathered. Dinner at Mario's Restaurant turned into an event as the news anchor, Walter Cronkite, sat with his friends only a few tables away.

JoAnne wanted to thank him for speaking at her son Doug's graduation from Dartmouth College, I discouraged her. "JoAnne, that would be gauche. He just wants to eat his dinner." She was hurt by my comment, which I realized later was not called for because she had been at the graduation and was a huge fan of Walter's.

The marina staff had made arrangements for a trip to Guatemala City, so we joined the group of cruisers on a launch ride to Flores, the nearest town on the highway, catching the local "chicken" bus out to the main highway. That name for the bus was earned by transporting many Indians and their chickens. Most of the group followed the instructions of the marina manager so we waited for the express bus to arrive.

"Can you imagine having a stewardess greet us with cold drinks?" JoAnne exclaimed once on the bus. "We have comfortable seats and TV, too."

"This bus certainly puts Greyhound to shame," I replied. "But, it's too bad that the couple from San Jose, California, got so impatient or didn't believe it would come."

After arriving in Guatemala City, JoAnne and I roamed the central area and found that the National Palace and the Cathedral Metropolitana were open. We visited both and saw an abundance of statues and ornaments of the Spanish Rococo period, the main style of the Colonial Period.

* * * * *

Chicken Bus

In the morning, we caught a different "chicken" bus, actually an old Blue Bird school bus, and rode it higher into the volcanic mountains to the southwest, headed for the city of Antigua. The crowded bus put JoAnne sitting knee-to-knee with Dr. Patrick Harpole, a physician from Walnut Creek, California. What a small

Maria in Antigua

world! He had just completed a volunteer assignment doing corrective surgeries on children of villagers living outside Guatemala City. We teamed up with him and settled into a basic small pension in Antigua.

The next day, we all set out to explore the fascinating old city filled with colonial buildings, churches, and Spanish language schools. Located in an earthquake zone, Antigua had many buildings that were in ruins, including the former capital building. The new capital was built in Guatemala City. In addition to its scenic location, Antigua is known for its Spanish language schools that attract students from all over the world.

After spending some time with us, Patrick became alarmed about JoAnne's persistent cough. "How long have you been coughing like this?" he said.

"Oh, months," said JoAnne. "This cough may have started when I began taking a new blood pressure medication."

"Your cough might be a side effect of the med," said Patrick. "I'll check with a pharmacy to see if a different medication is available for you."

Luckily, the cough disappeared after JoAnne began taking her new meds. We both agreed that Patrick Harpole should become our own doctor back home in California.

The next day, JoAnne and I moved to a nicer small hotel, the Santa Catalina Convent Hotel featuring a functioning bath, a large, sunny room, and a central courtyard opening through an arched gate onto the main shopping street. One day when we were walking into another courtyard across the street, a charming ten-year-old named Maria met us. Flashing her big smile, she held up hand-woven Mayan shirts. Maria amazed us by communicating in English, but she could also speak French and Italian along with her native Mayan and Spanish. She had learned these languages on the streets of Antigua where she commuted fifty miles each day from her village near Lake Atitlan to sell her goods. Buying two blue, yellow, and red striped shirts, JoAnne and I marveled at Maria's mastery of the art of selling.

Afterwards, I said to JoAnne, "I wonder how far she could go with some formal education?"

"I can imagine her being a translator at the United Nations," said JoAnne.

After renting a small car, JoAnne and I drove to Panahachel on the shores of Lake Atitlan surrounded by high volcanoes. The Mayan villages and the houses of North American ex-pats along the shore could only be reached by boat. As we boarded a motor launch for a trip out to the peninsula of San Antonio de Atitlan, we were amazed to find Patrick Harpole talking with two teenaged Mayan girls, Dolores and Rita, who had agreed to be his guides in their home town. They helped us find good bargains in the street market because they knew all the vendors and the prices that locals would pay.

We walked together uphill to St. James Catholic Church, dominating the town from its high position. Inside, we were dazzled by an abundance of gold. The girls then led us out a side door into a narrow street leading to a nearby house where a group of Mayan Indians were holding a special Mammon ceremony in a rectangular room. Mammon is an antichrist figure, perhaps the personification of greed and materialism who takes a human form in his scarecrow-looking body complete with a straw cowboy hat. "He" was being cared for by an elder of the Mayan Brotherhood, an organization that parallels the official Catholic Church. The elder was seated on a chair next to a table with a bottle of beer in the center of a smoke filled room. One elder chanted as other Mayans sat in a circle around Mammon burning incense. The participants were mesmerized and gazed at Mammon through the haze. The ceremony had an otherworldly feeling as smoke altered our vision. Each person seemed to have a special desire that they hoped Mammon would fulfill. For a dollar U.S., I was given permission to video the ceremony which seemed to have evolved from the ancient religion of the Mayas.

Dolores and Rita walked with us back to the boat before saying goodbye, having given us a very complete and most interesting tour of San Antonio de Atitlan.

"*Muchas gracias y Buena suerte!*" we said wishing them well.

"JoAnne, I could never have imagined being in a ceremony like that," I said, still feeling the effects.

*****

We drove our rented car through the countryside, passing small farms terraced into the hillsides. Their small whitewashed adobe houses were stained brown by rain-splashed soil. We stopped along the side of the road to video the panorama. While I was recording, two boys passed by on their way home from school. The older boy held a rope tied around the waist of the younger one. I guessed that perhaps they did this to prevent the younger from running out onto the highway and to assist him when climbing the steep hills.

We arrived back in Guatemala City and stayed at the Hotel Casa Blanca located next to the U.S. Embassy and not far from the airport. JoAnne and I flew out the next day to neighboring San Jose, Costa Rica, to visit our ex-cruising friends, George and Akiko. They had sold their thirty-eight-foot sailboat *Camille* after a disastrous trip off the Central American coast and settled on a one hundred- twenty-acre farm near Quepos on the Pacific Coast.

On the bus ride to Quepos from San Jose, the differences in living conditions and standard of living of people in Guatemala and Costa Rica became immediately apparent. Guatemalans generally seemed poorer, living in smaller and more dilapidated houses, while Costa Ricans seemed wealthier, living in more substantial-looking homes. One reason for this difference could be that the democratic Costa Rican government grants a low interest loan to anyone who has accumulated a one hundred dollar down payment to buy a cement block house. In this way a significant percentage of the population can own and improve their homes, often adding patios surrounded by trees, vegetable gardens, and flowering plants. The Guatemalan government seems designed to benefit the upper class, while using its right wing paramilitary forces to suppress the ongoing Mayan struggle to achieve more political and economic parity.

George picked us up at the bus station in Quepos, then drove us in his Toyota Land Cruiser, the "Costa Rica National Vehicle." We then drove fifteen miles inland toward the mountains where the home of him and his partner, Akiko, Rancho Viejo Marinero, "Old Sailor's Ranch," is located.

When we arrived, George and Akiko gave us a tour. "Our property extends over there to the base of the steeply rising coastal range," George said, pointing to the east. "In this small community, we're lucky that electricity and piped water are available. Our green-colored cement block house has three bedrooms, a living and dining area, a kitchen open to the back, and a cement bathroom with a shower. We love its location in this banana grove. This is a working rancho complete with twenty head of Brahma cows and many calves, a huge but gentle Brahma bull, three horses, and even a singing dog who creates a sound somewhere between howling and crooning."

Leading us on, George continued, "Let's walk this way to the two-acre pineapple field located by the stream flowing down from the mountains. Over there, you can see we have a grove of orange trees. The whole Rancho cost only $46,000 which is the amount we secured when selling our cruising boat, *Camille*."

"Wow, George, a place like this would cost a fortune back in California!" I exclaimed. "Seeing all of this almost makes me want to come down here and get back into my homesteading thing."

"Well, that would be great," said George. "You two would be wonderful friends to have as neighbors. Thrown in this bargain are the services of Ricardo, the hired man. He's been my strong right arm in managing the farm. Ricardo happily works for one dollar per hour which is a higher wage than most Costa Ricans receive." It was clear that Ricardo had really helped George make the transition from sailor to tropical farmer.

"We love our new home, the way of life we've created, and the new friendships with other ex-pats we've made living in the area," Akiko added.

As they showed us around their beautiful area, both JoAnne and I could feel a strong pull to join them as neighbors. Having already done my "homesteading thing," however, I thought that continuing our cruising would be more rewarding for us at that time.

*****

Once back in Guatemala City, we crossed paths with Guy and Deborah, our neighbors at Mario's Marina when we checked into Casa Blanca Hotel. We compared notes on inland travel before we flew off again, this time to Tikal, the ancient Mayan capital located in the northwestern part of Guatemala. With luck, we were able to stay in a lodge close to the ruins. On our first trip into the site with a guide, we walked out of the jungle into an immense clearing dominated by three huge pyramids rising out of the mist.

"This is like finding the skyscrapers of New York City materializing out of a jungle," I gasped.

"Yeah, it's rather mind boggling," said JoAnne. "How in earth did all these immense structures get here?"

Acropolises stood on mounds of earth on three sides of the site where passageways connected groups of buildings. Archeologists of the University of Pennsylvania had excavated the site between 1956 and 1969 after its earlier discovery in 1842. We climbed the one hundred-fifty-four-foot high Temple I, which had been restored after being extricated from the clutches of the tropical rainforest that lapped near the structure. The glyphs, however, did not fare so well because this local limestone was much softer than the stone used at Copan and had been worn down by many years of rain and blackened by mold. We walked away savoring our wonderment.

I woke up at dawn the following morning but left JoAnne still sleeping, while I hiked alone through the jungle. A troop of spider monkeys accompanied me overhead in the trees. Black headed trogans perched on branches showed off their long multicolored tails. Loud chachalacas created a racket higher up in the trees. Beautiful ocellated turkeys strutted along showing off their iridescent blue, yellow, and orange colored plumage.

I arrived at the base of Pyramid III in the dim light of dawn. After looking at its imposing two hundred foot height, I began my assent using roots and rocks for handholds. Finally reaching the ritual observatory on top, I was in time to witness the first glowing rays of the morning sun. Light streamed through the doorway illuminating the human and jaguar figures painted on the back wall. Awe swept over me as the power of the figures leapt out at me. Appreciation and astonishment followed when I realized the level of expertise and amount of work that the Mayans had used to create this experience for their high priests and for me, now following in their footsteps.

Looking out over Tikal, I saw the other pyramids rising out of a sea of dense green trees and vines as the sun rose higher, brightening the ground. At its zenith, Tikal had been an urban center for about 60,000 people. About one hundred-fifty tons of salt had to be imported each year because local salt sources did not exist. I looked out and saw that causeways radiated out from the center of Tikal providing access over the lowlands surrounding the site. Local water sources being scarce, Mayan engineers created collection and storage systems to trap rain water during the rainy season for their use throughout the year.

Following the Mayan fifty-two-year calendar cycle, old structures were torn down and filled with rubble so that more impressive buildings could be constructed with each new layer rising over the old. The size and scope of Tikal makes it one of the most impressive archeological sites on the planet! Being able to see and experience Tikal in person added depth to my understanding of how the ancient world functioned even though knowledge of it had been lost to us for centuries. In that context, perhaps the rise of our "modern" civilization is all the more impressive.

After this exhilarating experience, we flew back the next day to Guatemala City with enough time to connect with the brother of JoAnne's Berkeley friend Connie and his wife. Rolando and Rebecca live in a business district near the National Palace. Rolando is a mechanical engineer and owns a refrigeration parts business. He uses his expertise to design and build large refrigeration systems. Rolando also makes many trips to Miami to buy U.S.-made parts and other goods. Many other wealthy Central and South Americans make these frequent trips. Rolando and Rebecca treated us to a delicious steak dinner and we talked about our travels in their country and our trip by rental car from Antigua to Guatemala City.

"Wow, I'm really alarmed that you took an auto trip," said Rolando. "We Guatemalans don't go anywhere out of the city without an armed guard. There are many bandits and rebels in the countryside."

"Well, in our case, perhaps not knowing of all the dangers turned out to be a good thing," I said. "We blithely toured the countryside and fortunately didn't encounter any problems on the road along the way." And we could have been lucky—again.

* * * * *

The next day, we took the bus back to Flores, where a water taxi took us out to Mario's Marina and our reunion with *Aurora*. The two weeks away seemed more like a month. We had met so many people and seen so many new places. My next objective was to pick up a new Mariner Outboard Motor that I had ordered from a shop in Flores. We received the ten HP motor, right out of the box, for about eight hundred dollars, which is about half the price for the same engine in the United States. It seemed that the Guatemalan government did not charge import duties on outboard engines because they were vitally important to poor fishermen.

Back on the water again, we glided under the highway bridge into Lago Izabel. Our eyes soaked up the expanded horizon of mountain ranges in the distance and miles of green shoreline covered by dense trees entwined with vines in the foreground. After anchoring *Aurora* in a small cove, JoAnne and I relaxed in the cockpit. Waves of contentment swept over us as we watched the setting sun's changing pallete of yellow, orange, and red hues on the water and the distant mountains. Snuggling together, we exchanged smiles and allowed our bodies to revel in the moment.

In the morning, it was time to move on. We motored again down the Rio Dulce toward the Caribbean Sea, stopping in the late afternoon to anchor in the canyon. This gave us time to absorb more of its magic as flocks of birds flew in to find roosts in trees along the river's banks. We were happily immersed in nature.

27

HOW ABOUT BELIZE?

After a restful night, JoAnne and I continued down the Rio Dulce to Livingston where we checked out of Guatemala in a hurry because the tide was falling. At full throttle with a few bumps on the bottom later, we crossed over the dreaded entrance sand bar and turned left to head north across the bay to Punta Gorda, Belize, where we checked in with authorities. Deteriorating weather forced us to leave the open anchorage hastily and make for the barrier reef where a small cay offered shelter from the increasing wind and mounting waves.

By morning, the storm became a heavy downpour, obscuring our vision beyond the bow of *Aurora*. Radar waves bounced back, short-circuited by the rain drops blocking their path in search of islands or other solid objects. We had to reach Placencia to make arrangements for the visit of JoAnne's daughter, Betsy. Luckily, our new GPS succeeded in providing accurate latitude and longitude readings that enabled me to plot *Aurora's* position on the chart verifying our course. The rain finally stopped as we entered the anchorage between the Placencia Peninsula and an adjacent island.

We drove the dinghy at full speed, flying across the bay and landing at a small dock near the post office that had the only public telephone in town.

Suddenly a three-wheeled motorcycle roared up. "I'm Janice, the postmistress. How can I help you?" the woman driving it said.

"We're trying to make arrangements for my daughter Betsy's visit," said JoAnne. "We need to have Betsy's new airline tickets hand delivered to her in Belize City so she can fly into Placencia."

"Okay, I can arrange that," said Janice. "I have friends at the airport."

"Wow, thanks so much!" said JoAnne.

While waiting for Betsy's arrival, we discovered papaya milk shakes at Sonny's Resort, fresh bread from John the bread man, and a great fish dinner served by Brenda in her *palapa* restaurant. During another downpour, she brought out hot rum toddies as we dodged drips coming through the palm-thatched roof while waiting for her uncle to bring in the catch of the day in his canoe. Talk about fresh!

By morning, the rain had stopped, making it easier to motor *Aurora* up the canal to a new ship terminal being built by the U.S. Army Corps of Engineers. Leaving the dinghy on the shore, we had a short walk to the grass airstrip. Waiting for the plane on the veranda of a small hotel with revolving plantation fans overhead, we ordered cold beers. JoAnne and I imagined we were in the movie *African Queen*. Watching the two-engine plane land and taxi right up to the hotel's front door heightened our "right out of the movies" experience.

With a broad smile, Betsy stepped into the tropical heat saying, "At last, I'm really here. Have I got hugs for you guys!"

"It's been too long for me too," said JoAnne hugging Betsy.

"Yeah, it's great seeing you two together again," I said with a hug.

Taking the dinghy back to *Aurora* created enough breeze to cool all of us down a bit, in the heat of the tropics. Betsy had enjoyed being at the helm when sailing on *Aurora* on San Francisco Bay. She let out a whoop when seeing her lying gracefully at anchor.

Climbing aboard, Betsy said, "It's great to be back on *Aurora*."

That evening at Brenda's Restaurant, we heard about the impending arrival of an intense storm system sweeping down on Belize from the Gulf of Mexico. I knew we had to sail to a more protected anchorage. I alerted Bev and Dave on *Cloverleaf* by VHF radio, and we jointly made plans to move our boats early in the morning to the Pelican Cays where its anchorage was almost completely surrounded by land. With Betsy at the helm, *Aurora* glided into the lagoon with our new buddy boat. We anchored in sixty feet of water, deep for an anchorage. I deployed all of the available chain totaling two hundred feet with the anchor to secure *Aurora* to the bottom. Now the crew could relax. Hearing their laughter and giggles from the aft cabin, I knew that JoAnne and Betsy were having much needed mother-daughter time.

After dinner, Bev and Dave joined us for a weather-watching party on *Aurora*. We listened to reports on the High Seas Radio confirming that the storm consisted of 30-40-knot winds and 15-foot seas upgrading it to a gale. At about 1 a.m., we awoke to *Aurora's* rigging shaking in the 30-knot winds. After turning on the radar, I saw that *Aurora* was holding fast but realized that *Cloverleaf* was dragging her anchor, fortunately stopping just before reaching shore. JoAnne, Betsy, and I took turns on anchor watch through the night. I awoke at 5 a.m. when a second, stronger weather trough came through with sustained winds of 35 knots. Again our anchor held, as we maintained our position. We felt lucky to be in Belize rather than on the East Coast of the United States that had been pummeled by one hundred-mph shrieking winds. "The Storm of the Century" had caused nine deaths, severe beach erosion, and damage to many boats and marinas.

In the morning light, the wind and waves began to subside much to our relief. Staying put in our safe anchorage became "the thing to do." Responding to an invitation from Bev and Dave, we dinghied over to *Cloverleaf* for a day of board games and sharing experiences with these veteran cruisers. Owning their Cal 3-46 sloop for seventeen years had inspired many improvements and updates that made *Cloverleaf* seem like a much newer boat. Their travels had taken Bev and Dave to the Bahamas many times. This was their first trip to Belize, Guatemala, and Honduras in the Western Caribbean. Sharing this day with them was a welcome activity on a stormy day.

"Compared with *Aurora*, your main saloon is more like a living room with swiveling chairs and a real couch," said Betsy with a wink. "I could easily get used to this."

Back on *Aurora*, JoAnne saw that food was running low, so we decided to make a supply run in the morning to Dangriga, further north on the mainland coast of Belize.

Off under sunny skies in the morning, Betsy sailed in a 10-knot wind. "Wow, sailing here is amazing," she said. "The water is a crystal clear tinted blue and the sky has amazing white puffy clouds. I need to pinch myself to be sure I'm really here."

I dropped the anchor off the town opposite the school. Dangriga is a town populated by Garifuna people who sprang up on the island of St. Vincent when the shipwrecks of two British slave ships in 1685 forced the African survivors to swim ashore. These and subsequent Africans integrated rapidly into the indigenous Arawakan or Caribe societies through marriage, creating a new population of Black Caribes now known as the Garifuna people. French and British attempts at the colonization of St. Vincent in 1796 eventually caused the Garifuna people to flee. Fearing being enslaved again, they relocated to Honduras where some of their numbers migrated north to Belize.

Our friends Joseph and Myrtle Palacio, living in Belize City with their two children, were Garifuna. JoAnne met them at UC Berkeley when they asked for her services at the Foreign Student Office where she was an advisor. Joseph was pursuing a Doctorate in Anthropology while Myrtle was working on a Master's Degree in Business. We had made arrangements to stay with them when we reached Belize City.

Coming ashore in Dangriga, we passed scores of smiling school children jumping rope and playing games with great gusto on their lunch hour. Further along our way, we met Charles Gamboa, Myrtle's cousin who had been alerted to watch for us. Charles, a fast talker, happily volunteered to be our guide around Dangriga. We tuned our ears to Charles' Garifuna accented English. He helped us find all the items on our shopping list by going into almost all the small shops scattered along the dirt main street. Because Belize had been a British colony, everyone spoke English. Shopkeepers were eager to answer our questions about the types of food on display that were new to us.

Paradise Island

The light was beginning to fade as we made our way out to Bluefield Range where we carefully searched for the passes through the two reefs into the protecting the lagoon. Our *Belize Cruising Guide* bought from Nigel Calder, its author, whom we met in Dangriga, helped us through the "skinny" water where we found seven other cruising boats at anchor. In talking with cruisers on *Blue Ribbon* and *Locura*, we gathered suggestions of more interesting places to visit. One of these, Rendezvous Cay, was located on the barrier reef and became our first destination to visit in the morning. The white sand, small size, and waving palm trees captivated us, earning the title of our own "Paradise Island" in the clear blue sea. We sat in the shade of a palm tree absorbing the beauty.

"It's such a small island, but it's just the right size to fit into my mind," Betsy said. "When I need to go to a peaceful place in my thoughts, this is where I'll go."

"I hope you won't object to sharing it with me," JoAnne said.

After lunch, we headed through the reef into the deeper azure water of the Caribbean Sea. *Aurora* sailed north to Turneffe Atoll located about twenty miles off the coast of Belize. Turneffe Atoll is a series of small islands connected by reefs creating a very shallow central lagoon. Betsy steered *Aurora*, putting her engineering skills to use. I stood on the mast spreaders and called down directions that I discerned by reading the water color. We found a good spot to anchor without any annoying bumps on the bottom. This atoll is the largest and most biologically diverse in the Western Hemisphere. Nearby is a "Blue Hole" that extends hundreds of feet down below the water's surface. Unfortunately, time and the weather limited our exploration of the lagoon. Another norther roared through during the night causing the anchor to drag while we all began to feel that, "Hey, this is getting to be a bit too much!"

Betsy's two week's time with us had been disappearing at a rapid pace, so we sailed back through the barrier reef and made for Cay Chapel, the only marina in Belize having deep enough water to accommodate sailboats. Along the way, we motored into a skinny water area when I was again up on the spreaders trying to locate the deeper bluer water. Bouncing to a halt confirmed Betsy and JoAnne's decision that following my directions was a BIG mistake so they turned *Aurora* around. This was mutiny because I wanted to continue going forward, but their reading of the chart proved to be more accurate. Lucky for me, the problem of the light-hearted mutiny was soon resolved when we found Smitty, an old tug captain, now the harbormaster at Cay Chapel, who directed us to a slip. We were safe from the storm but not from thousands of biting flies. We fought back with chemical and physical warfare, driving the pests out of the interior of *Aurora* where we took refuge and waited until sunset when it was safe to return to the cockpit.

*****

The next morning, we took a speedboat to Belize City in the morning to visit Joseph and Myrtle's home and guesthouse on Hyde Lane near the market area of the city. The door opened with a loud cry, "Welcome, JoAnne and Betsy!" Myrtle rushed to them with open arms. Soon Aniki and Bina, their teenage children, joined us flashing their wide smiles.

"Wow, you kids have grown since your parents' student days in Berkeley," said JoAnne.

"Yes," said Myrtle. "Aniki is interested in criminology, and Bina is attracted to marine biology. Both are attending two-year colleges in Belize and are hoping to follow our example by studying in the United States or Canada."

Settling into their guesthouse, we had easy access into Belize City and its attractive street market. Later in the day, when Joseph returned home from his job as director of the Belize Campus of the University of the West Indies, we all gathered for dinner. JoAnne, Betsy, and I felt truly blessed to be encompassed by the warmth and love of the Palacio family.

Myrtle is a sturdy looking dynamo with her own business and computer school located in the house. She teaches young adults how to become good employees in a culture that is so laid back that being on time is not a cultural value. Creating employable people became one of Myrtle's most important tasks because computers were just being introduced in Belize in 1993. She is using her skills to create the first generation of computer operators there. Obviously, this is a "happening place."

*****

A day at the Belize City Zoo had been highly recommended since the natural habitats for its animals created a unique and informative experience for the visitors. We had an up close and personal encounter with a young jaguar who stood inches away from us on the other side of a wire fence. He seemed very interested in us, coming up to the fence while intently watching us.

I spoke quietly to him saying, "Nice kitty, nice kitty," as he purred enjoying my attention.

We hitched a ride back to Belize City in the van filled with health workers from Canada who were here training their local counterparts in the methods and principles of family planning.

Joseph Palacio is a tall handsome Garifuna man who had worked in the Belize Department of Antiquities before getting his PhD in Anthropology at UC Berkeley. Back at their home I talked with Joseph about the Mayans.

"Joseph, I'm really interested in the ancient culture of the Mayans," I said. "Would it be possible to visit Caracol? I read about it in *Time Magazine*."

"Just so happens that I know Arlen and Diane Chase, the archeologists excavating Caracol near the border of Belize and Guatemala," said Joseph. "I'll arrange a trip for us to visit there."

"That's great," I said. "I've really been looking forward to exploring Caracol."

Joseph secured permission for a private visit for all of us to the site that was not yet open to the public. I was thrilled! After a bumpy ride through the rolling countryside, we walked through the forest into the site. Joseph introduced us to the Chases who were sitting at tables sorting through pottery and other items found on the site. It felt like I had stepped into an *Indiana Jones* movie.

"Welcome to Caracol!" Arlen said. "This is our winter home where we are directing the excavation. Our students from the University of South Florida are doing the primary work helped by locals who do the heavy lifting. Cathy, a junior undergraduate student, will be your guide through the dig. Caracol had been the home of as many as 185,000 Mayans before 900 AD. Today's total population of Belize is only 185,000 people, an amazing statistic."

Cathy took us up to the top of a pyramid which opened the view over the tree tops toward Guatemala, a vast sea of green as

Joseph and Myrtle Caracol

far as our eyes could see. Walking further into the site, we followed her to a tomb that she was excavating with her partner.

I imagined myself being an archeologist and working alongside her.

"Be careful, don't stand too close to the edge. The soil is quite loose," Cathy warned. "You can see two emerging human skeletons and some grave goods sticking out of the earth. At the foot of the skeletons, do you see the edges of those pots materializing? We have to be ever so careful that we don't crush things as we remove the soil, inch by inch. This find is a thrilling event for us, two college juniors! What an opportunity to be here with Arlen and Diane who are such really knowledgeable teachers." Listening to Cathy, I couldn't help but wish that I could have had the opportunity of making important discoveries like this when I was in college.

Saying our goodbyes to the Chases and Cathy, we all drove back forty miles on a gravel road that felt bumpier than earlier. Finally we reached the main highway.

At one point, Betsy said, "Could we stop and cool off in that clear small stream running along the roadside?"

Joseph pulled the car over to the side of the road, and we all scrambled out and slid down the bank to the stream.

Shoes flew off and our hot feet and legs plunged into the cool water.

"Wow, that was welcome relief," I said.

* * * * *

This was the day that ignited the amateur anthropologist in me! Here I was delving into an ancient site uncovering clues as to how the Mayans lived. I wanted to understand more about how to put these artifacts together to create a picture of the Mayan culture.

Our final dinner that night had sad overtones because Betsy would be flying back to California the next day. JoAnne and I would continue our journey on *Aurora*. We said our goodbyes to the Palacio family who touched us with their hospitality, opening their guesthouse to us, taking us on the special trip to Caracol, and including us in family meals. With a few tears and many hugs, we sent Betsy by taxi to the airport.

"I'm beginning to miss her already," JoAnne said. "She's a great daughter and friend. I just love her smiles and ready for anything personality."

"I'll miss her too. She's a great crew member and lots of fun!" I said. "Besides, when you two are together, laughter reigns."

After gathering provisions in the central market, we took the speedboat back to *Aurora* at Cay Chapel.

The Mayan seaport site of Cerros was our next destination. It was off the beaten track, so getting there required navigating in depths hovering around six feet, giving us only two inches to spare. Seeking a sheltered spot south of Cerros, we ran hard aground and had to wait hours for high tide that allowed us to winch ourselves off using anchors I'd set in deeper water.

Cerros is set on a bluff overlooking a great bay that forms the border between Belize and Mexico to the north. Anchoring near the ruins, we took the dinghy onto a beach near the lone house of the Rangell family, the caretakers of Cerros. Here we met the mother and two children, later joined by son, David, who became our guide of this undeveloped site.

The information about the Mayas from the great book *Forest of Kings* by Linda Schele and David Freidel, combined with our imaginations and David's explanations, helped us to make sense of what we were seeing there. Archeologists had reburied most of their findings to prevent looters from pillaging the site so we saw only mounds of earth on the bluff overlooking the bay. The walled site on a narrow peninsula was chosen to provide protection for the Mayan inhabitants. We took advantage of the view to the north into the Yucatan. The Rangell family was single-handedly protecting and maintaining Cerros under the supervision of the government of Belize. JoAnne and I vowed to visit more Mayan sites on future visits to Belize and Mexico.

As we picked our way back to the main channel, we heard on the radio that *Locura* had run hard aground on its way to San Pedro on Ambergris Cay, our next destination.

Our trip was much smoother because the tide was rising, but as we traveled beside the barrier reef, some waves came crashing over it, hitting us with spray. The anchorage was just a wide spot behind the reef south of Ambergris Cay. Near the pass through the reef and over hard coral sand, I laid out most of our chain to provide weight and friction on the bottom. The sand was only a few inches deep over its solid coral rock base. Amazingly, *Aurora* held her position with the bow aimed into the 25-knot winds that generated huge swells breaking over the reef.

* * * * *

JoAnne and I joined Bev and Dave from *Cloverleaf* in exploring San Pedro's two main streets connected by a few cross streets. Everything there is on a small scale, and there were only a few other tourists. Good restaurants and fresh produce were our main rewards.

The winds and swells made going through the pass out into the Caribbean a dangerous proposition. We witnessed a forty-five-foot ketch trying to leave being tipped sideways in the swells so that its masts lay parallel to the water. The ketch did make it out but came perilously close to the sharp coral reef projecting out of the sea.

Watching this episode, I said, "No way José, I won't expose *Aurora* to that danger!"

"I'm not José, but you sure have my vote to stay," JoAnne said with a laugh.

We waited three days for the winds and seas to subside.

28

THE YUCATAN

Aurora followed *Cloverleaf* in a parade of cruising boats going out through the pass in the dangerous reef into the safety of deeper water. Leaving later than we did, Leroy and Caroline on *Jaime* were pushed sideways into the reef and suffered serious damage to their rudder. They were forced to remain in Belize for repairs. As our day progressed, the winds and waves grew higher causing *Aurora's* motion to become more violent. Having a faster boat, Bev and Dave were already at anchor so they helped us to navigate into the anchorage at Cayo Norte in the dark. Speaking by radio, Dave identified the blips marking other boats that we were seeing on our radar from his position inside the lagoon. I used that information to help find a safe place to anchor *Aurora*. JoAnne and I sighed with relief as our bouncy world was smoothed by the restful calm of the anchorage. There we joined *Lightheart* and *Deliverance*.

In the morning, we all navigated our boats toward Espiritu Sancto Lagoon on the coast of the Yucatan Peninsula. Entering the pass was an easy task. After settling in, I joined Bev skin-diving just inside the reef composed of large blocks of coral uplifted and jumbled along a line between the deep water outside and the shallow water inside. While swimming around one of the blocks, we came nose-to-nose with six five-foot long barracudas. Their mouths opened and closed to force water over their gills. Rows of sharp needle-like teeth made us gasp for breath, and jolts of fear unnerved me. No words were possible under water, but a quick point toward the boat said it was time to go. One barracuda accompanied us as we speedily swam back to *Cloverleaf*.

"Wow," I said, "I know Barracudas don't attack humans, but something primal takes over and kicks my flight mode into high gear."

"Yeah, I experienced the same feelings," said Bev. "I couldn't stop myself swimming away, full speed ahead." Exiting through the pass under full power in the morning, *Aurora* plowed into the higher swells because I wanted to shorten our time spent close to the reef. When I turned the boat to the north toward Isla Mujeres, *Aurora* fell sideways off the crest of the wave with a resounding crash that upset JoAnne's sense of equilibrium. She went below to regain her composure by meditating in the lurching boat. I continued to steer *Aurora* away from the reef. Soon, a group of ten-foot-long melon-headed whales (members of the dolphin family) joined us swimming close to the cockpit. They are larger than dolphins weighing about four hundred-forty pounds as adults. Their body is light grey and their dorsal fin is not quite as high as a killer whale's. They communicated with squeaks loud enough for JoAnne to hear through the hull from her position lying on the bed listening to a quiet tape while trying to meditate.

They seemed to be saying, "Come on up, JoAnne, everything is okay."

I called out, "JoAnne, you have some friends up here who would like to talk with you."

She came up saying, "I'm feeling much better." JoAnne was able to enjoy the presence of these beautiful creatures as they continued their unusual communication so close to her seat in the cockpit that she could smell their fishy breath.

She began talking to them. "Hi, friends, hearing and seeing you makes me feel much better. Having such beautiful creatures so close to me, wanting to communicate with me, dissolves my fear. If I needed you, you would be there to help me."

One of the whales turned its head toward JoAnne and seemed to be listening. A quick up and down nod of its head confirmed the impression. JoAnne let out a squeal of delight in response.

During the rest of the day, the weather moderated as we sailed north past the ancient Mayan seaport of Tulum, set on cliffs overlooking the sea, toward the south end of Isla Cozumel where we dropped our hook there in the lee of the island. In the morning, we continued sailing with all the forces of nature in harmonious action. The winds, Gulf Stream currents, and waves came together to push us toward Isla Mujeres. Under clear skies the water sparkled a brilliant turquoise. We were suspended in so much beauty. We felt so alive, so privileged, so fortunate. We were truly sailing the dream!

"Let's cherish this day in our memories of being surrounded by nature's most lavish bounties!" JoAnne gushed.

At the marina on Isla Mujeres, Bill Weh, my lifelong friend from Aurora, Ohio (the namesake of our boat *Aurora*) joined us for a month's visit with his traveling companion, Elliot, his teddy bear. When we saw the bear, we raised our eyebrows in wonder for a few moments, but looked at each other as if saying, "Oh well, that's Bill." We didn't know then that this trip to Mexico would be Bill's first and unfortunately last trip.

Finding a rental car during Easter Week took ingenuity, but we managed and were off on the ferry to the Yucatan. Once on land, we turned the car south to Tulum. When we arrived, we saw that the ancient site of Tulum was suffering the "assault of too many

Mayan Riveria

tourists" syndrome. Officials responded by roping off most of the fragile buildings at this critical seaport where Mayans had traded with Aztecs and other native groups. The views of the sea from the cliffs reversed our previous perspective from *Aurora* looking toward the land. We gazed instead at the passing sailboats. That night we stayed at a Mayan resort with *palapas* set in the dunes next to the beach. Our *palapa* was three stories high and built of poles lashed together with vines and covered with a thatched palm frond roof. It was swaying in an alarming manner in the 20-knot wind coming off the sea. Thank goodness we were sailors who were used to the to and fro.

The next morning as we were ready to go for breakfast, we looked down at the beach and saw a beautiful, nude young European woman. Three Mayan guys sitting on a log smiled and flashed the "thumbs up" sign of approval. A boyfriend or spouse also nude followed her. The same guys expressed their "thumbs down" disapproval.

"Wow, Bill, this is already an enticing morning," I said, smiling. "The young woman has quite a figure as you must have noticed."

"Yeah, I didn't realize that Mexico would be this interesting," Bill said, still watching the woman.

"How about the guy?" JoAnne chimed in. "He's cute and has nice buns! This is an equal opportunity experience for me too!"

After walking down the beach, we reached a large *palapa* restaurant belonging to the neighboring resort where we had a breakfast of omelets with beans and rice. Our eyes wandered over to a local artisan who had beautiful amber jewelry on display near our table. Attracted by his wide smile, we discovered his amber had reasonable prices. He used a most charming, low pressure approach in selling his wares that hooked us in. It was simple to find the right piece because JoAnne loved jewelry, and I had an eye for good design.

While driving across the Yucatan Peninsula, we found Loltun Cave, a large cavern created by underground streams that dissolved the limestone rock, leaving wondrous formations stained with colors created by water leaching through the limestone from above. Areas where the ceiling had collapsed allowed both light and vegetation to stream into the cave, creating striking points of interest. Mayans had used the cave for religious ceremonies in ancient times but also during the Mayan revolt in the late 1800s against the oppression of the dominant Mexican culture. Then, the cavern served as a refuge for the Mayans hiding from Mexican soldiers.

After exploring the cave, we drove to nearby Uxmal, the premier Mayan ruin in the southern Yucatan. We stayed at Hotel Villas Arquelogicas that had been used by the archeologists excavating Uxmal. We were enticed by the charming high ceilinged rooms and a swimming pool set in a tropical garden where we soaked up the unaccustomed luxury. In the morning, we hired a local Mayan guide, Ruben, to enhance our visit to the ruins.

"The rattlesnake is an important Mayan symbol of power along with Chac, the God of rain," Ruben began when we arrived at the site. "Those images that you see over there are carved into the limestone of the buildings and temples. Turtles also adorn some buildings, being the symbol of water. They play an active role in purifying water collected off the plazas and stored in cisterns in this dry climate. All the carvings, now over 1000 years old, are in an amazing state of preservation due to the lack of rain that would have eroded their surfaces."

Bill and I began climbing up the one hundred-foot tall Pyramid of the Magician using a chain installed to help keep our balance in following the narrow steep steps all the way to the top.

"Amazing!" exclaimed Bill. "What a view of Uxmal. There must be forty buildings out there set on a series of Mayan built flat plazas. It's breathtaking."

"Yeah, I'm impressed by the carvings that completely cover their walls," I said. "Just imagine how much time and effort the Mayans used to create what we are marveling at."

JoAnne called up while standing at the bottom, "Guys, I can hear every word you've spoken. How amazing is that?"

"Looks like the Mayans had mastered the art of acoustics when building this and other structures," I said. "This must have been how the Mayan priests and kings communicated with the masses

Uxmal—Pyramid of the Magician

from their lofty position up here on the pyramid while asserting their godlike control. I can't even imagine having that much power."

"Well, it might be fun to try," laughed Bill. "Let's start by issuing orders to our 'subject,' JoAnne."

"I heard that, Bill," said JoAnne. "I don't think you have *that* much power."

＊＊＊＊＊

On the road in the morning, we drove toward Merida, the capital of the Yucatan state. Arriving in Merida, we found a hotel facing a square that interlocked with other squares, providing open spaces for gardens and cafés in the center of this medium sized city. The streets were closed to vehicular traffic and squares were filled with street venders, musicians, and people on this Easter weekend. In one square we listened to Marimba music played by a large family of eight musicians, ranging in age from the dad down to a grandchild perched at the edge of the Marimba striking random notes now and then. We watched Mayan women with lovely dark, almond shaped faces accompanied by handsome, graceful men dancing their traditional dances to the music of guitars, trumpets, and large double basses.

Jorge, a disabled young Mayan, offered to be our guide. He led us into a government palace where a classical music concert was taking place. The palace walls were covered with large paintings depicting the cruelty imposed on the Mayans by their Spanish overlords. The native population was treated as if they were less than human beings. Unfortunately, this was a common belief and practice in the sixteenth and seventeenth centuries.

"I'm feeling the impact their cruelty had on the Mayans," Jo-Anne blurted out in anger. "It's overwhelming being surrounded on all sides by such horrible images."

We asked Jorge to join us for lunch at the hotel, giving us the opportunity to learn more about him. He had lost part of his leg in a motorcycle accident in which his girlfriend had been killed. Jorge told us about his experience.

"During my hospital stay, I became increasingly depressed until one day, a fellow disabled man put this choice before me—it's either life or death. Fortunately, I chose life which as you can see, I live with enthusiasm and purpose. I see that my own fight is part of a larger Mayan struggle for equal treatment in a society that is just now beginning to make improvements in its treatment of my people."

I was deeply touched by Jorge's plight. He was able to emerge from his darkness into the light of life, embracing whatever it had to offer.

*****

We could not leave the Yucatan without seeing Chichenitza, its largest and most restored Mayan site. Chichenitza flourished from the end of the Classical Period (about 1000 AD) when other Mayan centers were declining, until the arrival of the Spanish in 1519. Its celestial observatory made accurate observations used by the Mayans to create their calendar based on a fifty-two-year cycle—the long count, and the two hundred-sixty-two-day cycle—the short count. The Mayan Calendar is also an astrological calendar that marked propitious days for various events from starting wars to planting crops.

Chichenitza also had a ball court with sloping sides where a ballgame was played by opposing teams for recreation as well as ritualistic purposes. Often, the ballgame was used to settle disputes between communities. The losing captain might be sacrificed! The game was played with an eight-inch ball made of rubber. A small bat was used to hit it, while elbows and knees protected with leather were also allowed to strike the ball. Hitting a stone target on each side of the court was the object of the game. The earliest ball courts date from 2500 BC and are the sites of the first human sporting events.

After leaving Chichenitza, we all climbed down into a Cenote, a sinkhole in the limestone rock, that had filled with water and was once used by the Mayans as a sacred well. Bill and I swam in the clear cool water passing through shafts of sunlight streaming down from above. As we floated in the dancing water, we slipped back to ancient times.

"Just think about human sacrifices being thrown into this Cenote during the Mayan period," I said.

"Yeah, it gives me a creepy feeling," said Bill. "I wonder if there are bones under the mushy layer on the bottom?"

"Well, I'm not anxious to find out!" I said, ready to get out.

*****

After our dip in the Cenote, we drove into Cancun to buy provisions for our sail across the Gulf of Mexico to Florida. When we arrived back at Marina Paradiso on Isla Mujeres, we found that many cruisers had been collecting there to wait out a series of northers sweeping south down the Gulf of Mexico. The storms had eliminated the option of crossing the gulf. We all decided to play the party option which gave us the opportunity to get to know Don Weiner on *El Rubio* and Lister and Marion on *Deliverance*. Other friends on *Amigo, Livin, Watersmeet,* and *Cloverleaf* rounded out the cast of characters who gathered daily to analyze the weather forecasts and drink more than a few good cold

Mexican beers accompanied by mounds of tortilla chips and bowls filled with guacamole and salsa.

Standing around a small table in the bar, JoAnne and I joined Mar and Jan, owners of *Livin,* who had started their journey in Oregon. Mar had been a PBS radio announcer back home and had a booming bass voice with a laugh and belly to match. Jan had been interested in sailing since her childhood in Minnesota, our land of the Swedes.

"Yeah, Jan got me into sailing," said Mar, taking a sip of beer. "We've owned a number of boats that were platforms for lots of family fun. I'm not very mechanical, but I do enjoy sailing."

"Sailing has been a good thing in our lives," said Jan. "Besides we have lots of fun. Mar's laughs are contagious."

'I'll bear witness to that," laughed JoAnne. "So what's your destination across the Gulf of Mexico?"

"We're heading for Marco Island where my sister and brother-in-law have a great house," said Jan.

"Well, our destination is Naples, not far from Marco, where my mom lives," I said.

"Let's get together in Florida. The food at Mom's is great," said JoAnne.

*****

Marsha and Ewert on *Watersmeet* expressed concern about their trip. "Our autopilot has packed it up and we have the longest voyage of the group all the way to Galveston, Texas, probably a six-day trip," said Ewert.

"Not to worry," I said. "Just so happens that I bought a new AutoHelm 4000 auto pilot as a back up in Florida, and it's still in its box. I will lend it to you and will help you install it. I'd feel a lot better knowing you'll have a safer and more comfortable passage."

Providing lots of beers for *Aurora's* crew was one way Marsha and Ewert expressed their gratitude for my autopilot. After arriving in Galveston, *Watersmeet* would be loaded on a semi-truck to be driven across the United States and then to their home waters off Vancouver Island in British Columbia. We received the

AutoHelm in its box after we arrived in Naples, Florida, just as I expected, validating my belief that fellow cruisers could be trusted. We were a group dependent on each other for information, assistance, and comradeship.

29

ROUGH PASSAGE TO FLORIDA

Passage plans to Florida were in the works when we agreed to sail with Don Weiner on *El Rubio* as buddy boats. He was a single hander who had just taken on a young attractive couple, Carol Ann and Cameron from New Zealand, as crew. The underlying theory of buddy boating is that having another boat close by on a long passage multiplies each boat's chances of survival in an emergency situation. We all were listening to Herb, a good amateur weather man broadcasting from Canada who analyzes NOAA's forecasts, the satellite photos of the clouds and sea, and then prepares his own weather forecast. Herb reinforced our decision to wait for a break in the northerly storms.

Another factor in our route planning was the location of the Gulf Stream that swept in a northerly direction past Isla Mujeres and then turned east above the northern coast of Cuba. The Gulf Stream is a powerful river-like current in the Atlantic Ocean. It could boost our boat's speed by 3-4 knots, decreasing the time needed to make the crossing and reducing our exposure to bad weather. On the passage, we also hoped to stop at the national park at the Dry Tortugas, small tropical atolls forming the actual end of the Florida Keys, located about one hundred miles west of Key West.

With our plans in place for the four hundred-fifty mile voyage to Florida, we finally had a break in the flow of northerly storms, so we could cast off our dock lines. Our cruising friends gathered on the dock to wish us bon voyage. *Aurora* and *El Rubio* sailed out of the marina rounding the end of Isla Mujeres. There, we met left-over high waves from the storm that crashed into our boats, slowing our progress. After a unanimous vote of both crews, we chose the nearby Isla Contoy as our next destination, seeking shelter in its bay.

"I'm really upset that we're going to be close to the reef where that boat was lost," said JoAnne. Recalling our own encounter with a reef in Costa Rica increased her concern.

"But, JoAnne, we're two and a half miles from it," I pointed out. "We'll be okay. You could plot our position on the chart so you better understand where we are."

"Okay, it makes more sense now," JoAnne said, looking more at ease.

By the morning of April 20th, the waves had moderated enough allowing us to get underway again in a short good weather window, before the predicted arrival of a small norther. The wind shifted in our favor as we picked up the Gulf Stream heading into the shipping lanes north of Cuba. We were speeding along at 7.8 knots when we appointed Bill to be our head "dolphin trainer." He went to work lying on the deck at the bow looking down at a pod of dolphins and their babies swimming along with *Aurora* in the clear, bright blue water. Bill was captivated by the grace of their movements and the intelligent look on their faces smiling up at him.

"See them looking up at me and diving under the bow," Bill said with delight. "Too bad I don't have my hoop! I sense that they're ready for more advanced tricks."

"I bet they are," I said. "I saw three dolphins leap together in the Sea of Cortez."

On the second night at one in the morning, our idyllic voyage was abruptly altered by the arrival of the "small" northern, quoting from the weather forecast.

"So much for the accuracy of weather forecasts," I said sarcastically as the wind increased to 30 knots and the seas rose up to twelve to fourteen feet.

By morning's light, the seas were looking wild. We stared up at one and a half story waves as high as our mast spreaders. Their crests were being blown off by the force of the winds. Feeling seasick, Bill and JoAnne went below where they didn't have to look at

Bill in the Galley

the waves enveloping *Aurora* and sometimes crashing over her bow. Standing at the wheel, I saw that *Aurora* was proving herself a worthy boat by holding the course I set on the autopilot. She climbed up the large waves (the highest I had ever experienced) with a minimum of strain. Wow, I thought, *Aurora's* design for handling the Southern Ocean off Australia is being tested right now. I was proud of her and my knowledge of how to sail in these extreme conditions.

On *El Rubio*, Don called on the radio. "My boat is doing well, but Carol Ann, our young New Zealander, hasn't been able to keep anything in her stomach and she has a fever."

Captain Don, a general psychiatrist, was becoming alarmed with her acute dehydration and fainting.

"We're located about one hundred miles from land," Don said. "What are our options?"

"Entering the Dry Tortugas is too dangerous in this weather," I said. "Heading for Cuba, now a lee shore, won't work either. Landing at Key West is our best choice because its entrance channel is on the south side of the key and protected from the northerly winds."

"Yeah, I think you're right," Don said. "We'll have to soldier on."

During the third night on our way to Key West, Don called to tell us that our navigation lights were out. This was alarming because we were now in the shipping lanes. A swallow flew aboard seeking some respite from the storm. The tiny creature seemed unafraid, joining me by sitting on the pedestal guard just forward of my position at the wheel. His chirps kept me awake for awhile. But being very tired, I asked Bill to take the watch. I went below to rest. Later, I was awoken from my deep sleep by *Aurora's* abrupt change of course. I rushed up to the cockpit and found that Bill had dozed off on watch. A loud blast of a ship's horn awoke him just in time to make an evasive maneuver to avoid being hit by the oncoming freighter. That was a close call, I thought as my gut tightened.

"Wow, that was too close for comfort. I'm taking charge," I said emphatically. "I'll sail closer to *El Rubio* so we register being a stronger image on the large ships' radars. Right now, we have six freighters going west and two heading east showing up on our radar screen."

"I'm sorry, but I can hardly keep awake. Being seasick has done me in," said Bill as he went below.

JoAnne was awoken by the commotion and took over the radar watch.

The wind and waves had begun to subside, improving our outlook when JoAnne called the closest oncoming ship on the radio. "Large ship off my port bow, this is yacht *Aurora* under sail at Latitude 23.7 north and Longitude 83.85 west. Do you see me?"

"*Aurora*, this is the container ship *Maersk Victory*. I see you now. I'm changing course to port to avoid you."

"Thanks, *Aurora* will continue to hold her present course," JoAnne radioed back.

Seeing a break in the stream of ships, *Aurora* and *El Rubio* changed course to cut across both shipping lanes, steering to the north. This maneuver reduced our exposure to the big ships and put us closer to the calmer area created by the lee of the Florida Keys. About 2 a.m., our radar picked up the sea buoy marking the entrance channel to Key West and by 3:30 a.m., we dropped the hook among shrimp boats sheltering off Key West. Our voyage of three days and four nights covered four hundred fifty miles while skirting the north shore of Cuba.

Falling into a deep sleep in the calm waters was easy. The crew awoke about noon to find that I, Captain Karl, had been busy preparing a good brunch to celebrate our safe arrival.

"What's for brunch?" said JoAnne. "It's been a treat sailing with a captain who cooks."

"Well, the omelet for brunch has morphed into a smorgasbord since I added all of our fresh food to the menu," I said. Other cruisers had warned me that all the fresh food aboard would be confiscated by officials when we checked back into the United States. We enjoyed a well-deserved carefree feast bobbing among our shrimp boat neighbors.

*****

After motoring *Aurora* into the sailboat anchorage off downtown Key West, we dinghied ashore to visit customs and immigration officials, and the agricultural inspectors. Our smoked pork chops didn't pass muster, but because we had eaten all our fruit the only thing they wanted was our bag of garbage which we gratefully surrendered. We met Don and his crew outside the office and saw that Carol Ann was much better as she walked along the street. Don introduced us to his partner, Linda, a lovely blond nurse, who would join him on *El Rubio* for the trip along the East Coast of Florida to their home in Stuart.

While walking through town, we were intrigued by the large, old wooden houses surrounded by wide porches that reminded us of an earlier era when the pace of life was slow enough to encourage chatting between neighbors and passersby. This strong sense of history makes Key West stand out in my mind when compared to other Florida cities that are dominated by traffic whizzing along and strip malls. While visiting Harry Truman's Key West White House, we seconded his choice of this tropical location for his retreat located inside a lovely old military base. This was a place where he could unwind from the pressures of the presidency and have friendly poker games with friends and colleagues. Ernest Hemingway's house gave us further insight into the writer's life and his many relationships with women who had difficulty putting up with his sometimes black moods and his wandering ways.

Heeding our growling stomachs, we found a French restaurant with great food. We savored our delicious reward for the hard work and diligence in making a successful passage. How luxurious it was to have someone else prepare and serve the meals in a restaurant that was not bouncing through the water.

After settling into the anchorage, my first job was to replace the dysfunctional navigation lights at the top of the mast. To install the new unit purchased from a shoreside chandlery, I climbed the mast using the mast steps and then secured the tether from my safety harness through the top step and around the mast.

Suddenly, *Aurora* was rocked by the waves emanating from a passing parade of boats that forced me to valiantly hold on to the mast that was swinging back and forth in wide arcs. Sailors on other boats in the anchorage stopped what they were doing to stare up at me in amazement. Later, I heard that a number of people were placing bets on my ability to remain attached to the mast. When I heard that, I wished I'd been able to bet! Thank goodness I survived and successfully installed the new lights that would soon come in quite handy.

Our next destination was Naples on Florida's west Gulf Coast where my mom lived, and where we would take time to rehabilitate *Aurora* after her more than three years of sometimes strenuous cruising in the tropics. To reach Naples, we had to arrive in daylight because Gordon Pass from the Gulf of Mexico into Naples Bay was quite narrow and had few lights. Leaving from Key West in the late afternoon, we sailed north into Florida Bay, and when darkness fell, we saw the lights of twenty-four shrimp boats dotting the horizon. Luckily, they were all dragging their nets at a slow speed which made our navigation through them a little less

Karl—Top of Mast

tricky. Our navigation lights and radar made the passage dodging through the shrimping fleet a much safer experience.

As the sun began to rise illuminating the sky, *Aurora* was passing Everglades National Park and soon approached Marco Island where its many mansions stood out against the vivid green of the tropical shoreline. We'd been in radio contact with Bill's Uncle Al, a ham radio operator, who called my mom by phone to alert her to our expected arrival time at her next door neighbor's dock located on one of Naples' many canals. These neighbors, Mary Lou and Fenton, joined Mom in providing a warm welcome to the sailors "home from the sea." They helped us tie *Aurora* to the dock, signaling our reconnection to the land.

In the preceding eighteen months, *Aurora* had traveled 6,348 nautical miles (one quarter of the way around the world) from Puerto Escondido, Mexico, to Naples, Florida. It was now time for a celebration and serious boat work!

After seeing Bill off at the Fort Meyers airport, JoAnne and I moved into the guest room in Mom's seventh floor condo at the Glenview Retirement Residence, overlooking the Gulf of Mexico. We quickly adapted to the "demands" of luxury living. We established a daily routine of boat work after breakfast and moved our operations base into Mary Lou's porch following their return to the family home in Fenton, Michigan. I recruited Scott, the spouse of Mom's friend, and his young Mexican friend, Joel, to help with the project. Joel gave us the youthful energy and strength needed to insure forward momentum. Our team of four accomplished a massive amount of work during the five-to-six-day work weeks. JoAnne set up a work space on the porch where she worked on all the aluminum ports and hatches that we removed from the boat.

"I feel like I'm working in a boat factory," she said. "By the time I've cleaned and sanded these things down to bare metal and then go though the whole process of pickling, priming, and painting them with two to three coats of two-part Allgrip white paint, I should join the union!"

"Maybe I should join a union, too!" I added with a smile. "At least someone would pay me some wages."

With help from Joel and Scott, we installed: a new four burner stove with oven, a new sewage treatment system, a new head (toilet), the Autohelm 4000 autopilot, a new vinyl dodger, Bimini, and side curtains custom made for *Aurora* by a canvas shop in Naples. We also raised the boom twelve inches to reduce the danger of crew being hit. I sewed and installed a new sail cover, weather clothes, outboard motor cover, and BBQ cover. We washed the interior and cushions. We sanded worn areas on the cabin sole (floor) and then brushed them with three coats of urethane. The teak decks were cleaned and covered with three coats of Perma Teak Gold. When finished, we had created a better equipped *Aurora* ready for more miles of interesting sailing.

It was wonderful for JoAnne and me to return to Mom's each evening for needed showers, gourmet meals, and conversation in the dining room where we got to know many of her friends. Some of them stopped by to help with *Aurora* while others just came to see how the project was progressing. We learned on the radio that our friends Mar and Jan on *Livin* had become becalmed off Marco Island close to the finish of their trip across the Gulf of Mexico. They could not start their motor due to the starter being too loose to engage the flywheel on the engine. During the day, light winds blew them toward shore, but at night, the offshore winds blew them back away from shore. Finally, as their water and food supplies were running low, they called for help and were towed into Jan's sister's dock. Borrowing her car, they also stopped by to see us. We had become a local tourist attraction!

Deciding to reward our renovation team, JoAnne and I took them on *Aurora* for a test sail through the Naples canals and out into the bay behind Keewayden Beach State Park where we discovered a shelling paradise. The beach was lined with piles of shells that had accumulated up to a foot deep. Because the only access to the beach was by boat, not very many shellers had been there to search for special treasures. Having a picnic helped us thank everyone for all the diligent work done. This land break in our cruising adventure provided the much needed R&R for JoAnne and me as well as a wonderful chance to spend quality time with Mom.

PART III

FAMILY FRIENDS HOME

Upon leaving a place, parts of ourselves remain behind
Even though we go away
Those fragments can only be found by returning
In finding those fragments of ourselves
We can reopen the life we left behind
With all its possibilities

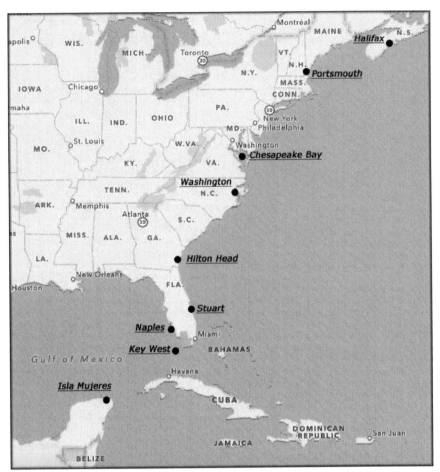

East Coast

30

SAILING UP THE EAST COAST

On July 1, 1993, JoAnne and I sailed the restored, classy look-ing *Aurora* north from Naples up the Gulf Coast past Sanibel Is-land where we turned the corner to Ft. Meyers Beach, choosing to anchor off the town in its protected bay. Leaving, however, be-came a lot more complicated when our anchor snagged on some-thing heavy on the bottom. The windlass was overpowered, leaving me in a muddle trying to get loose.

Joe, on a neighboring boat called over, "Do you need some help?"

"We sure do!" I said. Joe dinghied over to help.

"Give me a line from your largest winch in the cockpit and I'll hook it into the anchor chain," said Joe.

"Okay, it's taut. I'll keep cranking," I said. "Wow, look at the tangle of anchors and chains coming out of the water."

"I'll untangle them and place them in your dinghy so you can take them to shore," Joe said.

"Thanks for all your help, Joe. It's great having a fellow cruiser like you anchored close by." We were both determined to make the anchorage safer for future cruisers by hauling off the lost an-chors.

Finally freed, *Aurora* entered the Caloosahatchee River which divides Ft. Meyers on the south shore from Cape Coral to the north. Passing by Thomas Edison's winter home located close to downtown Ft. Meyers, we saw his large wooden mansion had a front porch looking out to his gardens lining the riverbank. Trees surrounded Edison's famous laboratory in the backyard. Edison had entertained presidents and industrialists such as Henry Ford at this comfortable winter hideaway.

As we motored east on the Caloosahatchee River, *Aurora* passed by the suburbs of Ft. Myers that spread out along the river where most homes had their own docks with boats attached. Along the way, we stopped to visit Bill's Uncle Al and Aunt Maybelle at their home near the shore. Al, our ham radio contact person as we crossed the Gulf of Mexico, was eager to meet us "in the flesh."

"It was great to talk with you and Bill out in the Gulf," said Al. "I'm so happy that you made it across in that storm. I was monitoring the weather buoy reports which confirmed that the highest waves varied between twelve and fourteen feet. Looking out at your boat, I'm amazed that she did so well."

"We're sure glad that you were there on the radio in case we needed help," I said. "*Aurora* was designed for conditions in Australia. She sure earned her keep out there!"

Al prepared a delicious dinner, giving us another sendoff before we continued east crossing the state of Florida. We arrived at Clewiston on the edge of Lake Okeechobee, the largest fresh water lake in Florida. We followed a dredged channel across the shallow lake, anchoring for the night on the eastern shore in a small bay surrounded by mangrove trees and the sounds of birds and animals.

Waking in the morning, I felt like having a swim and a bath, until I noticed that the "log" floating by in the brown tannin colored water had eyes. Alligators and swimming are not a good mix. Instead, I happily washed using water from the solar heated sun shower. Proceeding north along the shore of the lake, we found Port Mayaca and located the entrance to the St. Lucie River flowing east toward Stuart. Reading the chart, I realized that *Aurora's* total mast height would JUST fit under the railroad bridge. It did do that as the tip of the VHF radio antenna scraped along on the underside of the bridge.

"Whew, we made it!" we exclaimed, letting out a long breath.

Upon reaching Stuart, we anchored in St. Lucie Inlet right off downtown. A call to our cruising buddy, Don Weiner, brought him over to pick us up. He took us out to his modern house on Sewell's Point. We immediately felt at ease in its natural setting among palm trees and tropical plants growing everywhere in an unimproved yard. Don's partner, Linda, greeted us and showed us the house.

"I certainly made the right choice in not crossing the Gulf of Mexico with you guys because I get seasick!" Linda said. "I'm so happy that Carol Ann survived the passage and didn't become too dehydrated. Dehydration is really bad news for the blood pressure, kidneys, and bladder."

"I'm also happy you chose not to make the passage," said Don. "If you'd been there under those conditions, I would have had two patients on my hands."

We enjoyed Stuart's old fashioned downtown with an ice cream parlor (a cruiser's favorite) and good restaurants with Don and Linda. Later, JoAnne and I had ring-side seats on *Aurora* for the Fourth of July celebration. Fireworks exploded over our heads sending colored streams of sparks flowing down to the water.

Two days later, after filling *Aurora* with diesel at $1.09 per gallon (remember those prices?) we motored out of the St. Lucie Inlet into the Atlantic Ocean. We headed east to locate the Gulf Stream which increased our speed to 9 knots over the bottom. The seas were calm and the July weather was balmy. We were on a long arc following the flow of this "river in the ocean" along the east coast of the United States. We navigated with the help of the Gulf Stream coordinates supplied by the National Weather Service on the radio. JoAnne came on watch at 1:15 a.m. and saw two ships at 5 a.m. that passed in front of *Aurora* about eight miles away. She let me sleep until 7 a.m. when I awoke to a thunder and lightning storm dumping a deluge of rain on *Aurora* that caused the dodger's seams to leak. The accompanying 30-knot wind gusts required rolling in the jib to keep the boat from heeling excessively. I altered course to avoid lightning strikes ahead and disconnected all the electronics as a precaution.

An hour later, things had quieted down with only a few lumpy waves remaining to remind us of the violence of the storm. Off St. Augustine, Florida, I was watching a huge container ship as it passed near to shore from our location. I noticed small specks near the bow. Grabbing the binoculars, I clearly saw dolphins swimming up the huge rising bow wave and then diving off its crest in front of the huge ship.

"JoAnne, look at this," I said. "*Aurora* must seem like a bathtub toy for dolphins in comparison to a ship that large."

Later as JoAnne sat reading in the cockpit, she suddenly shouted, "A whale! Karl, can it tip us over?" A loud exhale of spouting water announced the presence of a whale surfacing right next to her.

"Where's the camera?" I said, hoping it answered her question.

Clambering up the companionway stairs, I saw the whale's back as it took three big breaths before diving down and away from *Aurora*. A check in our *Marine Mammals* book revealed that minke whales seem to be attracted to slow moving objects on the surface of the sea. That sure fit our description. The thirty-foot-long minke was about ten feet away from the side of the boat and seemed mighty large. It was our closest whale sighting to date.

* * * * *

Off Quinby Inlet, Virginia, we saw another sailboat on the horizon. Calling it on the VHF radio, we discovered that the boat was *Cinnamon Girl*. They were sailing in the company of our friends Guy and Deborah, on *La Coursaire*. After setting up a radio schedule, we were no longer so alone in the Atlantic Ocean one hundred miles from shore. Suddenly, thousands of flies enveloped the boat, perhaps being driven offshore by a heat wave currently blanketing the eastern seaboard. After diving down into the cabin, we shut the main hatch and quickly installed our screens.

"How in the world could flies even exist one hundred miles from land?" JoAnne wondered.

"I don't have a clue," I said. "It's quite a mystery to me."

Off New Jersey, ominous weather forecasts on the radio predicted that a strong frontal system was coming so we headed toward Shinnecock Inlet, Long Island. During that night, the radio squawked incessantly with emergency broadcasts that we really couldn't understand.

Nearer to shore, I called out, "JoAnne, do you see all those pieces of yellow foam floating on the water? I wonder where they came from?"

"I hope people around here aren't using the ocean as a trash dump," JoAnne said.

As we entered the Inlet in a small thunderstorm, three young Coast Guard members dinghied up and boarded *Aurora* to check our safety equipment (it was okay) but found that our radio license had lapsed and our vessel tax was unpaid.

One of the guardsmen said, "Do you know that TWA flight 800 exploded and crashed in the sea off Long Island last night? All three hundred-thirty people aboard were killed. What a tragedy!"

"We saw pieces of foam floating on the water and wondered where they came from," I said. "Wow, seems like the plane must have been blown to bits."

This was not the welcome we had anticipated after six days and nights at sea. We covered 1015 miles on our longest passage to date at an average speed of 6.8 knots, very good for a thirty-three-foot long sailboat! It seemed that Livengood Luck was still with us.

After finding a place to anchor in the shallow bay, JoAnne and I relaxed. We were amazed, however, that we didn't feel tired because of our easy trip and the routine of sleeping as needed using our flexible watch system. The "serious" storm had passed quickly, so we sailed out the next day toward Block Island along the Hamptons shore of Long Island. We passed many large estates whose green lawns reached down to the beach. Off East Hampton, our fish lure attracted a beautiful bluefish that proved to be delicious when barbecued. Sailing around Montauk Point at the end of Long Island, we entered Block Island Sound and made out Block Island on the horizon.

We found the entrance to Salt Pond, an inlet on Block Island, and sailed through its narrow entrance. Looking at the other anchored boats, we found our friends Guy and Deborah on *La Coursaire*. Soon, we were hiking ashore with them, stretching our sea legs and catching up with each other's lives since our time together in Guatemala. We developed a plan to meet again in Newport, Rhode Island, and invited them to attend our family reunion in Maine. Block Island's old cottages and colorful small towns gave us lots to see and great places to stop for lunch and, of course, beer.

Bob and Janet Bean, also part of our group of Central American cruising companions, sailed in and invited us over for coffee on their Cal 35 *Windfall*. Sitting at their raised dining table in the main salon gave us a great view of the anchorage. I was alarmed seeing *Aurora* slowly move by, dragging her anchor. Bob, an athletic ex-fire captain from Long Beach, California, was up in a flash and together we dinghied over and moved *Aurora* to a mooring ball that was more firmly attached to the hard bottom. While we were occupied, Janet mentioned to JoAnne that she had joined the "Woman Aboard" organization.

"I'm certainly qualified and would love to join," JoAnne said.

"Great, here's the address and phone number. We'll be Sea Sisters together. Jan on *Livin* also is a member," Janet said. "We're going north to Maine this summer and looking forward to exploring the islands and the rocky coast."

"Great, we're going to Maine for Karl's family reunion," JoAnne said. "We'll keep on the lookout for you guys on *Windfall*."

On *Aurora*, JoAnne and I marveled at our good luck in crossing paths with such interesting friends. Remembering meetings like that still ignites an afterglow of warm feelings and a smile.

Sailing west across Narragansett Bay, we arrived at Newport where my sisters, Margie and Leslie, met us. They had driven in from their home in South Glastonbury, Connecticut. JoAnne and I were swept into a luxury mode, staying at their hotel and eating out with them during tours of the magnificent "cottages" built by the very rich for their summer stays at the coast. Bellcourt Castle, one of these cottages, was palatial in scale. Its decorations seemed to flaunt its "robber baron" owner's wealth while competing in a massive game of keeping up with the Rockefellers. We were impressed that the architecture managed to be overwhelmed by the stuff inside, but the views out over Narragansett Bay were spectacular. We treated the girls to a daysail on *Aurora*, watching the racing boats pop out their colorful spinnaker sails on the downwind leg of the race.

Two days later, we joined Guy and Deborah for wet dinghy rides across the harbor to shop in Newport for charts of New England and Nova Scotia where we both intended to sail this summer. Eating and drinking at the old White Horse Tavern on Broadway dropped us into the haunt of many sailors who over the centuries felt at home in the place. One of these sailors was drinking at the bar so we joined him. Deborah sat next to him. He couldn't resist making a pass, probably attracted by her friendly smile and gorgeous looks. After Guy moved closer, he got the hint and gave us his card, perhaps as an explanation of his behavior. And I quote: JEFF BROWN, a legend in his own time, World Traveler, Soldier of Fortune, International Lover, Best Stud in Town, Virgins Converted, Sex Educationalist, Bars Emptied. While his judgment may have been lacking, the same cannot be said for his ego!

*****

After goodbyes, JoAnne and I left the sailing capital of the East Coast and joined a parade of more than twenty boats sailing northward up Buzzard's Bay toward the Cape Cod Canal. The canal was cut through the land where the hook shaped Cape Cod juts out of the mainland. Being a sea level canal, it has a current that forms rips or rapids caused as the tide attempts to equalize the water level between the southern and northern ends of the canal. *Aurora* was swept north by the current, reaching 10.5 knots over the ground. We were flying along!

Reaching the north end at Massachusetts Bay, *Aurora* sailed into mellow seas navigating toward Cape Elizabeth located north of Boston. Suddenly a black squall line hit us with 30-knot winds and building seas. Gloucester became our port of refuge. Its snug harbor protected us from the high waves while the wind howled and the rain pounded down. Man, the weather can change so rapidly, I thought. Thank God for Gloucester!

In the morning, the winds and seas subsided to a normal range. After finding the Annisquam River at the end of the harbor, we followed it north behind Cape Elizabeth until the river emptied into Ipswich Bay. Sailing along the coast of northern Massachusetts, we passed Newburyport where JoAnne's relative

Nathaniel Merrill landed in 1630 on the *Speedwell*, the second ship to bring Pilgrims to the continent of North America.

Crossing into New Hampshire, we sailed up the Piscataqua River, passing through the heart of Portsmouth. While waiting for a lift bridge to open, I became alarmed that *Aurora* was being sucked under the bridge by the strong incoming tidal current. After throwing the engine into reverse, I realized that it did not have enough power to halt the forward motion of the boat. We were so close to the bridge that turning around would not have worked either. In desperation, I blew our fog horn that caught the attention of the bridge tender, who raised the bridge deck just high enough to accommodate *Aurora's* mast as she was swept under it. Our waves and smiles expressed the gratitude that we felt as both of our hearts were still racing.

That was too close!

Surviving this crisis, I gave other bridges a wider berth as *Aurora* continued upstream to George Patten's Yacht Yard. We had a reservation to be hauled out for a much needed bottom cleaning and paint job. A hydraulic trailer was winched down a precipitous concrete ramp at high tide so *Aurora* could be floated onto it. Its hydraulic arms raised to cradle the boat securely, and the trailer and its cargo were winched up the ramp to the tractor. It was amazing to watch the tractor pull *Aurora* up the steep slope of the riverbank to the work yard to be deposited on a work cradle.

Examining the hull I called out, "Oh, my God, my bottom has blisters." Initially not understanding, JoAnne said, "Whose bottom has blisters?"

Fiberglass had not proved to be the impenetrable material that was advertised when it was first used to construct boats. It absorbs moisture, so blisters are a problem to solve because they can weaken the structure of the hull. The new "to do" list included replacement of the cutlass bearing, which required lifting up of the engine to make room to pull the propeller shaft into the boat, installing new motor mounts and a new wet exhaust for the Yanmar Diesel engine, and finally cleaning and waxing the hull. Our work was cut out for us.

*****

No More Blisters

The whole project consumed three weeks of hard work. My work duty, however, was made more pleasant by staying with Jo-Anne's nephew, Keith, and his spouse, Lynn, at their late 1800s cottage located at the Hedding Methodist campgrounds near Exeter, New Hampshire. The work crew grew when JoAnne's son, Douglas, and his family arrived from Halifax, Nova Scotia, and a cruising friend, Linda, and her husband, Mike, drove in from Ohio. They joined Greg, a professional boat worker from the yard, and me in the final push after the blisters had all been popped and then filled with epoxy. The whole hull was sanded six coats of West System Epoxy were rolled on as a waterproof barrier to prevent osmosis, and finally three coats of expensive Micron 33 anti-fouling paint were applied to keep the sea critters from making a home on the hull. Along with the realigned engine on its new mounts, the propeller shaft was now stable in its new bearing, and *Aurora* was in great shape for our continuing exploration of the "known" world. The old adage "boats are a hole in the water to be filled with money" certainly had a meaningful ring.

*****

Hooray! It was time for a sailing celebration as our expanded crew joined us for a daysail out to the Isle of Shoals about ten miles off the coast from Portsmouth. Our grandniece, thirteen-year-old Madeline, found her sea legs and learned how to steer *Aurora* into the harbor. French and English explorers discovered the Isle of Shoals early in our country's history. It had been a fishing community for most of the time, but today tourists staying at the large, old wooden Victorian hotel have replaced the fishermen. Artists spice up the island's mix of residents and show their works in a small museum on Harbor Street. Our crew enjoyed hiking on the shore and taking in the barren beauty of the jumble of rocks that made up the island. On the way back, Keith and Greg were having fun comparing stories from their stints in the Navy hunting Russian submarines during the 1970s.

"I was assigned to the Fire Control Center when the captain was at the point of launching an anti-submarine missile," said Keith. "Our missile cruiser had lost contract with a Russian submarine shadowing us. The captain felt we were in danger. If a missile is launched it rotates in circles until its radar detects a target. Then, it dives into the water to destroy the sub. But all of a sudden, the sub surfaced about two hundred yards in front of the ship. We immediately had to execute an emergency turn to port to avoid running it over." The crew on station with Keith let out a collective "Whew!" as everyone realized how close they had come to heating up the cold war.

"Wow, your story sure beats any of mine!" exclaimed Greg.

*****

Our sail north along the Maine Coast began the next day. Linda and Mike joined the crew sailing past the rock bound islands covered with pines and blueberry bushes, surrounded by the cold, blue waters of the North Atlantic. By late afternoon, we had passed Kennebunkport, reaching Richmond Island off Old Orchard Beach. There, we discovered a safe anchorage in the lee of the Island. A hike ashore limbered our sea legs as we watched the curling waves crashing into the rocky shore. Hiking made up for the disappointment later in the evening when heavy cloud cover blotted out the Perseid meteor shower, one of nature's most spectacular light shows. Away in the morning, we sailed around Point Elizabeth, marked by its tall black striped lighthouse, into Casco Bay off Portland, Maine.

Our destination was Sebasco Lodge located at the northern rim of the Bay. The Lodge provided essentials: hot showers, laundry facilities, and a restaurant where we had a farewell dinner with Mike and Linda. We met fellow cruisers Charlie and Ruth Wing, who work at the lodge during the short summer season. They cruise the Bahamas on their boat *Puffin* in the winters. We had some interesting conversations with them about the Bahamas which would be our cruising destination this winter.

Linekin Bay Resort was only a six-hour sail away. But, it took help from a friendly lobsterman to direct us the last mile through a maze of small islands and confusing coves before we saw a mooring off the resort's dock. The resort was chosen as the location for the Livengood/Colebrook Family reunion, drawing thirty-nine family members from all over the United States. JoAnne and I were assigned a cabin overlooking *Aurora* floating out in the Bay.

Sisters, Margie and Leslie, provided some excitement when Margie tripped, falling against a small sink in her room, dislodging it from the wall. A gush of water shot out from the broken waterline. Shutting the water off was a problem since there were no valves on the pipe. In desperation, our brother-in-law Pat jammed sticks into the pipes stemming the flow of water. Margie scurried to the office to alert the maintenance staff. By now the room was awash. Fortunately, a drier cabin was available. The scowls on the face of Mrs. Branch, the resort owner, made us feel that we were a group of naughty children. The food was very good and the wait staff consisted of smiling, college age, young adults that made up for Mrs. Branch's sour puss and strict rules about not changing tables. Imagine not being able to sit with different members of the family when you wanted to. I ignored the silly rule.

The family decided on an outing to Monhegan Island located fifteen miles off the coast of Maine. *Aurora* and the daily ferry were pressed into action hauling everyone out on a sunny bright day.

My grandson, Greg, stationed himself on the bow as lookout with his dad, Doug, standing close by, while his sister, Elise, steered the boat under my guidance.

Monhegan Island has a small permanent population of fishers and lobstermen along with a summer colony of artists founded in 1905 by Rockwell Kent. He painted the Island's stark beauty in an American modernist style. A transcendentalist and mystic in the tradition of Thoreau and Emerson, Rockwell found inspiration in the austerity and beauty of the wilderness. His training in architecture at Columbia gave him work as a draftsman and carpenter on the Island before his paintings produced enough income to provide for his needs. His presence on the island could be felt in the "fairy houses" made of bark and sticks populating the pine forests filled with wandering deer and chirping birds. Visitors' imaginations seemed to be charmed by the magical quality and serenity of the place. We gathered bark and sticks for our own "fairy houses."

The arrival of Guy and Deborah on *La Coursaire* for cocktails was a treat back at Linekin Bay. We were enthralled by the story of their stormy sail from Provincetown on Cape Cod to Nova Scotia. Caught by an unpredicted gale, *La Coursaire* was being blown into Cape Sable, Nova Scotia, a lee shore. They radioed the Canadian Coast Guard asking for directions to a safe harbor. The Coast Guardsman was reluctant to provide the information, perhaps fearing some sort of liability. Fortunately, fishers caught in the same storm heard their call and gave Guy GPS coordinates so they could rendezvous with them on the sea. In spite of the heavy fog and rain, *La Coursaire* was able to follow the fishermen's navigation lights into the safety of East Pubnico Harbor. The whole town came out to celebrate the safe arrival of their men at 3 a.m.! Deborah said they partied for a while, but exhaustion forced their retreat to bed. The hospitality flowed throughout their stay. Someone even lent Deborah and Guy a car so they could explore more of Nova Scotia. This story comes under the heading of "Sailors take care of their own!"

After a week of nonstop talking, playing, reminiscing, drinking, and eating at the reunion, my daughter, Leanne, and nephew, Steve, joined the crew on *Aurora*. As we sailed north past Pemaquid Light located on its rocky point, fond childhood memories flooded into JoAnne's consciousness. She had spent many summers with her Auntie Beth who lived at New Harbor close to the lighthouse. Auntie Beth was famous for her freshly caught mackerel breakfasts. Yum? Fish for breakfast?

We had a wonderful sail to Port Clyde and picked up a mooring securing *Aurora* among scores of lobster traps whose buoys sprinkled blobs of color into the distance across the water. This small fishing port was the home of Dorothea and Fred Belano, whose sailing adventures on their schooner, *RW Hopkins*, in 1910-13, were noted in Dorothea's diaries. Compiled by her son, they became the basis of a book, *The Log of the Skipper's Wife*. Their principal cargo was ice cut off fresh water ponds in Maine that they hauled to Rio de Janeiro to cool the summer drinks of rich Brazilians. Dorothea decided to live on the schooner with her husband and later her two children rather than face the censorship of an overbearing mother-in-law. Learning how to run the ship and most importantly how to navigate using a sextant and chronometer made her an indispensable member of the crew. In fact, when her husband, "Freddy Boy," fell ill, she and the first mate navigated the ship for over a week to its destination while the skipper recovered.

"I feel a strong kinship with Dorothea, and I'm thrilled to be anchored in her harbor. She's my kind of woman," said JoAnne. "I like the way she took over the ship and assumed her husband's role as skipper. Let's walk uphill, so I can take a close look at Dorothea's sea captain's house up there overlooking the harbor."

"I really admire Dorothea too," I said. "I love the Victorian look of the gingerbread decorations along the roof line of her house and the front porch sporting a white railing supported by turned spindles."

Taking a short morning sail the following day, we arrived at Metinic Island, anchored in its bay and dinghied ashore to begin a refreshing hike accompanied by the baaing of sheep as wheeling sea gulls swooped above us in the glorious weather. I began to wonder where Maine's much advertised fog had disappeared. By afternoon, we tied to the Rockport town dock next to a park containing old lime kilns used to create the plaster and cement employed in the building of Boston in the 1700s and 1800s.

Leanne left in the morning to begin her year at Vassar College. Steve, JoAnne, and I prepared for our twenty-five-mile voyage out to Matinicus Island, the easternmost inhabited island in the United States.

Sailing near Rockland harbor, we were surrounded by historic wooden schooners heading out for sails on Penobscot Bay. We counted a dozen of these magnificent ships flying all their sails on this calm day. Where else could you see more schooners on the water than any other type of vessel? I was transported back into the 19th century when schooners hauled cargo and passengers to outlying islands and towns along the Maine coast. In town, our treat was seeing the collection of Wyeth family paintings in the Farnsworth Museum. Their penetrating realism chronicled life on the Maine coast as their subjects communicated deep levels of feeling made visible through the skill and vision of the artists.

Sailing offshore to Matinicus Island, we picked up a mooring for twenty dollars in the center of the harbor. We had easy access by dinghy into town. From reading the *Island Journal* published in Maine, we learned about the state's off lying islands and that the schools on these islands were the key to the survival of the year around population. Children meant population growth and replacement of the older islanders. Matinicus had a good teacher for their one-room school house according to three boys from the mainland who talked with us.

"We're boarding out here with our aunt and uncle so we can attend school," one of the boys told us. "Our teacher is great, and we have small classes so we learn a lot!"

Summer residents round out the population of fishers and lobstermen who provide for their families by plying their trades in all sorts of weather. Life here is simple but intense, because everyone is exposed to the forces of the weather and the closeness of interpersonal relationships among the small permanent population.

In the morning as we released our mooring, a thick fog rolled in blanketing the harbor. Now was the time to really put our radar to work! But the radar showed it had other ideas by confronting me with a blank screen.

"Steve," I called out, "the radar's busted. I want you to be a lookout on the bow armed with the fog horn."

"Okay, I'll give three blasts if I see another boat," replied Steve.

We did have our GPS whose coordinates would show us where we were, but the real danger we faced was running into another boat or ship because visibility was limited to about twenty feet. Ghosting along in the thick fog, we came upon another sailboat.

"Ahoy, our radar is broken. Where are you headed?" I called out.

"I'm heading for Rockport and my radar is working," the captain called back. "Why don't you follow along in my wake to Rockport."

"Thanks, sounds like a plan to me," I said.

Close to Rockport, the fog magically lifted, allowing us easy entry into the harbor. Steve had done a marvelous job as lookout, a throwback to days of sail before electronics. After reminiscing about his 1991 visit on *Aurora* in the Sea of Cortez and swimming with the seals, we all went to bed early so Steve could catch his early morning flight.

Snuggling into bed, JoAnne and I talked. "I'm struck by the distances we have traveled," I said.

"Just think of the many unique experiences that crowd our recollections," said JoAnne.

"Indeed, we are sailing the dream!" I said.

The yachting center of Camden had the radar repair facilities we needed, so *Aurora* joined the mobs of summer people crowding into town and the harbor. This beautiful old seaport is filled with bustling shops, restaurants, a microbrewery, and a movie theater which we visited while waiting for the radar parts to arrive. Mega-yachts from England joined schooners and just plain sailboats and became our neighbors as we dinghied through the harbor or sat watching the vessels parade by from the cockpit of

Aurora. Old houses and churches became our shoreside "friends" as we absorbed local history in walks through this charming town. Kevin of Wayfarer Marine installed a new tuning board in the radar dome. I reinstalled the apparatus on *Aurora's* mast in preparation for our voyage to Nova Scotia where JoAnne's son, Douglas, and his family lived in Halifax.

31

ON TO NOVA SCOTIA

Remembering *La Coursaire's* harrowing passage to Nova Scotia, I stayed glued to the weather fax and the VHF marine weather forecasts for the Gulf of Maine and the coast of Nova Scotia. A good weather forecast predicting low winds and waves sent us off sailing across Penobscott Bay to Winter Harbor where the anchorage looked like a calm Canadian lake surrounded by pine trees lining the rocky shores. We set off at 8 a.m. the next morning to begin a two hundred-eighty-mile passage sending us past Bar Harbor, Maine, across the Gulf of Maine, and seaward of the Bay of Fundy that has enormous thirty-foot tides. We rounded Cape Sable at the southwestern end of Nova Scotia and proceeded to the northeast along its coast into St. Margaret's Bay finding Boutilier's Point where Douglas's brother-in-law Alan lived with wife Theresa and their children, Evan and Laura. We anchored right off their front yard.

Blessed by good weather, we arrived rested and dinghied into their dock for a warm welcome. Eleven-year-old Evan treated us to a lively rendition of Celtic fiddle music that had our hands clapping and toes tapping. Evan continued playing the fiddle as a teenager and later he attended the Berkeley School of Music in Boston. Our stay was cut short, however, by the predicted arrival of Hurricane Emily moving north in the Atlantic Ocean. A visit to the Nova Scotia Coast was on its track.

* * * * *

The safest place for *Aurora* would be in Halifax Harbor. We sailed into its Northeast Arm which offered the best protection from hurricane winds and also offered an extra bonus by being the home of the Royal Nova Scotia Yacht Squadron. The club's patron was Prince Philip, Queen Elizabeth's husband, which entitled the use of Royal in its name! We felt like royalty when the Yacht Squadron staff sent out a classic mahogany water taxi to pick us up. At the grand old club house, warm showers were made available to us.

After a phone call, the water taxi brought JoAnne's son, Douglas, and family out to *Aurora* where a happy reunion ensued. Douglas stands six feet, two inches tall while our daughter-in-law, Heather, is a more diminutive Scottish Ferguson. Our grandkids, Sarah, aged ten, and Jonathan, seven, complete the family. We were all drawn into the Squadron's Celebration of Venetian Night that featured two thirty-foot war canoes propelled by large crews of furious paddlers racing through the anchorage. Following the races, a sumptuous barbeque ignited our appetites as we joined club members waiting to fill their plates. The evening was topped off by a Lighted Boat Parade passing right next to *Aurora's* location on her mooring. To say that we were all royally entertained would be an understatement.

Joining the family, we drove down the coast to Lunenburg where we visited its fishing museum, illustrating the lives of our floating compatriots and spelling out the current crisis involving the collapse of the cod fisheries. Canada has stopped all fishing for these species in Canadian waters, effectively closing down an industry that had existed since the 1600s. Huge trawler factory ships with their gigantic nets had been killing every species of fish they swept up. Now was the time for *all* fishermen to pay for those who were too greedy. I feel that men sometimes have a hard time acknowledging that their actions have a major negative effect on the web of life.

* * * * *

On the way back from Lunenburg, we stopped at the home of Bill and Kristen Gilkerson, who were members of Doug and Heather's Tibetan Buddhist group in Halifax. We had an interesting chat and tasty lunch in their home overlooking Mahone Bay on the Atlantic Shore of Nova Scotia. Bill is a sailor, painter and illustrator of marine scenes, author of numerous books, historian, and an adventurer. Some of his historically accurate paintings of ships from the age of sail now hang at the United States Naval Academy in Annapolis, Maryland. His illustrations grace his own and other writers' books brimming with the history and adventure of sailing ships. Bill and I had an immediate attraction based on my sailing experience and desire to understand more about his work. His studio was filled with old Navy uniforms, muskets, and even a small cannon which were used as models for his drawings and paintings. Bill and Kristen sail their ancient cutter, *Elly*, off the coast and it gives them a sense of joy.

Hurricane Emily had now been downgraded to a tropical storm passing well south of Nova Scotia. We reluctantly began thinking about leaving since winter's breath could be felt in the drop of night time temperatures in early September. So much for summer in northern latitudes as JoAnne and I began to miss the tropics.

32

HEADING SOUTH FOR WARMTH

On September 6, 1993, we sailed out of Halifax Harbor south toward Casco Bay off Portland, Maine, in weather that seemed blessed by the gods. The unusual sight of a six-foot shark swimming on the surface and the arrival of an exhausted yellow warbler broke up our routine of reading, navigating, and cooking. The warbler, possibly having become separated from its flock flying south, stayed with us. It even flew down into the cabin and perched on my finger enjoying a free ride until we sighted land and he flew off free as a bird.

Landing at Jewel Island on the outer flanks of Casco Bay about ten miles from Portland, we found that the island lived up to its name. We hiked through its forests, coming upon gun emplacements and watch towers constructed during WWII to protect Portland from the threat of German U-Boats. I met a man who had sailed on wooden sailing ships during WWII. He patrolled the East Coast, looking for and reporting U-Boats so that U.S. torpedo dive bombers could find and sink them. Not registering on the U-Boats' sonar, the wooden hulled ships sailed without using engine power which reduced their chance of being seen or heard.

Our anchorage was not under attack, but was the center of the local lobster fishery. A pick-up boat, anchored close to *Aurora*, received the lobster catch from the incoming forty-foot-long lobster boats and delivered bait fish for their traps. I had a few dollars in my pocket when I dinghied over, enough money to buy us two right- out-of-the-sea lobsters, that made a delicious dinner.

Our next destination, Yarmouth, is located on the Royall River where it flows into Casco Bay. We found it after steering though "fields" of lobster traps marked by their colorfully coded pickup buoys that stretched out to the horizon in long rows. In essence, lobsters were being farmed because the small ones that enter the traps to eat the bait are thrown back by the lobstermen to grow larger. The really big lobsters comprise the breeding stock. The keepers, between one and two pounds, are sent to lobster pounds for sale or to the live tanks of restaurants around the country. Jo-Anne's friends, Lew and Peggy, gave us guest accommodations and a wonderful break from the "rigors" of cruising on *Aurora*. They loaned us one of their cars and offered guide services. We toured Portland's Old Town which was populated with three-and-four-story red brick mid-1800 buildings. Then we drove out to Cape Elizabeth that marks the southern edge of Casco Bay. We continued on to Prout's Neck where we found Winslow Homer's home at the end. He is my favorite American artist who painted lively watercolors of sailboats and their crews and seascapes spiced by waves crashing on rocky coasts.

We had docked *Aurora* at Yankee Marina. Yet, another hurricane threat forced us to leave and motor up the Cousins River to anchor the boat where she would be safely surrounded by land. *Aurora* did well until an extreme low tide caused by the hurricane heeled her over on her side allowing the bilge water to slosh up into the storage lockers. What a mess! When we returned, the marina was abuzz with activity as boats were being hauled for winter storage—in mid-September. This not so subtle message warned us to "Head south! Now!"

Four days later after an easy sail, we anchored in Plymouth Harbor, becoming neighbors of the *Mayflower II*, a replica of the original, as guests of the Plymouth Yacht Club. Soon we were joined by JoAnne's "kissin'" cousin, George, his wife, Ginny, an accomplished artist, their son, Jeff, and his wife, Kathy, along with assorted children for a sail on *Aurora*. It was a treat for them to get the feeling of being on *Aurora* that up to now had only existed in our letters and photos. For now, it was more family hospitality in Hopkinton, Massachusetts, punctuated by Kathy's strong Bostonian accent, great meals, and warm showers for *Aurora's* crew that were putting us on the verge of being "spoiled."

Feeling the pressure of a twenty-degree cold front, we retraced our track south across Massachusetts Bay to the Cape Cod Canal where this time the tidal current was flowing against us. The strength of the current forced me to implement the river running techniques I learned canoeing in northern Canada. Hugging the shore, where the current is the weakest, was the key as we pushed *Aurora's* Yanmar engine to maximum power through the ten-mile long canal. After passing the Massachusetts Maritime Academy on a hill at the end of the canal, we entered Buzzard's Bay. Here we made overnight stops at Cuttyhunk Island where we anchored off the front yards of million dollar houses and at Stonington Harbor inside the breakwater.

When we passed the mouth of the Thames River at JoAnne's old home of New London, Connecticut, her childhood memories switched into overdrive. She shared one of those with me.

"A life threatening incident occurred when my older sister, Pat, fell through the ice on a pond. Mom had forbidden us to skate there. My young friends and I had the presence of mind to form a 'human chain' to drag her out of the water. We built a fire to dry her clothes. My mom, Madeline, must never find out! And you better not tell her."

"Okay, I won't," I said. "I can imagine your mother's wrath even though it happened sixty years ago."

Soon, we were entering the mouth of the Connecticut River to tie up at the Old Lyme Marina under orders from sisters Margie and Leslie to visit them. We always obeyed those kinds of orders! After catching the incoming tide in the morning, we used the current to help us motor upstream for about fifty miles to our destination, the ferry landing at South Glastonbury. The ferry operators were amazed to see a sailboat so far from the sea and promised to keep an eye on *Aurora* as Margie zoomed up in her Jeep to collect us. Her home is on a ridge in a grove of trees with an orchard out back that opens up to a view of the skyline of Hartford filling the horizon. From their screened back porch, we could take in the view while relaxing with drinks in our hands. Conversation helped us catch up on family activities we'd missed. We'd been traveling for months on *Aurora* without the immediate communication we now enjoyed.

While spending time in South Glastonbury, founded in 1693, we learned the township was bought from Chief Sowheag for twelve yards of trading cloth. The old Brookside Tavern on Main Street served us an ample lunch, a delicious treat. Hiking in the Cotton Hollow Preserve, we came upon the ruins of George Stocking's gunpowder factory that had supplied the Connecticut Volunteers during the Revolutionary War. Remnants of old water mills also lined Roaring Brook that flows down into the Connecticut River. Along the river bank were leaf tobacco, corn, and vegetable farms while apple and peach orchards populated the hills, complementing the atmosphere created by Revolutionary War era houses lining Main Street. For us, this was a welcome connection to the earlier and more graceful life of our forebears.

On our way again we had an easy ride on the outgoing tide on the Connecticut River to Long Island Sound. Sailing south along the coast of Connecticut, we caught the incoming tide at Hell's Gate of the East River in New York that flows between the Bronx and Queens. There the river's current generated two-foot tall standing waves that we surfed on before being swept into calmer water. Seeing the United Nations complex and Battery Park at the end of Manhattan Island from the boat was a thrill. That was topped by the sight of a square rigger sailing next to the Statue of Liberty. What a day being so clear and bright. *Aurora* was sailing in one of the world's most famous harbors and I was her master. We'd come a long way, baby.

River traffic was lighter than anticipated. We felt sadness at the sight of Riker's Island's prison barges whose inmates were playing basketball on the barbed wire fenced top deck. These barges held the overflow of teenage inmates from the prison, reminding us that we live in a troubled society.

After rounding Battery Park at the end of Manhattan, *Aurora* was now in the Hudson River proceeding north upstream with the tide past the World Trade Center and Columbia University on Morningside Heights. JoAnne was thrilled to see International House in the distance, having worked at its counterpart on the UC

Berkeley campus for seventeen years. Winds from the south pushed *Aurora's* wing on wing sails as we gracefully sailed under the George Washington Suspension Bridge, past the Palisades on the New Jersey side of the Hudson, and finally to the Tarrytown Marina nestled at the eastern end of the Tappan Zee Bridge, where we took a slip.

After a good night's rest, JoAnne and I rented a car and drove off to visit my daughter Leanne at Vassar College located in Poughkeepsie also on the East side of the Hudson. Our trip to Hyde Park, the home of Franklin and Eleanor Roosevelt overlooking the Hudson, was brightened by a lavish display of red, yellow, and orange fall colors shouting out from the maples and oaks. After we arrived at Hyde Park, Leanne shared some of her insights with us.

"Dad, I just saw a PBS special that made clear the role of Franklin and Eleanor Roosevelt in leading the nation out of the Great Depression. I feel by seeing their home and museum in person has doubled the impact on me. Being a political science major, I'm also impressed by their commitment to the unemployed and poor." I listened intently to my daughter.

"Did you know that Eleanor was often the public face of Franklin's Administration and kept pushing for change throughout the long years of the Great Depression?" I pointed out. "I think that she was the most influential woman in America at that time."

Leanne continued, "I learned more about how decisions were made and how ideas such as Civilian Conservation Corps were put into action that employed many thousands of people whose work changed the face of America. Eleanor's example gives me hope that I can have a positive impact on society using my education and drive to succeed."

* * * * *

After saying goodbye to Leanne, we timed our departure from Tarrytown to coincide with the outgoing tide so *Aurora* was able to ride the current, sailing downstream past the Palisades and finally past the Statue of Liberty where the river traffic became fearsome. Ferries, sightseeing boats, tugs with their tows, and freighters kept us on our toes as daylight waned. After passing under the Verrazano Narrows Bridge, we made the turn into a channel toward Great Kill Harbor on Staten Island without incident.

"JoAnne, I just noticed that our GPS readings, the radar images, and the charts aren't agreeing," I said with alarm. "I'm not sure where we are! I'm feeling a bit disoriented, and it's getting dark. What should I do?"

"Do you see that light tower over there?" said JoAnne, "I think I can make out some numbers on it. Why don't you steer *Aurora* over to the light tower and maybe you can figure out where we are."

"Okay," I said. "Here we go. Well, the chart's longitude numbers are wrong so I entered the wrong coordinates into the GPS, and of course, we have been following them to an incorrect destination."

By now it was dark, so I reprogrammed the GPS to direct us to Great Kill Harbor. Luckily, we narrowly missed the breakwater as *Aurora* entered the harbor.

"Wow, that breakwater was a little too close for comfort," I exclaimed. "Let's anchor, have dinner, and get some rest."

Early the next morning, *Aurora* headed around Sandy Hook into the Atlantic Ocean, beginning a one hundred-sixty-mile overnight sail down the coast of New Jersey. The ocean was nearly smooth, and the winds blew over the stern quarter assuring us a mellow ride all day. Happy and relaxed, we watched a beautiful sunset fade into darkness populated with millions of stars. That night clearly answered the question of why people sail. Our senses basked in the starlight, as a 15-knot breeze filled our sails, driving us softly along through the calm sea. JoAnne and I snuggled in the cockpit sharing the sensory high and the love we felt for each other.

A breath-taking crimson sunrise graced the ocean at 6:47 a.m. Later that day, we sailed past the Victorian homes with intricate gingerbread decorations of Cape May, New Jersey. Turning into Delaware Bay, we caught the incoming tide surging northward toward the Chesapeake and Delaware Canal which took us into

Chesapeake Bay. Here warmer temperatures allowed us to open our hatches for the first time in a month.

JoAnne turned to me saying, "Indeed, we really are further south."

"Yeah, isn't that great!" I said with a smile as I took off my shirt.

St. Michael's, on the eastern shore of Maryland, was our first port of call in the Chesapeake. It was a very charming small town with Colonial era houses lining the streets. The sailing museum just off our anchorage was a big hit. The restaurant next to the museum served us mountains of blue crabs served on newspapers. Cracking and then picking the meat out of the shells was accompanied by large schooners of beer that floated our energy and spirits. After sailing over to Back Creek near Annapolis, we anchored off the Port Annapolis Marina which allowed us to use their dinghy dock and showers for a reasonable fee.

Here we were joined by JoAnne's nephew, Keith, spouse, Lynne, and their daughter, Madeline, who stopped by on their drive back to Boston from a visit to Keith's Dad in Charlotte. They stayed on *Aurora* and took us on a tour of Annapolis and the United States Naval Academy where Keith was able to reconnect with memories of his time in the Navy spent on a guided missile cruiser, USS *Sampson*, in the Mediterranean Sea. We saw two of Bill Gilkerson's paintings in the Naval Academy Museum: *The Bonhomme Richard* and *The Battle of the USS Constitution and HMS Java*. Bill's talent for representing the details of the ships, the rigging, sails, spars, masts, hulls, and guns spewing smoke and fire, was very impressive in creating an overall feeling of power and action. After the tour, Keith and Lynne treated us to a dinner at a wonderful seafood restaurant in this seafood mecca where we celebrated our third wedding anniversary.

The next day, we were off to the mid-October Annapolis (In The Water) Boat Show featuring many beautiful, but costly sailboats priced well beyond our reach. We also enjoyed shoreside exhibits. The owner of Neil Pryde Sails gave us a good deal on the installation of full battens on *Aurora's* spare mainsail. This improvement would help the sail create a better airfoil in the wind, increasing its power and our speed. Moreover, the full battens would make it easier to reef and to lower the sail after I installed new lazy jacks, small lines designed to catch the lowered sail.

Later, I would also install a used Windbugger, a rather large wind generator, that I had bought from another sailor at the Seven Seas Cruising Association picnic. Alas, the two and one half foot-long blades wouldn't turn in less than 20 knots of wind. After disassembling it, I greased all the friction points, so it did produce electricity at lower wind velocities and would prove itself useful in the windy Bahamas.

Guy, Deborah, Karl

When we met Guy and Deborah of *La Coursaire* at the boat show, they suggested renting a car together for a trip to Gettysburg to take advantage of the brilliant fall colors. The visit to the Cemetery Ridge Battlefield at Gettysburg was sobering as we learned that more than 51,000 Americans lost their lives there, more than in any other battle in American history. The untried General George Meade held the center of the line against Pickett's charge, while at "Little Round Top," Colonel Joshua Chamberlain's Maine volunteers secured the end of the line preventing its envelopment by the Alabama Volunteers. They saved the day.

Reading *The Killer Angels* by Michael Shaara and seeing the film *Gettysburg* made walking on that hallowed ground more meaningful and poignant as we passed monument after monument. Various states erected these monuments to honor their fallen soldiers. Often we walked in silence as Lincoln's eloquent words of the *Gettysburg Address* echoed in our minds.

*****

Leenigs

After arriving back on *Aurora*, we sailed south in Chesapeake Bay to Knapp's Narrows separating Tilghman Island from the rest of Maryland. *Aurora* ran aground there after I became confused and chose to go on the wrong side of a channel buoy. Was it red right returning? The engine could not move the boat and the falling tide made matters even worse. I signaled desperately that I needed a tow from the passing motor boats. Not one of them offered to help. So much for "stinkpot" sailors. Finally, one sailboat responded by slowly coming closer to us, so I could throw him a line that I attached to the bow cleat. With both engines racing, the line stretched and with a noticeable "twang" *Aurora* bounced off the sandbar into deeper water. We raised shouts of, "Hooray, hooray! Thanks so much!"

Turning up Harris Creek, we found our destination, the dock belonging to Fred and Karen Leenig, owners of *Hotspur*, whom we had met in Guanaja, Honduras. Again, we had a "home away from home" that gave us the opportunity to play catch up with our lives. Fred made us a wonderful Chesapeake soup from crabs caught in his traps at the end of their dock. Karen was pregnant with their first child and had just been ordered to bed by her doctor due to the high possibility of miscarriage.

JoAnne and I swung into action helping out with cooking and shopping for a few days while also doing some sightseeing on the Eastern Shore of Maryland. Oxford and Easton were charming old towns situated along the bay where the creeks create nooks and crannies that widen out to larger bodies of water surrounded by farms and estates. Horses filled the green pastures enlivening the landscape. JoAnne and I began thinking that this area might be a good place to settle down. Later in the Bahamas, we would hear the good news on the High Seas Radio that Karen and Fred were the proud parents of a baby boy, Greg. Later they adopted Mae from China.

* * * * *

Sailing across Chesapeake Bay, we located Little Creek Marina in Norfolk, Virginia, and found that our friends Mar and Jan aboard *Livin* had tied up in a neighboring slip. Their 1982 Cadillac, appropriately called "The Yellow Banana Boat," became our mode of transportation, fulfilling every cruiser's dream of having friends with a car. All the fun was cut short by news of yet another hurricane that was threatening North Carolina and was forecast to continue northward. Deciding that the marina was too exposed to the wind, we joined the Navy ships heading out—them to sea and us up the East River of Mobjack Bay—*Livin's* favorite hurricane hole. We anchored behind a sandspit over a heavy mud bottom that provided good holding ground for the two anchors I set in a V formation to secure *Aurora* when the rotating hurricane winds passed over. I was feeling prepared after tying down all the sails with extra lines.

The uptight owner of *Flight* dinghied over to almost demand that I remove all the sails and the dodger since he felt threatened by being anchored behind me. I did remove the roller furling jib and doubled the snubbers to the anchor chain, but felt removing the dodger would expose the cockpit and companionway to the force of the storm, limiting my ability to respond to any emergency. *Flight's* owner left grumbling, but I was the captain and felt that *Aurora* was ready.

I kept the first anchor watch using the readings on the GPS to verify that we were not moving. About midnight, JoAnne relieved me and felt 50-knot gusts that caused the boat to pull at the anchors, jerking and bucking as it changed directions. I slept through it all and upon awakening at first light found *Aurora* heading in the opposite direction next to our protective sandbar.

We had survived a dangerous night and a season filled with threats of hurricanes. The time to move on down the Intracoastal Waterway was now!

33

TREKKING ALONG THE ICW

It was the end of October and temperatures again fell, so we joined the southern migration of cruising boats and birds heading for Norfolk, Virginia, where the Intracoastal Waterway (ICW) begins. The ICW consists of dredged canals, rivers, and sounds connected together behind the beaches lining the southern Atlantic Coast of the United States. It allows shallow draft vessels to make the 1,000-mile journey from the Chesapeake Bay to Southern Florida protected from the waves and winds of the sea. For this protection, we gave up the freedom of steering *Aurora* with the autopilot. We had to hand steer in the narrow channels. Wildlife such as egrets, osprey, ducks, and deer were frequent companions along the banks. Even a swimming black bear joined *Aurora* in the Dismal Swamp Canal portion south of Norfolk. George Washington created the Dismal Swamp Land Company to drain the swamp to permit logging. He surveyed it and had the canal finished in 1805 for this purpose. We stopped overnight at an automobile/boat rest stop next to the canal along highway 17 where many car travelers stopped by to ask, "Where are you going? Do you sleep on the boat overnight?"

Eagles, ospreys, and great blue herons kept our eyes focused on the trees in this National Wildlife Refuge. It felt like we were in an upside down zoo with the creatures looking down on us as we navigated the canal through a tunnel of trees. The canal broadened out into the Pasquotank River which flowed south into Albemarle Sound at Elizabeth City, North Carolina, home of the "Rose Buddies." Founded in 1983 by Fred Fearing and Joe Kramer, the "Rose Buddies" decided to bring wine and cheese and fresh cut roses down to the boats tied to the docks. They also provide all sorts of information about Elizabeth City and the surrounding area. We felt warmly welcomed to this town that is rated as one of the top one hundred small cities in the United States.

As we crossed Albemarle Sound, the sky blackened as a long squall line raced toward us that sent me seeking shelter along the nearest shore. I dropped the hook and had just secured the snubber into the anchor chain when *Aurora* was hit with 50 knots of wind, heeling her over and stripping the loose chain off the windlass. Fortunately, the snubber stretched and the anchor held as we wildly swung toward shore. JoAnne struggled to corral the airborne charts in the cockpit just as Marine Harrier jets zoomed overhead lining up for their dive bombing practice runs. Cruising can be exciting!

In the morning looking west toward the end of the sound, we found the opening of the narrow canal leading to Bellhaven. Here, we were joined by tugs with their tows, crowding us close to the banks. If they didn't slow down in a more gentlemanly fashion, large sport fishing boats would create huge wakes that would cause *Aurora* to roll violently. I developed a method of dealing with this problem by slowing down and turning into the wake so *Aurora's* roll would be minimized. A few sharp words on the radio expressed my frustration and just perhaps would be heard by an oncoming boat causing it at least to think about slowing their speed. *Aurora* was able to make about sixty-five miles a day with the mainsail sheeted in tight which increased our speed and dampened the violent rolling because it acted like a wind break. Anchoring overnight meant finding a wide spot or creek off the main channel where we wouldn't be disturbed by passing boats or be a hazard to the navigation of other boats.

Running hard aground just before arriving at Beaufort, North Carolina, was complicated by the driving rain and 35-knot winds. Fortunately the bottom was soft and a powerboat from New Hampshire came by and pulled us loose from the grip of the gooey mud, reversing our bad luck with powerboats. Beaufort is a charming old town with city docks and other businesses oriented to cruising folks like us. We were joined by Deborah and Guy of *La*

Coursaire and Dan and Marty of *Vivid* for drinks at the bar where we each recounted our adventures. Deborah and Guy's stormy trip to Nova Scotia won them an extra drink in our competition for the best story. We arranged to pool our grocery lists and for shopping we used an old car provided by the marina.

"You know, Guy, this car looks like it's overdue for its final trip to the junkyard," I said.

"I hope it makes it to the store and back," said Guy. And by golly it just did!

While we were celebrating JoAnne's sixty-fourth birthday at the best restaurant in town, the Beaufort Grocery Company, Guy and Deborah were stopped from joining us by high waves in the harbor. Instead we included a charming couple, Sarah and John from Harker's Island, who were waiting for a table. Folks on Harker's Island which was founded in 1730 still speak a distinctive dialect of Old English.

On the ICW again, it was bridges, bridges, and more bridges. Their individual, specific opening times set the pattern of our days. Often we motored at full throttle to make an opening for some, while at other times we dawdled along because it would be a while before the next bridge's scheduled opening. Once, I asked the bridge tender to wait for a sailboat coming along behind us. Moving through as the bridge raised, we were passed by *Cursail*, a Morgan Out Island 41. The owners waved and shouted, "Thank you!" continuing along in their faster boat.

After anchoring in a bay off the channel near the U.S. Marine Base at Camp Lejeune, we were down below when the sound of a large helicopter brought us up to see what was happening. Dressed in suits with green fluorescent light bands outlining their bodies, Marines shinnied down a rope from the helicopter into a boat in the water. We became alarmed as a brightly burning flare kept drifting toward us, but soon the Marines sped up in a fast boat to pull it away. Quite a show demonstrating that the Marines are ready for most anything.

*****

Charleston, South Carolina, was our next long stop where we basked in its southern charm. Free van trips downtown from the city marina gave us access to the old slave market where descendants of slaves sold their baskets woven from reeds growing in the marshy areas we had passed before coming into Charleston Harbor. An eerie feeling came over me as I felt the impact of the place's history and imagined how these descendants felt working in the same place where their families were torn apart and sold into bondage.

From there we walked south through the French Quarter. We met and talked with an attorney in work clothes pushing a lawnmower along the street on his way home after mowing his mother's lawn.

Further along, we came to Battery Park with its huge cannons aimed toward Ft. Sumter that ignited the Civil War. Visiting Boone Hall Plantation outside of town, we were drawn into a reenactment of the Battle of Secessionville which occurred on June 16, 1862. Originally nine thousand Union Troops attacked a well fortified Confederate position defended by only five hundred Rebels on James Island. The Federals had to cross a narrow isthmus where the Rebels concentrated their cannon fire killing one hundred-seven Federal Troops.

At Boone Hall, four hundred Civil War buffs re-enacted the battle in a nearby field to the accompaniment of rifle and cannon fire. Historically accurate camps contained white canvas tents sheltering tailors, tinkers, and tarts. Some women were cooking in black iron pots hung over open fires, and others were enticing passersby in their low cut dresses, while barbers plied their trade under an adjacent tree. Immersed in this environment, I found it was an easy step to let my mind join the troops on the Union side of course. The sense of history is very strong in the South and the Civil War remains a topic of discussion. Being the loser is never an easy role to play.

* * * * *

Continuing south we stopped at the Palmetto Bay Marina at Hilton Head, South Carolina, the home of Larry and Carol Jordan, owners of *Amigo,* now tied to its permanent slip. We anchored *Aurora* off the Marina. Larry, a retired orthodontist, is now having too much fun selling boats while Carol is working as an interior decorator. They serve as hosts for their many friends from the Cruising Class of 1992-93 who have returned to the United States from Central America. It was party time.

Calm, warm weather greeted *Aurora* as we left the shelter of the ICW, sailing out the Savannah River into the Atlantic Ocean for a three hundred-fifty-mile passage to Stuart, Florida. During a night sail, JoAnne was on watch tracking a freighter on our radar when its course appeared to be converging with ours. She called the freighter on the VHF radio identifying *Aurora* as a sailing vessel and reporting our GPS coordinates, our location, then asking if they saw us.

After pausing to look at his radar, the ship's officer answered, "Yes," and altered his course to avoid *Aurora.* JoAnne let out a sigh of relief.

"That ship really does see us, so we don't have to give it an extra wide berth," she said.

On the second night of the passage off Cape Canaveral, looking at the chart I noted that we were close to a warning area that would be impacted as weather rockets fell back to earth. I called the Coast Guard asking if rockets would be fired tonight.

While they were checking, another voice came on the radio: "Watch out, here comes a weather rocket, rrrrrraaahhh."

These sound effects were quite good, but the prankster's efforts were short circuited by the Coast Guard operator who reassured us, "There is no rocket activity scheduled for tonight."

We laughed. "It seems that boaters do have a sense of humor!" I said.

The buoy located off St. Lucie Inlet came into view at 11:45 am the next day. Threading our way along the narrow channel toward Stuart, we found David Lowe's Boatyard in Manatee Pocket where we left *Aurora* for a month's rest while we visited my mom in Naples and flew to California for Christmas with our children.

34

BAHAMAS HERE WE COME

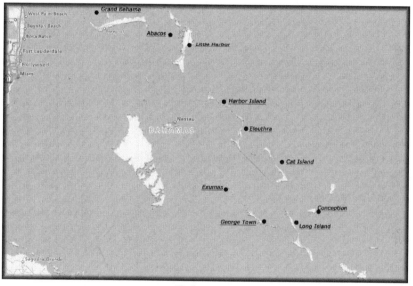

Bahamas

After returning to Stuart, Florida, in early January, 1994, we sailed on the ICW to Ft. Lauderdale where my daughter Leanne joined us in waiting for the weather to improve. We needed calm weather to cross the Gulf Stream to the northern Bahamas because the current would create high waves if it were opposed by the wind. On January 12 conditions were right so we left that evening and were able to transit through the reef in early morning light. Following Todd on *Loon*, we used the poles and arrows marking the winding passage through the reef, entering the shallow waters of the Bahama Banks. I steered *Aurora* north of Grand

Bahama Island to Great Sale Cay and anchored over a grassy, sandy bottom that did not provide good holding when tested by winds that gusted to 38 knots. A horn blast from *Pilgrim*, a thirty-two-foot trawler anchored nearby, alerted us that our anchor was dragging. Putting out more heavy chain solved the problem, and we settled into our spot one hundred-seventeen nautical miles from Ft. Lauderdale.

Leanne dove in the blue water and let out a shrill scream, "It's freezing!" as she furiously swam back to the boat. The water temperature had dropped to 66 degrees, much too cold for our tender bodies that had been spoiled by the warm waters of Central America. Marsh Harbor on Great Abaco Island provided a safe anchorage and a place where we could buy provisions and connect with a small plane that would fly Leanne back to Miami, then to Vassar in Poughkeepsie for the beginning of her spring semester.

We reconnected with Dave and Bev on *Cloverleaf* and joined these two expert Bahama cruisers in exploring the Abacos Island Chain where the shallow water between the islands and the outer reefs on the Atlantic side made for tricky navigating. Anchoring off Treasure Cay where Bev's brother owned a condo, we took our dinghies into town, coming upon a sunken yawl, *Xanadu III*, from Montreal tied to a concrete seawall along the way. I climbed aboard to investigate and discovered a ready to eat meal set at the table and no obvious signs of physical damage to the yacht. It seems that a hose or valve must have given way causing the boat to flood with water and forcing its abandonment. "Where are the people?" I wondered out loud.

We all continued south in the skinny water. After bouncing along on the sand berms (like waves of sand), we wiggled our way out to deeper water heading to Little Harbor in the middle of the island. Entering the harbor through a small opening, we anchored off Pete's Pub and Gallery operated by Peter Johnston, son of the renowned sculptor Randolph Johnston. Randolph operated his own bronze foundry using the "Lost Wax" method of casting to create graceful blue herons, arching dolphins, and swimming sea turtles. What could be a better pastime than drinking beer while admiring artistic representations of these creatures? The harbormaster brought us over a favorable weather fax and also a warning about thievery in Nassau Harbor, our next destination, which we filed under "Reasons to keep alert and to be aware of those who were walking the docks."

After less than an hour's motoring in the morning, the 9-12 knot wind came at 90 degrees over the beam of *Aurora* so we eased out the sails and had a mellow ride in the shelter of Eleuthera heading toward a twenty-four-foot tower off Paradise Island and into the Nassau Yacht Haven where we took a slip. We were greeted by Frank and Denise from *Cursail* whom we had waited for at a lift bridge on the ICW. Remembering *Aurora* they wanted to become acquainted with "considerate folks, like us." So over lunch at a cafe across from the Marina, we got to know each other.

"We're Frank and Denise, both IBMers, who spent their careers selling large computers," Frank said. "We bought *Cursail* when we retired so we could continue Denise's love of sailing. I'm a golfer and bring my clubs along."

"Yeah, I'm really proud of him," Denise said with a smile. "He's branched out into boat maintenance and mechanics and besides is sharpening his sailing skills. We're both enjoying the freedom of a sailing retirement and plan to head to the Caribbean in the future."

"It's great to be getting to know you. We'd enjoy being friends," said JoAnne.

"Our goal is seeing the Bahamas this winter and early spring. It's back to the USA after that," JoAnne said.

*****

Being at a dock again, I created a highly recommended second anchor system called a Bahamian Moor for deploying in narrow anchorages. The main heavier Bruce Anchor is set to the right, and then by driving the boat to the left and setting the second lighter Danforth Anchor, *Aurora* would be kept centered over the spot between the two anchors. Stretched between the two anchors, *Aurora's* swing would be minimized, keeping her from hitting other boats or running aground in shallow water which is in abundance in the Bahamas.

After five days of exploring the crowded capital, Nassau, we sailed southeast to the top of the narrow chain of Exumas Islands, the least populated in the Bahamas. It offered many good anchorages and beaches, but lacked drinking water.

Stopping at Allen's Cay, we fed the scores of iguanas that rushed out of the scrubby bushes to greet us. They gobbled up our potato and carrot peels and seemed especially fond of our leftover lettuce and cabbage leaves. We felt a bit like Dr. John Dolittle, created by Hugh Lofting, who could communicate with animals. Since these iguanas were very gentle and curious, they seemed to respond to our quiet voices. A group of the larger ones accompanied us on a hike to the other side of the island even though we showed them we had no more food. We enjoyed each other's company as they ran ahead of us to reveal their island. Our smiles were abundant.

Our next stop was at Highborne Cay, where *Infinity*, an elegant Broward 70 motor yacht from Biddeford Pool, Maine, was anchored. Coming by in her dinghy, Peggy invited us over to see the boat. Can you imagine seeing chandlers hung in the dining room of a boat!

"Peggy, I discovered the water we took on board in Nassau is brackish. Is the water on the Island okay?"

"No, it isn't, answered Peggy. "Here are two bottles of spring water. Why don't you come back tomorrow with two Jerry jugs. Todd, my captain, can fill them using the ship's huge water maker."

"Thanks so much! Your fresh water will probably save us from getting a urinary tract infection caused by the salt in our water," JoAnne said.

Further south was located the privately supported National Park at Wardrick Wells where we tied to moorings in a narrow anchorage having a rapid tidal flow. This island, along with the surrounding reefs and bays, is a protected Marine sanctuary serving as a nursery for groupers, conch, and many other species of marine organisms. A resident ranger patrolled the area to prevent fishers from encroaching into the protected area. At a Sunday night Potluck Supper, JoAnne and I met Paul and Marion from the Boston Area sailing on their yawl, *Ching Pai*. Paul was a Harvard grad who had run a Boston Adult Education Program, while Marion was a Psychotherapist who was developing her artistic talents as a painter of landscapes.

We sailed together off and on for three weeks. We swam in Thunderball Cave (of James Bond fame) at Staniel Cay where releasing dry oatmeal from plastic bags drew in hundreds of fish that swarmed around us in the shafts of sunlight streaming down through holes in the ceiling of the cave. The flashing colors and reflections of their scales created undulating balls of light pulsing in the water. Also at Staniel Cay, we were drawn to visit *Beluga*, the first Nantucket Island 33 like ours we'd seen. We dinghied over and met an older Fred and his young friend of the family, Julie. Fred's spouse had died so Julie, a violinist, decided to join him so he could continue cruising. The boat developed some serious problems after hitting the bottom coming into Georgetown Harbor in a rage (high waves breaking across the opening in the reef), which broke his rudder from top to bottom and caused leaks at the mast step. JoAnne and I wished them luck, feeling the stress in their situation. I made a note in our log to beware when we would go into Georgetown in a few weeks.

Frank and Denise on *Cursail* accompanied us to Black Point on Great Guana Cay further south on the Exumas Chain. After dinghying ashore, we received a warm welcome from a swarm of kids and their grandmothers all anxious to show us around. "See how the plants are being grown in holes hammered out of the limestone rock," one boy said, as we were touring a vegetable garden. "There isn't enough soil on the surface to grow much of anything. Food and plant scraps are used to create soil in the holes. Every plant must be watered by hand. There ain't much fresh water on the island."

"Wow, you guys really have to work hard to grow food," JoAnne said.

Captured in a procession of young boys walking toward the church on the highest point of the island, we were treated to a drum solo by Simon and an invitation: "Why don't y'all come to

Blackpoint Kids

church tomorrow. We'll come by the beach in the mornin' to git you."

Sure enough they showed up on time. We were welcomed by an enthusiastic congregation that broke into singing, clapping their hands to the joyful music played by Simon's dad on the keyboard accompanied by Simon on the drums. Bodies swayed, and women's large hats bobbed to the exuberant pulsating rhythms.

We became the center of the sermon as the preacher welcomed us, but warned us to pay attention to the weather. "You need to heed the power of God's fury."

We were aware of the impending arrival of a "Norther Front" from morning weather reports, but his emphasis raised the level of urgency as we could see black clouds gathering outside the windows.

We began to wonder, "When's he going to stop talking?"

Freed at last, we hurried back to our dinghies on the beach. We took a few kids out for a quick look at our boats before motoring out through the choppy waves in the pass for a short hop to Little Farmer's Cay.

The anchorage was surrounded by Little Farmer's Cay and offered us protection from the waves generated by the heavy Norther that hit during the night. The force of the wind, however, was not impeded by low islands, thus testing our anchor gear to the maximum. The storm would continue for three days causing quite a few episodes of "cabin fever" that finally drove us ashore. We discovered crab races at Terry's Bar where everyone placed their bets. His good cooking brought approving smiles to the women's faces. JR, a Bahamian wood carver, produced interesting primitive wood carvings that had a distinctive African style depicting native men and women. A treasure hunt was organized by the crew of the one hundred-ten-foot long Brigantine, *Faire Jeanne*. Guests aboard included a number of officers from the Canadian Navy who had served with the owner, Captain Tom Fuller, during World War II. Captain Fuller had built this fiberglass and steel ship in his back yard on the Ottawa River. He named it for his wife, Jeanne, laying the keel in 1978 and launching the ship in 1980. Tom had sailed over 150,000 miles with a professional captain and crew of six. *Faire Jeanne* had also been used as a deep water sail training vessel for more than 2000 young men. Their treasure hunt took us all over the island keeping our brains working at top speed as we competed with other teams to find the treasure which was a case of cold Klick Bahamian Beer.

As the end of the storm passed over the island, it kicked up more disturbance in the anchorage while we were ashore. Looking out, I saw *Aurora* swinging wildly and coming too close to the boat behind us. Dinghying back to *Aurora*, I saw that our neighbor *Lady Luck's* fiberglass VHF radio antenna had proved to be no match for our spinning Windbugger blades. Diving down to our Danforth HiTensile Anchor, I found the shank had been snapped in half by the force of the wind, and the anchor on *Lady Luck* had also dragged, creating a rat's nest of line and chain on the bottom. It was a struggle to pull the whole mess up to the surface where I could sort things out in our dinghy. We bought them a new antenna in Georgetown to make things right!

On our way again, *Aurora* and *Ching Pai* sailed through the reef turning south to Rudder Cut Cay and anchoring in an almost landlocked lagoon completely sheltered from the wind and a short distance from a concrete cistern filled with fresh water captured off the roof of an abandoned round building. It took many trips with an old wheelbarrow filled with our Jerry cans down at the dock. Five dinghy loads of water were necessary to top off our tanks. What a luxury it was having enough water in this saltwater desert. This island had been the home of a very rich person who built a large geodetic dome main house, an airport, and miles of roads. It sported a stretch limo rusting in front of the house. All of this faded opulence was falling into further ruin. It was rumored that the owner was languishing in prison due to being busted for drug sales or trading in junk bonds.

Sitting in *Ching Pai's* cockpit, Paul remarked, "What a shame that this beautiful island, with its palm trees, lush tropical plants and flowers, is going to waste."

"Yeah, why don't we turn the island into a resort featuring its spectacular beaches and a great natural harbor," Marion said.

"Wouldn't it be fun? Think of the neat people who would be attracted to an out of the way place like this," fantasized JoAnne. "Talk about pipe dreams!"

That night the quiet of the anchorage was shattered by a low flying airplane that just missed our masts before it zoomed off into the darkness.

We wondered, "Huh! What was that all about?"

As we were sailing south to Georgetown, the short, sloppy seas and high winds made for an unmellow day, to say the least. It was punctuated by a small tornado spinning out of a black rain squall near shore. Coming through the opening in the reef became more exciting as *Aurora* surfed off a wave and bounced off the bottom in the trough, creating quite a bang but fortunately causing no damage to the hull, rudder, mast, or rigging. Thank God our bump on the bottom was less forceful than that of Fred and Julie on *Beluga*. It seemed that knowing what might happen wasn't enough to prevent us from hitting the bottom. Our need to find shelter pushed us into the shallow pass in the reef and Livengood Luck might have prevented things from being worse.

Georgetown was the center of government and commerce for the Exumas and the gathering place for most of the cruising yachts in all the Bahamas. Cruisers are attracted here because the sweep of the Norther Storms stops above Georgetown located at the southern end of the Exumas Chain of Islands. Our arrival was timed for the beginning of the Cruisers' Regatta which this year, 1994, attracted four hundred boats. The grand size of Elizabeth Harbor made the accommodation of that many yachts along its beaches possible without having a parking lot feeling. Exuma Market served as a headquarters of sorts. Their crammed message board became another way of communicating for boats out in the anchorage. We planned a Central American Class of 1992 Reunion for those who sailed through the Panama Canal and up the West Coast of Central America—Dan and Marty on *Vivid* and Bob and Janet on *Windfall* joined the party. Reconnecting with friends was another rewarding aspect of cruising that deepened friendships.

A speedy dinghy was essential as our social life moved from boat to boat, one evening on *Cursail* and another on *Ching Pai* as we traded food, stories, and ideas for future cruising destinations. Frank and Denise were drawn to cruising the Caribbean while Marion and Paul were interested in continuing their exploration of Maine. JoAnne and I stopped by other yachts to check them out. We were thinking that we needed a larger boat for long term cruising.

One evening, while standing in line for a BBQ dinner put on as a fund raiser for the Episcopal Church, I overheard three guys talking about flying for the DEA, the Drug Enforcement Administration.

"Did you guys fly over Rudder Cut Cay recently?" I said.

"Oh, yeah, we sure did," one responded.

"Wow, you sure came close to our masts!" I replied.

"Not to worry, we had on our night vision goggles and could see you plain as day," he bragged. "Once, we flew our helicopter right on top of a small plane, forcing it to land on Rudder Cut Cay since we suspected it of carrying cocaine from Columbia." "Yeah, we got that one right! We arrested the pilot and crew," asserted another agent. "Did you know that the DEA also operates a number of Fat Albert Blimps that carry radar antennas high over the Bahamas which track small aircraft enabling us to find them and make these kinds of arrests?"

"Yeah, I've seen the blimps and kind of guessed that they were being used to spot planes," I said. "Nice talking with you guys! Happy hunting!"

The Regatta had two races which *Aurora* was in position to watch as about thirty sailboats crowded into a turn around a channel buoy. Then out popped the spinnakers for the downwind run as their crews struggled to drop and douse their jibs, securing them along the rail. All of this action was on the narrow foredeck as the boats bounced over the waves. Sometimes, it seemed that ballet dancers were doing pirouettes as the foredeck crews worked to maintain their balance and stay on the boat. From our cockpit, we cheered and held our breaths.

Water polo, swimming races, volleyball, and other sports were scattered about on the beaches surrounding the harbor. A fun Talent Show was put on which included a great Gospel Singer from the Georgetown Post Office and a cruiser's chorus. Lastly, a Dinner Dance at Cousin's Purple Palace combined good food with a great band from the Peace and Plenty Hotel so we all had a great time! We summed up all of this activity under the heading, "Americans certainly know how to organize fun things to do!"

*****

After saying goodbye to all our friends in Georgetown, we sailed alone on *Aurora* east to Long Island where we dropped the hook in a small protected bight behind Cape Santa Maria, at the end of the island. Looking out from the cockpit, I saw dolphins playing about one hundred feet from the boat, so I swam over to say hello. Three dolphins were swimming in lazy vertical circles in the water picking up pieces of coral from the bottom, carrying them to the surface, and then dropping the coral to watch it sink. At fifteen feet, I stopped moving toward them as they continued playing for an audience of one, accepting my presence. I was one of the guys and was thrilled to be in their watery environment watching these intelligent wild creatures just have fun!

In the morning, we rounded the Cape into one to three-foot Atlantic swells making a pleasant ten mile passage to Conception Island surrounded by its reef and deep water. We anchored *Aurora* in a bay on the sheltered west side, behind the reef. Conception Island is 2100 acres in size, uninhabited except for the seabird rookery and a hatching site for green turtles that has access to a large shallow inner lagoon. Skin diving was interesting in the reefs of Staghorn Coral that were overgrowing a wrecked ship stuck on the reef protecting the anchorage. The coral was populated with neon blue and golden yellow queen angelfish, blue and yellow torpedo shaped wrasses, and a few brilliant orange-red swordtails all swimming around and through the "horns" of the coral.

Floating above, I lazily watched as the fish performed their individual dances in tune with surges from the swells.

Early the next morning, the *Notre Dame DuCap*, a rusty, listing old fishing boat from Honduras, limped into the anchorage after hitting the reef during the night. Two men in a skiff were dispatched to *Intrigue* anchored nearby. After they left, we also dinghied over.

"Hi, we're JoAnne and Karl from *Aurora* anchored over there. We noticed that you had some visitors from the old fishing boat and were wondering what was on their minds?"

"Hello, we're Willy and Anne from South Africa. The two guys that stopped by are fisherman from Honduras who asked us for the course and distance to Long Island and then to Georgetown. We wondered how in the world they were able to get this far without adequate charts and navigation equipment?"

"Wow, doing that would be quite a feat! It seems plausible since they bumped into the reef during the night," I said. "We're from San Francisco and have circumnavigated Central America after going through the Panama Canal."

"We've come from South Africa via Miami and came to the Bahamas for a needed vacation," Willy joked. "I have two circumnavigations under my belt while Anne had sailed 'only' 28,000 miles."

"Yeah, the distances really mount up when sailing from the Southern Hemisphere to the Northern Hemisphere," added Anne.

"Why don't you come over for dinner and drinks?" asked Jo-Anne.

"What can we bring?" asked Anne.

We spent a great evening with these two interesting people who had spent many years sailing to places I'd only read about.

"How have you accomplished all your sailing on a tight budget?" I wondered. "And I might add with such a refreshing sense of style."

"Well, two of our secrets are catching lots of fish and not eating onshore very often," said Willy.

"We're not doing well at catching fish," said JoAnne, "but we haven't been eating out much in the Bahamas. So maybe we're halfway there."

* * * * *

Off the next morning with the wind on the stern quarter, I held out the jib with a spinnaker pole for a downwind run, trolling as usual. First a large barracuda took the lure and began jumping and splashing as I pulled it in. I was forced to use long needle nose pliers to remove the hooks from his gaping mouth filled with needle sharp teeth. Overboard he went since ingesting its flesh can produce ciguatera poisoning caused by the barracuda eating reef fish that have accumulated toxins. Soon a large king mackerel took the lure, but as I pulled it in a large shark chomped away half the fish which still left a good sized dinner for us at our anchorage in the bight off the Old Stone Pier on the South end of Cat Island. Maybe that fish was a half measure of Livengood Luck?

Cat Island is the birthplace of actor Sidney Poitier, where he lived on his parent's farm until he was ten years old. Overlooking our anchorage at Cat Island, we could see the Hermitage built by Fr. Jerome, a Catholic priest-architect, as his retreat and final resting place on the highest hill (two hundred-nine feet) in the

Fr. Jerome's Hermitage

Bahamas. The Hermitage is an austere structure built of limestone with a commanding view of the Island and the surrounding ocean. What an inspiring place. Here we felt "above it all" in a setting where meditating and praying came naturally as we sat engrossed in the scene. That mood was broken when walking further inland to the store, JoAnne and I noticed many abandoned homes of people who had gone to Nassau to find work. Outmigration presents a perennial problem of depopulation in the "Out Islands" of the Bahamas. Father Jerome, however, was able to be above the realities of everyday life.

Sailing north, we took advantage of the southerly winds that gave *Aurora* a chance to slide over the waves rather than crash through them. Arriving at Little San Salvador Island, we anchored off a long curving beach with one other sailboat off this otherwise deserted island. Ashore, we began to clean up the beach, as we had done on other islands, by picking up the plastic waste contributed by fishers, ships, and careless people on land. After filling two large black trash bags, we hauled them inland to a dumping spot established by earlier cruisers. On *Aurora*, we didn't have room to store that much trash.

Sailing a Dream

Plastic trash persists in the environment often entangling marine animals or when mistaken for food killing its victim by blocking their digestive tract. While swimming around the boat, I found a golf ball on the bottom which I retrieved and later presented to Frank (the golfer) on *Cursail* as a gift from (fellow duffer) King Neptune.

Arriving at Rock Sound, Eleuthera, we found its Homecoming and Easter Celebration in full swing right on shore opposite our anchorage. JoAnne and I had box seats for watching dancing and hearing the music as it continued late into the night. Attending the Episcopal Church on Easter Sunday put us into the action. We were dazzled by the women wearing their colorful Sunday best outfits complimented with large hats and roused by the choir and congregation singing Spirituals in close harmonies at full volume that lifted our spirits. Afterward, a tasty chicken BBQ sustained our physical bodies as we sat chatting with a Bahamian family. The Festival included the Royal Bahamian Police Band which played and marched their hearts out—we appreciated them as much as Queen Elizabeth had during their performance the previous week in Nassau. Eleuthera is a long narrow island, looking like a long bent stick on the chart starting in the southeast and continuing northwest which took three days to traverse by sailing close to the coast and stopping each night in a safe harbor.

Arriving at Spanish Wells, a small island off the top of Eleuthera, we had contacted Edsel Roberts, a pilot, by radio. He came aboard *Aurora* to guide us through the Devil's Backbone Reefs to Harbor Island. There, we would meet my mom, my three sisters, and a nephew for a week in a house. For me, having a pilot steering the boat was wonderful, since I didn't have to worry about hitting bottom in the shallow water.

Edsel is a raw boned gentleman who shared his history with us. "My ancestors fled from South Carolina at the time of the American Revolution, because they were Loyalists to the King George of England. Many islands of the Northern Bahamas were originally settled by Loyalists who brought their slaves with them thus populating the area. I just survived Hurricane Andrew in my home in Spanish Wells. I've never been so scared in my whole life."

"Sorry to hear about Andrew, Edsel," I said. "For us it was a lucky miss because we were further south. I can't imagine going through a hurricane out here. There is really no safe harbor or refuge! We're glad you survived."

Everywhere, we saw Andrew's devastation marked by uprooted trees, damaged houses, and destroyed boats driven high up on the beaches. The cleanup was progressing and most buildings were being repaired, but it was quite a challenge for people with few resources who must import everything.

Tying *Aurora* to Edsel's mooring off a marina at Dunmore Town on Harbor Island gave us a safe place to leave her while we stayed ashore in a comfortable house overlooking a pink sand beach on the Atlantic side of the Island. Mom, Margie, Leslie, Elaine, and Paul arrived the next morning along with two rented golf carts which transported us back and forth on the half mile ride into town for shopping, sight seeing, and eating at restaurants. This time would be a real vacation for JoAnne and me. Paul took a scuba diving course and became a certified diver while the rest of us took it easy, laughed a lot, played cards, accompanied Paul on a diving trip, and swam off the beautiful pink coral sand beach.

Waking up early as the sun emerged out of the ocean, we saw it fill the darkness with an orangey red glow that splashed onto the beach and then spread over the land. This mesmerizing experience was fueled with cups of strong coffee. The biggest challenge was organizing our lives around the power outages caused by problems in the undersea cable bringing power from Eleuthera to Harbor Island. The old generating plant was not up to the growth in demand. Sometimes it went offline, becoming overworked. Harbor Island was the most upscale island we visited, having good restaurants and shops for tourists and an interesting native population whose use of old English carried many old words and expressions that had their roots in Colonial America.

After seeing the family off on the small runabout ferry to the airport on Eleuthera, JoAnne and I moved back on *Aurora* and prepared to continue our voyage north, but the Yanmar "engine god" had other ideas. The engine started with some reluctance while the exhaust had a louder, hollow sound accompanied by backfiring. I thought that perhaps the valves were out of adjustment, so I used a feeler gauge to check. Trying to turn the engine over again produced a loud bang (not a good sign) and it stopped dead (a worse sign). Removing the head from the top of the engine revealed a piece of the valve seat (a metal ring) imbedded on the top of the piston. I made a frantic call to Fred, our friend in Maryland from *Hotspur*, who had years of diesel mechanic experience on his resume.

His over the telephone diagnosis was, "It's terminal. You have to remove the engine from the boat and take it to a garage that has a good diesel mechanic."

Swallowing hard and springing into action, I tied the dinghy to *Aurora's* side using its ten HP outboard motor to maneuver the boat to a dock at the Harbor Island Marina, a short distance away. Roger, the Kiwi born manager, literally gave us keys to the place, putting his fax and telephone at our disposal. Mike, an ex-British Royal Navy engineer from Ross's Garage, helped remove the engine block using my come-along (ratchet puller) tied to the boom supported by the main halyard. This task was accomplished after I had removed shelves of the galley and the cockpit floor that resided above the engine. Nothing is ever simple on a sailboat because every space usually serves more than one purpose. Mike and I held our breath as we swung the engine over the side of *Aurora*, lowering it into a wheelbarrow. We carefully pushed it up the dock to his waiting pickup truck on shore.

The damage to the lower end of the engine was limited to the piston, its rod, and bearing while the head was cracked. This was accounted for by the valve seat coming loose. Those problems forced me to order a new head from the Yanmar Parts Dealer in Florida for $1100. The good news was that when everything was installed, the engine would essentially be rebuilt and ready for many more hours of faithful work. It started right up and ran better than ever. The rebuilt engine made our two and half weeks of waiting, hard work, and money spent a worthwhile venture

Farmer Anthony

enabling us to continue our journey while bringing smiles to our faces and deep sighs of gratitude.

Aurora, being the only boat in the marina, became a minor tourist attraction. Conversations grew into parties and dinner invitations which helped us overcome the feeling of being trapped in paradise. Becoming acquainted with farmer Anthony, a large black man with a bushy beard, who grew vegetables down the road, JoAnne discovered a compatriot, an old soul. At last, we had some really fresh beans, lettuce, tomatoes and other goodies like fresh basil—which are quite unusual in the Bahamas since most "fresh" vegetables arrive once a week on the supply boat. Farmer Anthony, dressed in denim overalls and floppy straw hat, with a jolly countenance, had a presence that ignited smiles on our faces and bubbling laughter from out of our throats. We felt Anthony's connection to the earth, to people around him, and tasted it in his wonderful vegetables.

Seeing many attractive larger boats in Georgetown, JoAnne and I made the decision to sell *Aurora*. For full-time cruising, we needed more space. We used our waiting period to clear out the accumulated stuff which was given to a group of nursery school mothers to be sold at their next rummage sale. Those donations gave JoAnne and me good feelings about making a positive contribution to the Harbor Island Community.

Now ready to leave, *Aurora* joined *Island Fever* with Larry and Martha Barber aboard for the return trip through Devil's Backbone to Spanish Wells and then over to Royale Island where we anchored together. Going ashore we explored many beautiful (old) falling down stone buildings that seemed to have been well constructed, but now were in ruins.

Talking with a caretaker, he said, "A man built all this for his mistress."

Larry remarked, "She must have been quite a woman, if the story's true."

Over cocktails and dinner that night, JoAnne discovered that the Barbers were best friends with Vangie, her friend and former colleague at UC Berkeley. "Wow, the world just shrank a bit and it seems to prove that indeed only six degrees of separation exist between people," she exclaimed.

Both boats headed across The Tongue of the Ocean, a deep area of the ocean that separates the shallow islands to the east from the Bahama Banks occupying another shallow area toward Florida. We entered the Banks at Chub Cay and were able to follow GPS Waypoints safely through the night until reaching a wrecked lighthouse at the western edge of the Banks where I caught a thirty-six-inch yellowtail jack as our final gift from the Bahamas. Crossing the Gulf Stream was rougher than anticipated due to a shift of the south winds that opposed the water flowing north thus creating higher waves.

35

BACK IN THE USA

By 10 a.m., May 9, 1993, we had arrived at Ft. Lauderdale after a mellow one hundred-fifty-nautical mile overnight sail from Chub Cay. Our new temporary home recommended by other cruisers was located at Cooley's Landing on the New River. The new docks, air conditioned showers, and a laundry building there were like paradise for us sailors after spending five months in the Bahamas where shoreside facilities were nonexistent or minimal. A quick phone call to U.S. Customs checked us into the United States, so we were legal. Reviewing our continuous distance log, we found that we were now 11,105.9 nautical miles from Puerto Escondido, Baja Sur, Mexico, where JoAnne and I began this two and a half year voyage. Both of us felt surges of pride in having made this accomplishment.

"Looking back, JoAnne, I have successfully transformed my dream of cruising into reality," I said. "I'm thrilled that you chose be an integral part of this adventure. I am so proud that you over-came your fears and reservations to be with me. You helped make this an experience of a lifetime for me."

"Wow, I did it because I love you and you've hooked me on sailing. I'm also proud that I made the voyage without too many screams. I feel I'm now a much stronger and more competent person. Thanks for helping me achieve that!"

"Maybe it's trite to say this, but, you've come a long way, baby!" I said, giving her a hug and a long kiss.

Dan and Marty on *Vivid* were docked next to us and joined us for a celebratory dinner toasting our successful voyages and growing friendship.

They were selling their boat because the cost to transport it back to California was too much. Joanne and I wanted to sell *Aurora* to buy a larger, more spacious center-cockpit cruiser. Dan and I rented a car together to transport many pounds of books and equipment to a storage locker. On *Aurora* the mottled, discolored teak decks were crying out for attention. I was forced to use a belt sander to remove the impenetrable gooey mess and to return the deck to its light brown teak color and like new condition. What a job to do in the tropical heat of Florida!

Fortunately, the Russians had arrived. Our new neighbors had sailed in from Vladivostok by way of the Sea of Japan, after transiting the Indian Ocean, the Suez Canal, the Mediterranean Sea, and finally crossing the Atlantic to Ft. Lauderdale, more than three quarters of the way way around the world. Handsome Vassily had been the captain of a coastal freighter plying the North Pacific who had saved enough money to build their thirty-six-foot flush-decked wooden cruising boat. His spouse, Nellie, a beautiful woman and mother of eight-year-old Vanya and older son, Igor, the roller blade champ, completed the crew. Vassily joined me in the sanding task with gusto and expertise while Nellie helped out by accepting many of our open stores such as flour, brown rice, sugar, and canned goods so JoAnne could empty out and clean the storage lockers.

Nellie's bike had been stolen from its parking spot in front of *Aurora*. A few days later, Nellie walked Vanya to school where she saw the bike on the playground. Yelling, "That's my bicycle," she ran over and grabbed it from some boys who began tussling with her for it. The school principal called the police who impounded the bike and gave Nellie the location where it could be reclaimed. I took Nellie and an interpreter to the Police Station where she identified the undamaged bike with a broad smile.

JoAnne left for a well deserved break at my mom's in Naples. I continued to erase the effect of years of cruising off *Aurora*, making her a pristine example of a used cruising sailboat. Dan and I, now "temporary" bachelors, went out to dinner where our conversations centered on the next changes to our ever-changing lives. Dan planned to return home to Long Beach, California, where he would employ his tennis skills as a teacher and coach.

JoAnne and I decided to take up our friend Tom Schmidt's offer of a free place to live in exchange for remodeling work at his house in Mountain View, California. *Aurora* would be moved to a dock in someone's backyard at the end of a canal in Ft. Lauderdale, waiting to be sold to another star-struck sailor who could use her voyaging capabilities to realize his dreams. I felt nostalgic leaving my friend and voyage mate behind. *Aurora* had overcome the challenges confronting her and safely carried JoAnne and me over 11,000 miles, but it was time for a new chapter to be written.

*****

We flew to Mountain View, California, where we took over Tom's house, beginning its restoration by painting most of the rooms and doing remodeling work in the baths and kitchen. JoAnne and I spent loads of time with her mother, Madeline, who was in her nineties. We sharpened our gaming skills to keep up with her quick mind and maddening good luck. We all enjoyed our times together. Madeline often remarked, "I wonder why I am still here?"

"Because we love you and have so much fun together," we said.

One night after playing bridge with friends at her senior residence, Madeline suffered a massive cerebral hemorrhage and was found slumped in her chair in the morning. At her memorial, my mom played the piano while JoAnne, Betsy, and I talked about how Madeline affected our lives.

With her mom's passing, JoAnne and I thought about moving to the East to continue our sailing adventures. Our friends Marion and Paul on *Ching Pai* stopped in to tell us about the townhouse they bought at Pamlico Plantation near Washington, North Carolina. Pamlico Plantation is an adult community with its own marina, clubhouse, pool, and tennis courts set in pine woods along the Pamlico River in a rural area on the coastal plain. We were attracted to the location because the marina would finally give *Aurora* a permanent home. So far our attempts to sell the boat had been fruitless. Remembering that *Aurora* had been a good and comfortable cruising boat, we decided to take her off the market.

Our next step was to fly to Raleigh, North Carolina, where my daughter Leanne had relocated with some of her college friends. After seeing her, we rented a car for the two hundred-mile drive to Washington, the first town in the new United States named for George Washington. Founded in 1776, Washington was located right on the banks of the Pamlico River. Its old brick buildings created a charming downtown along Main Street.

Pamlico Plantation is located ten miles out of town and about a mile's drive through a Boy Scout Camp, off Bicycle Route 2. We drove in to find that eighty townhouses had been built in clusters along the river. We looked at a few before finding one offered for sale by its owner that overlooked wetlands, the clubhouse, and the Pamlico River where the marina reached out from shore. Being on the rear deck would place us in nature. Cypress trees and Spanish moss attracted birds while other critters lived in the marshy water. Another favorable feature for me was the large room off the carport on the ground floor that would serve as my shop while the living areas occupied the second and third floors safe from any flooding emanating from the river. As you can guess, it was a done deal so JoAnne and I moved across country in September, 1995.

We arrived in our old Dodge Caravan after nursing it through the desert and across the rest of the country. Paul and Marion whom we met in the Bahamas invited us to stay in their new townhouse. A welcome party was their first order of business where we met their friends who soon to become ours. John LaVake and his wife, Maureen, were an instant hit with us as John, Vice President of the Townhome Owner's Board, offered me a job maintaining the exteriors of the townhouses for the association. Maureen was the exercise leader for a group of about twenty residents. What a welcome! We had followed our instincts about the Plantation being a friendly place which paid off in making new friends who shared our interests in sailing and travel along with hobbies such as photography, water-color painting, sculpture, and wood-working that would enrich our lives.

Soon not having *Aurora* close by began to wear on me. I missed having her close by so I could work on her, spend relaxing time aboard, and most of all sail her. I hatched a plan to sail her up the Atlantic Coast from Ft. Lauderdale to Beaufort, North Carolina, and then up the Intracoastal Waterway to the Plantation.

My first thought was to call my friend and avid sailor, Donn Weaver in Berkeley, California. "Hey, Donn, this is Karl. I've got a sailing proposition for you. How about helping me sail *Aurora* to our new place in Washington, North Carolina?"

"Wow, more sailing in my life. Just what I need," Donn said with glee. "It's been months since I sailed with a friend in the Caribbean. I was beginning to feel the old itch again."

"Great!" I said. "JoAnne will work out the details and we'd like Barbara to come for a visit too. We'll keep in touch."

*****

We picked up Donn and Barbara at the Ft. Lauderdale Airport. JoAnne delivered us men to *Aurora* moored at Cooley's Landing while they stayed with her friends Roz and Glenn at Boca Raton. It was great to reconnect with *Aurora* again. My dream was no longer on hold. I had to clean the algae and fungus out of the fuel and water tanks that had been incubating for over a year spent in Florida's warm tropical climate. Bleach, green scrubbers, and rubber gloves were the required work implements to beat back "Mother Nature's" unwanted advances.

A week later on Friday, November 11, 1995, *Aurora* and the weather were ready. Donn and I sailed out into the Atlantic and into the Gulf Stream heading northwest along the Florida coast in an ocean much rougher than we had anticipated. Off Cape Canaveral, we were seasick as *Aurora* bucked up and down over the steep, choppy waves. Thank goodness, the wind finally clocked around to the south, moderating the waves and smoothing out our ride because we were sliding over them. Our tummies felt better, too. Our gentle interlude didn't last. We were still in the ocean near Ponce de Leon Inlet in northern Florida when a black squall line developed with 30-40-knot winds. We headed for shelter in the inlet. Slam! A 40-knot gust hit us. Back winding the jib held *Aurora* over on her side until Donn was able to release the main sheet, freeing the mainsail to allow the boat to right itself. Using GPS and radar to guide *Aurora* through the storm, we found the entrance to the inlet and located shelter along the inbound channel. We anchored and after a quick dinner, fell into bed exhausted.

In the morning, storm conditions made the ocean rough, so we motored north on the ICW to St. Augustine where we tied up to a dock in the municipal marina. We repaired the storm damage on the mainsail and the jib with our trusty sewing machine using heavy Dacron sail thread. By standing on the front bunk with my body emerging from the forward hatch and the sewing machine resting on the deck, I could mimic having a table in a sail loft that supported the sail allowing me to pull the fabric through the machine. Donn's help in guiding the sail was critical as we sewed down the ripped out seams and reinforced other seams that seemed weak. The success of our work on the sails validated the self-sufficient mantra that guided me and most cruising sailors. Away from marine services, cruisers must be able to fix or diagnose whatever breaks. By acquiring the knowledge and equipment necessary, I put the mantra into action, time and time again.

Leaving St. Augustine in the morning, we were greeted by a calmer ocean, but as we continued north along the Georgia and South Carolina coasts, the weather deteriorated again. Gale warnings off Charleston had us tacking inshore to be closer to shelter. *Aurora* responded to the higher wind speeds by heeling over further and by bouncing over the steeper waves. Suddenly, a loud bang echoed inside the boat. Going down the companionway, I smelled a sharp, biting acid odor coming from the battery compartment under the chart table. Something was very wrong!

"Oh my God, Donn," I yelled out. "I just opened the door to the battery compartment. There's a battery with its top blown off lying on its side spewing battery acid. Why did that happen?"

"You've got to be really careful," Donn implored. "Use latex gloves and wear glasses. The acid is strong and will burn your skin," he warned. I followed his instructions.

"Okay, Donn, I righted the battery and saw that it had not been properly secured. When the battery shifted, its cable was pulled loose causing a spark, igniting hydrogen that is a byproduct of battery operation. Great, now we have a damaged battery with some of its acid left inside it and no place to safely keep it from splashing acid out into the boat since *Aurora* is bouncing along in the waves. What should I do?"

"It looks like throwing it in the ocean is our best alternative," Donn asserted. I found some plastic to wrap around the battery and carefully carried it up the ladder to the cockpit where I threw it overboard. I wasn't happy about polluting the ocean, but considering the great depth and huge volume of water, it was literally like "a drop in the ocean."

"Donn, this has not been an easy trip," I said wearily. "Hopefully the weather will improve."

"I'm saying a prayer right now," said Donn.

Our prayers were answered as the wind shifted aft, parting the clouds to reveal a beautiful sunset complemented by a smooth sail through the night. We smiled in the cockpit, and I chuckled that Livengood Luck might have finally taken hold after our spell of bad luck. Arriving off the end of Frying Pan Shoals in the early morning, we closed in on Beaufort, North Carolina, where finding Buoy 2 put us in the channel that we followed into the harbor, sheltered behind sand dunes. After five nights and days of sailing six hundred fifty-two miles from Ft. Lauderdale to Beaufort, Donn and I relished having our feet on solid ground. We walked around town and then ordered a fresh fish dinner at the Beaufort Grocery Company located just up the street from the harbor.

Our last passage of the trip was from Beaufort to Washington, North Carolina, motor sailing in the ICW for another sixty-one miles to reach *Aurora's* new home on Broad Creek where we found its slip in the Pamlico Plantation Marina. Donn and I had survived a rough trip that tested our sailing skills but also deepened our friendship. After some recuperation time and a celebratory dinner at the best restaurant in Washington, Down on Main Street, JoAnne delivered Donn to the small airport in Greenville for the beginning of his own long flight home to Berkeley. Barbara had made the flight earlier to spend time with her mom.

Although *Aurora* couldn't say it, she was very happy to be home at last where I could work on her. A bike ride down the docks to her slip from our new townhome put her within easy reach. Neglecting my friend and fellow traveler *Aurora* was no longer an option for me. Her lonely time in Florida had been hard on her. It was not the way to treat a good friend and carrier of my dreams. I redoubled my commitment to her and to continuing my dream of cruising the world.

PART IV

AN OCEAN OF NEW POSSIBILITIES

By being able to expand the world outside ourselves, we create room to enlarge the world inside our minds and to discover what else may be possible in our lives.

North Atlantic

36

PREPARATIONS FOR CROSSING ATLANTIC

Living in North Carolina allowed me to expand my sailing dreams. Why not cross the Atlantic Ocean to Europe, a place that has always fascinated me with its cultural complexity, history, and quaint beauty? After finishing graduate school in 1962, I spent seven weeks traveling in an old Renault through France, Italy, Austria, and Germany. I yearned to return someday. Maybe now was the time.

If I had read Washington Irving's *The Sketch Book,* written in the early 1800s, however, I might have had second thoughts about traveling over the Atlantic Ocean. He compares traveling by land with its "continuity of scene" that connects one to home, to the crossing of an ocean.

"But the wide sea voyage severs us at once. It makes us conscious of being cast loose from the secure anchorage of settled life, and sent adrift upon a doubtful world. It interposes a gulf not merely imaginary, but real, between us and our homes—a gulf subjected to tempest and fear and uncertainty, rendering distance palpable, and return precarious."

Irving's words poetically describe his impression of such a voyage; however, I had been to sea and had the experience and skill to put them in a modern context where most of the "what ifs" can be mitigated. I rationally considered making such an ambitious effort. *Aurora* was a sound boat that would be up to the 3,000-mile crossing. After I had done some needed major maintenance and purchased more specialized equipment, the voyage would be doable. Yes, I was ready for my next voyage of a lifetime!

Finding a crew proved to be an easier task than I had thought. I first called Donn Weaver in Berkeley who had helped me bring *Aurora* up from Florida to Pamlico Plantation. "Cross the Atlantic? Yes, I'd love to," said Donn. He had his own thirty-nine-foot wooden sloop that he raced in San Francisco Bay. Given his extensive sailing experience and our good friendship, I designated him co-captain. I trusted his ability and his judgment.

My nephew, Steve, was the next on my short list. He was quick to answer the question, "How would you like to sail across the Atlantic?"

"Wow, of course," he said. "I've been wanting to sail on *Aurora* ever since my trip in the Sea of Cortez. Besides, I need a break from the loneliness of building classical guitars alone in my shop."

Steve's strength and stamina would be appreciated by the older members of the crew. Being a quick learner and very competent with tools, he could perform any task with minimum supervision.

JoAnne's nephew, Keith, was another obvious choice because he loved sailing and had enjoyed cruising on *Aurora* in Maine. Keith was still working as a soils engineer in Boston but wanted to crew from *Aurora's* home in North Carolina to Bermuda where his family could join him for a short vacation. We now had a crew of four to Bermuda, but one more person would be needed for the long 1,700 mile passage from there to the Azores.

I made a call to Tom Schmidt in California. He and his girlfriend, Gina, crewed on *Aurora* during the tough passage from Acapulco to Northern Costa Rica and from the Panama Canal through the San Blas Islands to Cartagena, Columbia. Tom made vital contributions to those passages.

"Yeah, I'd be happy to join the crew from Bermuda to the Azores," said Tom. "Then I'll fly on to France to attend the Twenty-four Hours at LeMans Formula One Auto Race."

Everyone I had asked said an emphatic "Yes!" *Aurora* had a good crew to make the month-long sailing passage to Portugal. I was thrilled to see my dream coming true—again!

With our target date for departure May 1998, I began retrofitting *Aurora* in the fall of 1997. My trusted companion had been used hard, and her sixteen years of age were showing on her decks, in her mechanical and plumbing systems, and her bottom, again pocked with blisters. I took *Aurora* to a boatyard across the creek where I would work on her for the next six months.

Following recommendations by friends, I hired a local marine surveyor to go over all the boat's systems, literally with a magnifying glass at times, to detect any signs of weakness. Most of the engine hoses needed replacement as did the sea water intake hoses that cooled the engine. Much of the fresh water plumbing system was replaced with new, nylon reinforced tubing. As the surveyor checked each system, I would complete the recommended repairs, then have him examine my new work, ensuring that I did it right. He would next check another system. The electrical wiring was upgraded with new circuit breakers added to conform with modern standards.

The black, rubbery Thiokol used to seal the spaces between the planks of the teak deck had lost its elasticity and was allowing water to leak into the ceiling below. Not a good sign. Many hours were required to remove it using a narrow chisel to remove the Thiokol, then to tape off the gaps, prime them, squirt in new material, pull up the tape, and finally sand off the residue. It was a "labor of love" that pushed my patience and my back to their limits. When I bought *Aurora*, I had wanted a fiberglass deck, but that option was not available at the time. Even with all the deck work, *Aurora* was worth all the effort.

A crane removed the mast so it could be sand blasted before I spray painted it with a special two-part marine paint that made it look and feel like new. Before reinstalling the mast, the stainless steel stays holding it up were replaced to be sure they held fast during the stresses imposed during crossing the Atlantic.

I am going to include many of the detailed steps that were necessary to prepare *Aurora* for the Atlantic crossing. They had to be done thoroughly, thoughtfully, and accurately. Our lives would depend on it!

It was now time to equip *Aurora* for her most demanding challenge where she would be a thousand miles from the nearest land. A neighbor sold me a used Switlik six-man life raft in a hard fiberglass container. I through-bolted it onto the deck just forward of the mast where it would be accessible in an emergency.

A 406 EPIRB (Emergency Position Indicating Radio Beacon) was mounted near the companionway. It would signal our location in an emergency and broadcast our special ship's number registered with the US Coast Guard. The crew could grab the EPIRB as we abandoned ship so that rescuers could locate us floating in our raft on the empty ocean. The registration gave emergency contact numbers of family so they could be called to verify that we were indeed sailing across the Atlantic.

Another critical piece of equipment, an automatic antenna turner for the High Seas Radio, was installed in the aft cabin where it attached to the back stay antenna. A new "Little Wonder" Reverse Osmosis WaterMaker was an essential piece of equipment installed on a shelf in the head. It was plumbed into the sea water system, its source of raw material, and then into the fresh water system where its product of fresh water would be sent to its own special tank. Having a water maker insured that the crew would have enough water to drink with some left over for quick ship showers designed to keep the crew's odors within tolerance.

After removing the worn-out aft storage box, I fabricated two new boxes out of marine plywood that were curved at the ends, allowing passage between them to the dinghy mounted on the stern. The new boxes were strong and waterproof, and were given coats of white two-part paint to match the hull color.

All through the long days of work, many friends from Pamlico Plantation stopped by to lend a hand or assess the progress being made. When I began popping the blisters in the hull, a whole group of workers suddenly appeared. This job was familiar to most boat owners because grinding out the blisters to solid fiberglass created a sense of satisfaction, having overcome something that was eating away at the hull. Together, we were giving birth to a stronger and safer boat that was now seventeen years old.

Finally, after six months, work on *Aurora* was completed. Back into the water she went and I drove her to a slip within sight of the back deck of our house.

JoAnne had also been busy buying dried and canned food that would feed an ever hungry crew on the way across the Atlantic. Her most delicious buy was canned stewed chicken, pork, and beef made on a farm in Ohio. This "delicacy" would become the basis of many tasty meals. The problem of keeping all the food dry in a damp environment was solved using a Seal-a-Meal device that sucked most of the air out of a special plastic bag filled with perhaps rice or lentils. The machine then melted the plastic together forming a water and air proof seal. It also kept spare parts dry and protected, ready for use.

JoAnne, known as the "Stowage Wizard," filled every inch of the small storage spaces with food. She even produced a stowage diagram so the crew could find what they needed. As May approached, I was feeling more frantic since items on the "done" list were being replaced by even more things on the "to do" list. A call to Donn Weaver solved the problem.

"Donn, great that you're here! Let's go right to work. Our first task is sewing a sun cover for the dinghy. I designed it to keep the dinghy from collecting water on high seas."

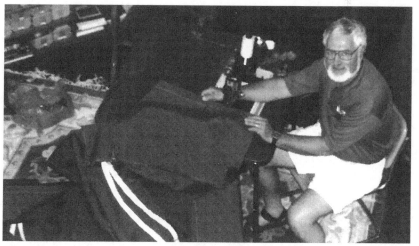

Karl Sewing

Next, we modified the mainsail cover by adding lazy jacks lines tied to the mast. They secure the sail preventing it from flopping on the deck when being reefed or lowered. The radios and the two GPSs were checked. All of these electronic devices would be essential to making a safe, successful voyage.

"Auto," the Autohelm Auto Pilot, was put through its paces steering *Aurora* to a set of latitude and longitude coordinates that we had entered in the GPS. Auto was able to communicate with the GPS and understand what it was saying! Because we would be sailing for weeks toward a set of GPS coordinates in the open ocean, Auto would be a valuable member of the crew who only ate electricity but wouldn't drink any of our precious beer. In addition, the crew on duty would not have to stand and steer at the wheel, but could read or talk with occasional glances at the horizon to be sure our way forward was free of ships or floating containers.

The two nephews, Keith and Steve, arrived next and were assigned to help JoAnne with her stowage duties. Soon, *Aurora* was ready for her voyage and the crew was ready to party!

Friends Tony and David Ritchie threw a lively bon voyage party at their house overlooking the Pamlico River that

Bon Voyage

overflowed with fellow sailors living at the plantation. Donn, Keith, and Steve were made honorary members of the Pamlico Plantation Yacht Club as well as being "adopted" by many of our closest friends. We all felt the love and caring imparted to us with the champagne bon voyage toasts and in the deep conversations expressing critical advice and best wishes. My heart was filled with gratitude that so many friends were there for us.

I raised my glass for a toast. "I want to take this opportunity to thank everyone for their help in preparing *Aurora*, especially Jo-Anne whose provisioning will insure the crew has full stomachs. All of you have become vital parts of the effort needed to complete my sailing dream. In a real sense, *you* will be crossing the Atlantic with me and my wonderful crew."

JoAnne stepped forward. "While you're doing the guy thing of sailing across the Atlantic, I'll be flying to Bermuda, then later to Lisbon, and returning to spend time on *Aurora* in the Azores. Let's all toast to a safe voyage!"

"To a safe voyage!" everyone cheered. The next day at about 10:00 a.m., the crew loaded their personal gear on *Aurora* as the dock filled with well wishers. Friends Carol Jean and Cherry

Keith, Karl, Donn, Steve

climbed aboard to wash the wind screen. They were almost shanghaied by the crew. Casting off our lines, swinging into the channel, *Aurora* was on her way to cheers from our friends, the blaring of boat horns, and the loud boom of the hairspray-powered-potato cannon fired by Kenny, the plantation's best cannoneer. Fortunately, we were out of range!

Kenny

Looking back at them, I was amazed that all those friends could fit on the dock. I was deeply moved and honored by their presence. We all had lumps in our throats as we pulled away, while trying to focus on the tasks at hand so that *Aurora* would move out proudly.

It took two partial sailing days to reach Beaufort, North Carolina, where we would enter the Atlantic Ocean. Arriving there in the afternoon, I maneuvered *Aurora* into a slip at the municipal marina strung along Front Street. After checking in and having a beer aboard, I took the crew out for a tasty fish dinner at a restaurant opposite the boat. Here, we toasted to our successful voyage. A few of us made last minute phone calls home to reassure our spouses that yes, we were ready to leave in the morning for our five-day sail to Bermuda. Returning to *Aurora*, we were drawn to live music streaming out of a bar on Front Street. Keith and Steve wandered into the bar, while Donn and I walked slowly along the waterfront back to the boat. We both wanted to get a good night's rest.

My last words to the crew were, "*Aurora* will be leaving at 9 a.m. in the morning. Be sure that all of you are aboard!"

37

IT'S A BIG OCEAN OUT THERE

My wish to have a good night's sleep was thwarted by the empty V-berth in the front of *Aurora* where Steve should have been sleeping. Like a nervous father, I kept waking up hoping to see my nephew in his assigned bunk. My hope was not fulfilled.

The rest of the crew was up early, brewing coffee, making scrambled eggs and toast, while also waiting for Steve to reappear. About 8:45 a.m., Steve ambled down the dock to a chorus of "Where have you been?"

"Oh, I met a girl whose father owns a boatyard," Steve said casually. "We got talking about boats."

"Yeah, sure!" we replied.

Everyone was now on board and yes, it was time to head out of Beaufort Inlet into the Atlantic Ocean. The crew cleared non-essential items off the deck and readied the sails.

"Okay, Steve, cast off the dock-lines," I said. "Wow!" I shouted out. "Here we go. Next stop Bermuda!" Following the ship channel, we soon cleared the harbor entrance and sailed northeast off of the Cape Lookout light, our last connection with land for the next five days. Beyond the cape, the bottom began to rise so I checked our small scale Ocean Chart which did not have enough detail. The shallower water was not really indicated, but breakers off our port (left) side told us that a shoal extended many miles to the seaward off the cape. A more easterly course was set as the sails filled and began pulling *Aurora* and heeling her to the starboard (right) side. It was a thrill to have the wind propelling the boat on this six hundred-mile passage to Bermuda. *Aurora* was in

Keith in Action

her element showing off her stuff. Smiles lit the faces of the crew. This was ocean sailing at its best.

In the daytime, the crew's watch assignments were informal as long as one person took the responsibility of keeping an eye out for other ships. The cockpit was covered by a dodger of white vinyl waterproof material that kept us out of the sun and dry if it should rain. If stormy, side curtains could be attached, further protecting the crew and the companionway steps leading below. Water sloshing below was a definite "no no" because our instruments were mounted on the bulkhead and the charts lived on the chart table located next to the companionway.

Cooking meals was a shared duty with one primary cook and one helper who worked from the meal plan prepared by JoAnne. We ate our fresh food first, then we prepared meals with the dried and canned stores. Besides the usual favorite of spaghetti and salad, canned meats over noodles became hits with the crew. Beer was rationed to one per meal so that all hands would be able to react if the situation demanded. Breakfasts included my favorite granola with yogurt that I made from powdered milk using two teaspoons of the old batch as starter for the new. Lunch was soup and sandwiches made with store bought bread until it ran out, then beer bread was mixed and baked in our propane oven. Snacks included fruit, apples and oranges that kept well out of the refrigerator along with secret stashes of favorite candy bars brought by crew members to "keep up" their energy.

My special job everyday was to contact our volunteer weather man, Herb Hildenberg, on 12.359 kHz using the marine high frequency radio at 20:00 GMT (Greenwich Mean Time). Talking to Herb, I would first check *Aurora* into his Transatlantic Weather Net, giving him this information:

"Herb, this is *Aurora*. Our current position is 32 degrees 15 minutes north latitude and 85 degrees 24 minutes west longitude, our course is 110 degrees magnetic, and our speed is 5.5 knots (nautical miles per hour). Wind speed is 12 knots from northeast, air temperature is 68 degrees while the ocean temperature is 72 degrees, wave height is 4 feet coming from the north." I would give him a report of any noteworthy problems. Herb had our United States Coast Guard Float Plan that listed our intended schedule as well as a complete description of *Aurora* and names of the crew.

Later in the broadcast, Herb called *Aurora* back and gave us a specific weather forecast for our part of the Atlantic Ocean. It was based on his reading of the satellite photos of the cloud cover and the surface weather reports from the yachts strung out across the Atlantic Ocean. Herb did an amazing job in predicting wind speeds and directions, often calling the wind shifts within an hour of their occurrence. Herb was our critical verbal connection to land, and his weather predictions were essential to our well-being on the sea.

Fishing was another part of the voyage plan that we hoped would supplement our food supply. I attached a deep sea rod to the stern rail and its line and lure streamed out behind *Aurora*. The fish, unfortunately, were not in on the plan. After a few hours, we didn't catch one fish. Then, Steve discovered the problem.

"Damn, something big bit through the nylon leader," Steve grumbled. "I'll put on a wire leader. It should hold 'em." He looked again later. "Karl, the line is slack and it looks like a monster broke it," Steve said with exasperation.

Soon, we were out of lures and leaders. In a crisis conference, the crew agreed that we were attracting some mighty big fish. If we managed to keep one on the line, it would be almost impossible to land it. The deck was five feet above the sea and our landing net was designed for smaller fish so we stopped fishing. No fish were caught between Beaufort and Bermuda.

Sailing on the big ocean so far from land was both relaxing and at times exhilarating. When we were feeling *Aurora* move with the wind and feeling the waves lift and then slide under her, the rhythm of the sea enraptured our beings. As the wind speed and wave heights increased, however, *Aurora* responded by going faster, heeling further, and bouncing through the waves. Holding on to something solid became our task at hand. Moving inside the boat required being in sync with *Aurora's* movements. From time to time, the realization that she was only a tiny speck on the vast ocean would float into my head, jarring me and humbly putting me in my place. We each held onto our own significance dearly, but in the ocean's eyes we were insignificant. Thank goodness for our radio lifeline to Herb and through him to the Coast Guard and the web of ships and planes that would know *Aurora* was on the ocean and would respond if we needed help. Knowing that helped me keep things in perspective and my mind at ease.

A major mishap occurred when the mainsail jibbed, meaning the wind came from behind the sail and violently flipped it over the boom from one side of the boat to the other. The sail accelerated across the boat, but was stopped short by the main sheet, placing great strain on both the sail and the boom. A loud crack announced that the sail was ripping, starting at the leach, the outer edge, following the seam right to the mast. About one-third of the sail was unusable which would slow our progress toward Bermuda.

Struggling to control the sail and boom, I yelled, "Steve, pull in the mainsheet so the boom is centered so it can't move too far." He followed my instructions.

"Okay, the tear followed the seam nearest the bottom of the sail," I said. "Help me pull the upper part of the sail down to the boom using the second reef line. We'll tie the torn part to the boom with the reef ties."

We now had a smaller but functioning sail again, so back on course we went. Examining the sail, I realized that the company I contracted with to clean and evaluate the sail's suitability for making an Atlantic crossing had really only performed the cleaning part of the task. The leach tape on the back edge of the sail was tissue paper thin and easily tore in my fingers. We had to pay close attention to the wind speed and reef the mainsail down further if conditions got wilder. Realizing how vulnerable to damage the sail was, I decided I must have a new leach sown on by a professional sailmaker in Bermuda. It seemed that a little drama was necessary to keep us on our toes!

Reading the guide books about Bermuda gave us some vital information on where we were headed. The islands were discovered by the Spanish in the late 1500s, but settled by the English in 1609. St. George's Town was founded in 1612 and is the oldest continuously inhabited English town in the Americas. The Islands total fifty-three square miles lying on a ridge that has been covered with coral reefs more than six hundred miles from the nearest land, Cape Hatteras, North Carolina, located about fifty miles north of *Aurora's* starting point, Beaufort, North Carolina. British English is the language used by most people which would force us to sharpen our listening habits and to speak clearly.

Right on time the Island of Bermuda appeared as a blurry spot on the radar set to its maximum range of twenty-four miles, then about twelve miles out we picked up flashes of light from St. David's Light on the northeastern part of the island just below our destination of St. George's Harbor. Through the night, these flashes became our aiming point along with the GPS coordinates. By morning, we saw the Island and with the binoculars began searching for St. George's Channel. We eventually found a narrow entrance into the harbor that had been blasted through the limestone rock that formed the island rising from the reef below. Following our harbor chart, I steered *Aurora* to the customs dock on the land side of the cruise ship terminal. We deployed our fenders and tied to a dock for the first time in five days having sailed six hundred-fifty miles under generally ideal condition.

I put in a call to sailmakers Steve and his wife, Suzanne. They agreed to come to the dock to pick up the sail on a national holiday so we could stay on our loose sailing schedule. Taking off the sail involved the whole crew including Keith who accidentally stepped into the open hatch over the aft cabin, straining his knee but not breaking any bones. I think we were all more than a little punchy after being at sea. Even the dock seemed to be moving under us.

Donn, JoAnne, Karl, Steve

After moving *Aurora* to the St. George's Dinghy and Sport Club docks, I abandoned ship to join JoAnne and my mom at Aunt Nea's Guest House where a king-sized bed replaced the aft bunk. The delicious breakfasts eased us into the day. It was wonderful being with JoAnne again. Her anxiety about the passage melted away as we had time to share our experiences with each other. Being apart was always difficult because we had spent most of our time together on *Aurora* or at home at the plantation.

Keith joined his wife, Lynne, and daughter, Madeline, at the Pink Beach Club where they too slipped easily into the luxury of a cabin overlooking the beach. Donn and Steve set their own routine after soaking up the two dollar showers to wash off the last crystals of salt caught on their hair and bodies. Soon, they were ready for dinner out with Mom, JoAnne, and me. Strolling through the narrow, wandering lanes of St. George's Town, we found the restaurant recommended by Auntie Nea.

Later on a cab trip around the island, we saw estates looking out to sea, testifying to the heights of luxury living on Bermuda, that has the highest GDP in the world. This income is earned from tourism and high finance. Mom was having a great time surrounded by her family. She took part in the repartee as witticisms flew back and forth when our youngest member Steve practiced his art of loosening laughter from those nearby.

Later in the week, sailmakers Steve and Suzanne returned the mainsail after sewing on a doubled leach strip of acrylic sail material and re-sewing the torn seam. They suggested that we sew an additional row of stitches on each seam. Following their recommendation, I stood in the forward hatch using the Pfaff light duty industrial sewing machine powered by a small 110-volt electric motor while Donn fed the sail into the machine as I guided it under the needle. The sail was about thirty-six feet high by twelve feet long at the bottom.

"Donn, I'm feeling overwhelmed by this job. It seems like we're sewing miles of seams," I complained.

"But, Karl, aren't we 'real' sailors?" Donn said with a wink.

So being real sailors, Donn and I finished the job with feelings of satisfaction. Tom Schmidt, our new crew member, had arrived and was assigned the task of feeding the sail slugs (plastic slides that attach the sail to the mast and boom) into their correct slots. I pulled the sail up the mast and Donn helped guide the repaired and much stronger sail into its working position. Steve was off being Steve, avoiding the whole exercise!

Too soon, our allotted week in Bermuda was over. JoAnne and Mom, our shoreside support group, bid us bon voyage from the dock as *Aurora* headed for the diesel dock to top off our tanks. In less than a month, JoAnne would be joining us in the Azores. At the fuel dock, we met the crew and boat with whom I had traded our rod and reel for some Wahoo steaks. Fortunately, we collected the steaks before they could sail off; they were fresh and very good barbecued, making the trade worthwhile.

Sailing out of the harbor, *Aurora* was on her way to the Azores, a passage of 1,700 miles, our longest open water passage. Information from Herb that afternoon on the High Seas Radio mandated an immediate change of course from the northeasterly direct course to Flores in the Azores to an easterly course following the 32 degree latitude line toward Madera. Herb had been charting a string of strong storms marching across the Atlantic at 50 degrees of latitude. Had we continued on the northeasterly course, *Aurora* would have been exposed to 50-knot winds and giant seas. Thank you, Herb!

About an hour later, Steve alerted me: "There's a sailboat following our old course into potential danger."

"Okay, I'll put out a call on the VHF radio," I said. "Calling sailboat heading northeast, this is *Aurora* off your starboard side at 33 degrees north and 63 degrees west. Please come in."

Soon a young woman's voice with a heavy French accent responded. "This is Frauke on *Explorateur*, over."

"This is Karl on the sailboat *Aurora*. I have some very important weather information for you, over."

"I will wake the captain. One moment please," Frauke responded.

Soon a response came back: "I am Luc, the captain of *Explorateur*. Bon jour. What is your weather information?"

"Luc, have you heard a recent weather forecast, over?"

"No, we have only a short wave radio and can only listen, but have not heard a current forecast, over."

"Luc, our weatherman, Herb, warned us that a group of gales are crossing the Atlantic to the north of us. He advised us to sail a course of 90 degrees to the east until we are closer to the Azores, over."

Luc responded, "Thank you so much, Karl. We'll set our course to the east, over"

"Have a good trip and we will look for you in the Azores," were my final words.

38

THOUGHTS ON THE PASSAGE TO THE AZORES

Karl on HiSeas Radio

As we sailed across the Atlantic, I wrote this letter to family and friends detailing many days of our journey and my reflections.

On June 1, the fourth day from Bermuda, we have 1,377 nautical miles remaining to sail before arriving at Flores, the westernmost island of the Azores group. Flores is also the farthest north island at 39 degrees latitude. We are using the spinnaker on an easterly course of 32 degrees latitude to avoid a developing gale north of our position. *Aurora* is sailing well in 7-8 knots of wind off our starboard beam with the main vanged out to port and the spinnaker poled out to starboard, moving easily at 5.5 knots. I am amazed that we are going so fast in such light air. We are in an area of high pressure surrounded by flat seas and mostly sunny skies. A bonus popped up on the horizon—a ship that I was the first to sight. My winnings were two dollars from the ship-sighting pool. Is it possible to make this voyage pay for itself after all?

We've all settled into a mellow routine of three-hour night watches with time for much reading and talking, and I might add bits of nap taking. *Aurora* is functioning very well with all systems performing and no major surprises. The solar panels are producing 4-5 amps of electricity when the sun is high. While not enough power to keep up with the ship's electrical usage, it does stretch out the time before the Yanmar is called upon to again produce a surge of 12-volt power to top up the batteries. The Little Wonder WaterMaker makes six gallons of fresh water per hour but also draws so much electrical power that the engine must be run to support its appetite.

Life is more relaxed out at sea. I am beginning to have time for reflection and pondering the universe. The immensity of the ocean, its lack of reference points, the infinite series of waves all create a transcendent experience which opens the mind to new possibilities. I am feeling so fortunate that I'm here following my dream. Writing about being here is icing on the cake for me. I have to stop this reverie now to kill the sugar ants that invaded the boat in Bermuda and keep insisting on making *Aurora* their home.

Communicating with Herb, our weather forecast occupies my late afternoon hours. He provided *Aurora* with a detailed routing plan to avoid the 50-knot gales that are raging to our north off the Gulf of St. Lawrence. The crew feels that Herb is not only a "weather god," but also a "weather overlord" since he insists that we religiously follow his information format and directions.

On June 2, our mellow time deteriorated as wind speeds and wave heights have increased forcing the crew to tie two reefs in the main and to roll in the jib, thus balancing the boat. In the night, Donn and I were visited by a rogue wave that came over the

Mail Bag

bow and rolled down the deck sloshing through our open aft cabin hatch, soaking both of us, the pillows, bedding, and mattress. All of this at 1 a.m. What a mess! Cooking and moving about *Aurora* have become difficult, so following the "one hand for the ship" mantra is now a necessity.

June 3, we opened the mail bag created by our friends from Pamlico Plantation. They sent wonderful poems and thoughts that are truly inspirational. What a unique way for our friends to be on the voyage, in spirit if not in substance. The crew have been awed by the creativity and caring sent to us in the mail bag. Our other connection with home is through single side band radio contacts with Linda Neiderbuhl, our neighbor at the plantation on Tuesday and Thursday mornings when news is exchanged and our positions verified. The ocean is enormous, but these contacts keep us from feeling "lost."

June 3—It's been a fixer-upper type day. The water-maker is now working at top efficiency after I removed the air locks in the sea water feed line that choked off the flow to the pressure pump. The wind bugger is now history because the propeller blades flew off, bouncing on the aft solar panel, into the ocean. In 30-knot winds, Steve was attempting to control its wild oscillations with a bungee cord while turning it into the wind to slow it down. The five-foot-diameter prop assembly came loose from its shaft just missing Steve. Thank God it flew into the ocean and not into the cockpit where we were all sitting. We have first aid equipment but just imagine the damage those heavy blades would create as they spun at 500 r.p.m.s. It would have been a disaster! Looks like Livengood Luck was with us. While the windbugger produced good amounts of electricity, it was just too heavy and dangerous. We cursed "Bugger Bob," its creator, for not designing a safe way to slow or stop its propeller!

June 4—Back to the more mundane. Steve installed a working fan in his forward cabin referred to as "Steve's Cave." He is happier to have moving air because all the hatches and ports are dogged down in these lumpy seas. Four days from now Herb promised better weather. Perhaps *Aurora* can turn north again so we can open the hatches to allow air into the interior of the boat to dry it out. Dampness has been seeping into our lives, replacing the ants.

June 5—We are approaching the half-way mark on the chart. We are anticipating opening the bottle of champagne from Maureen and John tomorrow when blue skies should appear. I'm amazed when I think about this small sailboat racing along through the sea. We're controlled by Auto and occasionally by Steve at the helm, driven by the free winds toward our destination. Being able to ride the winds and seas in my own vessel instills a deep feeling of satisfaction in me. Being able to harness the forces of "Mother Nature" is based on my intimate knowledge of the boat's dynamics and systems used to control her passage through the water. Adding to this is the challenge of planning all aspects of the voyage, and in my case, restoring and strengthening *Aurora* for duty on the "Big Ocean." Fulfilling all of these tasks completes the picture of why sailboat cruising is such a passion for me.

In the background, sounds of Errol Garner playing the deep dissonant chords that make his jazz piano so unique are enhancing my experience. Feelings like these more than compensate for the discomforts and challenges experienced along the way.

Voyaging gives me time and space where I can grow, learn, and change.

June 6—Unfortunately the mellow weather promised by Herb has yet to appear, although the skies are brightening a bit. Hanging on to the boat is still a priority while the champagne rests cold in the refrigerator. Even though we are on our easterly course along 32.51 degrees north latitude, we are still making one hundred miles a day toward Flores which hasn't moved from its position at 39 degrees north. When we do turn north, the miles made good toward the destination will increase because *Aurora* will be heading directly to Flores.

The crews' reading and sleeping quotients are rapidly being filled up as many issues of *Cruising World* and the *New Yorker* are becoming shop worn, passing from hand to hand. Water races by the portholes in the hull as yet another wave breaks under us. Our heightened sensation of speed is produced by the motion of the boat because we lack an external reference point, such as an island on the horizon or another boat. Winds have been gusting to 30 knots which seems fine with *Aurora*. The crew's projects are all on hold for now with our weather senses being strained, looking for favorable signs.

Auto decided that its drive belt was just too tired for duty last night. In heavy seas, it began to slip. We were all hoping "he" could make it to dawn, but the belt just gave up. The trusty crew sprang into action with Donn taking over steering while Steve and I removed the steering wheel from the pedestal. Quickly, we removed Auto from the wheel, then reinstalled it so Donn could regain control of *Aurora* as she hurtled through the night at 6.5 knots in seven-foot seas. Placing Auto on the chart table, aka the "operating table," Tom and I disassembled the outer case to expose the broken belt, which we replaced. Auto back together now, Steve reinstalled it back on the wheel. A collective smile and sigh announced that Auto was steering again! None of us could imagine the tedium of hand steering for nine hundred-seventy-eight miles.

June 7—Greeting us in the morning, the sun is accompanied by more wind and waves as *Aurora* is flying along between 6.5 and

7.5 knots. The seas are more friendly but still sent us skidding off the occasional bigger wave. We are beginning to think Madeira directly east off Africa might be our destination, because Herb thinks we shouldn't turn northeastward yet due to gales to our north. His last words were "Maybe on Monday?"

The crew got tired of waiting when Herb gave other boats the go-ahead to turn north. We decided to head for Flores. About 5:30 the next morning, Donn woke me saying, "Karl, the second reef line has chaffed through releasing the aft edge of the sail putting stain on the reefing points tied down to the boom."

"Okay," I said. "I'll harness up." I struggled to bring the main under control, but the 25-knot winds and ten to twelve-foot seas created quite a balance problem in addition to causing the sail to whip around.

"Donn," I yelled. "The slides holding the sail along the boom are breaking. Wow, the last one held on but all the force is on the last reef point sewn on the sail. It just tore out of the sail. Oh my God, we have a huge tear in the sail!"

I lashed the injured sail to the boom. We continued sailing at 5.5 knots using only the power of the jib. The heavy weather forced us to wait before tying in a third reef, so the sail could be raised again.

"You know," said Steve, "Herb must have been watching when we decided to head north. So he let loose his weather demons to punish our misbehavior."

What the incident did tell me is that chafe is our enemy and must be watched for every day. This truth applies to ocean sailing when the sails and other gear are deployed unchanged for days. The weather is still on the heavy side, although the sun and barometer are both up.

Hoisting the main again was a success with Donn steering, Tom advising, and Steve and I installing the new third reef line that pulled the extra sail down to the boom. The sail looked good and began drawing as *Aurora* responded by picking up speed. Traveling at 7.4 knots with the jib also reefed in 22 knots of apparent wind is very good for a thirty-three-foot boat! The seas have smoothed out a bit causing *Aurora's* motion to ease. We may yet sample the champagne.

One joy of cruising is wearing shorts and going barefoot all day long. Some of the restraints of civilization and polite society have fallen away as being comfortable becomes a priority although a constant struggle. Steve is taking advantage of the drop in the wind and seas to fish. We ate the last bit of salami, so desperation is setting in. A lone dolphin visited this afternoon as if to encourage us by raising the possibility of fish. Everyone is now thinking fish! A nice dorado would be great; a tuna would be welcome; while the large teeth of a wahoo might scare us, it would be good eating. In addition, the champagne would complement a fresh fish meal. "So, Steve go for it!" I said. Later he came below for a beer and a head call indicating his serious interest and effort.

Well, no fish volunteered for our dinner, but Tom worked hard to create a good tandoori turkey dinner over rice with carrots and onions. The canned meats JoAnne stocked for us have been most appreciated. Herb finally released us to turn north. As the seas smoothed out, we poled out the jib to catch the wind coming over *Aurora's* stern quarter.

June 9—In the morning, we found the sun breaking through thin clouds with the spinnaker deployed to gather in the light winds. We have three hundred-forty-six miles to reach Flores. The barometer is up to 1023 MB as we enter the newly forming Azores High. Out came the sleeping bags, towels, and blankets for an airing out, while the crew lounged on the forward deck, soaking up the sun's rays. What a great feeling of being in light trade wind conditions where the previously lumpy seas have been transformed into large rollers which easily slide under *Aurora*. Most important, the sun showers heated up, so crew can get really clean, improving the "aroma" below decks. *Aurora's* now pleasant motion has released smiles and sighs of relaxation—our well earned reward for the past days of rough seas.

Heavy winds have now given way to no wind and flat seas as we move further into the Azores High. The barometer now reads 1031 MB, the highest I have ever seen! We are motoring with our engine, Yanni, chug, chug, chugging along; everyone is listening for any signs of its discomfort. Water in the diesel is being eliminated by the Raycor filter so again we are replacing the paper elements. Thanks to Marion and Paul for the gift of a case of filters!

Steve has won another ship point by sighting whales five hundred yards off the starboard bow. Just their plumes of exhaled air were visible as they ignored our calls and whistles inviting them over for a visit. Next time we'll stop *Aurora* and turn off the motor to see if they respond. Small sea turtles swam by closer to the boat which added to our sense that there is life in this huge expanse of water. Up to now, we had only seen odd bits of flotsam: floats, paper, some plastic that Steve caught on his fishing line.

Although the ocean surface covers so much of the Earth, we can readily appreciate its enormity by moving through it at 6-7 miles per hour. Over the radio another boat reported a lost container floating closer to the Azores, reminding us of the unseen or barely visible dangers that lurk out here. These containers have fallen off huge container ships in rough weather and can easily sink a sailing vessel possessing no defense against these stealthy "beasts." Only six inches of their structure remain visible above the water.

Motoring continues to be our way of life as Yanni's constant throb fills our ears and bodies. The winds have deserted us. Due to our being two hundred miles from Flores, the official five dollars per person pool has a 3:00 p.m. deadline for each crew member's estimate of when we will first sight land. I have a slight advantage because the "Captain Program" has visibility estimates in the computer, but Steve, the Bermuda sighting winner, has youth and sharp mental acuity in his favor. Flores has both a 2,700-foot mountain and a lighthouse, so the time of day is a critical factor in making the estimate. I am glad to have chosen Flores as our landfall in the Azores. Its remote location from the central group of islands means it has fewer visitors. Its small rock bound harbor might be daunting because we have been warned not to anchor near the quay where the holding is poor. So *Aurora* will anchor farther out in the harbor.

This is our last full day at sea with two sailboats and a freighter being sighted already. Pia on *Ilha Azul* called on the radio to chat, our first call in over a week. She is also motor sailing two miles off our port beam heading for Flores. Their friends on *Springer* are in port and report only four boats at anchor. They hit a whale twice, possibly sustaining some damage. I will talk with *Springer's* captain after our arrival to determine what happened. Whales are a hazard if you are silently sailing while they are sleeping on the surface.

Tonight, we will be celebrating Donn and Annita's tenth wedding anniversary with a dinner of clam linguini, cole slaw, lemon-poppy seed muffins, and, at last, champagne! I will give "Yanni" a well deserved rest so we can enjoy soothing dinner music. Not too shabby for a small boat in the big ocean taking advantage of a favorable current that is pushing *Aurora* a knot faster.

June 11—Everyone's anticipation of our landfall is rising. A pod of white-sided dolphins just visited causing more excitement. The crystal clear water is giving us a ringside seat to their antics as they make *Aurora* their big toy.

The sight-a-ship pool now has Karl 4, Tom 4, Donn 2, and Steve 2. We promised Steve extra points if he catches a fish, hoping to heighten his flagging motivation after many fish-less days. Donn is five dollars richer after winning the sighting Island contest. He was on the first watch of the night when he saw tiny flashes from the lighthouse, sparkling on the horizon. Those of us still awake let out quiet cheers as to not wake our compatriots.

June 12—*Aurora* made her landfall on Flores at Lajes rather than Santa Cruz, based on the recommendation of the port captain. Arguing with Port Captains is not "in the book," but we did sail by Santa Cruz Harbor deciding that he was right due to its exposure to the winds and waves from the south.

Lajes is a nice small harbor with a huge breakwater offering protection for us and the container ships that stop here. Volcanic cliffs line the north side while the town was located above a beach. The opening to the harbor was to the east. Holding was good in fifteen to thirty-five feet of water. The water was vodka clear and Steve swam ashore rather than waiting for the rest of us to get the dinghy launched and underway. Climbing up a ladder to the pier, we wobbled as our feet made contact with solid ground. Our bodies still swayed to the rhythm of the boat. A cheer went up, "We've made it! By God, we're here at last!" I felt very proud of *Aurora* and her crew. I glowed with the satisfaction of having completed the 1721 n.m. passage in fifteen days with *Aurora* under my command. I had put together all the pieces needed to make the voyage possible. I was stoked!

The friendly officials made checking in a breeze in spite of their limited facility in speaking English. My problem was standing on the dock which I felt was undulating at an alarming rate. The concrete remained stable as usual, but my body continued the motion it had become accustomed to for the past two weeks. People ashore have been quite friendly and the island is beautiful—verdant green, accented with many flowers: lilies of golden yellow with red spots, purple and burgundy hydrangeas, and fiery red flowers we couldn't identify. Seeing so much color after weeks of looking only at the monochromatic sea was such a feast for our eyes searching for the stimulation of different shapes and colors.

We had a large and tasty fish dinner at Restaurante Flores that we found on a half-mile walk toward Santa Cruz. Its owner, Paula, was brought up in Fall River, Massachusetts. The fresh fish was grilled in butter and garlic, accompanied by boiled potatoes and rice, and set off by a garden fresh green salad. Local beers were raised in toasts to each other and our grand accomplishment! Of course, we sailors had lots of ice cream for dessert. Thank goodness, the walk back to the boat was downhill!

Back on *Aurora*, the crew had the time and inclination to review the trip to Flores. We had proved that four guys can survive on a thirty-three-foot boat after two weeks at sea! *Aurora* had some broken equipment but no broken people. We all got along well, had fun, and shared the ship's duties. We had no close calls with ships or other objects in the water, had arrived safely, ready to see more of this wonderful Earth. As a crew, I felt we have done a great job. My dream, another one, came true!

June 13—Communicating with *Springer* in the morning, we learned that their Amel 41 ketch had hit a forty-foot whale in daylight going 6.5 knots, bringing the boat to a complete stop. The two masts went twang, but held their vertical position. The whale blew, then sounded, diving straight down. There was no blood so it seemed the whale was not injured. The problem for any crew is seeing a dark object floating mostly submerged, on a dark sea. The only damage to *Springer* occurred when a line broke connecting the aft-edge of the keel with the skeg that supports the rudder. The impact to the hull produced no damage which speaks volumes about the strength of this French-built yacht. Everyone who heard about this incident just shook their heads in wonder hoping that their own boats would survive the same experience in similar good condition.

We found a friendly taxi driver, Caesar Fonseca, who had worked in Canada for many years. We all set off in his Peugeot touring the island having the same volcanic nature as all the other islands of the Azores.

Caesar told us about the island and its people. "Most of the people are farmers who live in town and commute to their Holstein milk cows that are pastured and milked in small plots of land separated by walls of volcanic rock higher up in the mountains. These walls are ablaze with the bright colors of hydrangeas and rock roses creating a checkerboard pattern when viewed from up here. Many people have American connections because 15,000 Azoreans emigrated mostly to New England where they worked as fishermen. There are currently 16,000 cows, 4,584 people, and with Paula being pregnant one more is coming!"

Our tour came to a halt when a herd of cows blocked the road as a laughing group of kids drove them to a new pasture nearby. Ahead, on the side of the volcano was a lava formation that looked like organ pipes rising from their base to about one hundred feet up the cliff. Coming upon an old mill used to grind grains, we followed its water source up to a deep blue crater lake. Heading over a ridge, Caesar took the road that plummeted toward the ocean where a small resort with a black sand beach was filled with families bravely swimming in the 60-degree water.

Provisioning *Aurora* was our next priority so we trudged uphill strengthening our sea legs and eyes that absorbed the flowers' colors. Two grocery stores competed for our business, but one has Luis who speaks English and seems to pop up whenever we have questions or problems. He went to his house to pull fresh onions from his garden and gather fresh eggs because none were available in his family's store. His dad then gave us a ride down the hill with our load of groceries and two Jerry cans of diesel. The kindness of the people here is part of the island's culture in which the community functions as a caring entity, supplementing the limited physical resources due to its isolation.

Arriving on this island and meeting its people was an immediate reward for the hard work of the passage of 1700 miles. Being able to go to out-of-the-way places and make new acquaintances was an important part of my dream. The sailing, with its rewards of relaxation and challenges, pushed my boundaries as my sense of self expanded to encompass all that happened and all that was demanded. I was able to rise to these occasions integrating all of my studies and practical knowledge to accomplish the fifteen-day crossing of the Atlantic from Bermuda to Flores, Azores, on *Aurora*, my trusted companion and vehicle for achieving my dreams.

39

EXPLORING THE AZORES

Aurora's anchors held as a weather front came through, generating 35-knot winds and white caps in the harbor. By the morning of June 17, the large surging waves signaled that leaving was our best option. *Aurora* sailed out with her triple reefed main into a weather trough that trailed the front, producing gusts into the mid 20s, continuous rain, and lumpy seas; it was not a great day to be sailing.

At dawn the next day, the islands Ilha do Faial and its close neighbor, Pico, popped up from the sea. They are the two central islands of the Azores. Out came our spinnaker to capture the now lighter air. It did not survive the stronger winds that gusted close to the island. The top of the sail split apart. *Aurora* was not having good luck flying her old sails! A huge, black basalt monolith marked the entrance to the harbor at Horta, the capital city of the island.

Motoring in toward the reception dock past other sailboats, *suddenly* we heard, "*Aurora, Aurora,* I am Luc, come and see us after you have checked in." Luc was the captain of *Explorateur* who changed course based on the weather information I radioed to him.

I yelled back, "Luc, Luc, great to see you in person. We'll come over later."

When checking in, we discovered that we had reached the true crossroads of the Atlantic where 985 sailing vessels had arrived the last year, 1997, during their Trans-Atlantic voyages. France contributed 254 to England's 251, while 98 made the United States a distant third. All the officials as well as the marina administration had offices at the reception dock which made the entire checking in process a breeze. The marina was jammed with boats so we rafted up against a boat tied to the wall and waited for a slip in the marina to open up. Next, we headed over to *Explorateur* to meet Luc and Frauke. Wine and goodies were the order of the day. After introductions, Luc told us that their passage had not been as easy as ours.

Frauke and Luc

"Even though there was reduced wind on the easterly route, two lower stays on our mast broke, forcing me to climb the mast to the spreaders to install two strong lines to replace the stays. We felt fortunate indeed that the mast did not fall or crumble and that we made it to Faial where the stays can be replaced. If we had continued northeast on our original course into the gale force winds, chances are that the mast would have fallen, and we would have been at the mercy of huge waves. I don't know if we would have survived. Thank you, so much, Karl, for alerting us to the dangerous weather to the north. I offer a toast of thanks to *Aurora* and her crew!"

I toasted our new French friends. "*Aurora* and her crew drink to your successful voyage and our lasting friendship." Our friendship would continue when we met again in Paris.

For Tom, it was his time to grab a taxi for the airport to catch a flight to France where he would join other spectators at the Formula One road race at Le Mans. After Tom left, Peter's Sport Café was our next stop for drinking glasses of cold beer, collecting our mail, and gathering helpful advice, all dispensed with good cheer in many languages. Peter offered good food at a reasonable cost that reflected the local economy. The café became sort of a fraternity house for sailors who felt right at home, allowing new friendships to develop and old ones to deepen as paths crossed. Peter watched over his place with bemused smiles as he greeted many old friends.

"You know, Donn, I have a satisfied feeling of being in the right place after having done all the work of getting here," I said, sipping my beer. "I think we should follow tradition here and contribute an old American flag and a Pamlico Plantation Yacht Club flag to the flag collection on the Café's walls." We did just that. Steve and Donn put up the flags. We stood back and looked at our flags on the wall, alongside those from sailing boats from all over the world.

Wind Mill, Pico in Distance

"Great," Donn exclaimed. "*Aurora* and her crew are now members of Peter's fraternity whose membership requirement is a long ocean passage!"

At the suggestion of Robert, a new tall English friend, we rented a car and set off together to explore the island. Faial is a much drier island than Flores and has earned the nickname of Ilha Azul, "the blue island." The name is fitting since hedgerows of blue hydrangeas play hopscotch on the hillsides and blue lakes lie at the bottom of volcanic craters scattered on the slopes of the mountain.

*****

The drive out to Ponta Capelinhos turned out to be a three-café journey that kept our crew awake, then nourished, and finally cooled down. We stopped to admire the views and climbed down to an old lighthouse partially destroyed by the 1958 volcanic eruption. Adding land to the western end of the island, that eruption is well documented by a photo exhibit at Capelinhos. The subsequent pounding of the seas that had washed away half of the original cone is shown in many dramatic photos. On the way back to Horta, we stopped by an old, crumbling stone cottage with a great view of the slopes down to the sea. We all agreed that it would be a great fixer upper project for Donn, the retired architect.

Steve abandoned *Aurora* and us for camping in a meadow close to town where he could spend unencumbered time with a young Canadian ballet dancer that he had met. Donn and I were alone on the boat. I spotted a cruising boat leaving its slip on a floating pontoon so we quickly moved in to fill its spot. Now having electricity Donn and I pressed the old Pfaff sewing machine into service to repair the tear in the main and to rebuild the blown out spinnaker. Showers ashore were $1.20 with soap and towel included. Our slip rate was six dollars per day and included water and power, a great bargain when compared with prices in the United States.

Wandering around the harbor, we came upon the famous racing sloop *Bolero,* designed by L. Francis Herreshoff, the premier

U.S. naval architect from the 1920s-1950s. Its hull shape and graceful sheer lines evoked thoughts of speed even as it rested tied to the dock. Further on was the British ketch, *Mariette*, constructed in 1915, possessing more shining brass than seemed reasonable, thus guaranteeing the professional crew endless work. Its old winches were huge, over eighteen inches across, and were needed to pull in the large jib and mainsail. Watching a tuna boat unload, we were almost sickened by the rotten smell of the fish, and the realization that most of it would have to be thrown away. Small container ships lined the quays bringing all the stuff needed to sustain the island's population and its cadre of visitors.

Many Azoreans having connections to the United States were very happy to help and converse with us in English. Local sailboat owners directed us to good restaurants and needed local services. Because we were in the minority, making friends from other countries is a plus and in our case, would lead to a cruising base in Paris. Having Steve aboard opened up many possibilities. Using his interest in chess as an opening gambit, he made many new friends. Steve elected to stay at Horta while Donn and I prepared *Aurora* for sailing to Ihla de San Miguel where JoAnne would soon arrive on a flight from Lisbon.

* * * * *

Sailing to San Miguel to pick up JoAnne became an interesting exercise in both trying to predict the weather and then reacting to it. Choosing to navigate the Canal do Sao Jorge between Pico and Sao Jorge, the southwest winds made Pico our destination. When shifted northwest, however, we headed to Velas on Sao Jorge. As we were approaching its tiny harbor, the winds changed to the southeast making the harbor entrance untenable as waves crashed through the opening. Dominated by the wind gods all day, we were forced to sail on through the night, cook dinner at sea and suffer the unhappy camper syndrome. Fortunately, the wind gave out before we did and the moon came up, rescuing the night as Yanni droned on.

Luck was with us as we sailed a distance of one hundred-eighty miles. The winds picked up in the morning, bringing

San Miguel into view from fifty miles out. Our arrival at 9:00 p.m. was not a problem because the sun was still well above the horizon. The young man who helped us raft up at the reception dock also hustled rental cars from McAuto that turned out to be the least expensive rentals on the island. Immigration and customs officers arrived in the morning with Leonora taking the lead. Her easy command of English provided us with detailed information on the island.

Checking into the marina took longer than anticipated because the government was just talking over its management. *Aurora* was the first vessel logged onto the new computer system by Lourdes at the keyboard while the programmer and I watched her input our information on their Windows operating system. We made an expensive mistake sending out our laundry—a medium sized bag cost twenty-four US dollars! The marina provided full services with a large salt water swimming pool and a café with coffee, beer, ice cream, and light food. Market prices were very reasonable with fresh tuna at $2.77 a pound. On the international beer scale, a medium-sized bottle cost $.41 in the market and $.83 in the café making the Azores a very attractive destination for beer drinkers. The mild climate with daytime temperatures in the low 80s dropping to low 70s at night with low humidity completed the alluring picture.

Using our rented Ford Fiesta, Donn and I picked up JoAnne at the airport on July 3rd after her flight from Lisbon. Full of smiles and hugs, she brought good news of securing a slip for *Aurora* at this year's 1998 Lisbon World Exposition outside Lisbon on the River Tagus. JoAnne had enjoyed a great reception in Lisbon from her son Bruce's friend, Rosa, who took her everywhere including to dinner with her family.

After settling in on *Aurora*, JoAnne and I made up for being apart for more than a month. As we held each other in the aft cabin, some of the worry she felt during *Aurora's* long passage to Flores came out in sobs of relief and joy.

"You know," she said, "I have confidence in you and your abilities, but your being so far from land had me on edge."

"You're right, we felt the isolation of being a tiny speck on the ocean and felt our vulnerability acutely when things were going wrong," I said. "But, I felt your love and concern. It helped me though the rough spots knowing that you'll always be there for me."

"Well, we're together again and it's time to celebrate with Donn," JoAnne said. "You two guys are really something else."

"Calling Donn," I said. "Let's break out that cold bottle of white wine."

In the morning, it was time for some serious touring on the island's narrow, rough roads. The blooming hydrangeas kept our eyes and cameras busy as we headed over the mountain to Sete Cicades (Seven Cities) located in the crater of a large volcano where two lakes came together. Towns lined the shores as valleys spread behind them leading up to the crater's rim towering above. Finding a restaurant on a side street, we had a tasty lunch sitting on the patio while absorbing this unusual and spectacular landscape.

Driving north to the coast, we found St. Peter's Church in Capelas enlivened by a beautiful recording of monks singing chants. At Rabo de Peixe, a fishing harbor and old whaling town, a statue of a whale and whalers stood in the town square. At the museum, we saw the long dories that the whalers rowed out to chase the whales. Old movies showing their harpooning and capture put us in the action. Whaling was an exciting and bloody business that thankfully stopped, but also dashed my desire to buy scrimshaw.

Furnas, located in an area of volcanic activity in the mountains, was the destination on our second day of touring. The volcanic heat under the ground was used to cook meals in holes dug down into the hot soil. Enterprising persons monitored the holes, charging picnickers for using them to cook their one pot meals. The town had very narrow streets filled with many cars bringing visitors to see the beautiful park and home built by Thomas Hickling in the mid-1800s when he was consul to the Azores from the United States. Trees and plants are full grown, interspersed with ponds and waterways that lead visitors down magical paths splashed with colors and views of town. A hotel was located on a stream bordering the park and would have been a nice stopping place to soak in a hot mineral water spring located in a cave up the mountain at Possa da Beija. Having our own accommodations on *Aurora*, we returned to Punta Delgada, taking a number of detours around the bridges washed out in winter floods.

Sailing back to Horta again, we encountered shifting and varying winds from the north caused by the effects of the Azores High that sent us to the south coast of Pico at Lajes do Pico which offered the best protection and space to anchor. About 5:20 a.m., a loud crashing noise jolted us out of bed. Waves left the boat shaking. At first, it felt like a boat had bashed into *Aurora* or that the volcano had erupted; then all was still until dogs began to bark and babies started to cry.

I looked toward *Aurora's* bow just as Donn's head popped up though the open hatch.

"What was that?" I yelled. "Whatever it was sounded like a freight train."

"Can you hear the rocks falling off the side of the volcano?" said Donn. "We sure received quite a jolt."

"Something very big just happened," I said. "But the volcano isn't belching much smoke. It's all very puzzling."

Lights went on, but we heard no sirens. In the morning light, we saw smoke rising along the shore which could have been from vents of the volcano. Later, however, we determined that the smoke seemed to be from garbage being burned along the shore.

When we arrived in Horta, an excited staff member told us that a violent tectonic earthquake had occurred under the sea between the Islands of Faial and Sao Jorge causing major damage on Faial. It left 1,500 people homeless, about 10% of the island's population. Eight people had died. Thousands of old stone houses came crashing down. Whole villages were flattened on the north side of Faial where we had toured only a few weeks ago. A cruising couple from Holland decided to donate the use of their vacation home to a needy family rather than staying on the island.

We were okay, but where was nephew Steve? Just then he came sauntering up and looked fine.

"Steve, you look okay," I said. "But what happened where the earthquake struck?"

"Well, a few stones hit my tent in a valley near Horta," he said. "No damage was done and as you can see I'm doing great."

The marina had some settling and cracking but no other damage.

Luiz greeted us at the marina office and directed us to a slip with a view of downtown, the fort, and the park. Lush green hills surrounded Horta undamaged.

Steve continued camping and stopped by to introduce his new set of friends including Anna, a cute marine biology student. She was studying sharks using the marine laboratory at the end of the harbor. Anna would keep us up to date on the effects of the earthquake and the fear generated by the aftershocks.

"Many people moved to parks rather than risk sleeping in their apartments," she said. "The earthquake was so violent that many people are still traumatized."

Our being from Northern California allowed us to keep things in perspective, having experienced the violent 1989 Loma Prieta earthquake and its aftermath. We learned that another one of Steve's friends, Dirk, from Holland, was waiting for his girlfriend,

Margriet and Dirk

Margriet, who was sailing single-handed from the Dutch Antilles in the Southern Caribbean, a 3,100-mile voyage, to Horta. She was long overdue and the light winds near the Azores would not be of much help.

A day later, Margriet was finally able to make radio contact, enabling Steve and Dirk to find her and to tow her into the marina using our trusty Avon dinghy and its strong outboard motor. Over beers and munchies on *Aurora* later, we had a debriefing as the terror and vulnerability she felt on the trip became clear and sobering. Margriet's young face showed the fear and tension she had felt. Her arms hugged her chest while Dirk rubbed her neck and shoulders. There was a moment of silence as we imagined what Margriet had encountered.

"Early in my voyage, the engine failed, limiting my ability to generate electricity or to maneuver the boat in periods of no winds," she said. "I had a hair-raising experience during a windless night when a liquid gas carrier did not acknowledge my radio calls nor my bright lights on my sails as it was bearing down on a collision course. In desperation, I fired a red meteor flare at the ship which finally turned about one hundred feet away. I'm still shaken."

"After sailing long distances, I'm humbled by your experience and just so thankful that you survived and are with us today," I said.

"Margriet, I don't want you to sail alone over such long distances," Dirk insisted.

"Yeah, you're right," she said. "I've accomplished my single-handed sailing goals. From now on we'll sail together. I've experienced enough danger to last a lifetime!"

We all nodded in agreement.

Our last official act in Horta was painting our boat's signature on the marina wall as many boat owners had done before us. Donn designed a small mural with *Aurora*, the goddess of dawn, sailing into a sunrise and affixed the crew's names and the date of June 1998. We all felt proud of our accomplishment, and this mural placed us in the context of our peers who had made similar voyages. The sailors who had left their marks on this wall have

Aurora's Signature

created a visual sailing history. The Azores are truly the crossroads of the Atlantic.

Three days later, we were forced to drag Steve away from Anna, because we had to meet JoAnne's scheduled airline departure to Lisbon from Ponta Delgada on San Miguel. Talking with Anna, it became clear that she was quite aware that Steve was a "here today and gone tomorrow" kind of guy. Only part of that assessment by her was due to the fact that he had arrived on a cruising boat.

Angra Do Heroismo on Terceira was our next port of call. Angra is a beautiful city surrounding a large deep bay, the best natural anchorage in the Azores. We anchored in thirty feet of water off Club Nautico, a white building located just below the fort built by Phillip II of Spain when he defeated the Portuguese.

We found that the club house was a great place to hang out with local sailors. Over beers we learned that although the fort may have protected the harbor from foreign fleets, it also protected the Spanish from the islanders who were none too happy about being under Spanish domination. The club members were a laid back group watching the World Cup Soccer finals while cheering for France and ignoring the plight of their former colony, Brazil. Pica-Pac, a pork dish, served in a medium hot sauce with great bread as both appetizer and the main meal. Sitting on the patio overlooking the bay, we ate Pica-Pac washed down with draft beer. What could be better!

Angra and its lush parks, imposing forts, and historic buildings demanded more time than we had, but the friendly *tourismo* office staff outlined a short itinerary which included an important stop at the bakery next to the city market. As if Angra was angry with our cursory visit, our anchor refused to come up. We deployed Steve who dove in to find it hooked on an old foundation section that had been dumped into the bay. Diving down with a line, Steve tied it to the chain, and then we led the line to the large sheet winch which provided enough side pull to forcefully dislodge the anchor.

Sailing away overnight, our return to Punta Delgada felt like a homecoming with Lourdes there to greet us again. We joined the thirty-five-boat fleet of the British Royal Cruising Club in the crowded marina. Members had just sailed 1,200 miles for an *outing* here on San Miguel. They were a jolly bunch who answered our questions about the meaning of all their different flags and burgees (yacht club flags). The British seem to have plenty of both!

40

ON TO PORTUGAL

After taking JoAnne to her plane to Lisbon, Donn, Steve, and I provisioned *Aurora* and readied her for our passage to Portugal. We were a crew of three, a better number for a thirty-three-foot sloop like *Aurora*. On July 15, 1998, we sailed out of the harbor around the end of San Miguel and then headed due east toward Lisbon. To help pass the time profitably, we looked for mermaids. Steve was the most consistent and persistent looker. Perhaps, his needs were more urgent than ours. Was that an *advantage* of growing older?

We were encompassed by the Azores High where the light winds died during the night requiring motoring. During the day, the high provided 8-12 knots of apparent wind coming at 45 degrees to the course of *Aurora* that propelled us at 3-5 knots toward our destination. We were connected to our "weather god," Herb, whose precise forecasts covered the whole North Atlantic Ocean. One day, he was watching a tropical wave off Africa which he thought would not develop into a hurricane.

In the calm weather, baking a batch of granola is a big event. I issued orders that the crew was not to grab more than two handfuls at a time. Steve is the worst offender, perhaps driven by his high metabolism and his capacity to eat most everything, but he's fun, however, likes to steer to keep busy, and stays awake on his watch. Our ongoing chess tournament offered islands as prizes. Steven won Corvo, the smallest of the Azores, but I played him to a draw in the second game, so maybe there was hope for me. Later I won Flores where we first touched land coming from Bermuda and a larger island than Corvo. While Steve is a much better chess player, in that game I had the Livengood Luck.

The sun was out in full force, but the wind had gone to the north so we hove to (backed our sails) allowing Steve to dive off the davits using the remnants of the Wind Bugger for balance. The water seemed very warm so Donn and I took turns joining him in the bright blue water about 2,000 feet deep.

It was a beautiful day, no critters bothering us and no wind moving *Aurora*. While I was in the water, however, an eerie feeling rose into my consciousness. I felt vulnerable being suspended in so much water. Perhaps, I was feeling fears loosen from my subconscious. But, what was in the depths below me? In the more rational world, with no birds, fish, and dolphins, we seemed to be floating in a watery desert.

Later in Lisbon a scientist on a British ocean research ship would confirm that, "The Azores High creates a body of warm water due to the intense solar radiation that floats on top of the cooler, richer water where all the sea creatures live." I was relieved to hear his explanation because the lack of sea life implied to me that the ocean was dying.

There was still no wind after five days although Herb kept promising us some—perhaps he isn't the weather god after all. Fortunately, Yanni chugged on or we could have been out here forever!

"It feels like we're on the smooth waters of Lake Gitchegumee rather than in the midst of the Atlantic," I said. "I wonder if we will have enough fuel to motor to where the wind is? We must save enough diesel to charge the batteries and to motor into port."

Donn, trying to put my mind at rest, said, "You know *Aurora* uses only a half gallon of diesel an hour so we should make it."

I continued to make detailed estimates of our diesel reserves that helped calm my incipient anxieties. Steve, having given up on spotting mermaids, turned to fishing. Perhaps his stomach won out over his libido. Donn shut down the engine, so we were now sailing "wing on wing" at 4 knots with the wind coming over the stern at 6-8 knots while Auto was steering the boat. JoAnne and Donn's wife, Annita, might have to wait an extra day or two for our arrival just as sailors' wives have done forever, hoping their men would return from the sea.

*****

As we were nearing the Portuguese coast, the wind was steady and building as a front moved in behind *Aurora*, and coming our way so the boat's motion was still quite comfortable. The sun remained buried behind clouds while Captain Karl cooked mushroom soup with toasted cheese and ham sandwiches for lunch. My liking to cook has allowed me to create good meals. French toast for breakfast and even two loaves of beer bread in the oven. I called in to Herb giving him our local weather observations. I wasn't sure our radio transmission would get through because we were about 3,000 miles from his residence in Toronto. But my transmission made it. I heard him which gave me a connected feeling to counter balance the feeling of our "being a tiny speck in the ocean" reality. Being on the only boat you can see, day after day, contributes to that feeling. Without our usual connections to society, to cities, to land and its beauty, my mind wandered into the enlarged space wondering where do I fit, what is important, and where do I go from here. Fortunately, my dream provided some of the answers as did my relationship with JoAnne who was a fellow traveler. I knew that I wanted to deepen my understanding of people and cultures of the world that I would encounter.

*****

Last night, we had a 3 a.m. jibbing drill when the topping lift holding up the spinnaker pole for the jib wrapped around the roller furling, near the top of the mast. The boat must have rolled in the waves causing the line to go slack and then become entangled in the roller furling.

"All hands on deck!" shouted Donn.

Steve and I stumbled up to the cockpit from deep slumber. We unwound the topping lift line while Donn continued to steer. We, however, could not reclaim our rightful places in bed as the glow of sunrise began to creep over the horizon. In morning's light, we launched the repaired spinnaker that was soon pulling us along at 5.7 knots in 11 knots of apparent wind.

"Would the spinnaker repairs hold?" I said. "This time we'll take it down early if the winds increase rather than wait until it's too late." The spinnaker did hold together, validating our sewing skills.

Approaching the coast, we hatched a new pool. How many ships or boats would we see at one time within twenty miles of Portugal? My guess was ten, Donn's five, and Steve's eight. Steve's guess was closest with seven ships coming at us in the shipping lane off the Portuguese Coast.

"Steve, you are awarded 2,000 escudos, the equivalent of ten beers as your prize," I said in my most ceremonial voice.

A change in the engine's r.p.m.s woke me up that night. I saw that a ship was coming rather close to us.

"Should I steer in front of that freighter or go behind?" said Donn from the cockpit.

"Donn, let's go behind," I decided.

I always choose the least risky option especially when in a little sailboat with something large bearing down on us. But judgments can get cloudy in the dark early morning hours.

"Auto," our auto-pilot navigator, bless his mechanical brain, really got screwed up last night as it gave up steering us in the right direction. Auto was sending out random compass readings, making it impossible to steer the course we had set. I tried all the "fix Auto tricks" but to no avail. So, I brought up the old Auto 3000 brain unit and wired it into the 4000 motor drive unit, but it wouldn't keep a course either. We did what true sailors did of old, we hand-steered through the night until my wide awake brain focused on the problem. I moved the 3000 brain unit away from the cockpit speaker that had a magnetic field. Voila! The old Auto began steering correctly so the crew could return to more creative and less taxing endeavors like napping, writing, and listening to music.

*****

About 10:30 a.m., we made our landfall at Cascais, Portugal, located where the River Tagus flows into the sea. I anchored in the bay near a fisherman whose boat was named *Aurora*.

"Wow, what a coincidence," I said. "It almost feels like a homecoming."

Donn, Steve, and I dinghied into the yacht club and I called JoAnne at her hotel in Lisbon. Donn and I agreed to meet our wives at the marina after a night's rest. In the morning, we motored upstream on the Tagus past the marble Henry the Navigator monument, past

Navigator Monument

the city of Lisbon installed in layers on its hills, and past the freight and cruise ship docks lining the waterfront. We had crossed the Atlantic, and I felt welcomed by Henry who looked down on *Aurora* as if to say, "I knew you could do it." His advancement of navigation made Portugal's voyages of discovery possible and in a sense made our voyage feasible because his advances underlaid the systems we relied on to safely cross the Atlantic.

Working against heavy currents, crossing under famous bridges, we reached Expo Marina about 5:30 in the afternoon, fascinated to have trees, buildings, the outer signs of society within our view from the river. Our vision became more focused by having many colors and shapes to observe compared to the expanse of the ocean that had been our universe for a week.

While trying to drive *Aurora* into her slip, I yelled out, "Oh my God, we're being carried downstream by the current. I'll increase the engine revolutions in reverse. Oh no, we're rocketing into the slip. Steve, do something!"

Thank God, Steve's expert lassoing of the dock cleat stopped our forward motion averting a certain damaging crunch.

* * * * *

An hour later, JoAnne and Annita arrived And were welcomed with heartfelt hugs and kisses from their husbands. "I really enjoy holding you in my arms," I whispered in JoAnne's ear. "I promise that there will be no more of these long separations. We belong together here on *Aurora* and at home."

They brought a precious cargo of champagne, so the celebration was on.

"Well, I'm so happy to be reunited with my lovely wife," said Donn, beaming. "Here's a toast to those who kept the home fires burning."

"I'd like to toast to the health of my mentors and friends, Donn and Karl," said Steve as he raised his glass.

"I'm so thankful that we're all here together on the other side of the Atlantic," I toasted, feeling humbled by the experience. "It is a grand accomplishment that we did together! I must say that we are a great crew. Each of us made our voyage a safe and memorable trip. I'm so thankful for you guys helping me realize more of my dream!"

"Guys, I appreciate your skill and enthusiasm that made this voyage possible," said JoAnne. "I felt better knowing that you were with Karl and that together you would keep each other safe. Knowing Steve, I want to thank him for adding his boundless energy and humor to the mix. I'm sure you kept things light and made the trip that much more interesting. But what about mermaids? I heard you were looking for them."

"Well, you'll have to ask the mermaids," said Steve. "My charms failed to lure them close to *Aurora*."

"You know, you guys look very good after spending a month at sea and more than two months on *Aurora*," said Annita. "I know that sailing is Donn's passion and I can see the joy on Karl and Steve's faces. You guys are something else!"

"You got that right, Annita," I said. "I'm feeling so elated that I could burst. What a reunion this is. The whole voyage was so gratifying to me."

* * * * *

Annita and Donn later left for their own planned exploration of Portuguese villages in search of records of her ancestors who had migrated from Portugal to Brazil.

Afterwards JoAnne and I taxied to her hotel for our own celebration! Steve was left to his own devices on *Aurora* where his cave in the V berth was home. I advised him to check out the beautiful, dark-haired young women manning the marina's check in desk. Knowing Steve, he did.

* * * * *

Back at the Expo Marina on *Aurora*, I was having some time to reflect on our incredible voyage: *Aurora* had crossed the Atlantic Ocean with no injuries to the crew, and only minor mechanical problems; our old sails that bore the brunt of high winds were damaged but repairable and completed the voyage; the voyage lasted thirty sailing days and covered about 4000 statute miles that equal 3476 nautical miles; the average day covered 117 n.m. at an average speed of 4.9 knots; *Aurora* was not trying to set speed records or take chances so we reefed early with the goal of having a comfortable trip; we did stay dry and had enough water for frequent showers, and very importantly we ate well and all the crew got along together.

As captain I felt satisfied that I kept the ship running well without being overbearing since the decisions flowed easily with input from the crew. But the final decisions were mine, being owner and captain and the one who knew *Aurora* most intimately. The passage across the Atlantic validated the need for all the preparation of *Aurora* and myself. Together, we made it happen. *Aurora* proved herself again as the vessel capable of carrying me and my dreams out into an expanding world.

My deep sense of inner calm was buoyed by feelings of accomplishment and pride. I have successfully sailed my dream! What is next for JoAnne and me?

Dream! Dream! Dream!

PART V

EXPANDING THE DREAM

By allowing your mind to expand into new places
By allowing your heart to open and express
Its love to those you meet
By allowing your dreams to precede you
Into the new realities you encounter
You will live life to the fullest

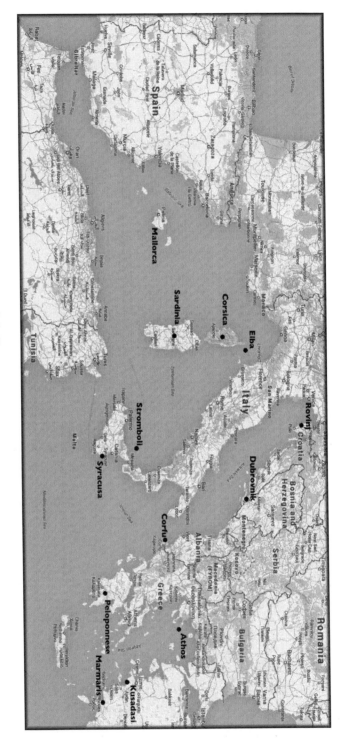

Mediterranean

41

EUROPE HERE WE ARE

1998—After arriving in Lisbon and settling in at Marina Expo for a month, our sailing adventure continued. Steve, JoAnne, and I sailed south along the Algarve Coast of Portugal. Steve and I enjoyed the views of topless bathers on the beaches. At Sagres, home of Henry the Navigator's school, Steve left us and *Aurora* to become chess teacher and crew with a family heading for Gibraltar in a fifty-foot schooner. He was anxious to reach Granada to begin making guitars again. Parting from Steve with hugs and tears, we felt like we were losing a son.

Our friend Elmo and his girlfriend, Cathy, joined us to find the navigable limits of the Guardiana River that forms the border between Portugal and Spain. Making our way upriver, we saw the damage from a huge flood the past year caused by heavy rains and the uncoordinated release of water from upstream dams by Portugal and Spain. We heard of cruisers at anchor who were swept into orange groves above the river, but none lost their lives. We learned that cruisers who were constantly crossing by dinghy between the two countries had finally led the authorities to open the border and drop immigration formalities. We sailed to Spain and motored up the Guadalquivir River to Sevilla where we arrived at *Aurora's* winter home of Puerto Gelves. We made a new friend, Enrique Berends, who was publicizing the port. He helped us make all the necessary arrangements for storing *Aurora*.

* * * * *

A world of possibilities now opened up with *Aurora* in Europe. On *Aurora* JoAnne and I used our time to begin an intimate exploration of Portugal, Spain, and the countries bordering the Mediterranean on *Aurora*. Our dream expanded. In subsequent years, JoAnne and I sailed *Aurora* into the Mediterranean Sea during the six months centering on summer. Each summer our crew was augmented by family and sailing friends who wanted to share our adventures and have more time on *Aurora*. As we progressed further into the Med, we found new places to store *Aurora* for the winter months. Guests often volunteered to help prepare her for the new season. JoAnne and I welcomed the help and savored our deepening relationships with them.

1999—SAILING INTO PAGEANTRY AND HISTORY

We participated in an amazing Easter week in Sevilla, observing men carrying huge statues of the Holy Family on platforms on their backs to the beat of drums as reverent crowds silently watched. John and Maureen, sailing friends from Pamlico Plantation, joined us for the Spring Horse Fair set in a large tent city that brought out beautiful horses and riders prancing down the streets followed by magnificent carriages carrying fairgoers. Huge tents available by invitation only were loaded with food, drink, and music. Enrique's girlfriend, Pepa, was our ticket of admission. We dined and danced, exhilarated being with other fairgoers.

Returning to the Atlantic down the Guadalquivir, we anchored at Cadiz to sample sherry and watch the beautiful Lipizzan horses strut their stuff. Breeding Lipizzaners began in 1580 in Austria when Spanish Andalusians were bred to local Karst horses that had a high stepping gait. Sailing past Cape Trafalgar, we could almost feel the heat of the battle where Admiral Horatio Nelson defeated the combined French and Spanish navies in 1805.

The Straits of Gibraltar presented a challenge with its strong currents. Shipping lanes filled with ships of all sizes were being squeezed through the narrow strait. We docked in the marina next to the airport where runways were filled with military planes preparing to stop the civil war in Yugoslavia. After having a banana snatched out of my hand by one of the Barbary apes living in the cliffs, we toured the famous Rock of Gibraltar, honeycombed with defensive tunnels. We then sailed south across the straits to

Ceuta, a Spanish port on the African side. Taken by bus inland, we became immersed in Moroccan bazaars where vendors had the upper hand. Taken into a Berber rug shop, we were exposed to some of the world's greatest salesmen. The many rugs in my home prove it! Sailing deeper into the Med on the Spanish side, along the Costa del Sol, we stopped and rented a car to explore the Puebla's Blancas in the coastal mountains. Friendly JoAnne was invited into a cave house. The owner gave us all an intimate tour of his house that dated back to Neolithic times.

John and Maureen left us to tour Europe on their own. JoAnne and I bused to Granada to reunite with nephew Steve. He had completed a year of guitar making in this city of guitar makers, while improving his Spanish with the aid of a Spanish girlfriend. Steve joined us on *Aurora* and nephew Keith arrived soon after in Cartagena where we met him walking toward *Aurora* at her berth. Sailing out to the Balearic Islands off the coast, the four of us explored Formentara and Ibiza before arriving at Mallorca. Steve again jumped ship to join the paid crew of a large wooden Spanish racing sloop. Later in the summer while celebrating a victory party on his boat, Steve had the pleasure of following tradition when asking Juan Carlos, the King of Spain, to remove his shoes before coming aboard. Steve's boat had defeated the King's boat in a close race that day. Keith's wife, Lynne, and daughter, Madeline, joined us briefly for day sails and island tours before they all headed back to Boston.

Alone again, JoAnne and I sailed to Minorca, finding narrow slots in the tall cliffs that opened into small bays with sand beaches and ancient cave dwellings overlooking the anchorages. At Cuitadella, we joined the festival for their patron, St. John. Huge horses with their sometimes diminutive riders pranced through the streets rearing up when brave onlookers raced forward to touch the horse's heart. Sailing to Barcelona over three days, we docked at Porto Vell where our dock-mates warned us to beware of the tricks and scams used by Gypsies. Wouldn't you know that over the course of a week, the Gypsies tried all of them on us, but since we were prepared, all our possessions remained where they belonged. My daughter Leanne and one of her girlfriends joined us for a magical exploration of the world of Gaudi represented in his buildings, a fantastical park, and his awe inspiring La Sacrada Familia church.

Later in October, we laid up *Aurora* in winter storage at Port Ginesta near Barcelona.

Back in North Carolina, a conversation with my doctor about chest pains I felt when pulling up the anchor led to an emergency insertion of three stents and an overnight stay in the hospital. I did very well following the procedure. I went on a camp reunion canoe trip on Lake Temagami, Ontario, a week later and have led an active life for fifteen years, thriving on regular exercise and a low fat diet.

2000—CHOPIN, GEORGE SAND, NAPOLEON, ODYSSEUS, MARCO POLO

We returned to Porto Ginesta to embark on a new season. My to do list eventually numbered twenty-three tasks as I prepared *Aurora* for more sailing in the Med. The job I dreaded most was cleaning out the sewage treatment tank—a three hour operation. Oh yes, boats are fun! JoAnne's daughter, Betsy, joined us in Barcelona to revisit Gaudi's fluid modern architecture. On an overnight sail to Mallorca, Betsy took her turn on the watch crew, and we arrived in Porto Pollensa the next day. Renting a car, we found the cottage of Frederic Chopin and his girlfriend, George Sand, overlooking the sea. Searching for privacy and better health in 1838, they had come here to write music and novels. Chopin wrote twenty-three preludes while Sand created *Winter in Majorca*. Now a museum with concert hall, it was a thrill to hear Chopin's music played on the estate.

When Betsy's engineering design work in California called her home, JoAnne and I sailed to the fortified port of Mahon Bay in Minorca where the English fleet was stationed in the 1800s. Keith again joined the crew. It seems that his sailing habit had formed and we loved it. While *Aurora* was berthed to a floating island in the bay, a boat neighbor asked for help finding parts for his engine. I gave him my resource material and also met his lovely wife. The next morning, I couldn't help but notice that she was showering in the nude just opposite my cockpit. Keith came up to enjoy the view.

Sailing to Sardinia, we found ourselves in the middle of NATO maneuvers. Keith took command, confirming our position with the nearest destroyer that informed us we were safe from the shelling of the nearby small island and from helicopters and hovercrafts swarming around us. His past navy persona was reactivated, so he found glee in every moment. Keith left us in Puerto Chervo, Sardinia, to meet his wife, Lynne, on mainland Italy. After the weather settled, JoAnne and I sailed to the Island of Elba. We toured the residence where Napoleon lived when he was exiled in 1814 and from whence he escaped in 1815, only to be defeated at the Battle of Waterloo, then sent to St. Helena in the south Atlantic.

Sailing north up the Tyrrhenian Sea, we moored at Livorno where Keith and Lynne rescued us from the hardships of cruising. We stayed with them in a monastery at San Pietro located in the hills above Lucca. The view from the loggia overlooked the vineyards then swept out toward Lucca. There, its tall defensive towers stood out, having protected their owners from neighbors and invaders alike.

My college age nephew, Paul, and his boyhood friend, Andre, caught up with us in Flumicino, the port of Rome. On an island off the coast, fireworks were shooting up toward us so in return, I shot up some of our old parachute flares. Everyone on board winced as they drifted in over a crowd on shore. No screams were heard so they must have burned out in the air. Capri satisfied the boys' need for exercise as they ran to the top of the island. JoAnne and I rode the cogwheel railway to Alex Munthe's wonderful estate perched on the side of the cliff facing Mt. Vesuvius on the Italian coast. Having Paul and Andre aboard fully filled our young energy quotient, with laughs overflowing.

Further south we picked up Don and Liz, Pamlico Plantation sailing neighbors, and sailed out to the Island of Stromboli, anchoring off a black sand beach on the side of the volcano. A wind shift during the night sent us drifting into the all encompassing blackness, quickly terminating our sleep. We were in the Aeolian

Islands named for the God of the winds, and our dragging anchor experiences on several occasions proved it. Sailing through the Straits of Messina between Italy and Sicily, we battled the same incredible currents that had dogged Odysseus but made progress toward Syracusa. We fancied ourselves also ignoring the famous sirens' calls. On Don and Liz's last day, poor holding in the harbor caused *Aurora* to swing into the pier's rock wall, but the crew of a Maltese boat ran over and held us off the jagged rocks until it could drive the boat out to deeper water. I vowed to visit Malta one day.

Donn Weaver, my friend and co-captain on the Atlantic crossing, rejoined us for our sail around the heel of Italy toward Otranto where strong winds and high waves impeded our progress. As we were bashing along, the Italian Coast Guard wanted to board *Aurora*. I refused their request, knowing we would be in danger if their large ship came alongside. I told them that we were going to Otranto. They never did check out *Aurora*. (A week before, one of their men had been killed when boarding a boat smuggling Albanians to Italy.)

We had a mellow overnight sail across the Adriatic to Dubrovnik where we fell in love with Croatia and with Sandra, my sister's pianist friend, who grew up there. Just imagine walled cities and polished cobblestone streets dating back many centuries where Marco Polo and thousands of others had trod. Friendly people were anxious to help us, glad we were visiting their country after the terrible civil wars that tore the former Yugoslavia apart.

When Donn departed, we were joined by Sandra and her husband, Steven, who helped us explore the northern Dalmatian Coast. Sandra had grown up in Yugoslavia under Tito and was trained as a classical pianist. She is now living with her husband in the San Francisco Bay Area and teaches piano and gives the occasional classical concert. They added a spirit of lightness and liberation to *Aurora*, sometimes dancing naked on the deck. Steven jumped into the sea for a last swim just before we docked in Zadar where they would leave us.

JoAnne and I sailed *Aurora* north to Rovinj and then made a day sail's trip to Venice where Frank and Denise, friends made in the Bahamas, accompanied us in a week long, intimate exploration of the city spread over many low islands, crisscrossed with canals, and hovering just above sea level. Finally, we sailed *Aurora* back to Rovinj, Croatia, and put her to bed for the winter.

2001—CIVIL WAR, DELPHI, OLYMPUS, KALAMATA, AND A NASTY RAT

Maureen and John LaVake flew with us from Pamlico Plantation to Rovinj in April to begin the new cruising season. A week later after a lot of work, we began sailing down the Dalmatian Coast of Croatia in the Aegean Sea. A side trip up a river took us east to Krka National Park where a series of falls are growing higher as the dissolved calcium in the water sticks to plants. We were about halfway across Croatia and talked with a traumatized man selling ice cream. The Serbs attacked this idyllic place in an attempt to cut Croatia in half during the civil war. After showing Dubrovnik to Maureen and John, we sailed together off shore fifty miles to avoid Albanians trying to flee their Stalinist regime that continued his repressive ways long after his death in 1953. We heard shooting in Albania just before we arrived in Corfu, Greece.

Keith joined us again after the LaVakes departed. We sailed south in the Ionian Sea to Zakinthos Island where we took a ferry to Delphi in the Gulf of Corinth. The famous oracle of Delphi had drawn seekers from all over the ancient Greek world. Standing on the mountainside amongst the ruins and kneeling by the sacred spring, we felt the power of the place. After Keith returned to home and work, JoAnne and I were on our own. We sailed across to the Ionian Sea to the Peloponnese and visited Olympus where the original games were held. I ran down the track without competition or the crowd's cheers. Just being in these ancient places set our imaginations loose.

After sailing around the end of the Peloponnese, we turned north to Kalamata where I learned to like black olives. Akkos and Gloria, sailing neighbors from Pamlico Plantation, joined us as we sailed along the coast and out to nearby islands. After stopping to see an ancient fortress town of Momemvasia located on an island dominated by a huge rock monolith, we discovered that a rat had stowed away on *Aurora*. She announced her presence by chewing up our *Time Magazine*. A few days later, I saw her in the aft cabin and shot my shoe at her, but missed. She ran under the door to the toilet and over JoAnne's feet accompanied by loud screams. Akkos and Gloria decided to abandon ship the next day. I did catch the rat a few days later and found her nest under our stove. She must have been pregnant. What a mess she could have created by eating the insulation off the boat's wires and chewing up other unimaginable things.

We left *Aurora* in a boatyard at the end of the Corinth Canal. Completed in 1893, digging the four miles long canal must have been a difficult feat, because over one hundred feet vertical of material had to be removed to create this sea level canal. We were now in the Aegean Sea and had satisfied more of our desire to experience the ancient places so vital in the formation of western culture.

2002—TEMPLE OF POISEIDON, MONKS ON PATROL, ISTANBUL, WONDERFUL TURKEY

Donn Weaver rejoined us and helped prepare *Aurora* for the new season. We discovered that the deep cycle batteries were not holding their charge. This was a major problem, because they powered all the electrical circuits on *Aurora*. Piraeus, the port of Athens, had the batteries we needed. After ordering the batteries, JoAnne, Donn, and I then took an overnight ferry trip to Santorini, sleeping in cabins for only 33 Euros each. Our villa rooms just outside town were also comfy and cheap. Walking the streets of Thira treated us to spectacular views of the crater and the stucco houses with blue domes stacked like blocks glued onto the cliff face. Three old windmills at the end of the island dripped with charm.

Back on *Aurora*, we completed all our work and set off down the Athens peninsula, anchoring opposite the Temple of Poseidon (built in 444 BC) and accessing it by dinghy. Walking through the lovely ruins, we paid our respect to the God of the seas. Sailing up the eastern side of the peninsula, we conducted a ceremonial burial at sea of an old Zenith computer and Donn's broken watch as symbols of the modern culture that have influenced our lives. Perhaps, Poseidon was using them to keep up to date? In Kyriaki, we met Manolos, a retired merchant marine officer, now a restaurateur, who gave JoAnne, Donn, and me a good fish dinner with wine for 36 Euros. Skepolos was an island in search of new residents. Older people have been left behind as the young have gone off in search of work. Foreigners looking for second homes were filling the void.

Sailing north to Thessaloniki, we battled winds and waves flowing down the Aegean. When we were secure in its marina, Donn left for home in California. Marion and Paul, sailing friends from North Carolina, then joined us as we explored the far reaches of the northern Aegean. Sailing along the monastery-filled Athos Peninsula, we anchored off a spectacular monastery that seemed to be hanging by threads attached to the cliff face. While we were swimming off the boat to cool down, the monk police motored up, objecting that our wives were bathing in their one piece suits in sight of the cloistered monks. He ordered us to move immediately. We were shocked. Later, we discovered the whole monk-filled Athos peninsula is off limits to the fairer sex.

*****

Marion and Paul left us at Thasos, and JoAnne and I sailed south to Lemnos, a Greek island off the coast of Turkey. A fisherman came over to warn us of an approaching storm and to suggest that better shelter was located across the bay. A few days later, we sailed to Bozcaada, a Turkish island located opposite the Dardanelles. We felt as if we had entered a different world where people were more friendly and more interested in us. These wonderful feelings grew as our time in Turkey lengthened. More fresh fruit and vegetables could be found in the bazaars, too. I used my river running tactics in the Dardanelles, staying close to shore where the shallows slowed the current that always flowed out toward the Mediterranean. We could see that we were actually moving faster than an old Russian freighter fighting the current in deeper water.

The Sea of Marmara was mellow and inviting so we sailed all the way to Istanbul's marina at Atakoy where Carolina friends Sue and Jim Taylor connected with us. The domes and minarets of the mosques scattered through the city give the place an other-worldly feel. The Blue Mosque and the Aga Sophia immersed us in the history and beauty of the place. Walking in the Spice Market and the Grand Bazaar, we could feel the beating heart of Istanbul. On a ferry trip through the Bosphorus, we joined a flood of ships going to and from Russia and the Black Sea. Its history is told by the buildings lining the shore.

Sailing southeast across the Sea of Marmara, we reached Zeytinbagi, side-tying to a wall. Walking through town after buying vegetables, we saw men drinking tea and playing dominos on small tables scattered along the street. Looking out of town, we could see women hoeing vegetables in the fields. We observed this role reversal elsewhere in rural Turkey. On the next morning, Sue, Jim, JoAnne, and I boarded a bus for Bursa, the historic end of the Silk Road.

Silk and items made from silk are the major products of Bursa. An enterprising young man convinced me that my dusty leather sandals needed to be cleaned and polished. What a good job he did making them look like new!

Arriving back in Zeytinbagi, we were stopped in the street by the owner of the fresh produce stand. Tables were brought out, tea was sent for, and we became the main attraction as English speakers came over to translate. And the questions flew. Where do you come from? Where are you going? How do you like Turkey? Why did you come so far to visit us in this small town? Our abundant smiles and direct answers had everyone enthralled. What an interesting turn of events!

Sailing southwest toward the Dardanelles, we anchored off a beach but were waved off and yelled at by the women swimming with their children. This was an opposite reaction compared to all the friendliness we had been experiencing in Turkey. Confused, we pulled anchor and found a more secluded spot. Later, the same group of women now wearing black burqas with their children in tow passed by on a trail above the beach and waved greetings. Suddenly, we got it. The women were in bathing suits away from men, and then we showed up, intruding on their day of freedom from being covered head to toe with hot burqas.

Swept by a strong current out into the Med, we were motor-sailing southward when the motor suddenly quit. Checking the fuel tanks, I realized that I'd been ignoring them, and they were just about empty. Looking toward shore I spotted a marina protected by a stout stone breakwater and gave a great sigh of relief. Sailing over, we made it through the entrance and had just enough fuel to angle into a wall where we side-tied *Aurora*. Looking around the marina, we realized that there was no fueling station. I walked behind us to a large shrimp boat to ask about where to find diesel fuel. The captain's son, Ahmad, who spoke English, told us that a gas station was about twenty kilometers away. After talking with his dad, he said, "I'll find someone to take you there." A half hour later, a man in a station wagon drove up and motioned to come with him. Armed with four jerry cans, Sue, Jim, and I got into his vehicle.

At the service station, I filled our jerry cans and told our benefactor to fill his station wagon with fuel. On the way back to the marina, he stopped by a field of tomatoes being picked by a group of women. He returned with a large shopping bag filled to the brim with red, ripe tomatoes which he gave to us. We thanked him and soon arrived at *Aurora*. JoAnne and Sue realized that we could never eat that many tomatoes, so we divided them in half and took a bag to our friends on the shrimp boat. They thanked us and in a short time Ahmad returned with a large platter of shrimp and sliced tomatoes. Our welcome expanded when we tried to buy shrimp from the boat in front, but they insisted on giving us a bag.

Next, Jim climbed the hill overlooking the marina to have a drink at a restaurant. Again, his money was refused and free drinks poured by the owner, who it turned out was the kind man who'd driven us to the gas station. We had dinner there later and were invited into the kitchen to pick the fresh fish for our meal.

The meal was excellent, topping off a generous day. Being immersed in this culture of sharing and concern for others, we all felt welcome and warm inside.

Sailing along the Turquoise Coast of Turkey, JoAnne looked at me and said, "You know, I've had enough of this sailing life. It's time to do something else."

"You're right," I said. "How about buying a canal boat in Holland? We've been talking about it for quite a while." We agreed to pursue the change. JoAnne's presence was central to my life and the voyages of *Aurora*. Honoring her request was easy for me to do. JoAnne really made living my dream possible for me, since mine was a dream to be shared!

I would miss *Aurora*, as she had done her part in carrying my dream forward. But more than that, she also had been my companion. She was a classy, sleek boat, yet tough enough to handle bad weather. She was our comfortable and inviting home on the sea where JoAnne felt comfortable as long as the heeling was not extreme.

Our season ended in Kusadasi where Sue and Jim helped us to put *Aurora* up for the winter. All of us bused to Jimmie's Place, a small hotel near Emphasis. We hired a teacher as our guide, and he provided information as we toured those amazing ruins of buildings that were begun by the Greeks and completed by the Romans. The two-story stone library was a standout. We learned that a tunnel was dug from it to the brothel across the street, providing weary readers with another form of diversion. A Turkish haircut for Jim and me gave us the new experience of having the hairs in our ears singed off by cotton balls dipped in alcohol and set alight. We survived the experience although Sue and JoAnne looked on doubtfully.

When we returned home, we were alerted by friends at Pamlico Plantation that they had seen a great steel canal cruiser. It was owned by an American couple and would be for sale in 2003. JoAnne and I were attracted to the blue and white steel motorboat, thirty-four feet long and twelve feet wide, that we saw on their website.

2003—A NEW WAY OF TRAVELING, ENGINE ALMOST DIES, CAPPADOCIA, ST. NICHOLAS ISLAND

Stopping in Holland, JoAnne and I found that the canal cruiser exceeded our expectations. After taking an overnight cruise with the owners, we decided to buy it at the end of that summer. We continued on to Turkey and put *Aurora* up for sale. Tom and Gina joined us for the launching of *Aurora*. It became a nightmare when the Yanmar engine belched black smoke and ran very roughly. Consultation with a mechanic revealed that he thought the engine was shot. A new engine could be delivered in three weeks, much too long a time, because Gina and Tom only had three weeks of vacation. I ran the engine some more, and it still started okay, so I decided to take a chance and make our trip south down the Turquoise Coast. Gradually, the black smoke turned into a more normal grey color and the old engine functioned quite well despite having given over a thousand hours of service.

Before Gina and Tom left we drove a rented car to Cappadocia, where the early Christians fled to escape the Romans. They built underground cities in the soft volcanic Tufa which above ground has been shaped by wind and rain into weird mushroom and phallic shapes. A thrilling hot air balloon ride gave me a bird's eye view as we skimmed over trees and ridges, dropping down into valleys and slipping by minarets while dogs barked and goats bleated.

Continuing on to Bodrum, we found our slip was located in the shadows of the Castle of St. Peter, built by the Knights Hospitaller beginning in 1402. It is a well-preserved example of late Crusader architecture. Here, JoAnne and I began sorting out and giving away a lot of the stuff that had been accumulating on *Aurora*. We felt good knowing that our stuff would go to people in need. I gave my scuba gear to a charitable group helping disabled people learn to dive.

Don and Betty Ann, neighbors from the Plantation, joined us for ten days of sailing and schmoozing where we learned about their Peace Corps teaching in Afghanistan. Their students and their families greatly valued the education they provided. Next, Keith rejoined the crew and we sailed further south to Gamier

Adasi, where a line to shore kept the boat safe in the narrow passage. Ashore, Keith and I hiked up to the ruins of a church and monastery on St. Nicholas Island. St. Nicholas lived here in the third century. A one hundred-meter-long covered walkway allowed the monks to meditate in the shade.

Turning north, we located a slip in the marina at Marmaris and found Adelina, a yacht broker, who agreed to help us sell *Aurora*. Our new engine arrived and I installed it in the place of our trusted old Yanni. Adelina sold the old engine to a fisherman while agreeing to watch over *Aurora* during the winter. JoAnne and I returned to Holland and completed our purchase of *Livngood*, our thirty-four-foot steel canal cruiser that had been updated and lovingly cared for by her previous American owners. We were ready to make the next transition in our floating lives. *Aurora* was sold to a British petroleum engineer working in Kazakstan who used her for floating vacations in the Mediterranean.

A DRAMATIC TURN OF EVENTS

Early in the morning on January 15, 2005, while we were sleeping on a houseboat in Sausalito, JoAnne had a massive heart attack. She could not be resuscitated. I called Betsy, JoAnne's daughter, who hurried to the hospital and we both stood in shock as her body lay on the gurney, grieving her loss and saying our goodbyes.

JoAnne and I had lived an intimately connected life on *Aurora* and ashore. Losing her so suddenly forced me to go inside myself where I found all those connections, the layers of memories, and her love that I felt in my heart. Over time, I put together these aspects of her life and created an inner mosaic of JoAnne. I carried that mosaic forward, knowing that we had led an incredible life together where she overcame many fears, from shouting, "If you think this is fun, you're crazy" as six-foot waves crashed into *Aurora* off Puerto Vallarta, to her guiding *Aurora* though the night as I slept in an intense electrical storm off Panama. JoAnne led a life where she expanded her world and used her skills as a foreign student advisor to become a "good American" to counter the then prevailing image of the "ugly American" projected by too many Americans overseas. JoAnne's basic love for humanity and life was expressed in the *interest* she showed when encountering new people. Feeling her openness, those she met were drawn to her. For me, her love and willingness to join me on the quest to follow my dream of cruising the world made all the difference in my life!

A call to my daughter Darsie revealed that her own dying husband, Greg, had just seen JoAnne in a vivid dream that very morning. He said that he saw "JoAnne standing in a tunnel of blue light wearing a blue dress." She told him, "You can have a little more time." Greg died later in the afternoon, succumbing to the lymphoma he'd been battling for fourteen months. My family suffered a double loss that day.

I'd known Betsy as long as JoAnne and I had been together. We were friends who knew each other well. Betsy and I planned two memorials for JoAnne, one at International House where she had worked on the Berkeley campus and the other at Pamlico Plantation in North Carolina where we lived. Betsy and I spoke at both of them. We worked together to sort out the myriad of details in need of attention when a loved one passes. We cried on each other's shoulders as we grieved and reminisced.

Betsy loved sailing on *Aurora*. She'd had spent more than a month sailing on her in San Francisco Bay, Belize, and off of Spain. She also had spent two weeks in 2004 on our canal cruiser, *Livngood*, that JoAnne and I bought. Betsy loved to travel as much as I did. Betsy had degrees in art therapy and counseling, but the lack of jobs in her field forced her to fall back on using her drafting skills, developed to help pay for her college education. She lived in Sonoma County, north of San Francisco, and worked as a civil engineering designer using computer aided design. Her latest work for wineries in the famous Napa and Sonoma Valley regions of California included designing roads, parking, water and waste water infrastructure, and wine caves and tasting rooms.

After discovering our mutual attraction, Betsy and I got together. I asked her to accompany me during the summer of 2005 on the canal boat in France. When her civil engineering company refused to give her a leave of absence, I encouraged her to retire and join me as my partner on *Livngood*. Betsy's engineering mindset made her the perfect pilot for *Livngood*. She undertook the critical docking and locking maneuvers with skill while I secured the lines to bollards and cleats. We were a great team. Our relationship deepened over the summer, and we married in June, 2006. *Livngood* proved herself to be a very good boat over the next ten years as Betsy and I traveled along with good friends and family on the canals and rivers of Holland, Belgium, France, and Germany.

In the fall of 2006, Betsy and I bought a 1981 Catalina 36 sailboat. We named her *JoJo* in memory of JoAnne, my wife, and her mother. We renovated *JoJo,* making her a safe and handsome sailboat that we sailed all over San Francisco Bay, up the river to Napa, out the Golden Gate to Point Reyes and down the coast to Half Moon Bay. We actively participated in the Catalina 36 sailing group. At Point Reyes, we dinghied ashore from our anchorage in Drake's Bay to find a huge, 2000 pound male elephant seal resting on what became known as "losers beach." He had been beaten off by more massive bull seals when he attempted to mate with members of their harems. He did seem a little depressed and didn't mind that we came so close to him. Perhaps, our company was better than nothing for him.

I was hoping that Betsy would again connect with her artistic talent. She is now actively pursuing creative expression, drawing and painting portraits and landscapes using charcoals, watercolors and oil. She has sold a number of her paintings and has exhibited in many shows. Her paintings have been displayed in pubic buildings were we live in California. Betsy is teaching a Portraiture class in the Art Association studios in Rossmoor.

42

RETURNING TO AILIGANDI

In 2010, Betsy and I accepted an invitation from our friends Denise and Frank to help them sail their forty-eight-foot Tayana sloop from Panama to Costa Rica. Being in Panama gave me the opportunity to return to Ailigandi village. Betsy used the Internet to find Dad Ibe Lodge located on a small island east of Ailigandi Village. I was ecstatic! Dad Ibe which means "Sunrise" in English is owned and managed by Osiris and her father. Following our sail with Frank and Denise north along the Pacific coast to Costa Rica, we flew back to Panama City and stayed in a B&B overlooking Allbrook Airport. At 5 am, we arrived at the airport and were greeted by Osiris. Her father checked in boxes of produce to fly on the Havilland Otter twin turbo prop plane taking us to a landing field near the island of Ailigandi. As we dropped down over the peaks of the Darien Mountains, the pilot banked the plane, making a steep turn just over the tops of the palm tree jungle. The palms became a blur out the plane's side window as we made a smooth landing on the concrete runway that had been constructed by the Kuna.

As we stepped off the plane, a small brown-skinned man came forward to greet us. He shook our hands and said, "I'm Sam. I will be your guide for the time you are with us at Dad Ibe."

The boat driver, Oswaldo, picked up the supply boxes from Osiris off the runway, and we walked to the nearby dock where an outboard powered *panga* was waiting. Heading toward three islands on the horizon, I could see Ailigandi Island to the west just off the Darien Peninsula.

Dad Ibe

As we got closer to Dad Ibe, a realization struck me. "Betsy, this is the island group called Islandia where I anchored Aurora eighteen years ago. Somehow you've found the same spot while searching the Internet. I'm really blown away! I'm back in 'Paradise.'"

"Wow, I guess I inherited your Livengood Luck," said Betsy with a smile.

Settling into our thatched bungalow, one of only three on Dad Ibe, we learned that we would be the only guests staying on the island. After we had eaten a tasty lunch of fried fresh snapper, Sam and his young helper took us by boat to Ailigandi Village. Beginning our tour of the island, we walked through the new hospital staffed by both Panamanian and Kuna doctors. In the village square a statue of Simral (General) Colman looks out toward the school also named in his honor. The statue stands paying homage for his leadership of the Kuna fighting force that he prepared to confront the invading Panamanians in the 1920s. Walking further into the village, Sam introduced us to a woodcarver, John, who was creating carved wooden plaques painted with bright colors. We visited Sam's elder sister in her dark hut, and she showed us two brightly colored *molas* she had sewn, costing only ten dollars each. We liked them, and her low price cinched the sale.

Walking along, I mentioned my friendship with Eladio Anderson. Sam looked at me with bright eyes, saying, "Eladio is my best friend. Eladio has moved to Panama City with his wife and son, Irving, but lately he has had problems with dizziness. He's getting treatment from a traditional Kuna healer on the neighboring island of Achutupu."

"We'd really like to see him," I eagerly replied.

"Okay, we can go there tomorrow," said Sam.

Sam and Kids

We continued walking toward Eladio's blue stucco house surrounded by a flock of children, some of whom were Sam's grandchildren and others who were attracted by this gentle man and to us, the strangers in their midst. No one was at home, but as we turned to leave, Evelyn, Eladio's daughter, walked up returning from teaching her second grade class.

Sam introduced us, and Evelyn said with a big smile on her face, "I remember you from a long time ago when you came to this house."

"Evelyn, I'm so happy that you remember me!" I said with a smile. "I'd like you to meet my wife, Betsy." I felt like a circle in my memory had been reconnected.

"I'm so happy to meet you," said Betsy. "It's great to be here in Ailigandi, a place that Karl loves and wanted to return to."

Evelyn was doubly pleased that we also would be visiting her father the next day. We talked for a while about her life and children before saying our goodbyes. Back at the boat dock, as we waited for Oswaldo to return, Evelyn arrived and handed us a piece of paper with her address. Children again surrounded us, all waving goodbye as we climbed down into the boat and began motoring back to Dad Ibe. The cool breeze relieved us from the dripping humidity of the hot tropical air.

Back at Dad Ibe, our top priority was to go snorkeling. Sam asked a young man, also named Oswaldo, to get us skin-diving masks and fins. He was assigned to accompany us around the island to insure our safety in the water. The cool, clear, crystal-like water was refreshing. Circling the island, we realized it was actually the top of a coral reef that had collected sand over time. The living parts of the reef were composed of a kaleidoscope of bright colors and shapes with brain and staghorn corals and sea grass spread out below us. The sea was pulsating with sgt. majors, yellow and black angelfish, neon blue lunar wrasse, turquoise parrot fish, long skinny trumpet fish, and even deadly lion fish bristling with narrow long fins capable of injecting poison into any careless passerby. We were living atop nature's aquarium. The view was also accessible by looking down from the overhanging back deck of our bungalow into the lapping water below.

After our swim, Eric and Katherine, the Swiss couple aboard *Windsong* who were anchored near *Aurora's* old spot joined us, accepting our morning's invitation to come over for cold drinks. We sat in chairs on the sand under the shade of an open *palapa* talking about their cruising experiences that started in 2002. After buying and renovating the Tayana thirty-seven-foot cutter sloop, they traveled in it through Central America, Cuba, Trinidad, and Venezuela. This was their third trip to the San Blas Islands, which they

Day's End

really love. We shared our many sailing adventures while enjoying being members of the same informal "cruising fraternity."

After Eric and Katherine returned to their boat, Betsy and I took our places for dinner in the palm roofed, open air dining room suspended over the water. The cook and her assistant brought out heaping plates filled with shrimp, red peppers, and onions in a red sauce. Yum! As we ate, we enjoyed the blending oranges and reds of the sunset reflecting on the sea. After we had finished our feast, the staff left the island and went back to their homes on Ailigandi. Two young men remained as caretakers to stay with us on the island overnight. Our evening's entertainment was provided by a spectacular lightning storm over the ocean accompanied by black storm cells dumping sheets of rain on the Darien Mountains. Soaking up the blissful quiet and beauty of being alone on the island, we sat under the palm trees with smiles spreading across our faces and our bodies relaxing.

In the morning, Sam came by *panga* and took us to Achutupu (Dog) Island to visit our friend Eladio. On this traditional island, we first had to secure a landing permit for five dollars per person from the Chief's Office. After paying the fee and signing in, we walked through the village. A red-scarfed Kuna woman with two children rushed out to show us her *molas* hanging from a pole. The younger girl carried a tree branch where three baby green parrots and two yellow parakeets sat on its branches. A tiny marmoset monkey tied with a string rested on her shoulder. The woman came on quite aggressively, almost demanding that we buy something since we were taking their pictures. Sam urged us to continue toward the water's edge where we found the small palm frond covered house where Eladio was staying.

I greeted Eladio but wasn't sure that he remembered me at first. But as I told him about my visit back in 1992, repeating some of the stories I told you, the reader, of my first time in Ailigandi, he began to smile. Showing him the pictures we had just taken of his daughter Evelyn brought more smiles.

Eladio said, "My grandson is now going to college. Would you sell some of Eloisa's *molas* so we can help pay for his college?"

Big smiles followed my answer, "Yes, of course, my friend!"

Two women caring for Eladio brought us cool drinks. They were fascinated that I knew Eladio and had returned to see him after so many years. The good news was that Eladio had been cured of his dizziness by the traditional shaman and would soon be returning to Ailigandi in a few days. Sam was very relieved and was happy that he would be seeing his friend more often and soon!

Away from the group, standing under a tree, Eladio discussed his cure with Sam. Later, I learned that vertigo is a very complex condition that western doctors have only limited success in treating.

We motored past the end of the island where Eladio stood on shore waving his goodbyes. We all waved as tears swelled in my eyes.

Back at Dad Ibe, the cooks and other staff stood scanning the horizon looking for sailing *cayucas* (canoes) returning from their day of fishing. They were hoping to find some fishers who had had good luck. The paddlers on the first two *cayucas* passed by, shouting out, "Sorry, no fish today," but the fisherman in the third cayuca came straight into the beach and amazed us with his catch. The bottom of the dugout canoe was covered with crawling colossal crabs, snapping lobsters, and a great grouper. Soon a procession carrying sea creatures clutched in small Kuna hands moved

Full of the Sea's Bounty

across the island to the bridge and into the kitchen-dining *palapa*. Betsy and I put our order in for broiled lobster which arrived on a platter at its succulent best when dipped in hot lemon butter accompanied by fresh vegetables and fruit.

Sam drew up a chair to join our conversation. "As a young adult, I worked in a U.S. Army mess hall and was accepted by the GIs who took me to dances on the Post, also allowing me to tag along on other off duty trips," he said. "Later, when I returned to Ailigandi Village, I met Ken Knight, a Peace Corps volunteer. Together, we formed a skin diving club, and he taught young Kunas how to dive with a spear to catch lobsters and fish. In the 1980s, Ken again visited Ailigandi and promised to return someday on a sailboat." Sam was still waiting.

Sam continued his story. "When I was thirty-five years old, I accepted an arranged marriage with a fifteen-year-old girl whose family chose me after conferring with my family. This type of marriage is no longer common, but young girls' mothers still have a strong influence on their choices of a spouse. Most young women no longer wear the colorful traditional beaded leggings and arm bands favored by older married women, but some continue to have nose rings."

"Sam, It's really great getting to know more about you," said Betsy. "Thank you."

After lunch, Sam took us back to Ailigandi by boat where we discovered the trading ship had arrived from Colombia and was tied up at the main dock. We joined a line of Kunas who were using their coconut credits ($.15/coconut) to buy plastic containers and other household items. I wanted to buy one of their sturdy colorful hammocks which would cost me fifteen dollars cash since I had no coconut credits. I had only ten dollars in my pocket, so Sam generously offered to put his name on the ledger to advance me his credits which I later paid him back in cash. From Ailigandi, Sam took us a mile across the water to the Darien Peninsula where we followed a stream penetrating into the jungle. Stopping at the site of family burial plots, we found that each family's plot was covered by a *palapa* with a thatched roof.

"Each departed Kuna is buried lying in their hammock suspended between two posts and then covered with earth," Sam told us. "The dead person's favorite cups, plates, and other things used in life are placed on top of the grave. Families visit at times to commune with their departed family members and make offerings."

Walking further upstream, Betsy said, "It feels like we've entered the Garden of Eden."

The land was divided into family plots where mangos, papayas, and bamboo grew wild, and where Cayuca trees towered above us along the stream. The larger three to four foot diameter Cayuca trees were felled when the family needed a new canoe. The center of the tree was burned out to speed up the carving process of creating a canoe that when finished can last for forty to fifty years becoming a major family asset. Further along the trail, we walked over a three-inch PVC pipe lying on the ground. Sam told us that it is carrying water down from a spring higher up an adjacent mountain and crossing under the lagoon to a large water tower on Ailigandi. The creation of this water system was one of the results of Ken Knight's and other Peace Corps volunteers' work in the 1960s.

We were beginning to feel the effects of the heat and humidity in the jungle, when we came upon the rusting carcass of an old green farm tractor. It had been brought to this "Garden of Eden" by Donnie, a Christian missionary, about twenty years earlier. Donnie was hoping to increase the Kunas' agricultural production by clearing a larger area of land in the jungle for planting corn, beans, and other crops using the assistance of this tractor.

After Donnie left and the tractor broke down, it just stopped and now lay abandoned, rusting into a ruin in this culture without mechanics. The Kunas returned to planting their small garden plots and tended them using hand tools.

"You know, modern ways don't necessarily mean progress for an isolated culture like this so finely attuned to their environment," Betsy said. "Even though cell phones are a big hit, today, most of the older ways of living are not changing."

Hiking back through the dense jungle, we reached the river mouth, jumping into the *panga* to escape from the oppressive heat of the jungle. Sam took us further west along the coast where we delivered a letter to a woman who was collecting beach gravel to be used in the water filter for the community drinking water system. Each family has communal assignments dictated by the chiefs and elders that contribute to the welfare of the whole community. On our way back along the coast, our driver, Oswaldo, began trolling for fish with a line dragging behind the *panga*. Suddenly, he began catching fish, one after another. First three gold-spotted, iridescent blue sierras, then more smaller fish were hooked just outside the surf line where the water begins to roil creating bubbles. Soon, we had enough fish to provide dinners for everyone on our Dad Ibe island. Talk about fresh caught fish. Nothing tastes better!

After our hearty fish dinner, the staff performed a simple, undulating Kuna dance accompanied by pan flute music, attracting Betsy into the circle of swaying women and men accompanied by much laughter and gaiety. The dance was their way of saying goodbye. Hugs followed.

A huge iridescent orange moon rose over the island to the east and sent its shimmering rays flickering across the water to scatter warm light on the white beach sand. Taking in deep breaths, we absorbed the peacefulness of the moment as the palm trees rustled in the warm breeze. Betsy and I reflected on the connections we had made here with Eladio and our guide. When Sam arrived each morning with other staff from Ailigandi, he would sing softly outside our cabin, "Good morning, my friends, I love you!"

We'd call back, "We love you, Sam."

As a person, Sam was so much more than just our guide. He was a philosopher who spread the "Good Man Philosophy" throughout the village. He had forged his practice by following the Golden Rule while integrating in the thoughts and ethics of his mentor, Dr. Norman Vincent Peale. This approach to living a "good life" made Sam a respected elder in his tribe. We witnessed his effect in Ailigandi as everyone wanted to shake his hand and greet him with their wide smiles.

"Betsy, for me being back with the Kunas has created an inner canvas on which my past images and memories are mixed with a rush of colors and new impressions to create a collage of sights, sounds, and feelings," I said. "They have warmed my being to its core while evoking an even deeper feeling of happiness and fulfillment."

"Wow, how poetic," Betsy replied, smiling.

EPILOGUE

I opened this book with the tragic story about losing *JoJo* on a reef in Carmel Bay, near Monterey, California. *JoJo's* loss devastated me. I had spent many hours of planning and working to make her a safe and comfortable sailboat. Sailing her was my way of carrying the dream forward that I had lived with JoAnne and was now sharing with Betsy. With *JoJo* gone, my dream was shattered along with my hard earned feelings of competence as a sailor.

To cope with my loss and grief, I decided to write about the dream that changed my life. As I wrote, I retraced my voyages on *Aurora* where I had moved my dream into reality. I wanted to regain those parts of my core that had been damaged. Writing this book helped me to put those pieces of the dream back together, while revisiting this all important and encompassing chapter in my life. I took the opportunity to delve deeper into my experiences—to feel the feelings and to think the thoughts that until now lay in the shadows of memory. By writing and reflecting, I was able to reconnect to the deeper meaning of my life.

Sailing can be a demanding pursuit, but for me, it is ultimately relaxing and mind expanding. Being on a boat, a vessel of beauty performing well, is exciting to me. By harnessing and staying in tune with nature's forces on the water, you and your boat are in motion and become one. Motion propels you through external space and time, but also opens up internal space for thoughts, ideas, and feelings to surface and become conscious. In my case, sailing sets in motion an interior dialogue where new goals, directions, and interests begin to develop. My sense of what is important in life takes on clarity, becomes more focused, and has an *expanded* and a *deeper* meaning. The things I remember most fondly are the experiences of love and laughter that money can't buy. Reconnecting with friends lodged in my memories brought up many *warm feelings*: of being with Peetie and Bob at Puerto Escondido; of learning more about Jacques and Mariam and their Mexican friends in LaPaz; of working in Chena's shop in San Blas; of the incredible encounter with a mermaid who swam out to *Aurora*; of drinking Margaritas with Len, Loretta, Ed, and Julie in Puerto Vallarta; of joining homesteaders Elan, Bella, and Natalie on their island off Panama; of becoming friends with Eladio and Irwin in the San Blas; of being helped by Dr. Juan in Cartagena; of joining farmer Anthony in his quest for fresh vegetables in the Bahamas; of accepting Paula's good food and warm hospitality in the Azores; and finally meeting Enrique who took us under his wing in Puerto Gelves, Spain. Immersion in history and learning through travel has invigorated my mind and created a deep respect for other cultures, religions, and customs. I feel at one with all that is good in human hearts, residing everywhere in the world.

By slowly defining and then following my dream, I found that in my daily life I was able to realize a greater, more finely tuned expanded and important focus. I learned that daily actions can be taken to push your dream forward in the midst of all the "have-to's" of life. In the midst of the seemingly mundane daily concerns, small steady steps can be taken toward the goal—in my case it was cruising the world.

I hope that you, the reader, will take away the underlying message of saying "Yes!" to your dreams. Personal goals are a very important aspect of living a fulfilling, successful, and productive life. Preparation, study, practice, and fortitude are needed to actualize a dream. The rewards are in the journey where competence grows as well as the sense of accomplishment. Along the way, I discovered a deeper, quieter place within myself where I could go in times of crisis or contemplation. Here, I was able to laser focus my mind on the problem or situation, create solutions or explanations, and apply all my physical and mental strength to correct the predicament or to create a new understanding. With travel, the more you know going into a new place, the more you gain when you are there.

Looking back over my life has been a *rewarding* experience. I feel strongly that, yes, I'm living a good and meaningful life. I am a stronger, more committed, and interesting person for having followed my dream. I feel more alive and engaged with this miracle we share, called life.

I will leave you with how the journey of a dream worked for me. First, I allowed the dream to germinate in my mind. Then I acknowledged that the dream was important. Next I began creating a path leading to fulfilling my dream. Finally I took the steps on that path necessary to make the dream become a reality. And along the way, my life became filled with love, laughter, learning, and a lot of Liven*good* Luck!

So I encourage each of you to dream, dream, dream!

23894701R00283

Made in the USA
San Bernardino, CA
04 September 2015